MW01088014

Anthology of Spanish American Thought and Culture

UNIVERSITY PRESS OF FLORIDA

Florida A&M University, Tallahassee
Florida Atlantic University, Boca Raton
Florida Gulf Coast University, Ft. Myers
Florida International University, Miami
Florida State University, Tallahassee
New College of Florida, Sarasota
University of Central Florida, Orlando
University of Florida, Gainesville
University of North Florida, Jacksonville
University of South Florida, Tampa
University of West Florida, Pensacola

ANTHOLOGY OF
Spanish American Thought and Culture

Edited by

Jorge Aguilar Mora, Josefa Salmón,
and Barbara C. Ewell

University Press of Florida

Gainesville · Tallahassee · Tampa · Boca Raton

Pensacola · Orlando · Miami · Jacksonville · Ft. Myers · Sarasota

First cloth printing, 2017
First paperback printing, 2020

25 24 23 22 21 20   6 5 4 3 2 1

Library of Congress Cataloging-in-Publication Data
Names: Aguilar Mora, Jorge, editor. | Salmón, Josefa, editor. | Ewell,
Barbara C., editor.
Title: Anthology of Spanish American thought and culture / edited by Jorge
Aguilar Mora, Josefa Salmón, and Barbara C. Ewell.
Description: Gainesville : University Press of Florida, 2017. | Includes
index.
Identifiers: LCCN 2016035945 | ISBN 9780813062884 (cloth) | ISBN 9780813068336 (pbk.)
Subjects: LCSH: Latin America—Civilization. | Spanish American
literature—History and criticism. | Spanish Americans—Social life and
customs. | Civilization—Spanish influences.
Classification: LCC F1408.3 .A615 2016 | DDC 980—dc23
LC record available at https://lccn.loc.gov/2016035945

The University Press of Florida is the scholarly publishing agency for the State University
System of Florida, comprising Florida A&M University, Florida Atlantic University,
Florida Gulf Coast University, Florida International University, Florida State University,
New College of Florida, University of Central Florida, University of Florida, University of
North Florida, University of South Florida, and University of West Florida.

University Press of Florida
2046 NE Waldo Road
Suite 2100
Gainesville, FL 32609
http://upress.ufl.edu

Contents

Illustrations

Map

Editors' Note

For the sake of brevity, the editors have occasionally omitted notes that were included in the original (Spanish) texts as well as in some published translations. Moreover, we have silently amended obvious mistakes in those original texts, including accidentally omitted lines and passages. We also sometimes insert (in angle brackets) remarks on the appearance of an original manuscript such as deletions, translator's or editor's clarifications, or marginalia. In any event, the editors assume full responsibility for any lingering errors, despite every effort to be accurate. Names and phrases in UPPERCASE cross-reference entries elsewhere in the anthology.

Acknowledgments

As with any major scholarly project, this anthology was only possible with considerable help, from individuals and from institutions alike.

Our most significant debt is to two generous donors, Renan Bu Contreras and Monica A. LeDee, whose contributions supported many of the original translations that we commissioned. We are grateful to Karen Anklam, development officer for the College of Humanities and Natural Sciences at Loyola University, who helped to identify our convergent interests and linked our project to their support. We are grateful to the Department of English for financial assistance at a critical time. Josefa Salmón also wishes to thank the Council for International Exchange of Scholars for a research grant that allowed her to dedicate considerable time to this anthology.

We are, of course, especially grateful to Loyola University New Orleans, home institution for two of us, and to our College of Humanities and Natural Sciences. Both its present dean, Maria Calzada, and her predecessor, JoAnn Cruz, shared our enthusiasm for this project and supported us with their time, resources, and funding assistance. We also appreciate the support of the chairs of our academic departments, especially Kate Adams, Chris Chambers, and John Biguenet. Both Josefa Salmón and Barbara Ewell deeply appreciate the ongoing support of their professorships, the Rev. Guy Lemieux Distinguished Professorship and the Dorothy H. Brown Distinguished Professorship, respectively, which covered both travel and publication costs. As former colleagues, both Father Lemieux and Dorothy Brown would have been pleased with our volume.

In fact, many members of the Loyola community helped to bring this anthology into being. Chief among them are the capable administrative assistants who really make our departments run smoothly: Avia Alonzo in the Department of Languages and Cultures and Heidi Braden and Carey

Herman in the Department of English. Along with their usual deft handling of the paperwork, they also supervised the student workers who did much of the necessary scanning, copying, and printing: Kurt Schratwiesier, Asia Cleggett, Destiny Simms, and Stewart Sinclair. No faculty member at Loyola could ever accomplish anything, however, without the cheerful and resourceful assistance of Tootie Buisson and Jayme C. Naquin, assistant controllers in the Office of Finance and Administration. We also gratefully remember our friend and colleague, Harold Baquet, university photographer.

Good librarians are behind the success of any scholarly project, and we have benefited from the excellent assistance of the staff at Loyola's J. Edgar and Louise S. Monroe Library and its Special Collections and Archives, especially Elizabeth Kelly, as well as the resources of the Latin American Library of Tulane University and the expertise of its director, Hortensia Calvo, and her fine staff, particularly the assistance of research and instruction librarian, Jade Madrid.

Loyola students Molly Alper and Stewart Sinclair provided valuable research assistance, while Tulane University student Estefania Flores assisted with locating images. We are also indebted to Sarah Kuczynski at the University of North Carolina and to Jerry Speir, who served as primary editors for many texts. We could not have included so many instructive and beautiful images without our photographers, Jennifer Saracino, Froilán Urzagasti, Matilde Mamani, Ava Cartner, and Jerry Speir.

While many of our selected texts were available in English, many more were not. The inclusion of these works was made possible by a talented group of translators who worked diligently to create accurate and graceful texts: Henry Sullivan, Charles Becker, Nathan Henne, Isabel Bastos, Marvin Liberman, Sarah Taylor Cook, Jacinto Fombona, the late Daniel Castro, Marta Edwards, Carlos Jáuregui, and our colleague in the English Department, John Biguenet, who provided timely assistance with a difficult poem.

We also greatly appreciate the generosity of several fellow scholars and other professionals who gave us permission to use their work, including Harry E. Vanden and Marc Becker, Elena Poniatowska, Antonio Turok, Gary Urton, Javier Nuñez de Arco, Marie Jose Paz, Teresa Gisbert, Marta Cajías and Silvia Arce, Verónica Cereceda, Carlos Jáuregui, Antonio Saborit, Jorge Valverde, María Cristina Monsalve, the heirs of Rafael F. Muñoz, Sociedad de Beneficencia de Lima, the Luciano Tapia family and Álvaro García Linera. We also appreciate the generous cooperation of the School for Advanced Research (SAR) Press, the Fundación Ezequiel Martínez Estrada, the Secretaria de Cultura of the Instituto Nacional de Antropología e Historia (INAH), the Museo de la Ciudad de México, and the Fundación Antropólogos del Surandino (ASUR).

Of course, our deepest thanks go to our editors and staff at the University Press of Florida—Sian Hunter, Catherine Nevil Parker, Stephanye Hunter, and our copyeditor, Gillian Hillis—and to former editor Amy Gorelick, who first agreed to review our manuscript. We are also particularly grateful to the two anonymous readers, whose meticulous attention to detail and thoughtful comments were invaluable in improving the manuscript. We can gratefully acknowledge Gene H. Bell-Villada here and hope that the other still-anonymous reader will recognize the positive results of her or his very considered critique.

Finally, each of us has specific personal debts of gratitude that we can barely begin to repay here. Jorge and Josefa want to thank several professional colleagues who contributed to this project in any number of indispensable ways: Fernando Unzueta, Harry E. Vanden, Cynthia Garza, Oscar Vega, Gary Urton, Ava Cartner, Guillermo Delgado, Elizabeth Boone, Martín Mendoza Botelho, Jennifer Saracino, Antonio Turok, Marcelo Uribe, Paola Nieto, Josefina Moguel, María Gabriela Mizraje, Roberto García Bonilla, Juan Carlos Fernández, Kris Lane, Maureen Shea, and John Charles. Jorge would like to thank Lauretta Clough, his son Diego Aguilar Canabal, and Saúl Sosnowski for their presence and support. He would also like to acknowledge Josefa and Barbara for their wonderful collaboration in this anthology.

Josefa is grateful to Jorge for his friendship, wisdom, and exemplary scholarship, and to Barbara for her friendship, her love of good writing, and her indispensable help with this anthology. She is indebted to her family for their constant loving support: Nilda Salmón, René Villavicencio, Virginia Salmón, Gedby Rojas, and her nephews Martín, René, and Fidel Salmón. In New Orleans, she can always count on the affection and help of colleagues at Loyola and at Tulane University, especially Robert Dewell, Isabel Durocher, Cassandra Mabe, Peter Rogers, SJ, Alice Kornovich, Hillary Eklund, Nathan Henne, Uriel Quesada, Eileen Doll, Guillermo Delgado, and in Bolivia, Alba María Paz-Soldán, Mauricio Souza, Gilmar Gonzáles, Sulma Montero, Froilán Urzagasti, María Luisa Talavera, Vanessa Alfaro, and her friends Antonio Gómez and family. She also wishes to acknowledge her long friendship with Daniel Castro and to honor Daniel, whose death coincided with the completion of this manuscript. Finally, without Sebastián and Sofía Edwards-Salmón, her son and daughter, no project would even be possible.

Barbara is primarily grateful to her remarkable colleague and friend, Josefa, who invited her to become part of this project and who, with Jorge, taught her volumes about these incredible texts and their contexts. Whatever she has brought to this project, in fact, owes much to her teachers, too numerous to name, who loved good writing and shared their pleasure in finding the right words. She also wants to acknowledge the inspiration of her colleagues in the Department of English and in City College, who are always doing something interesting, and the loving support of her five sisters and their families—for whatever she's doing. As for her partner in life and dearest friend, Jerry Speir, who seems to think she can do anything (but arithmetic), there are no right words to convey her gratitude for his unfailing love and support.

General Introduction

The history of thought in any culture can never be understood simply as a sequence of ideas. Ideas are never discrete: they are not distinct from the language in which they are expressed, and language itself cannot exist without ideas. Recognizing this interdependence (which does not always match thought with its representation) is fundamental to comprehending any culture, particularly one that is unfamiliar. In tracing the thought and culture of Hispanic America, we have been especially cognizant of the ways that thinking and expression are inherently linked, as well as by the notion that every thought embraces its particular form of expression. Sometimes a thought can only be articulated in a very specific way; and while a picture may be worth a thousand words, words do not substitute for images. Images embody their own specific meanings, just as words convey their own very precise significance. A history of thought is thus necessarily a history of the languages and symbols that convey ideas. Guided by these principles, this selection of visual and linguistic texts outlines the thought and culture of one very remarkable region, Hispanic America.

In tracing any such history, one is soon struck by the ways in which ideas both persist and regenerate themselves. The Book of Ecclesiastes famously insists that there is nothing new under the sun, but humans also experience the world as continually renewing itself, as though life were being created afresh at every moment. Ideas themselves appear and disappear, returning because they are needed and then fading away once they have fulfilled their purpose. As history presents new problems, old ideas often provide their solutions. What makes a great thinker is precisely that ability to grasp "old" ideas and apply them in reenergizing ways, as if their force had never been depleted. This transformative recycling of thought directly counters the conventional notion of newness as what is trendy or fashionable. But novelty in that sense actually embodies an explicitly modern perspective, one that privileges the present moment and current events, rather than recognizing the value—indeed, the persistence—of what has come before. The genuinely new occurs when a familiar concept is profoundly recuperated, when events of history or remarkable personalities direct the powerful light of what had seemed always to be—the "nothing new" of Ecclesiastes—to this unique moment and context. Only in this paradoxical way is the world fully revitalized and made new through what has always been present. This timely transformation of the old simultaneously signifies a moment of beginning. And just as the new historical context reaffirms the vitality of the old idea, that idea imparts to that moment an originality and a sense of beginning. In this way, the great beginnings of history always enunciate a memory, recollecting an event from the past and furnishing it with a new direction and fresh implications.

Reflecting on this interaction between the new and the old offers a particularly useful way to approach the history of thought in Spanish America. Pre-Hispanic cultures were firmly rooted in the belief that ideas do not change, since nature was conceived as a repetition of phenomena (or at least that is how these cultures viewed nature) and the gods themselves as unchanging concepts. But each new culture that emerged in Mesoamerica or the Andes interpreted these unchanging principles in new ways. Tradition and belief were thus continuous and the same but also always renewed and different. For example, at the heart of today's Mexican nation, there has been a succession of distinctive cultures. If we consider only those we know most about—the Teotihuacán, the Toltecs, the Nahua—it is clear that each group added new elements to the nucleus of a solid ideological organization that probably derived—as best we can tell—from the Olmecs, who had inhabited the Mexican coast in today's states of Veracruz and Tabasco. Of course, the Olmec culture, which flourished in the second millennium of our era, was quite possibly the heir of even more ancient cultures.

Another instance of how a basic concept can be reconfigured—even re-created—in different contexts by different peoples is the 260-day calendar, which was adopted by all Mesoamerican cultures. That the origins of this unique calendar remain unknown attests both to its distant antiquity as well as to its effectiveness, providing the basis for solar, lunar, Venusian, and various other time-keeping systems. What remains constant is how the measure of 260 days combines two other fundamental units in these cultures: the 20-day period and the number 13. While the significance of these particular numbers remains unexplained, anthropologists speculate that the vigesimal system appears frequently throughout the world because one could use the fingers and toes to count. And while we still do not know why Mesoamerican peoples combined the vigesimal system with the number 13, this calendar reappears throughout the region from a very early period.

This transformation of old ideas by the needs of the present continued into the modern era and the incorporation of the Americas into European perspectives. The conquest of the Americas, for instance, marks one of the major events in world history, changing the parameters of knowledge even as it altered global economic and social conditions. At last, the world could be conceived as complete and whole, a single and singular home for all humans. But the conquest had a devastating impact on the Americas: millions of Indian peoples died from wars, from the relentless exploitation of their labor and resources, and especially from the infectious diseases carried by Europeans. Culturally, the conquest provided a new historical terrain for Indian beliefs and traditions. Construed from European perspectives, long-standing native practices and views became reconfigured: sometimes destroyed, occasionally preserved, but often assimilated and combined with the conquerors' own traditions, constituting new versions of many old beliefs.

Many of these uneasy reconfigurations wrought by the conquest seemed to stabilize during the Colonial period. The historiography of this era often suggests ideological immobility, a time when the region's knowledge and thought were paralyzed by pervasive and stultifying Catholic dogma. But this was not entirely the case. Many inhabitants of the New World were quite informed about the ideological, scientific, and technical currents of the Old World. Indeed, some Spanish Americans knew more about Europe's scientific discoveries than many cultured Europeans, a point amply demonstrated in the late seventeenth century when Father Kino, an Austrian-Italian Jesuit, confronted CARLOS DE SIGÜENZA Y GÓNGORA in Mexico City. When they met, they discussed the significance of the comet that had appeared in the Western Hemisphere in 1618. Kino's arguments were based in the belief that comets were divine signals, but Sigüenza y Góngora argued that they were only physical phenomena much like the revolution of the planets.

One European idea uniquely and powerfully changed by its incarnation in Spanish America was the Baroque. Manifest typically as a style and an aesthetic, the Baroque was in fact a distinctive worldview, one that accommodated elements that were not necessarily harmonious or congruent. The most influential version of the Baroque was undoubtedly that disseminated by the Society of Jesus, a religious order that arrived in Spanish

America shortly after the Council of Trent (1545–1563). That decisive assembly of Roman Catholic theologians and clerics was convened to address the threats posed by Protestantism; its edicts marked the beginning of the Counter Reformation, which included a renewed emphasis on the power of the senses, especially in religious imagery. The Spanish Crown adopted both doctrine and aesthetic with particular fervor, as did one of its subjects, Ignatius de Loyola, who founded a religious order to advance those intentions. From its inception, then, the Society of Jesus—better known as the Jesuits—coupled those Counter Reformation goals with Baroque expression.

The power of the Baroque is evident even in attitudes toward conversion. As part of their intent to convert Indian populations, the Franciscans (another powerful religious order) initially maintained the messianic hope that Christ's return would occur once their evangelizing mission was complete. Since their apostolic goals included the recovery of the cultural texts of those they proselytized, they continued that practice even after it became clear that mass conversions were not hastening the final days. Nearly three decades later, when the Jesuits arrived, they too assumed the task of collecting testimony and artifacts, but in keeping with their Ignatian spirit, they also sought to understand the culture, so that they might better assimilate its elements into a Catholic perspective. Supporting their persuasive efforts with compelling images, the Jesuits evolved a distinctive Baroque objective: pursuing an integration of all the unique elements of the New World into its profoundly Catholic view. As a style and as a worldview congenial to the Jesuits, the Baroque thus became an active locus for religious syncretism and cultural hybridity. Though constructed of familiar components, the result was a deeply original culture: Colonial Spanish America.

So profound was the mark of the Baroque on the region that even the violence of the nineteenth century's anti-Colonial reaction and the incipient wars of independence could not erase the impact of the Baroque and its associated ideas that had spread through Jesuit education. But the first half of the nineteenth century also introduced a new form of hybridization: the merging of Romantic and Enlightenment ideas (especially between 1800 and 1848) with the Baroque and Neoclassical thought that still prevailed in Spain. This fertile confluence of ideas was complicated by the difficulty that the new Spanish American nations had in finding a political identity in the contexts of an oppressive colonial past. At least in principle and with only one exception, the new governments were founded as republics rather than monarchies. But the widespread reluctance of the Church, the wealthiest creoles, and the military to surrender their institutional privileges unsettled the formation of these new nation-states and generated numerous debilitating civil wars. The transition from colonialism to independence was hardly peaceful, though the fundamental elements of Hispanic America remained in place, even as new forms of government slowly evolved.

By the end of the nineteenth century, the belief in rationalism and the priority of experimental science dominated not just the Americas but much of Western thought. Sometimes known as "positivism," such notions shaped the directions—or at least the aspirations—of these new Hispanic nation-states. As a reaction to positivism, Spanish America, in the final decades of the century, generated its own genuinely new perspective: *modernismo*. Not to be confused with the later Modernism of the English-speaking world, *modernismo* served as a transition between the materialist perceptions of positivism and the radical outbursts of the avant-garde. Reflecting on issues of national identity and on the forms that were appropriate to the unique history and status of Hispanic America, *modernista* writers like José Martí and Rubén Darío were not only exceptional poets, but thinkers of international importance. They helped to confirm the ideological foundations of the Hispanic nation-states, so that with the emergence of international Modernism, writers and artists and thinkers of this region rivaled in sophistication the best in any language. César Vallejo, Vicente Huidobro, JORGE LUIS BORGES, and Pablo Neruda are a few stars in an impressive constellation of world-class authors. Political thought was no less exceptional in this era, producing critical works like *Creación de una pedagogía nacional* (1910) [Creation of a National Pedagogy] by the Bolivian FRANZ TAMAYO, *El payador* (1915) [The Minstrel] by the Argentinian Leopoldo Lugones, and *Cesarismo democrático* (1919) [Democratic Caesarism] by the Venezuelan Laureano Vallenilla Lanz. These ruminations about national identity are more part of *modernismo* than of the avant-garde movement and are the foundation of several crucial essays of the twentieth century: EZEQUIEL MARTÍNEZ ESTRADA with his masterful *Radiografía de la pampa* (1931) [X-Ray of the Pampa]; Fernando Ortiz's *Contrapunteo cubano del tabaco y del azúcar* (1940) [Cuban Counterpoint: Tobacco and Sugar]; and OCTAVIO PAZ in his *El laberinto de la soledad* (1950) [The Labyrinth of Solitude].

In the course of the century, however, the novel gradually began to subsume the reflective functions of the essay, particularly in the generation that flourished in the 1960s, known as the Boom. Anticipated by *Hombres de maíz* (1949) [Men of Maize] by Guatemalan Miguel Angel Asturias (one of the most artistically complete works of national identity), the novels of the Boom generation constitute an unrivaled set of texts about Latin American identity and represent a major contribution to world literature. The brilliant novel *Cien años de soledad* (1967) [One Hundred Years of Solitude] by the Colombian Gabriel García Márquez, for example, remains one of the most important works of the second half of the twentieth century in any language.

By the end of the twentieth century, Latin America was producing an impressive array of discourses, reflections, novels, and poems with worldwide significance. One revealing trigger for this literary groundswell was the Cuban Revolution (1959). That singular event demarcated a new moment in the history of Spanish America, another instance of old ideas being recycled to resolve a problem of the present. The restless emergence of people redefining themselves in contemporary contexts generated various political crises throughout the continent, including military dictatorships, the division of nations like Colombia, and civil wars throughout Central America. These crises produced immense economic disruption and social tragedy, with thousands dead, but they also gave rise to innovative political and cultural experiments. The collective effect of that chaos was the virtual erasure of national boundaries, making Latin America seem a single nation despite a stunning range of discourses, reflections, and experiences. But as inevitable and subsequent crises developed, such as the economic collapse in Argentina (1998–2002), Hispanic America became regionalized again, isolating its countries despite the new globalization stimulated by the Internet and other novel forms of communication, including social media. Once more, Hispanic America is in the process of reinventing itself for the present, building upon its unique history and remarkable cultures.

In selecting the texts for this anthology, we have tried to follow an often ill-defined path in the history of Spanish America: the path of identity. Trying to balance the canonical and indispensable with lesser-known and equally valuable works, we have tried to answer one basic question: "Who are we?" That question and some possible answers have been formulated in many different ways throughout the complex history of this extraordinary region. Our choice of texts reflects our efforts to represent a full range of perspectives, often from lesser-known writers, but without losing sight of the larger, sometimes less obvious patterns that have shaped—and continue to shape—Hispanic American identity. In emphasizing the frequently overlooked contribution of the Jesuits to Latin American culture, for example, both colonial culture and the political thought underlying the movements for independence become more comprehensible. Moreover, in the twentieth century, Jesuit thought and influence have had profound consequences for the theology of liberation—a contemporary theological movement native to the region. Other political movements at the end of the twentieth century have also been shaped by that Jesuit heritage, including the Mexican "Zapatistas," who emerged in 1994 and who continue to be a decisive political phenomenon, perhaps no less so than the Cuban Revolution.

The omission of noteworthy writers in this anthology was inevitable. Confronted with the impossibility of including all important writers and thinkers, we opted for giving priority to originality of thought rather than to the social importance of an author's work. This was the case with two important figures: José Enrique Rodó and Mario Vargas Llosa. While Rodó's *Ariel* was perhaps the most-read book in twentieth-century Latin America, we found its ideas better represented by the work of SARMIENTO and a political essay by RUBÉN DARÍO, in which he traces the opposition between the United States and Latin America from a political rather than from Rodó's idealist or cultural perspectives. Likewise, to Mario Vargas Llosa's defense of neoliberalism or "democracy," we have preferred the work of contemporary writers who are less-known but more deeply inventive, many of whom have emerged in critical and unique circumstances, such as Bolivia's Luciano Tapia and Álvaro García Linera, whose texts conclude our anthology.

Another difficult exclusion is that of José Vasconcelos. As a philosopher, Vasconcelos's lack of a clear method produced only mediocre thought, while his famous notion of the "cosmic race" is inescapably racist, disguised as the expression of "Americanism." His remarkable multivolume autobiography, *Ulises criollo* (1935) [Creole Ulysses], *La tormenta* (1936) [The storm], *El desastre* (1938) [The disaster], *El proconsulado* (1939) [The proconsul], however, is rare in Latin American culture, conveying a heartbreaking story with unparalleled honesty. Nevertheless, we did not feel that necessarily short excerpts would adequately demonstrate his originality, and we acknowledge here our regret at having reluctantly omitted this prominent and deeply influential figure.

Finally, we must note an obvious and unfortunate self-imposed limit in our efforts to trace the history of thought and culture in Latin America: the exclusion of non-Spanish-speaking territories, particularly the Portuguese. Having sought to provide both an introduction to a number of basic cultural texts as well as an examination of different ideological productions from several perspectives, we found it impossible to include such very different histories in a single volume with any coherence or depth. As with any anthology, ours is necessarily partial and incomplete. Even so, by including both familiar and unfamiliar texts and by highlighting some vital common threads, we hope we have provided students and scholars with new insights into the cultural identity of this fascinating and varied region, the Spanish Americas.

1

The Pre-Hispanic Period

Here at the beginning of the third millennium of the Christian era, most Westerners can barely imagine a worldview reliant on myth and cyclical time. Although it has been a mere five hundred years since the majority of human societies relied on narratives of a mythic past and ostensibly time-less rituals to explain and define reality, today we inhabit a very different ideological moment. But we cannot fully comprehend the texts and images of this first section without trying to recover the distinctive worldview that generated them. While many factors shaped the self-conception of pre-Hispanic societies in the Americas, two prominent features are particularly distinctive from our own. The first is their identification of natural phe-nomena with personified divinities; the second is their conception of labor both as a means of survival and as a form of worship.

While the Mediterranean cultures that generated the Western world were roughly contemporary with pre-Hispanic civilizations, their geo-graphical conditions were decidedly different. Arising on the perimeters of an inland sea, saturated and intersected by numerous trade routes, the Greek, Jewish, and Roman civilizations were, from their inceptions, char-acterized by frequent contact with other cultures and different worldviews, including Hindu and Persian as well as Egyptian and other African em-pires. As a result of such interactions, these great Western civilizations de-veloped distinctive ways of appropriating and transforming foreign values and even oppositional attitudes as they sought to resolve the tensions of living with—or surviving—cultures different from their own. Because pre-Hispanic societies in the Americas were largely isolated from such cultural interactions by two vast oceans, they never developed the adaptive skills and flexibility that were fundamental to surviving the utter foreignness of the Spanish invaders.

The major pre-Hispanic cultures that the Spanish encountered—the Inca, the Nahua, and the Mayan—were, in fact, the products of centuries-long cultural evolution, not constant cultural interaction. By the time of the conquest, the ancient Mesoamerican and Andean civilizations had been slowly transformed into the dominant (and dominating) military and economic power structures of the Incas and the Aztecs. But the relatively recent emergence of those powerful "empires"—barely over two hundred years in either case—only confirms that they were building on earlier cultures that had been tested and solidifying for centuries.

Though we often think of culture as limited to religious and artistic structures, culture is in fact a way of understanding the world that permeates all the social and economic aspects of a community and that is reflected in both individual and group behaviors. Religious rites, everyday life, food production, the construction of temples and artifacts, the exchange of goods and the transmission of knowledge—all were interrelated in these pre-Hispanic cultures, and separating out any of these elements would have threatened the integrity of the society as a whole.

When the Spanish arrived in America, there were, of course, many cultures, not just the three or four that we usually recall. But the processes of Spanish conquest and evangelization encouraged an identification of "major" cultures, distinctions that greatly facilitated the imposition of a colonial power that persisted for over three centuries. One immediate consequence was the misleading image of a handful of paramount, pre-Hispanic cultures that were "more civilized" and thus worthy of preservation. The first generation of missionaries clearly held such a view, regarding these "major" cultures as superior to others who were deemed "minor" simply because they had been subjugated by those dominant groups or who merely had smaller populations. Another constructed measure of that superiority was the similarities with Christianity that the missionaries thought they perceived in the history and organization of these "major" civilizations, thus aligning these American cultures with their own model of superior civilization.

Among the most consequential of those perceived similarities were mythological and legendary figures that, for many Spaniards, demonstrated an early Christian presence in the Americas. The widely known god Quetzalcóatl, for example, was frequently identified with St. Thomas, the apostle renowned for his global wanderings after the death of Christ. By linking Thomas with this popular Mesoamerican god, the missionaries could reaffirm the veracity and fulfillment of the Gospel's injunction to spread the news of Christ throughout the world. That those Christian teachings had apparently been abandoned for fifteen centuries merely helped to explain away the many disparities in these symbolic figures and social customs as the effects of temporal erosion from their obvious Christian origins.

Another crucial explanation of these similarities was the notion of providential evolution; that is, any society worthy of survival would necessarily evolve the social and mental organizations appropriate to Christianity. Accordingly, the Nahuas, the Incas, and the Mayans were judged to be just those kinds of societies, having arrived at the stage of civilization where all that was lacking to achieve full humanity was espousing the true religion: a perfect opening for energetic evangelizing. That the many accounts of similarities between Christianity and the "major" pre-Hispanic cultures included flagrant logical and obvious factual contradictions did little to discourage their widespread adoption by these eager interpreters.

The Spaniards, for example, simply could not imagine that the cross would represent anything but Christ's crucifixion—even among non-Christians. Accordingly, when they found crosses in the Americas, they could only conclude a Christian presence. Some missionaries thought that the change in the meaning of the cross since the first Christianization could only have been the work of the devil. Only evil forces would explain the shift from signifying Christ's sacrifice to representing the four cardinal points, which the cross meant in Mesoamerican cultures. Such determined reconstructions of native cultures frequently recur throughout the many Hispanic texts by historians, chroniclers, and missionaries of the period.

One of the most famous instances of these reconstructions and its effects concerns the figure of Quetzalcóatl in Mesoamerica. While the Spanish were quite experienced at adapting unfamiliar experiences to their own cultural frameworks, the isolation of pre-Hispanic cultures essentially rendered members of the latter unable to question many of their basic convictions. Thus when confronted with anomalies they could not at first explain—like pale men with beards and guns mounted on horses—they simply fit them into one of their own familiar categories, such as divinities. In the case of the Aztecs—one of the many peoples that made up the more extensive Nahua culture—the conquistador Hernán Cortés even became identified with a very specific god, Quetzalcóatl.

The mythological history of this god made the transfer plausible. Though Quetzalcóatl had left his people, he had promised to return from the East. He would be known by his whiteness (a color identified with the East) and the bulge under his chin (a well-known characteristic of the god of the wind). As the various chronicles note, Cortés's pale skin and beard were duly recognized as markers of the god. Moreover, his heavy Spanish armor and helmet, which would have looked like a mask to the Indians, further confirmed Cortés's deity: the Nahua gods never appeared with their true faces, but only disguised.

Even as the chronicles confirm the identification of the Spaniards as gods, they also record the Indians' realization that these strangers were not really divine. Such profound psychological oscillations between identifying a human figure with a god and then fully appreciating its human status have not yet been adequately explained. Nonetheless, this conflation represents one of the most decisive moments in the conquest and eventual colonization of America.[1] It also helped to define the unique way that Catholicism developed in Spanish America, fusing Christian and pre-Hispanic images and beliefs into a distinctively syncretic system, one that shapes faith and religious conviction in profound ways even today.

That syncretism is manifest in another key misidentification of Quetzalcóatl—not by the natives, but by the Spanish themselves. Many missionaries were convinced that Christianity must have arrived in America with one of the original disciples, and the belief soon became widespread that behind the divinity of Quetzalcóatl lay Saint Thomas, the man who supposedly brought the gospel to the Americas. The chronicles of Meso- and South America abound with references to the supposed traces of St. Thomas, including the "footprints" of his sandals in stone. The importance of Quetzalcóatl as a founding presence even survives in the official Mexican flag: the eagle devouring a serpent is a common representation of Quetzalcóatl, whose name means "plumed serpent."

If Quetzalcóatl was a particularly noteworthy divinity, his representation was hardly uniform among pre-Hispanic cultures. While the Aztec and others considered him a god, some Mesoamerican societies viewed him simply as a legendary figure, specifically a ruler of Tula,[2] whose kingdoms flourished in central Mexico between the tenth and twelfth centuries. For

---

1   That many missionaries believed in St. Thomas's American presence is confirmed by an anonymous author of the appendix titled "Noticias cronológicas del Cuzco" [Chronological notes on Cuzco] in Manuel Mendiburu's *Apuntes históricos del Perú* [Historical Sketches of Peru] (Lima: Imprenta del Estado, 1902). The lives of both CARLOS DE SIGÜENZA Y GÓNGORA and FRAY SERVANDO TERESA DE MIER were shaped by their belief in St. Thomas's American mission. See also Jacques Lafaye, *Quetzalcóatl and Guadalupe: The Formation of Mexican National Consciousness, 1531–1813* (Chicago: University of Chicago Press, 1976).

2   Located a few miles north of Teotihuacán, northeast of Mexico City, Tula was the Toltecs' principal city, reaching its prime between the tenth and eleventh centuries. Tula and its royal lineage were appropriated by other cultures as part of a legendary golden age, surviving in Mayan and Nahua lore well after the twelfth century.

them, Quetzalcóatl was a particularly merciful king who, having been exiled for opposing human sacrifice, promised to return. A similar myth occurs in Andean culture, where Quetzalcóatl is known as Wiracocha, a god who became identified with the local conquistador, Francisco Pizarro.

This conflation of divine, legendary, and semihistoric qualities in both Quetzalcóatl and Wiracocha is instructively manifest in the *Popol Vuh*, the sacred book of the Quiché culture, located in what is now Guatemala. While the narrative of the *Popol Vuh* begins with purely mythological accounts of the formation of the universe, it shifts readily into legends and concludes with datable historical references. This progression from the mythical to the historical, through the legendary, clearly exemplifies how knowledge accumulates in these pre-Hispanic cultures. Since there are no divisions among these varied types of information (myths, legends, facts), there is no basis for doubting their patently mythical foundations. Instead, myths become the frame of reference for the next (legendary) stage of comprehension, while the legends then establish the credibility for the final stage, which we understand as history. These successive framings do not imply a misunderstanding of the essential differences between myth and legend or between legend and history, but their interdependence does foreclose the kind of questioning or self-consciousness that would allow those distinctive ways of knowing to function more flexibly and more independently as information.

Associated with these interrelated accounts of the past is the decisive role of tradition in pre-Hispanic societies, which, in turn, offers a clue to one of its most disquieting features, the prominence of human sacrifice. In a civilization in which mere survival entailed enormous challenges, the crucial role of the past in sustaining all life is directly apprehended. Such a thin margin of survival demanded continuing gratitude to the ancestors, a gratitude embodied in the myths themselves, which manifested an appropriate devotion to the ancestors and to their stories. But the interlinking of gratitude for survival with the immediate fear of extinction also helps to explain the complexity of sacrificial rites in pre-Hispanic culture. For how can one thank the gods for the grace of survival if not with its most precious result, human life? And how does one suppress the growing fear of extinction, if not with sacrifices that emphasize the fragility and tenuousness of that life?

In addition to such primal motivations, sacrifice in pre-Hispanic cultures is also related to their notions of divinity. The Mesoamerican pantheon is a complex family of gods, differentiated not only by the natural elements (including sun, moon, planets, stars, water, fire, earth, air, sky, underworld, wind, night, and day) but also by the different forms that these elements assume: thus the god of rain water is distinct from the god of lake water, or that of river water or the water of the ocean. Even physical phenomena, such as movement or earthquakes, are represented by separate divinities. Such distinctions are even further refined: in the Incan pantheon, for example, there were discrete gods for the sound of thunder, for the appearance of lightning against the sky, and for lightning's impact as an electric discharge.

However, the significance of perhaps the most critical figures in the Inca pantheon, the stellar objects, remains largely mysterious to us. Of course, every civilization has sought, in the scattered and chaotic distribution of stars in the sky, some order that would explain both origins and destiny. But while Western culture has inherited a fairly similar version of those heavenly arrangements, Mesoamerican and Andean cultures viewed the starry sky quite differently and, indeed, from the southern hemisphere, the Andean peoples literally saw "another" sky altogether. While dissimilar constructions of the firmament are most obvious in the Incan pantheon, such differences are equally significant for Mesoamerican cultures since their mythologies are also shaped by their way of "seeing," that is, of arranging and ordering the stars in the sky. The shape and implications of these images are described in several of the texts included in this section.

One instance of this "seeing" the heavens so differently involves one of the most moving and dramatic accounts in Mesoamerican mythology, the narrative that explains the creation of the world as the sacrifice of many gods jumping into a fiery pit. Such sacrifice on the part of the gods underlines the enormity of the debt that these peoples perceived toward their precursors. If the gods sacrificed themselves, how else could people thank them for the creation of the world, except by comparable sacrifice? Moreover, the two most critical inhabitants of the skies, the sun and the moon, were not simply passive creations (as in many Western religions) but transformations of gods. Two divinities who jumped into the universal fire were miraculously changed into the two fundamental stars that give life to the world. Any failure of those heavenly bodies would be testimony to the death of the gods themselves—thus intensifying the sense of debt and fear on the part of the humans who had to rely on those luminaries for their very survival.

From these twinned emotions of debt and fear and their implications for understanding the divine, however, emerges the second critical dimension of Mesoamerican culture, the notion of work as an expenditure rather than a means of exchange. "Labor" in pre-Hispanic cultures was not a commodity, something that could be exchanged for money or a salary. It was a way of living, a way of expending energy in order to guarantee the world's existence and its harmonious continuation. Key to comprehending the historical behavior of these societies is recognizing that any excess of production was not directed toward an exchange of goods or an accumulation of wealth or even acquiring luxuries. On the contrary, excesses were obtained to support religious rites, to pay one's debt to the gods. The construction of enormous pyramids and roads, the mining of precious metals, and the fashioning of exquisite religious artifacts elicited great expenditures of labor and capital throughout Mesoamerica. But the most precious surplus in a marginal economy was always human life.

Paying this fundamental debt and giving thanks for survival evidently entailed the deaths of many human beings; on numerous occasions, thousands were sacrificed in a single ceremony. But such bloodshed, disturbing today, does provide an index of the magnitude of fear that defined these cultures. Any deviance in the behavior of the sun and moon, for example, would clearly bring chaos. To avoid such an unholy possibility, these two stars had to be offered the indispensable energy contained in human life and materialized in the palpitations of the human heart.

This identification of gods with stellar bodies and the human gifts that were required to sustain their life-giving presence not only explains human sacrifices but also elucidates another perplexing feature of Mesoamerican cultures: warfare as a source of sacrificial victims. On the one hand, paying a blood-debt to the gods required a greater and greater production of excess within the society; but supporting that increasing debt, especially among the Nahuas, also generated a spiral toward self-destruction, since that payment compelled an increasingly unmanageable consumption not only of labor but of human lives. Additional sources had to be found. One response to that necessity of additional sacrifice was *guerras floridas* or the "flower wars." In these calculated conflicts, capturing warriors alive was the point. The conquered were battle trophies that would contribute to sacrificial rites, their blood giving energy to the sun, keeping it moving and preserving the order of the universe.

While such ritualistic battles echo the Greek practice of declaring a truce in order to celebrate the Olympic Games, the Greeks' payment of the debt to the gods was symbolic; human energy was expended in games rather than in the surrender of human life on the altar. The Nahuas and the Mayas paid their obligations to the divine order far more literally. For pre-Colombian societies, religious ritual incarnated rather than signified its referents. In contrast to Western cultures, in which a symbol and what is symbolized are separate entities, with different qualities and natures, pre-Hispanic peoples identified the symbols of the gods with the gods themselves. An image of a god was at once image and reality: the depiction of a god was the god itself as well as what the god represented.

Human sacrifices were literal offerings of life in gratitude for the creation of the world. Likewise, sacred places, such as the pyramids, were not simply reproductions of mythic locations—they *were* those places reincarnated and physically present. Indeed, for the Incas, the structure of the Tahuantinsuyu, with its careful division of *ceques* or paths, was the terrestrial manifestation of time itself.

Another, somewhat counterintuitive, example of these literal connections between the physical and nonphysical worlds were the "costumes" that provided visual representations of the gods. Rather than symbolic portrayals, the divine masks were manifestations of the natural phenomena that the gods embodied. For Mesoamericans, physical phenomena could never become abstract or merely symbolic of the divine reality that they manifested. The divine and the physical were indistinct. There was, for example, no perceived separation between earth and sky. For the Incas and others, there was no break or distance between what was immediate and what was remote. The sky was attached to the earth and one could reach the Via Lactea or Milky Way directly from the ground. There was simply no division between the world of symbols and the other world of symbolized entities.

Such a view of natural phenomena did not, of course, allow for the construction of what we now call the "scientific" perspective. Pre-Colombian people, for instance, had an astonishing knowledge of the planetary and stellar universe and could predict phenomena hundreds or thousands of years in the future. But they were never able to abstract from those detailed observations the concept of cause and effect. Such a notion, comprehended by Western cultures in the sixteenth century and promptly applied to all other aspects of human experience, provided a key to the rationalism and experimental science that underlies our contemporary worldview. Appreciating these conceptual differences offers us an essential bridge between pre-Hispanic cultures and our own, and the texts that follow can help deepen our understanding of this critical interpenetration of the literal and the symbolic that defines the extraordinary world of pre-Hispanic America.

Mesoamerica

Despite much debate, there are very few undisputed conclusions about the origins or even the antiquity of Mesoamerican peoples. Almost every year, new archaeological and anthropological discoveries challenge accepted theories and raise new questions about when, and by whom, the Americas were settled.

One oft-repeated theory is that the ancestors of the American peoples crossed the Bering Strait from Asia. But that notion, which relies heavily on perceived similarities between Indian and Asian languages, overlooks an important mid-nineteenth-century survey of the different languages spoken in Mexico, indicating that the majority of those 150 documented vernaculars bore no resemblance to Asian tongues. Moreover, the notion of migrations from the north does not explain one of the oldest cultures in Mesoamerica, the Olmecs, nor one of the least studied, the Otomí, neither of which bears much evidence of Asian influence.[3]

In fact, the Olmec civilization offers important clues to the erratic and uncertain ways that the successive cultures developed. Often considered the "mother culture" of the region, the Olmecs settled along the Gulf of Mexico around the second millennium BCE. Though they seem to have disappeared around 500 BCE, elements of their culture persisted throughout Mesoamerica, suggesting that the Olmecs never truly vanished, but were gradually dispersed and integrated into successive societies across the region. Many Mayan and Zapotec sites, for example, include evidence of direct contact with the Olmecs, such as the ceremonial center of Monte Albán in Oaxaca. Though Monte Albán was a Zapotec site after 400 BCE, Olmec cultural elements remained integral and active aspects of the culture—not simply legacies of a distant past.

The common notion that Mesoamerican cultures replaced one another in a clear temporal sequence (that is, that the Olmecs were succeeded by the Zapotecs, Classic Mayas, and Teotihuacán, who were then followed by the Toltecs and Post-Classic Mayans, and finally the Nahuas, and within them, the Aztecs) cannot account for such cultural overlap. Rather these relationships can be better understood as a complex series of transformations and relocalizations of earlier traditions. The sheer diversity of what we now call Classic Mayan civilization—roughly spanning the first thousand years of the Christian era—itself suggests that the older Olmec culture was being

---

3   The Otomí people are not Nahua, and while their history is unknown, they are believed to be native to the Olmec region.

dispersed and transformed across the subcontinent. At Classic Mayan sites, for example, such as Palenque, Tikal, and Copán, earlier settlements that had once been united by a single tongue later evolved separate languages.

Even the two primary Mayan languages (the Huasteca, which spread across several modern states of northern Mexico, and the related tongues of the Yucatán peninsula and the Chiapas highlands) emerged in regions that were adjacent to the original Olmec territories, suggesting direct contact. So while it has been convenient to identify Mesoamerican cultures as a succession of societies in well-defined geographic regions, the interactions between and among peoples was clearly far more complex, both temporally and spatially.

But even if older cultures were dispersed in uneven ways, the northern migrations, which occurred in several different waves, did have a significant impact. The influential Nahua culture, for example, that flourished in the twelfth and thirteenth centuries, probably originated on the shores of the Colorado River, near the present-day borders of Utah and Colorado in the United States. The most famous of the Nahua, the Aztecs, were simply the final migrants to arrive on the shores of Lake Texcoco.

The diversity of these successive migrations, arriving over centuries, together with the erratic persistence of older cultures, like the Olmec, continues to make it difficult to attribute specific elements to specific peoples. Even the geographic range of these cultures makes generalizations problematic: spreading from the coasts of Veracruz (the Olmecs) to Yucatán-Highlands (the Mayas), to Oaxaca (the Zapotecs) and to the center of Mexico (the Teotihuacán and later the Toltecs at Tula and the Nahua at Texcoco). These latter are the best known, but even among the most familiar, like the Maya and Nahua, there are significant gaps. No one knows, for instance, what language was spoken in Teotihuacán, a powerful city that, at its apogee, around 500 CE, had a population of one quarter million souls. And certainly no one (as yet) understands the origin of many fundamental myths and customs, like the 260-day calendar around which the Nahuas and Mayas organized their cultures. What we do know is that, despite the ravages of conquest and colonialism, the people of this region managed to maintain more than 150 languages well into the nineteenth century, indicating both the strength and sophistication of their diverse cultures.

As we study Mesoamerica, then, we need to keep in mind how much remains unclear, including many cultural relationships, myths, deities, and even basic cosmologies. In this section, we have singled out only two of the dozen or so sophisticated cultures that coexisted (not always peaceably)

Figure 1.1. Olmec head. Museo de Antropología de Xalapa. Photograph by Luis, Chilangomex.wordpress.com. By permission of the Instituto Nacional de Antropología e Historia.

over the centuries. The Maya were probably the most powerful civilization in the area, leaving remarkable monuments across what are now Mexico, Guatemala, Honduras, and Belize. Even so, scholars have only recently begun to unravel some Mayan mysteries, including its glyphs and the marks of its cultural predominance. In contrast, we know a good deal more about the Aztecs, primarily because they became the "representative" Mesoamerican culture for their Spanish conquerors. But that culture was itself deeply shaped by a very particular history. And while its characteristics are often assumed to be generic, they were the result of distinct migration patterns as well as the specific place where they settled: the central basin of Mexico, or what is now Mexico City. By studying these two cultures and observing their singularities as well as their shared sensibilities, we can perhaps get some sense of the complexities of this distinctive region.

In Context | Olmec Head

Olmec civilization has long been a puzzle for both archaeologists and historians. Flourishing on the eastern gulf coast of present-day Mexico, this culture has been credited as the "Mother Civilization" of Mesoamerica, with scholars tracing its origins as far back as the second millennium BCE. Many myths and institutions unique to Mesoamerica, including the 260-day calendar,[4] together with certain agricultural and cultural practices, originate with the Olmecs.

Creation and Metamorphosis of the Mayan World: The *Popol Vuh*

Chicago's Newberry Library owns the manuscript of *Popol Vuh*, written in two columns, one in Maya Quiché, and the other, a translation into Spanish. Composed at the beginning of the eighteenth century (1703), this famous text is the work of Francisco Jiménez, a Dominican priest from Chichicastenango, Guatemala. According to his account, the Maya-Quiché text was copied from another—now lost—document, probably written in the middle of the sixteenth century, around 1550.

All translations of the *Popol Vuh* are based on this unique Maya-Quiché text, although some translators, convinced that the priest made too many mistakes in his transcription of the lost original, have used other sources for its myths, such as codices, and even contemporary versions—alive in the memory of the Mayans.

The fact that a document such as the *Popol Vuh* exists at all is a direct result of the Spanish conquest. Its famous accounts of the creation of the world and the formation of Mayan civilization (particularly the domestication of corn, which was essential to Mesoamerican life) were, of course, deeply inscribed in the Mayan codices and were constantly reelaborated in religious ceremonies—even as they are today. But the creation of a discrete text was a by-product of the Spanish challenge to native rule.

The *Popol Vuh* was actually the inventive response of a single group of Mayans, the Quiché, in adapting to the pressures of the Spanish conquest. A major reason for its composition (which internal evidence suggests occurred in the mid-sixteenth century) was to demonstrate to the King of Spain the legitimacy of Quiché territorial rights: what better way to justify the claim to one's lands than by recounting the history of the people in that place from the very beginning of the world?

The "continuous story" of the Mayan annals—the myths recited in the

---

4   The Mesoamerican peoples actually used at least four calendars: the solar, resembling the Gregorian calendar; the lunar, echoing the Jewish and Christian determinations of moveable feasts, like Yom Kippur or Easter; the Venusian, tracking the appearances of Venus; and the 260-day calendar, which relies on a combination of numbers from one to thirteen and the names of twenty different days, such as rabbit, knife, death, and reef. It served as the basis for ritual ceremonies, but its origins remain unknown.

Popol Vuh—did not in their original form have a clear narrative sequence. For the Mayans, the sagas of the different gods and heroes simply did not occur as a single story line. Accordingly, the initial chapters of what we know as the *Popol Vuh* do not follow a chronological sequence. But its tales of heroism and sacrifice for the sake of creation remain compelling, both in their imaginative scope and as revelations of the deepest values of the Mesoamerican people.

Among the more unusual features of Mesoamerican and some Andean mythologies is the notion that the world was not created once. Since the gods were not infallible, they continued to correct their creation until they achieved the equilibrium of each moment. But even that equilibrium was precarious. Mesoamerican peoples never got over the deep feeling that the universe was in a constant process of metamorphosis, always risking annihilation.

One reason that the gods never abandoned their creation is that they were intrinsic to it, transforming themselves into essential elements of nature: sun, moon, stars, earth, water. The land of mortals thus always touches the sky, extending into the realms of the immortals and the underworld of the dead. Mythologies are not simply stories about how that natural world works, but also manuals for the individual and for society about how to gain access to that sky and that underworld. The *Popol Vuh* superbly manifests those qualities, as both a narrative of how the world was created and a guide to traversing those boundaries. The term "popol vuh" translates as "council book," underlining its function as a manual for community leaders responsible for determining rituals and activities and appropriate forms of social behavior.

The excerpt here recounts the creation of the earth and heavens as a result of the death of the twin brothers Hunahpu and Xbalanque, who return from the dead in a different form from what they were before "dying" at the hands of the gods of Xibalba, the kingdom of Death. As two young vagabonds, Hunahpu and Xbalanque eventually deceive the gods of Xibalba and cause their deaths so that the brothers can create the sun and the moon.

This passage also exemplifies another basic concept in Mesoamerican thought, that of duality—duality refined by its embodiment in twins. As the story indicates, mere brothers had failed to trick the gods of Xibalba in their plan to create the world. Those who don't fail are the twins, Hunahpu and Xbalanque. "Twinness" is distinct from simple brotherhood. Twins are both the same and different. Moreover, their sameness is both material and spiritual, while their difference is also spiritual, without ceasing to be the same.

One example of that refined duality is that while the twins eventually overcome the lords of the dead, surviving all of their trials and, in the process, creating maize, the very basis of human life, they do not want to overcome death itself. Instead, they themselves undergo death in order to transform themselves into the sun and the moon, establishing the lasting order of the universe. In Mayan mythology, these two heavenly bodies are essential for the equilibrium of the universe, confirming how, in Mayan thought, natural objects are conceived not merely as symbols of the gods, but as the physical consequences of a divine metamorphosis. The materiality of the divine is thus established by the myth itself. Matter, in such a view, is never purely mechanical, nor simply an inert and inanimate mass, as became the case for most European cultures after the scientific revolution. The Mesoamerican material world exudes the spirituality of the twins: the sun and the moon who have sacrificed themselves to create the universe and who are, at the same time, a tangible effect of that very creation.

The text is part 3 from *Popol Vuh: The Definitive Edition of the Mayan Book of the Dawn of Life and the Glories of Gods and Kings*, translated by Dennis Tedlock (New York: Touchstone, 1996), 130–38. Reprinted with the permission of Simon & Schuster, Inc., from *Popol Vuh*, translated by Dennis Tedlock. Copyright © 1985, 1996 Dennis Tedlock. Digital permission granted by Ward & Balkin Agency.

And Here It Is: The Epitaph, the Death of Hunahpu and Xbalanque

Here it is: now we shall name their epitaph, their death. They did whatever they were instructed to do, going through all the dangers, the troubles that were made for them, but they did not die from the tests of Xibalba, nor were they defeated by all the voracious animals that inhabit Xibalba.

After that, they summoned two midmost seers, similar to readers. Here are their names: Xulu, Pacam, both knowers.

"Perhaps there will be questions from the lords of Xibalba about our death. They are thinking about how to overcome us because we haven't died, nor have we been defeated. We've exhausted all their tests. Not even the animals got us. So this is the sign, here in our hearts: their instrument for our death will be a stone oven. All the Xibalbans have gathered together. Isn't our death inevitable? So this is your plan, here we shall name it: if you come to be questioned by them about our death, once we've been burned, what will you say, Xulu, and you, Pacam? If they ask you:

'Wouldn't it be good if we dumped their bones in the canyon?'

'Perhaps it wouldn't be good, since they would only come back to life again,' you will say.

'Perhaps this would be good: we'll just hang them up in a tree,' they'll say to you next.

'Certainly that's no good, since you would see their faces,' you will say, and then they'll speak to you for the third time:

'Well, here's the only good thing: we'll just dump their bones in the river.' If that's what they ask you next:

'This is a good death for them, and it would also be good to grind their bones on a stone, just as hard corn is refined into flour, and refine each of them separately, and then:

'Spill them into the river,
sprinkle them on the water's way,
among the mountains, small and great.'

you will say, and then you will have carried out the instructions we've named for you," said little Hunahpu and Xbalanque. When they gave these instructions they already knew they would die.

THIS IS THE MAKING OF THE OVEN, the great stone oven. The Xibalbans made it like the places where the sweet drink is cooked, they opened it to a great width.

After that, messengers came to get the boys, the messengers of One and Seven Death:

"'They must come. We'll go with the boys, to see the treat we've cooked up for them,' says the lords, you boys," they were told.

"Very well," they replied. They went running and arrived at the mouth of the oven.

And there they tried to force them into a game.

"Here, let's jump over our drink four times, clear across, one of us after the other, boys," they were told by One Death.

"You'll never put that one over on us. Don't we know what our death is, you lords? Watch!" they said, then they faced each other. They grabbed each other by the hands and went head first into the oven.

And there they died, together, and now all the Xibalbans were happy, raising their shouts, raising their cheers:

"We've really beaten them! They didn't give up easily," they said.

After that they summoned Xulu and Pacam, who kept their word: the bones went just where the boys had wanted them. Once the Xibalbans had done their divination, the bones were ground and spilled in the river, but they didn't go far—they just sank to the bottom of the water. They became handsome boys; they looked just the same as before when they reappeared.

AND SO ON THE FIFTH DAY THEY REAPPEARED. They were seen in the water by the people. The two of them looked like catfish when their faces were seen by Xibalba. And having germinated in the waters, they appeared the day after that as two vagabonds, with rags before and rags behind, and rags all over too. They seemed unrefined when they were examined by Xibalba; they acted differently now.

It was the only Dance of the Poorwill, the Dance of the Weasel. Only Armadillos they danced.

Only swallowing swords, only Walking on Stilts now they danced.

They performed many miracles now. They would set fire to a house, as if they were really burning it, and suddenly bring it back again. Now Xibalba was full of admiration. Next they would sacrifice themselves, one of them dying for the other, stretched out as if in death. First they would kill themselves, but then they would suddenly look alive again. The Xibalbans could only admire what they did. Everything they did now was already the groundwork for their defeat of Xibalba.

And after that, news of their dances came to the ears of the lords, One and Seven Death. When they heard it they said:

"Who are these two vagabonds? [Hunahpu and Xbalanque] Are they really such a delight? And is their dancing really that pretty? They do everything!" they said. An account of them had reached the lords. It sounded delightful, so then they entreated their messengers to notify them that they must come:

"If only they'd come make a show for us, we'd wonder at them and marvel at them," say the lords, "you will say," the messengers were told. So they came to the dancers, then spoke the words of the lords to them.

"But we don't want to, because we're really ashamed. Just plain no. Wouldn't we be afraid to go inside there, into a lordly house? Because we'd really look bad. Wouldn't we just be wide-eyed? Take pity on us! Wouldn't we look like mere dancers to them? What would we say to our fellow vagabonds? There are others who also want us to dance today, to liven things up with us, so we can't do likewise for the lords, and likewise is not what we want, messengers," said Hunahpu and Xbalanque.

Even so, they were prevailed upon: through troubles, through torments, they went on their tortuous way. They didn't want to walk fast. Many times they had to be forced; the messengers went ahead of them as guides but had to keep coming back. And so they went to the lord.

AND THEY CAME TO THE LORDS. Feigning great humility, they bowed their heads all the way to the ground when they arrived. They brought themselves low, doubled over, flattened out, down to the rags, to the tatters. They really looked like vagabonds when they arrived.

So then they were asked what their mountain and tribe were, and they were also asked about their mother and father:

"Where do you come from?" they were asked.

"We've never known, lord. We don't know the identity of our mother and father. We must've been small when they died," was all they said. They didn't give any names.

"Very well. Please entertain us, then. What do you want us to give you in payment?" they were asked.

"Well, we don't want anything. To tell the truth, we're afraid," they told the lord.

"Don't be afraid. Don't be ashamed. Just dance this way: first you'll dance to sacrifice yourselves, you'll set fire to my house after that, you'll act out all the things you know. We want to be entertained. This is our heart's desire, the reason you had to be sent for, dear vagabonds. We'll give you payment," they were told.

So then they began their songs and dances, and then all the Xibalbans arrived, the spectators crowded the floor, and they danced everything: they danced the Weasel, they danced the Poorwill, they danced the Armadillo. Then the lord said to them:

"Sacrifice my dog, then bring him back to life again," they were told.

"Yes," they said.

When they sacrificed the dog
he then came back to life.
And that dog was really happy
when he came back to life.
Back and forth he wagged his tail
when he came back to life.

And the lord said to them:

"Well, you have yet to set my home on fire," they were told next, so then they set fire to the home of the lord. The house was packed with all the lords, but they were not burned. They quickly fixed it back again, lest the house of One Death be consumed all at once, and all the lords were amazed, and they went on dancing this way. They were overjoyed.

And then they were asked by the lord:

"You have yet to kill a person! Make a sacrifice without death!" they were told.

"Very well," they said.

And then they took hold of a human sacrifice.

And they held up a human heart on high.

And they showed its roundness to the lords.

And now One and Seven Death admired it, and now that person was brought right back to life. His heart was overjoyed when he came back to life, and the lords were amazed:

"Sacrifice yet again, even do it to yourselves! Let's see it! At heart, that's the dance we really want from you," the lords said now.

"Very well, lord," they replied, and then they sacrificed themselves.

AND THIS IS THE SACRIFICE OF LITTLE HUNAHPU BY XBALANQUE.

One by one his legs, his arms were spread wide. His head came off, rolled far away outside. His heart, dug out, was smothered in a leaf, and all the Xibalbans went crazy at the sight.

So now, only one of them was dancing there: Xbalanque.

"Get up!" he said, and Hunahpu came back to life. The two of them were overjoyed at this—and likewise the lords rejoiced, as if they were doing it themselves. One and Seven Death were as glad at heart as if they themselves were actually doing the dance.

And then the hearts of the lords were filled with longing, with yearning for the dance of little Hunahpu and Xbalanque, so then came the words from One and Seven Death:

"Do it to us! Sacrifice us!" they said. "Sacrifice both of us!" said One and Seven Death to little Hunahpu and Xbalanque.

"Very well. You ought to come back to life. What is death to you? And aren't we making you happy, along with the vassals of your domain?" they told the lords.

And this one was the first to be sacrificed: the lord at the very top, the one whose name is One Death, the ruler of Xibalba.

And with One Death dead, the next to be taken was Seven Death. They did not come back to life.

And then the Xibalbans were getting up to leave, those who had seen the lords die. They underwent heart sacrifice there, and the heart sacrifice was performed on the two lords only for the purpose of destroying them.

As soon as they had killed the one lord without bringing him back to life, the other lord had been meek and tearful before the dancers. He didn't consent, he didn't accept it:

"Take pity on me!" he said when he realized. All their vassals took the road to the great canyon, in one single mass they filled up the deep abyss. So they piled up there and gathered together, countless ants, tumbling down into the canyon, as if they were being herded there. And when they arrived, they all bent low in surrender, they arrived meek and tearful.

Such was the defeat of the rulers of Xibalba. The boys accomplished it only through wonders, only through self-transformation.

AND THEN THEY NAMED THEIR NAMES, they gave themselves names before all of Xibalba:

"Listen: we shall name our names, and we shall also name the names of our fathers for you. Here we are: we are little Hunahpu and Xbalanque by name. And these are our fathers, the ones you killed: One Hunahpu and Seven Hunahpu by name. And we are here to clear the road of the torments and troubles of our fathers. And so we have suffered all the troubles you've caused us. And so we are putting an end to all of you. We're going to kill you. No one can save you now," they were told. And then all the Xibalbans got down on the ground and cried out:

"Take pity on us, Hunahpu and Xbalanque! It is true that we wronged your fathers, the ones you name. Those two are buried at the Place of Ball Game Sacrifice," they replied.

"Very well. Now this is our word, we shall name it for you. All of you listen, you Xibalbans: Because of this, your day and your descendants will not be great. Moreover, the gifts you receive will no longer be great, but reduced to scabrous nodules of sap. There will be no cleanly blotted blood for you, just griddles, just gourds, just brittle things broken to pieces. Further, you will only feed on the creatures of the meadows and clearings. None of those who are born in the light, begotten in the light will be yours. Only the worthless will yield themselves up before you. These will be the guilty, the violent, the wretched, the afflicted. Wherever the blame is clear, that is where you will come in, rather than just making sudden attacks on people in general. And you will hear petitions over headed-up sap," all the Xibalbans were told.

Such was the beginning of their disappearance and the denial of their worship,

> Their ancient day was not a great one,
> these ancient people only wanted conflict,
> their ancient names are not really divine,
> but fearful is the ancient evil of their faces.

> They are makers of enemies, users of owls,
> they are inciters to wrong and violence,
> they are masters of hidden intentions as well,
> they are black and white,
> masters of stupidity, masters of perplexity,
> as it is said. By putting on appearances they cause dismay.

Such was the loss of their greatness and brilliance. Their domain did not return to greatness. This was accomplished by little Hunahpu and Xbalanque.

AND THIS IS THEIR GRANDMOTHER, CRYING AND CALLING OUT IN FRONT OF THE EARS OF GREEN CORN they left planted. Corn plants grew, then dried up.

And this was when they were burned in the oven; then the corn plants grew again.

And this was when their grandmother burned something, she burned copal before the ears of green corn as a memorial to them. There was happiness in their grandmother's heart the second time the corn plants sprouted. Then the ears were deified by their grandmother, and she gave them names: Middle of the House, Middle of the Harvest, Living Ears of Green Corn, Bed of Earth became their names.

And she named the ears Middle of the House, Middle of the Harvest, because they had planted them right in the middle of the inside of their home.

Kings as Gods, Gods as Kings: The Temple of Inscriptions

The Temple of Inscriptions was believed for centuries to be a place of worship until 1948, when the tomb of Pakal was first detected beneath its stone floors. One of Palenque's greatest kings, Pakal had had the building constructed in the decade before his death in 683 CE. Its name derives from the detailed account that Pakal left about his personal lineage and the succession of Palenque's kings, as well as a description of Pakal's funeral ceremonies. Though the temple itself was already celebrated for its extensive

Figure 1.2. Temple of Inscriptions, Palenque, Mexico. Photograph by Tato Grasso (2007). License CC BY-SA 2.5. By permission of the Instituto Nacional de Antropología e Historia.

glyphs, King Pakal's sarcophagus was only discovered in 1952 by the Mexican archaeologist Alberto Ruz. Containing several symbolic artifacts, including a jade collar and a richly ornamented jade death mask, the king's tomb yielded critical information that has helped to reformulate notions of Mayan pyramids.

Pakal's tomb is located at the bottom of the pyramid; a vaulted stair leads to the upper temple, where the various panels of glyphs and figures are inscribed. What is distinctive about this stepped pyramid is its obsession with regal history, an obsession partly revealed by two recorded deviations from patrilineal custom. The most important recognizes Pakal's mother, Lady Zac-Kuk who ruled from October 22, 612 CE, until her death on January 1, 643, long after her son's official enthronement on July 29, 615. But she is portrayed in the temple not simply as a queen but as the Mayan mother of creation, her deified status strengthening Pakal's claim to the throne and thereby marking this striking departure from the usual patrilineal order.

The temple's pyramidal shape replicates the cosmic mountain and the world tree that connected the three realms: the underground kingdom of the dead, Xibalba; the human world that flourished through the blood sacrifice of the kings; and the immortal regions of the heavens. In contrast to Andean myths, where creation occurs at a specific place, in Mayan belief, creation could have materialized wherever pyramids re-created the sacred spaces of the mountain, the forest, and the cave, and where it had been facilitated through the bloodletting of the king. The king himself thus functioned as the WORLD TREE linking these three realms. Moreover, like the twin gods in the *Popol Vuh*, Pakal at his death would go to Xibalba, and like them, confront the lords of the underworld, deceive them, and then die, resurrect, and return again to the human world.

Until the discovery of Pakal's entombment, Mayan pyramids were not viewed as funerary temples, but only as ritual spaces. With the recent identification of other pyramids that also had served as tombs, that notion is being revised. As the inscriptions at Palenque demonstrate, pyramids often had a double function, reaffirming the interpenetration of myth and history in Mayan culture. Thus the dead ruler replicates the mythic journey of the twins of the *Popol Vuh*, even as he completes his personal passage into and beyond death. The ceremony of his burial recorded in the glyphs both prepares and enacts this sacred journey even as it documents the history of a very specific individual, Pakal.

The Mayan Cosmos: The World Tree

In both Mesoamerican and Andean mythology, the universe is spatially continuous, with no separation between the underworld, the earth's surface, or the region of the stars. Among the many astronomical phenomena that corroborated such spatial continuity was the Venusian cycle of appearance and disappearance. And associated with that heavenly cycle was the image of the great world tree.

In recurring cycles of 584 days, Venus appears and reappears in the map of the sky. Mayans interpreted the regular disappearance of Venus as its voyage into the world of the dead. At the end of that journey, Venus would reemerge first as the morning star (before dawn) and then as the evening star (after sunset). The planet's cycle represented a complete passage through the universe: emerging ahead of the sun, it crossed the earth toward the underworld, where it fought with the dark lords; eventually it would reappear at dusk, behind the sun, only to disappear again, waging constant battle with the enemies of light and in recurring apotheosis as the sun's loyal companion.

The cycles of Venus represented for Mesoamericans the duality of duality itself: both a heavenly star and a fighter in the underworld. Its travels through the underworld echo the journeys recorded in the *Popol Vuh*, first

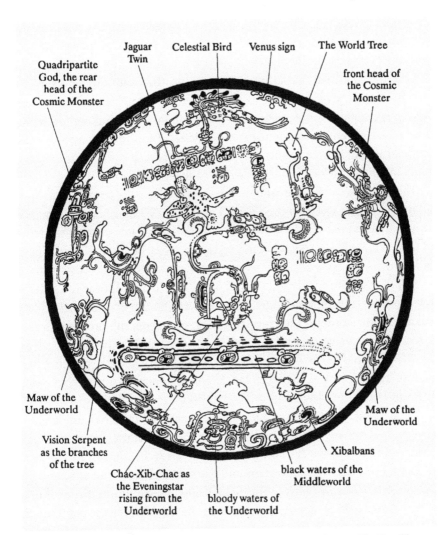

Figure 1.3. The Mayan cosmos: The World Tree. From *A Forest of Kings: The Untold Story of the Ancient Mayas* by Linda Schele and David Freidel (New York: William Morrow, 1992), 70, fig. 2.4. Copyright 1990 by Linda Schele and David Freidel. Used by permission of HarperCollins Publishers.

by One Hunahpu and Seven Hunahpu and later by the twins Hunahpu and Xbalanque.

In representations of the Mayan universe, the planet Venus emerges from the underworld at the point where it rises from the earth's surface on its way back to the heavens. This continuity between realms is represented by a great world tree, whose roots are embedded in the underworld and whose trunk merges with Venus's body—now represented as the evening star rising from that underworld—and whose highest branches mingle with the great bird of the sky.

Like the Venusian cycle, the tree embodies the continuity and the diversity of the universe. From its trunk, near the earth's heart, two giant branches extend toward the horizon, becoming the two arching forces, or jaws, of nature: one of creation and one of destruction. These great branches form a heavenly circle connected to the earth, revealing the fundamental unity of being and becoming throughout the universe.

This representation of duality that becomes a figure of oneness was also adopted by the Aztecs. In the AZTEC SUN STONE CALENDAR, for example, two serpents encircle the universe, their heads meeting at the base of the circle, opening their enormous jaws to reveal between them the face of Venus.

Another significant representation of the World Tree appears on Pakal's tombstone in the TEMPLE OF THE INSCRIPTIONS at Palenque. There Pakal himself occupies the place of Venus, traversing the universe in the form of a great tree extending from the underworld to the heavens. For the Mayans, in dying we all reproduce Venus's crossing and experience her duality. In fact, just as the tree's two branches, creation and destruction, reach out to encircle the horizon (both in Pakal's tomb and in the Sun Stone Calendar), Pakal's position in the place of Venus indicates our fundamental duality. Humans too are both destroyers and creators: we are made of corn, eating to survive and to reproduce ourselves. In contrast to Western thought, however, Mesoamericans understood this duality not as a concept but as a process. Constantly in the making and being undone, duality is not a mental image to be applied to objects in the world but is the continuous transformation of all being. Indeed, for Mayans, there are no fixed abstractions, only transformations. That is why the equilibrium of the universe remained so precarious and why its people lived in such constant anxiety.

For Mesoamericans, the world is in constant metamorphosis. Nothing is given for all eternity, and everything justifies itself by constantly creating and being created, by destroying and being destroyed. The Venusian cycles of duality, closely connected with the encircling expanses of the World Tree that links all levels of the universe, serves to demonstrate one of the more enduring and fundamental constructs of the Mesoamerican world. Without churches or doctrinal canons, there nonetheless reigned a profound and coherent vision of how all being constitutes a vital, if tenuous, process.

Aztec Cosmogony: The Birth of Life and Death in The Myth
of Huitzilopochtli

The birth of Huitzilopochtli, the hummingbird of the South, is the Aztec
myth par excellence. Myths usually tell of origins, testifying that everything
has a beginning: but the myth of Huitzilopochtli is the beginning of all
beginnings (fig. 1.4, 34).

In the mythology of the Nahua (and thus of the Aztecs, who shared their
culture), the world was created five times. An imbalance in the harmony
of nature had destroyed each of the previous worlds, or Four Suns, as they
were called: the first was consumed by devouring beasts, the next by winds,
then fire, and finally rains. The fifth Sun, our world, was founded on motion—natural energy—but any excess of motion would result in its destruction as well. In our Sun or era, therefore, everything depends on the steady
maintenance of movement, and thus the Nahua, like most Mesoamericans,
were obsessed with the consistency of natural phenomena, especially the
movements of the heavens—the stars, the sun, the moon, and the planets.

In many versions of the Nahua creation story, the sun and moon were
originally fashioned with equal intensity, so that there was no night, no
equilibrium of opposites, no duality. To achieve the necessary balance, the
gods threw a rabbit up to the moon.[5] The rabbit's impression on the lunar
surface dimmed the moon's original brightness and made it secondary to
the sun, so that there could be night. But in the Nahua creation myth that
features Huitzilopochtli, what is emphasized is the essential conflict that
creates equilibrium and keeps the world in motion. Huitzilopochtli is both
the sun and the god of war because the sun must constantly wage battle
against all the obstacles that threaten its daily course across the heavens. He
is both movement and stillness, exactly like a hummingbird that stays in
one place while beating its wings. He is also the symbol, the essence of the
current Fifth Sun, a period when humans must do whatever is necessary to
maintain the regularity or the stillness of Nature, knowing at the same time
that creation is in constant movement.

According to the Aztecs, Huitzilopochtli was the son of COATLICUE, the
Mother Earth, whose body is encircled by a skirt of snakes, her face formed
by two opposing serpents (fig. 1.5, 37). She is, in one sense, the feminine
aspect of her elder son, Quetzalcóatl, the god of duality, whose visage is likewise represented by two serpents, adorned with feathers as on the AZTEC

5   Gutierre Tibón, *Historia del nombre y de la fundación de México* (Mexico City: Fondo de Cultura
    Económica, 1975).

Figure 1.4. Birth of Huitzilopochtli. Illustration reprinted by permission of the School for Advanced Research (SAR Press) from "Book III: The Origin of the Gods," number 14, part IV in *Florentine Codex: General History of the Things of New Spain*, translated from the Aztec into English by Arthur J. O. Anderson and Charles E. Dibble, eds. (Santa Fe, New Mexico: School of American Research, 1952), 39. No part of this material may be printed, reproduced, transmitted, in any form or by any means, electronic or mechanical, including any information storage or retrieval system, without written permission from the School for Advanced Research (SAR Press).

CALENDAR STONE. The energies of Quetzalcóatl, who combines the opposites of earth and air, are thus divided by the Aztecs between the figure of his mother Coatlicue (with her serpents) and her posthumous offspring, Huitzilopochtli (the feathered hummingbird). In fact, Coatlicue was miraculously impregnated by a mysterious ball of feathers, giving birth to her twin sons, Quetzalcóatl and Xolotl. Embarrassed by her mother's pregnancy, Coatlicue's daughter COYOLXAUHQUI (fig. 1.6, 38) incited her four hundred brothers to attack their mother. At the moment of her decapitation, her son Huitzilopochtli sprang full-grown from her womb, adorned in feathers, holding a sword of fire, ready to defend his mother. He promptly cut off Coyolxauhqui's head and tossed it into the sky as the moon and then scattered his brothers, the Centzonuitznaua—the innumerable stars (literally the "four hundred rabbits")—across the heavens. Just as the image of Quetzalcóatl is split into separate figures, the Aztecs also set apart the Nahua moon—the luminous star, whose brightness is dimmed by the rabbit stamped on her surface—from the other major light of the night sky, the Milky Way or the Centzonuitznaua.

As the myth reveals, the killing of enemies meant not their obliteration but their dispersal, the destruction of the unity that might allow them to rival the divine sun's brightness. This phenomenon is emblematized in the ruins of the TEMPLO MAYOR in Mexico City. When Huitzilopochtli shattered the moon into pieces, it fell to the foot of Coatepec, the mountain of serpents. The pyramid, which represents Coatepec, has at its base a low relief depicting the moon in fragments, tangibly embodying the myth and expressing its significance.

The myth of Huitzilopochtli, perhaps more than any other constituent of Aztec culture, expresses most forcefully the oppositions that are central to its character: the tiniest bird represents the most impressive star, the sun—magnificently potent but never omnipotent. Arrayed with feathers (the sun's rays are often visualized as wings), sun and bird are both suspended in the air by their own powerful energies. Huitzilopochtli is the beginning of the beginning because he personifies primal energy and essential motion. The sun's light is not its essence, but only a weapon against enemies and rivals. The fundamental element is movement itself, wielding its power throughout the universe, allowing everything to proceed in order and harmony. Even so, nothing guarantees this motion; even the sun might at any moment be forced from its orbit, bringing universal chaos and the catastrophic end of the Fifth Sun.

Since Mesoamerican peoples wrote in ideographs rather than with alphabets, the account included here, like many other texts of this era, was the creation of the Spanish missionaries. Many works that survived in oral tradition were eventually written down by collectors like BERNARDINO DE SAHAGÚN. This particular text also indicates the commonality across Mesoamerica of many elements of Huitzilopochtli's birth, despite its close association with Aztec culture. Most prominent is the prediction that Huitzilopochtli's mother would bear a son who would come from her womb wielding a sword of fire. But despite these and other shared features, Huitzilopochtli's name—the hummingbird of the South—suggests that the god had not in fact been with the Aztecs at the beginning of their southward migrations. Instead, the deity had emerged in the vicissitudes of their journey, protecting them as they sought a new home where they would find "an eagle devouring a serpent"—an image of another god with different origins, Quetzalcóatl himself, who would also become part of the Aztec pantheon.

Symbolized Space: The Templo Mayor and the Original Place of Birth and Death (Mexico City)

As the last great empire preceding the Spanish conquest, the Aztecs have defined many of our assumptions about Mesoamerican civilization. However, the culture of this impressive nation drew on several sources. Even as the Aztecs took power in the central valley of Mexico, they apparently began to revise their own history, aligning it with the millennial traditions of the peoples they had conquered along the shores of Lake Texcoco. The complexities of that cultural heritage are reflected in the most important building in the ancient city of Tenochtitlán, the Templo Mayor.

In Mesoamerica, the principal edifices for the public practice of sacred rites were typically pyramids and ball courts. At the summit of the Templo Mayor, in the heart of the Aztecs' capital city, there were two temples, one dedicated to Tlaloc, the rain god, a traditional divinity throughout Mesoamerica, and the other to Huitzilopochtli, the primary god of the Aztecs. These two temples reflect the double heritage echoed in the myth of Huitzilopochtli, which includes elements that were clearly part of an adopted culture. In the version collected by BERNARDINO DE SAHAGÚN, Huitzilopochtli's mother—Mother Earth incarnated as a serpent—is impregnated by the feathers of a bird. This fusion of bird and reptile is a well-known motif of the region around Lake Texcoco—Quetzalcóatl, the plumed serpent. In Huitzilopochtli, aerial and terrestrial elements unite to

Figure 1.5. Coatlicue. Museo de Antropología e Historia, Mexico City. Photograph by Jennifer Saracino. By permission of the Instituto Nacional de Antropología e Historia.

represent the duality of the universe, a basic structure of Mesoamerican thought. That duality is further expressed by the place where Huitzilopochtli was born, Coatepec, "the mountain of serpents": both where Mother Earth resides and the earthly point of contact with the sky. Repeated in architectural terms, the pyramid physically symbolized that mountain in earthly

Figure 1.6. Coyolxauhqui. Museo del Templo Mayor, Mexico City. Photograph by Jennifer Saracino. By permission of the Instituto Nacional de Antropología e Historia.

contact with the heavens, while the temple of Tlaloc deliberately personifies the element of rain, which likewise ties together the earth and the sky.

In addition to these mythological allusions to a syncretic culture, the Templo Mayor also reproduces the combinations of Mesoamerican and Aztec history in other more cyclical ways. There were, in fact, three calendars that defined social and historical time in Mesoamerican life: the solar, the ritual cycle of 260 days, and the Venusian. These three calendars operated in parallel and the first two only coincided every 52 solar years, implying the end of everything.

Mesoamerican peoples lived with the anxiety of not knowing if the world would actually continue its regular course. At midnight of the final day of those coinciding cycles, all the fires in the kingdom were extinguished and all perishable utensils broken. Then the people waited for the passing of the Pleiades constellation through the zenith. If this passage occurred, the universe would continue its course harmoniously. In celebration, a New Fire was lit in a specific place in the valley (now located in a Mexico City neighborhood still called El Cerro de la Estrella—"Star Hill") and taken back to all homes. To further reflect the potential end of everything, the Templo Mayor itself was also renewed. Or rather, as twentieth-century excavations have revealed, especially the discoveries of the 1970s and 1980s, the temple was destroyed and rebuilt several times. In figure 1.7 (40), the sculptures decorating the old pyramid are facing the wall of the new pyramid on the left.

The ruins of the temple reflect layers of destruction and renovation since the beginning of the fourteenth century, precisely the moment when Aztecs arrived in the valley of Mexico. Though primarily a site for important public rituals, the Templo Mayor embodies the complex cultural history of the Aztec people and those they conquered: a mythic, historical, and material testimony to the continuing survival of the world.

The Aztec Sun Stone Calendar

The Sun Stone, also called the Aztec Calendar, is a circular basalt block weighing 25 tons and measuring three and a half meters (12 feet) in diameter (fig. 1.8, 42). Together with an equally famous piece, the COATLICUE (Woman of the Serpented Skirt), the Sun Stone was rescued in 1790, during excavations at the foot of the western bell tower of Mexico's cathedral. Though it is widely held that the Calendar was originally located in the Pyramid of the Templo Mayor, the site of its discovery casts doubt on that notion—along with the popular belief that the cathedral itself was constructed on top of the main building of the Aztec city. The latter is clearly not true.

Despite a great deal of speculation about the intricate figures carved on this stone, many interpretations are contradictory if not incomprehensible. However, coherent results can be gleaned about three of the innermost circles and about the outer circle that frames the whole. In any strict sense, the stone is not a calendar, but a symbolic and spatial representation of time. For Mesoamerican cultures and more specifically for the Nahua, which included the Aztecs, time and space were inseparable; time had a spatial form (the circle) while space itself was not static but dynamic, changing through the course of time.

Figure 1.7. Templo Mayor. Detail. Mexico City. Photograph by Jennifer Saracino. By permission of the Instituto Nacional de Antropología e Historia.

The stone can be read from the outer circle toward the center or from the center outward. The directions are complementary, though some of the circular stripes still resist interpretation. The central circle contains the mask of a god, the Sun, staring straight ahead, open-mouthed, a sacrificial knife hanging from its lips. There are three stones on its forehead and two earrings, marking the first occurrence of the number five. The stone in its entirety represents the Fifth Sun, or the fifth world, the fifth creation of the universe. Designated "suns" by the Nahua, each of the four previous creations had been successively destroyed by natural elements: jaguars, winds, a rain of fire from the volcanoes, and flood. Figures of these four elements fill the second ring, around the Sun's mask, each framed by squares. On either side of the Sun's mask are two eagle claws, identifying the sun as an eagle and the eagle as the sun. Each claw grasps a human heart, giving the sun-eagle the vitality to keep "flying" through the sky each day and cross into the world of the dead every night.

But if the four previous creations each have a protagonist, a day when they were created and a day when they were destroyed, who is the protagonist of the Fifth Sun? On what day was it created and, most crucially, on what day would it be destroyed? The Calendar answers these questions with one of the most fascinating concepts of Nahua—and Aztec—mythology. The contour enclosing the images of the four previous creations suggests a curious figure: a circle with four prolonged quadrangles pointing in four different directions. It is a circle that has been "tied up," the squares like the extremities of a ribbon tying the circle. This configuration represents *movement*: the sun is conceived as a sphere in "tied up" movement, prevented from leaving its orbit or its course. Any disruption of the regular movement of the sun would certainly bring chaos, but movement is essential to life. As the fifth world was created and is sustained by movement, so will it be destroyed. And the Calendar names the day: "Four-Movement."

Nahua constructs the names of days from two elements: first, a number from one to thirteen, and, second, the name of an object (like an obsidian knife), or an animal (a tiger or a deer) or a concept (movement, death). There are twenty such names, occupying the next circle in the stone, including the sign for movement—the tied-up circle. The combination of thirteen numbers with twenty images makes for 260 names, the number of days in the ritual calendar. Merging the ritual and solar calendars means that only four of the 260 days can start a year and only four of them can end one. The "movement" day (coupled with any of its thirteen numbers) is not among those starting and ending days. Thus a year ending in a day named

Figure 1.8. Aztec Sun Stone Calendar. Museo de Antropología e Historia, Mexico City. Photo by Paul Drozd (2011). License CC BY-SA 3.0. By permission of the Instituto Nacional de Antropología e Historia.

"Four-movement" is an anomaly, signaling the end of an era, of an entire Sun.

While the next circles have not been satisfactorily interpreted, the outer circle is clear enough. At the edge of the world lies the fire serpent, or the plumed serpent, the representation of the god Quetzalcóatl, who appears in the sky as the planet Venus. Since Venus's orbit makes it appear as the Morning or Evening Star, announcing the rising or setting of the sun, Venus is the stellar manifestation of duality. Venus's movements, looking at each other in profile at the bottom of the stone, form a face. As with Coatlicue, whose sculpture was originally found next to the Aztec Sun Calendar, the "woman's" face is formed by the literal confrontation of the two serpent heads.

The movement of the two serpents leads to other stars that rise from the serpents' faces as Venus's protruding plumes or *penachos*. It has been suggested that these protrusions represent the Pleiades, the constellation that must pass through the zenith on the night that ends a fifty-two-year cycle. so, then the final meaning of the stone is revealed: space is time, time is space, and both are united by motion.

The Andes

To visit the high Andes, to see its towering mountains and view the immensity of Lake Titicaca, is like traveling back in time and space. In this high Andean plain (12,500 feet/3,811 meters), known as the Altiplano, on the shores of Lake Titicaca (3,232 square miles/8,372 square km), which stretches across the borders of Peru and Bolivia—in this timeless and mysterious place, according to Andean myth, civilization was born.

The names here still tell their stories, such as Lake Titicaca, which in Aymara, the language of the southeastern Altiplano, means "rock of lead." "Titicaca" thus marks the spot where Wiraqocha, a principal Andean god, plumbed the depth of the lake waters and established the center of the universe. In that watery point he identified the axle that connects the three *pachas*, or divisions of time and space, that make up the Andean cosmos. These were *alaxpacha*, or the world above, the place of the sun and the time to come; *akapacha*, or the surfaces where we walk, the present; and *urinpacha*, the world below or that which transports us to the past. The three *pachas* are interrelated and complementary, and unreflective of any moral or ethical hierarchies.

At the heart of this mythic location, where the universe was founded, lies the city of Tiwanaku (or Tiahuanaco), whose origins date from around 1500–1200 BCE. One of the primary stone monuments of this ancient city is the Gateway of the Sun (figs. 1.11 and 1.12, 47, 48), where one can still observe the god Wiraqocha ensconced at its center. The Aymara name for Tiwanaku was Taypicala, or "the rock in the center." Thus the city and its famous portal are the stone that was the foundation of the universe.

The societies that developed in this Andean region and their history are complex. But among the most ancient is the Chavin culture (1400–200 BCE), which spread from the Peruvian highlands into the coast and valleys, establishing a pattern of development that many subsequent societies followed. The Tiwanaku culture flourished between 45 and 700 CE in an era classified as the urban period, which was marked by the appearance of several other cities, including Khonkho, Wankane, Pajchiri, Lukirmata, and Ojje. That culture left great granite and sandstone monoliths that proclaim their inhabitants' extensive knowledge of the movements of the sun, carefully measured in the layout of stones. Tiwanaku artistry is also evident in metalwork, especially in bronze, as well as in weavings and in pottery, with a distinctive Tiahuanacota style. In fact, Tiwanaku and the later Huari civilization (which flourished between 600 and 1000 CE) are recognized as producing the two most important pottery styles of this early period.

Another distinction of these Andean societies was a system of cultivation that John Murra calls a "vertical control of a maximum of ecological tiers"; that is, a system that allowed different *ayllus,* or community groups, to have control over their lands from the Altiplano down to the warmer valleys. In this way, they had access to a variety of products from different ecological tiers. Potatoes, quinoa, and *habas* (fava bean) would grow in the highlands, while coca and various fruits flourished in the warmer valleys of the Yungas region, which is located along both the eastern and western slopes of the Andes mountains. Animals of the Altiplano, especially the *auquenidos* family—llamas, alpacas, vicuñas, and guanacos—provided wool, meat, and dairy products.

This agricultural and economic system, connecting upper and lower regions, reflected a deeply holistic view of the cosmos. As elsewhere in the Americas, geography and the natural world were intrinsic to the myths and history of the people of the Altiplano. Their social structure echoed this division. The basic political and social unit, the *ayllus,* thus consisted of two parts, an upper half, called *alasaya,* and a lower section, called *urinsaya* (*urin* means "lower" in Quechua). This pairing reflected the cosmic division of the upper *alajpacha* (the world above) and the lower *urin* or *urinpacha* (the underworld), as well as the relations between genders, men (the upper) and women (the lower). Indeed the entire territory of the Tawantinsuyo (*suyo*=parts, *tawa*=four) was separated into four sections, with each half divided into a lower and upper part, reflecting these multifaceted relationships through all dimensions of reality.

The following visual and linguistic texts offer a sampling of this complex and culturally rich society, providing some glimpses of the perspectives of a people inhabiting one of the highest places in the world.

Taypicala, or the Stone in the Center: Tiwanaku

The ancient Aymara name for the city of Tiwanaku, about twelve miles from Lake Titicaca, was Taypikala, "the stone (*kala*) in the center (*taypi*)." As the "center of the world," Taypikala not only marked an equilibrium point for the two halves of the Andean universe, but as these three monuments—the AKAPANA PYRAMID, the ESTELA BENNETT, and the GATEWAY OF THE SUN—reveal, both the city and the lake epitomized the founding elements of the cosmos.

Figure 1.9. Akapana Pyramid, Tiwanaku, Bolivia. Photograph by Arthur Posnansky. Javier Nuñez de Arco Photographic Archives, La Paz, Bolivia. By permission of Javier Nuñez de Arco.

The Akapana Pyramid, which lies half-buried in the midst of the ruins of Tiwanaku, is a stepped pyramid composed of seven platforms with an open courtyard at the top. There was an intricate drainage network, which moved water alternately in and out of the structure, replicating the natural flow of water through a mountain, specifically that of the Quimsachata Range nearby. At one time surrounded by water, the Akapana Pyramid, like the vast lake nearby, thus embodies the cosmic mountain, the central axis that supports Wiraqocha in navigating the three pachas or levels of the universe.

As Tiwanaku expanded its boundaries through conquest, the *huacas* or divine objects of the subjugated peoples were brought into the ruling city and many of them were placed in the semisubterranean temple located beside the Akapana Pyramid. Among its notable treasures was the Bennett Monolith or ESTELA BENNETT (fig. 1.10, 46). (The stone was named for Wendell C. Bennett, the archaeologist who first explored the area in the 1930s; the monument is now housed in the Tiwanaku Museum.) The largest of several large carved stones at the site, the Estela Bennett measures 7.3 meters high and weighs 20 tons. Encoded on the surfaces of its huge stylized body is a unique representation of a twelve-month sidereal-lunar agricultural

Figure 1.10. The Estela Bennett, Tiwanaku, Bolivia. Photograph by Arthur Posnansky. Javier Nuñez de Arco Photographic Archives, La Paz, Bolivia. By permission of Javier Nuñez de Arco.

Figure 1.11. Gateway to the Sun, Tiwanaku, Bolivia. Photograph by M. H. Water (2007).

calendar, emphasizing the importance of agrarian culture and marking the sacred time of the site.

Also near the Akapana Pyramid, in an area known as the Kalassaya Temple, is one of the most famous monuments of Tiwanaku, THE GATE-WAY OF THE SUN. Carved with ideographs like the Estela Bennett, this ten-ton piece of granite represents the creator god Wiraqocha in several related ways. Primarily, this massive portal recalls how the creator god produced the great agricultural civilization of Tiwanaku in the vast high deserts of the Altiplano, underlining the necessary and life-giving cooperation between the divine and the natural world. Wiraqocha embodies a fundamental principle of Andean culture: namely, reciprocity—between humans and their environment, between the living and the dead, and among peoples. The agricultural calendar inscribed in the Gateway elaborates this reciprocity by highlighting Wiraqocha's identification with the planet Saturn, the measurer of time. In the agricultural calendar, which indicates the seasons and the rhythms of planting and growth and harvest, Wiraqocha measures out the substance of life itself. And through another of his names,

Figure 1.12. Gateway to the Sun, Tiwanaku, Bolivia. Detail. Photograph by Arthur Posnansky. Javier Nuñez de Arco Photographic Archives, La Paz, Bolivia. By permission of Javier Nuñez de Arco.

Tunapa Wiraqocha, or the bearer of the millstone (*tuna*), Wiraqocha also controls the millstone that moves the universe, the planets, and the Milky Way across the sky, generating those heavenly motions that the calendar faithfully tracks.

The Myth of the Fox's Tail: Ethnoastronomy and the Manuscript of Huarochiri

What has been called the Manuscript of Huarochiri is in fact oral testimony of pre-Hispanic peoples, transcribed from the Quechua language and first edited by a priest, Father Francisco de Ávila, around 1608. It was later translated into Spanish by the Peruvian writer José María Arguedas and by the French anthropologist Pierre Duviols in 1966. Father Ávila's original interest was his desire to uncover the location of the many *huacas* that the Indians worshiped, hoping to uproot these "pagan" cults and gain access to the treasures buried with them. The English translation by anthropologists Frank Salomon and Jorge Urioste includes stories of an ancient mythic past and the impact of the Spanish arrival on these beliefs. The selection here recounts the story of the flood and how, long ago, the fox got its tail wet.

In Andean cosmogony, the world was conceived as *pacha*, in which time and space are inseparable. The destruction of one world was a *pachakuti*, simply a "turnover" of space and time, with one "world" or *pacha* being overturned and another beginning. According to myth, there will be five *pachakutis*, each involving a different form of destruction. The myth of the flood depicts one of these destructive moments, that of water.

One of the most remarkable explanations of this myth has been developed by William Sullivan in *The Secret of the Incas* (1996), in which he examines the close links between the narrative and actual astronomical observations. The llama, for instance, corresponds to the constellation that "runs from the star Epsilon Scorpius, in the 'tail' of the Western constellation Centaurus," while the "eyes of the llama" can be identified as Alpha Centauri and Hadar (32). Sullivan observes that the name of the mountain is Vilcacoto, with *vilca* meaning sun and *coto* meaning pile or the Pleiades, referring to the pile of seeds or planting time. The man and llama escape to this "Sun Pleiades Mountain" or the heliacal rise of the Pleiades (35), a critical moment in the agricultural calendar.

Sullivan then connects the mythic flood to the June solstice, suggesting an analogy between Vilcacoto, the highest mountain in the world, and the solstice, as the place of the sun's "northernmost location in the stars" (Johanna Broda, cited in Sullivan 36). By observing the heliacal rise of the Pleiades at the Harvard-Smithsonian Astrophysical Observatory for the latitude of Cuzco thirty days before the June solstice, as the myth indicates, one finds that the year 650 CE corresponds with the heliacal rise of the Pleiades on Julian date May 20, 650 CE (39). As for the Fox constellation, which generally appears at the December solstice, Sullivan explains that its presence in the June solstice has to do with the phenomenon of precessional motion (figs. 1.13 and 1.14, 50). "[T]hey would also have been aware that a change in the heliacal-rise date of *any* star or object—as for example, the Pleiades—meant a change in that of *every* other star or object." Accordingly, at the December solstice of the same year, the Fox constellation would be seen rising above the horizon, "with the exception of his tail, sunk now—owing to precessional motion—beneath the horizon, soaked, bedraggled, and blackened in the rising waters of the celestial sea" (44).

Sullivan's ingenious explanation of this myth in contemporary astronomical terms makes visible the strong connection between Andean as-

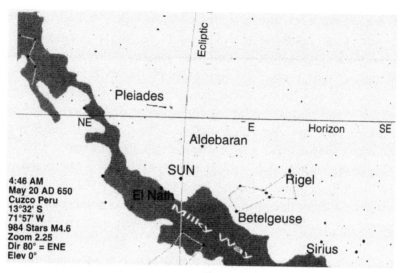

Figure 1.13. Rise of the Pleiades, May 20, 650 CE, one month before the "flood."
From William Sullivan, *The Secret of the Incas: Myth, Astronomy and the War
Against Time* (New York: Three Rivers, 1996), 372, fig. 2.6a. Copyright © William
Sullivan. Used by permission of Crown Books, an imprint of Random House, a
division of Penguin Random House. All rights reserved.

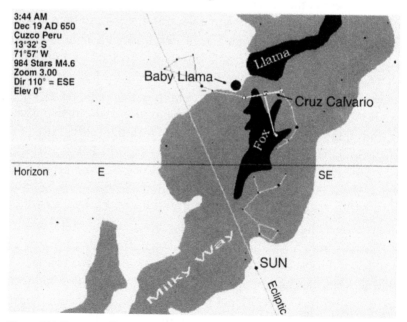

Figure 1.14. Fox constellation, December solstice 650 CE. From William Sullivan.
*From William Sullivan, The Secret of the Incas: Myth, Astronomy and the War
Against Time* (New York: Three Rivers, 1996), 375, fig. 2.9a. Copyright © William
Sullivan. Used by permission of Crown Books, an imprint of Random House, a
division of Penguin Random House. All rights reserved.

tronomical knowledge and the world below, clarifying the interdependence of the actions of animals in both realms. The Huarochiri Manuscript makes this relationship very explicit in all its myths, including the concept of *camay*, which Salomon explains as the infusion of life from above, as when the Llama constellation touches and infuses being into the llamas below (16).

The text here is from Frank Salomon and George L. Urioste's *The Huarochiri Manuscript: A Testament of Ancient and Colonial Andean Religion* (Austin: University of Texas Press, 1991), 52–53.

What Happened to the Indians in Ancient Times When the Ocean Overflowed

Now we'll return to what is said of very early people. The story goes like this.[6] In ancient times, this world wanted to come to an end.[7]

A llama buck, aware[8] that the ocean was about to overflow, was behaving like somebody who's deep in sadness. Even though its <crossed out:>[father] owner let it rest in a patch of excellent pasture, it cried and said, "In, in," and wouldn't eat.

The llama's <crossed out>[father] owner got really angry, and he threw the cob from some maize he had just eaten at the llama.

"Eat, dog! This is some fine grass I'm letting you rest in!" he said.

Then the llama began speaking like a human being.

"You simpleton, whatever could you be thinking about? Soon, in five days, the ocean will overflow. It's a certainty. And the whole world will come to an end," it said.

The man got good and scared. "What's going to happen to us? Where can we go to save ourselves?" he said.

The llama replied "Let's go to Villca Coto mountain.[9] <margin, in Spanish:>

6　Text shifts at this point from witness to reportive validation. (All notes to this text are from Salomon and Urioste.)

7　*Cay pachas puchocayta munarcan* 'this world wanted to come to an end': *puchocay* means the ending of something that has an intrinsic conclusion (as, for example, the finishing of a task), not a truncation or accidental end (González Holguín 293).

8　The prescience of llamas: (see chapter 18, sec. 221–222 in Salomon and Urioste), on llama divination, where the animal's body is credited with containing signs of the future.

9　A mountain today called by this name exists 12 km northwest of San Damián, between modern Huanre and Surco (Treacy, John 1984:18, unpublished paper, Madison, University of Wisconsin, 1984). Villca Coto may be the same *huaca* mentioned in Salomon, chapter 23 (sec. 301), the most beautiful one at the Inca court in Cuzco.

[This is a mountain that is between Huanri[10] and Surco.][11] There we'll be saved. Take along five days' food for yourself."

So the man went out from there in a great hurry, and himself carried both the llama buck and its load.

When they arrived at Villca Coto mountain, all sorts of animals had already filled it up: pumas, foxes, guanacos, condors, all kinds of animals in great numbers.

As soon as that man had arrived there, the ocean overflowed.

They stayed there huddling tightly together.

The waters covered all those mountains and it was only Villca Coto mountain, or rather its very peak, that was not covered by the water.

Water soaked the fox's tail.

That's how it turned black.

Five days later, the waters descended and began to dry up.

The drying waters caused the ocean to retreat all the way down again and exterminate all the people.

Afterward, that man began to multiply once more.

That's the reason there are people until today.

Regarding this story, we Christians believe it refers to the time of the Flood. But they believe it was Villca Coto mountain that saved them.

Disorder and Order: Jalq'a and Inca Textiles

In many parts of the Americas and specifically in the Andean region, textiles were not seen as objects of art that are produced for the market. Instead they are understood as an intrinsic part of the body, as subjects (rather than objects) that carry a message, as a text that speaks of the person's being, of one's identity. That quality becomes inherent in the textiles themselves, whose woven designs have become part of a communal identity that stretches back through the centuries.

The first weaving here (figure 1.15), for example, is from the Jalq'a communities, near the city of Sucre in Bolivia. Though men and women from these villages still wear their traditional dress, with designs that predate the Spanish invasions, the practice is fast disappearing. The garment itself is a

---

10 Modern Huanre is 5 km south of San Bartolomé (IGM Hojas Topográficas serie I:1000,0000, Lima: Instituto Geográfico Militar, 1970–1971).

11 The modern (former *reducción*) town of San Gerónimo de Surco is 17 km north-northwest of San Damián at 2,300 m above sea level, sheltered in the Rímac valley (IGM Hojas Topográficas serie I:1000,0000, Lima: Instituto Geográfico Militar, 1970–1971).

tunic, or *aqsu* (in Quechua), or *urku* (in Aymara), typically worn on special occasions.

While these Andean textiles functioned as a constituent of personal and communal identity—an identity deeply embedded in the material designs—they also articulated elements of the Andean cosmos. To understand the ways that textiles function in Andean communities is to appreciate a unique vision of the world.

Andean textiles have divine origins. According to the myths, when the creator god Wiraqocha formed all nations out of mud at Tiwanaku, he painted on their bodies the distinctive clothing they were to wear; he then ordered the people to go underground and come out at the places he had prescribed, each clad in their distinctive ethnic attire. The first beings to emerge were venerated as *huacas,* or divinities, arrayed in their specified clothing. The *huacas* thus confirmed the divine source of these unique textiles, and the shared dress of a particular group thus became the sacred wrapping that signaled their ancient origins and established the communal identity of those who wore them.

The first textile, the JALQ'A WEAVING, full of animal figures, is a particularly fascinating example of the complex history that particular designs represent (fig. 1.15, 54). In the colonial period, animal designs were often prohibited by the Spanish because they thought that the *huacas,* depicted as animals, were being worshiped instead of the Christian god. But in the isolated Jalq'a communities, these ancient designs survived. The representation of animals incorporating other animals inside their bodies, for example, very likely dates from pre-Inca and pre-Hispanic times. According to textile authority Verónica Cereceda, these strange creatures (two-headed quadrupeds with wings and serrated backs—identified as *khurus*) were wild animals as well as the fantastical beings that appear in visions on days of mist or in solitary places. In his colonial chronicle, Inca descendant JOAN DE SANTA CRUZ PACHACUTI describes these same creatures, explaining how winged quadrupeds with ears and tails, "and on their backs . . . many spines like fish," appeared in Cuzco during the time of Pachacuti Inga Yupangui. The ancestor then named his son Amaro Topa Inga, commemorating the fact that at his birth the fiercest of wild animals were thrown out of Cuzco, bringing order to the city.

The Jalq'a textile thus not only incorporates the untamed *khurus* as mythic animals that belong to the Uku Pacha, the underworld, but the design also alludes to Inca legend and history, recalling, in this instance, the powerful order occasioned by the birth of Amaro Topa Inga. The weaving

Figure 1.15. Jalq'a weaving. Photograph by Froilán Urzagasti. Courtesy of Verónica Cereceda, Museo de Arte Indígena ASUR, Sucre, Bolivia.

Figure 1.16. Inka unku from the Isla del Sol, Bolivia. Photo from Teresa Gisbert, Silvia Arze, Martha Cajías, *Arte textil y mundo andino* (La Paz: Plural Editores, 4th ed. 2010), 127, fig. 83. Courtesy of Teresa Gisbert and Silvia Arze.

becomes a rich repository of Andean knowledge, allowing myth, legend, and history to accumulate and mingle in a single text(ile).

In contrast to the Jalq'a piece, most Andean textiles reflect the traditional division of space into two parts: the *pampa*, both the open plain and a space in the textile without designs, and the *pallai*, the part with designs. The word *pallai* derives from the Quechua word meaning "to choose," that is, to choose the threads to make the figures. Typically, the *pampa* represents the space without culture, the untamed regions, while the *pallai* is the cultured space, the site where gods and meaning reside. And while the Jalq'a textile makes no clear division between *pampa* and *pallai*, the borders effectively create a cultured space that contains the wild animals, bringing order out of potential chaos.

The second example, the UNKU WEAVING (fig. 1.16), represents a more abstract version of Andean textiles. Also pre-Hispanic, dating from the Inca period, this *unku*, or poncho, has a forceful design of black and white checkered space against a red background. The checkered space, a familiar motif in indigenous coats of arms in the colonial period, represents the Andean social and political space: the center with its four cardinal points of the Tawantinsuyu recalling the Inca state with its four quarters. The chessboard squares of the poncho further suggest the family relationships among the different social groups.

The Quipus: Mnemonic Threads

The *quipus* (knotted threads) is one of the most efficient mnemonic methods used by Andean peoples, particularly the Incas (fig. 1.17). Performing many of the functions of the alphabet, the different threads tied to a principal cord represented (in the types of knots and varied colors) complex relationships and quantities with respect to any number of referents—an object, a social group, or a specific place.

The *quipus* provided an extremely sophisticated method of registering information: every kind of quantity and measurable relationship could be represented by the *quipus*. However, the knots and threads only made sense to those who knew what object was being counted or represented; the *quipus* was a mnemonic device rather than an independent medium. This apparent weakness was also a strength: without the persons who knew what a particular *quipus* represented, the threads became meaningless or inscrutable; but for the comprehending reader, the *quipus* was an incomparable form of ciphered communication.

The *quipus* obviously depended on living memory to communicate its messages. Like oral communication—a related form of transmission among the Andeans—the *quipus* had similar virtues and deficits. In such systems, the chain of memory is what keeps the transmission of information functional. As long as the chain remains intact, the message keeps its original force and selective power, since only those who know the message and their listeners can appreciate its real meaning. But when that chain is broken, both the *quipus* and the oral communication are stripped of their significance.

A great deal of information acquired and utilized by the Incas was dependent on this critical chain of memory. Such knowledge was often the result of thousands of years of accumulation, sometimes embodied in forms reaching far back to the earlier peoples in the Andes: the perfect stone architecture with its seemingly superhuman dimensions; the complex social organizations represented by the *ayllus*; or the astonishing construction of agricultural terraces in the steepest slopes of the Andes.

The arrival of the Spanish broke that critical chain of continuity in almost all areas of Andean life. As a result, the *quipus* lost its readers, the

Figure 1.17. Chachapoya/Inka *quipus* found at the site of Lake of the Condors, northern Peru (ca. 1500 ce), Centro Mallqui, Leymebamba, Peru. Photo courtesy of Gary Urton.

architecture and terraces their builders, the *ayllus* its organizers. Although remnants of these intricate and sophisticated constructions remain as witnesses to the coherent and complex civilizations that produced them, that crucial supporting knowledge, so dependent on human memory, has been lost, perhaps forever.

Guaraní Culture and the Origins of Language

One of the more singular beliefs of the Tupí-Guaraní people was that language was created before the universe itself. This priority of language over material being has several important consequences, most significantly perhaps in a distinctive construction of good and evil. For the Tupí-Guaraní, humans have not been expelled from a paradise because of some original sin or error. Instead, everything is imperfect from the beginning, and evil is part of the fabric of the world. Evil is real and ever present. But since gods coexist with humans rather than preside over the world from a distant empyrean, humans have immediate access to divinity through very concrete actions—sacrifices, prayers, rituals. The field of salvation is thus not relegated to an afterlife but remains here in this world. What mediates this relationship—between the human and the divine, the living and the dead, the visible and the invisible, past and present—is language itself. Words connect us to all that is or can be.

Such a conception of language is echoed in the centrality of the shamans or priests in Tupí-Guaraní culture. The shamans are the keepers of the words, transmitting through an exclusively oral tradition both critical knowledge and religious understanding. Without their sacred words, without language, the people themselves cannot exist.

The following account of the foundations of human language comes from one Tupí-Guaraní tribe, the Mbyá. For centuries, the Mbyá have resisted repeated attempts at colonization and religious conversion, costing them countless lives, the loss of territory, and drastic constrictions in the quality of their existence. But in spite of this marginalization—or perhaps because of it—ethnologists have found Tupí-Guaraní traditions and beliefs remarkably intact among the Mbyá.

In the mid-twentieth century, the ethnologist Leon Cadogan managed to be adopted as a member of the Mbyá as a shaman. In that role, he collected numerous myths, prayers, and legends that he eventually published in two important compilations: *Ayvú Rpytá* and *Ywyrá Ñéery.* "The Foundations of Human Language" belongs to the first of these compilations.

The original text is from *Literatura Guaraní del Paraguay*, prologue and edition compiled by Rubén Bareiro Saguier (Caracas: Biblioteca Ayaucho, 1980). The excerpt here was translated from the Spanish by Josefa Salmón with revisions by John Biguenet, Barbara Ewell, and Marta Edwards. Italics in parentheses are in the Spanish translation from the Guaraní.

The Creation of Ñamandú and the Foundations of Human Language

I

Our true Father Ñamandú, the First,
From a small portion of his own divinity,
From the wisdom contained by his own divinity
And from the depths of his creative spirit
Engendered the flames and the light mist.

II

Having arisen (*taken human form*),
From the wisdom contained by his own divinity,
And from the depths of his creative wisdom
He conceived the origins of human language

From the wisdom contained by his own divinity,
And from the depths of his creative wisdom
Our Father created the foundations of human language and shaped it as
Part of his own divinity.
Before earth existed,
In the midst of primordial darkness
Before the knowledge of things,
He created what would be the foundation of human language (*or the foun-
dation of future human language*)
And our First, True Father Ñamandú
Made language part of his own divinity.

III

Having conceived the origin of what would become human language
From the wisdom contained by his own divinity,
And from the depths of his creative spirit, he brought forth the foundations
of love (*of one's neighbor*)
Before earth existed
In the midst of primordial darkness,
Before the knowledge of things,
And from the depths of his creative wisdom he conceived the origins of
love (*of one's neighbor*).

IV

Having created the foundations of human language,
Having created a small fragment of love,
From the wisdom contained by his own divinity,
And from the depths of his creative wisdom
The beginning of a single sacred hymn he brought forth in his solitude.
Before earth existed
In the midst of primordial darkness,
Before the knowledge of things, the beginning of a sacred
hymn he brought forth in his solitude (for *himself*).

V

Having created, in his solitude, the foundations of human language;
Having created, in his solitude, a small fragment of love;
Having created, in his solitude, a short sacred hymn;

He pondered deeply about who might share the foundations of human
 language;
About who might share the small fragment of love (*for one's neighbor*)
About who might share the series of words that made up the sacred hymn.
Having pondered deeply, from the wisdom contained by his own divinity,
And from the depths of his creative wisdom
He created those who would be the companions of his divinity.

VI

Having pondered profoundly
In the wisdom contained by his own divinity,
And from the depths of his creative wisdom
He created the Ñamandú (*plural*) with a great heart (*brave*).
At that same moment, he also created the bright reflection of his wisdom
 (*the Sun*).
Before earth existed, in the midst of primordial darkness,
He created the Ñamandú with a great heart,
To father his future children,
To father truly the souls of his many children, he created the Ñamandú with
 a great heart.

2

From the Conquest to the Consolidation
of Colonial Society, 1530–1640

The Conquest of the Americas was not really a single event or even a period that can be precisely dated. The conquest certainly began when the Spanish arrived in the unfamiliar territory they eventually named "America." It ended around the middle of the nineteenth century, although it could be said that it persists in other forms. The process of settlement was not homogeneous across the continent, and even Spain and Portugal, the two countries whose territorial claims had some legitimacy, at least in Europe, actually occupied relatively small areas of these huge land masses. But, by the beginning of the seventeenth century, key regions were under colonial control, principally the center of Mexico and most of the territory formerly under the rule of the Incas.

The two primary instruments of the conquest were military campaigns and Christian conversion. The encounter between Europeans and the indigenous peoples of the Americas was extremely violent, producing disasters of unprecedented proportions. Scholars believe that in the most populated regions of Spanish America, native inhabitants were reduced by more than 80 percent within a hundred years of the first invasions. In the Caribbean, the reductions were precipitous: by the time BARTOLOMÉ DE LAS CASAS published his book *Brevísima relación de la destrucción de las indias* [A Short Account of the Destruction of the Indies] in 1552, barely sixty years after the first landings, there were virtually no native people left on any of the principal islands: Hispaniola (now Haiti and the Dominican Republic), Cuba, Jamaica, and Puerto Rico.

Military actions alone could hardly have caused such human devastation. The indigenous population was also assaulted by epidemics of diseases that had been unknown in the New World, by forced labor, by a decrease in birthrates, and by mass suicides, all provoking deep demoralization and disillusionment in entire societies. Adding to such misery, the Spanish began encouraging the widespread use of alcoholic beverages. Previously such intoxicants had only been utilized in rituals or for special occasions; alcohol now became an instrument of forgetfulness, sought out by the Indians themselves to allay their overwhelming despair. One modern historian has described the conquest as the longest massive drunken interlude in history. To that dismal point, others have noted that rapes of women exceeded that in any previous historical period.

Less visibly violent, conversion was also an essential tool of the conquest. In the Papal Bull *Inter Caetera* (1493), Pope Alexander VI had granted Spain and Portugal territorial legitimacy under the condition that the native populations would be converted to Christianity. Conversion became a legal obligation, for without it, there would be no justification to subdue these "discovered" territories; indeed, the brutal force that the colonizers employed was seen as divinely authorized.

In fact, colonization was not really Spain's objective and the term itself is inexact. There was never an intention to populate these new kingdoms with European settlers. Both the immediate and long-term goal was simply the extraction of precious ores, exploiting the local work force to do so. Despite such crass intentions, however, the foreign conquerors soon acquired an attachment to their occupied territories along with an ambition for power. And as early as the mid-sixteenth century, many settlers themselves began to harbor thoughts about breaking away from the crown and establishing their own kingdoms. BARTOLOMÉ DE LAS CASAS recognized these treacherous aspirations and wrote a letter to Charles V recommending that he not allow the conquistadors to remain in America; Las Casas shrewdly advised the king to recall these prominent men back to Spain, under the pretext of rewarding them for their efforts. Once there, they would not be allowed to leave the country. Such warnings went unheeded and in some places rebellions against the king often occurred.

If colonization became equated with conversion, the reasons for Christianization were no less ambivalent. The missionaries themselves were divided by two primary guiding—somewhat competing—principles that led to different approaches: some held the view that the conversion to Christianity was a long-term, perpetual project of dissemination of the faith; others believed that the "discovery" of the Americas was a sign of Christ's imminent return, portending the end of the world. Those in the latter group, the "millenarianists," were less interested in destroying or refuting indigenous religions than in imposing Christianity quickly, since Judgment

Day was so near. BERNARDINO DE SAHAGUN was initially among this group, although by the end of his life his ideas had changed dramatically.

All missionaries faced an intellectual dilemma in their task of conversion. How could one reconcile the apostolic injunction to spread the Gospel across the world with this newly found continent full of unconverted pagan peoples? That the apostles might have disobeyed Christ's command to disseminate the faith worldwide was inconceivable. An ingenious solution to that incongruity was the notion that the natives of America had already been converted in apostolic times. The necessary evidence for that early evangelization soon began to appear. There were frequent testimonies about finding miraculous stone "footprints" of an apostle, usually Thomas. Others identified the ancient gods of Incan and Mesoamerican myths as oblique versions of the apostle and his deeds. Moreover, many missionaries began to see indigenous practices as merely transformations of original Christian customs and institutions, following centuries of neglect and the loss of contact with the rest of the Christian world. EL INCA GARCILASO DE LA VEGA offers a notable example of those who believed that Christianity was original to the Americas.

The selections in this chapter highlight the enormous production of textual accounts of the conquest, one of the most momentous events in modern history. The appearance of a New World stimulated great curiosity among Europeans, who were just beginning to grapple with the novel constructions of reality generated by the Renaissance. Official reports to sovereigns and semiofficial accounts became the basis for reconfiguring the horizons of the Old World even as they shaped the otherness of the New World into more familiar and ultimately more subjugable patterns. The conquest of the Americas thus materialized in these early texts as much— and perhaps more enduringly—as in the often violent encounters they reflect.

Christopher Columbus (1451–1506)

Born in Genoa, Italy, in 1451, Christopher Columbus eventually left his native land for Portugal, becoming a sailor and trader with a radical notion about sailing west to Asia. Though very few knowledgeable Westerners still believed that the Earth was flat or that sailing west would bring one to its edge, Columbus was convinced (incorrectly, as it turns out) that Asia was much closer than most contemporary scholars believed, and he energetically sought funding to prove his plan. Eventually, Isabella the Catholic,

Queen of Castile, agreed to support the expedition, though her husband, King Ferdinand of Aragon, officially demurred—and thus Columbus's "discovery" of the two continents occurred under the flag of the kingdom of Castile and not that of Aragon. Columbus set sail with three ships on August 3, 1492. A little more than two months later, on October 12, he made landfall in the Bahamas, revealing that, in fact, between Europe and Asia there was a whole New World, the Americas.

Though Columbus himself never recognized that he had found another continent, the event proved revolutionary for the entire Western World, which would never see itself the same again. The consequences for the Americas and its people were not so positive.

Leaving thirty-nine of his men in a small settlement on the coast of present-day Haiti, Columbus returned to Spain as a hero. A year later, in October 1493, he set out on his second voyage, lasting three years, with a large fleet of seventeen ships filled with 1,200 colonists. Though Columbus made two more voyages (1498–1500 and 1502–1504), these later expeditions were quite troubled, as Columbus was unable to find much treasure or to maintain order among the new settlers. Accused of mismanagement and deprived of his wealth, Columbus died in Valladolid in 1506.

Columbus wrote a very popular account of his first voyage in 1493 that circulated in many editions and translations throughout Europe. That first letter and the subsequent accounts of his other voyages clearly establish the pattern of encounter between Europeans and the American peoples for the next three centuries: the racial and economic hierarchies Columbus depicted became foundational to Spanish colonial society. Columbus's primary intent, of course, was to describe the territory and people to his financiers, the Queen of Castile and the King of Aragon, but he also communicated a vision of an unfamiliar world, inhabited by people with strange beliefs. Columbus's letters were focused on his intent to impress his royal readers, promising both the prospect of converting many souls to Christianity and the acquisition of great quantities of precious metals. At the same time, his confident accounts inevitably incorporated the perils and hardships of his journeys, as well as reports of the startling natural phenomena and new social realities that he and his men were encountering every day.

The selection here, from Columbus's second expedition (October 1493– June 1496), was written by Diego Alvarez Chanca, the Queen's physician, who accompanied the colonists and described their experiences. This excerpt recounts the return to northern Haiti, where Columbus found that the Spanish men he had left during the first expedition had disappeared.

The detective work required to discover if the men were still alive or how they had died reveals much about the cultural misunderstandings that marked these first encounters—even with native translators, who had been brought to Spain as captives to learn the language. As the Spanish speculate about why the men were killed, their possible explanations underline the social and psychological contexts that shape the realities of these initial contacts. Columbus recalls the earlier negotiations he had made with the local chieftain, Guacamari, to protect the thirty-nine men he had left in this alien territory, but his inferences about the events on shore are full of suspicion and potential threat. Indeed, testimonies of the Indians themselves reveal a more complicated record, including the taking of four wives by some of the Spanish men as well as conflicts with Guacamari himself.

These early chronicles are distinctive in part because at this point the power of the Spanish settlers remains dependent on the goodwill of the native inhabitants, on whom they must rely for survival. Even so, we see how Columbus cannily uses barter and wine to collect information about the whereabouts of his men or to locate precious metals. The dangers of alcohol are immediately evident in these chronicles, which relate how some of the natives, made drunk on the ships with Spanish wine, drowned on the way home in their canoes. Alcohol and gunpowder, the latter used here mostly to intimidate the locals, eventually proved decisive factors, both in the military expeditions that soon followed as well as in the perpetuation of colonial power in the Americas.

The selections are from the translation of R. H. Major, *Four Voyages to the New World: Letters and Selected Documents* (New York: Corinth Books, 1961), 44–51.

From **The Second Voyage of Columbus (1493–1496)**

As we went on making our observations on the river and the land, some of our men found two dead bodies by the river's side, one with a rope round his neck, and the other with one round his foot: this was on the first day of our landing. On the following day they found two other corpses farther on, and one of these was observed to have a great quantity of beard; this was regarded as a very suspicious circumstance by many of our people, because, as I have already said, all the Indians are beardless. This harbour is twelve leagues from the place where the Spaniards had been left under the protection of Guacamari, the king of that province, whom I suppose to be one of the chief men of the island. After two days we set sail for that spot, but as it was late when we arrived there,[1] and there were some shoals, where the admiral's ship had been lost, we did not venture to put in close to the shore, but remained that night at a little less than a league from the coast, waiting until the morning, when we might enter securely. On that evening, a canoe, containing five or six Indians, came out at a considerable distance from where we were, and approached us with great celerity. The admiral believing that he insured our safety by keeping the sails set, would not wait for them; they, however, perseveringly rowed up to us within gunshot, and then stopped to look at us; but when they saw that we did not wait for them, they put back and went away. After we had anchored that night at the spot in question,[2] the admiral ordered two guns to be fired, to see if the Spaniards, who had remained with Guacamari, would fire in return, for they also had guns with them; but when we received no reply, and could not perceive any fires, nor the slightest symptom of habitations on the spot, the spirits of our people became much depressed, and they began to entertain the suspicion which the circumstances were naturally calculated to excite. While all were in this desponding mood, and when four or five hours of the night had passed away, the same canoe which we had seen in the evening, came up, and the Indians with a loud voice addressed the captain of the caravel, which they first approached, inquiring for the admiral; they were conducted to the admiral's vessel, but would not go on board till he had spoken to them, and they had asked for a light, in order to assure themselves that it was he who conversed with them. One of them was a cousin of Guacamari, who had been sent by him once before: it appeared, that after they had turned back the previous evening, they had been charged by Guacamari with two masks of gold as a present; one for the admiral, the other for a captain who had accompanied him on the former voyage. They remained on board for three hours, talking with the admiral in the presence of all of us, he showing much pleasure in their conversation, and inquiring respecting the welfare of the Spaniards whom he had left behind. Guacamari's cousin replied, that those who remained were all well, but that some of them had died of disease, and others had been killed in quarrels that had arisen amongst them: he said also that the province had been invaded, by two kings named Caonabó and Mayreni, who had burned the habitations of the people; and that Guacamari was at some distance, lying ill of a wound in his leg, which was the occasion of his not appearing, but that he would come on the next

1 The admiral anchored at the entrance of the harbor of Navidad, on Wednesday, the twenty-seventh of November, towards midnight, and on the following day, in the afternoon, put into the harbor. [Trans. note.]
2 The Bay of Caracol, four leagues west of Fort Dauphin. [Trans. note.]

day. The Indians then departed, saying they would return on the following day with the said Guacamari, and left us consoled for that night. On the morning of the next day, we were expecting that Guacamari would come; and, in the meantime, some of our men landed by command of the admiral, and went to the spot where the Spaniards had formerly been: they found the building which they had inhabited, and which they had in some degree fortified with a palisade, burnt and leveled with the ground; they found also some rags and stuffs which the Indians had brought to throw upon the house. They observed too that the Indians who were seen near the spot, looked very shy, and dared not approach, but, on the contrary, fled from them. This appeared strange to us, for the admiral had told us that in the former voyage, when he arrived at this place, so many came in canoes to see us, that there was no keeping them off; and as we now saw that they were suspicious of us, it gave us a very unfavourable impression. We threw trifles, such as buttons and beads, towards them, in order to conciliate them, but only four, a relation of Guacamari's and three others, took courage to enter the boat, and were rowed on board. When they were asked concerning the Spaniards, they replied that all of them were dead: we had been told this already by one of the Indians whom we had brought from Spain, and who had conversed with the two Indians that on the former occasion came on board with their canoe, but we had not believed it. Guacamari's kinsman was asked who had killed them: he replied that king Caonabó and king Mayreni had made an attack upon them, and burnt the buildings on the spot, that many were wounded in the affray, and among them Guacamari, who had received a wound in his thigh, and had retired to some distance: he also stated that he wished to go and fetch him; upon which some trifles were given to him, and he took his departure for the place of Guacamari's abode. All that day we remained in expectation of them, and when we saw that they did not come, many suspected that the Indians who had been on board the night before, had been drowned; for they had had wine given them two or three times, and they had come in a small canoe that might be easily upset. The next morning the admiral went on shore, taking some of us with him; we went to the spot where the settlement had been, and found it utterly destroyed by fire, and the clothes of the Spaniards lying about upon the grass, but on that occasion we saw no dead body. There were many different opinions amongst us; some suspecting that Guacamari himself was concerned in the betrayal and death of the Christians; others thought not, because his own residence was burnt: so that it remained a very doubtful question. The admiral ordered all the ground which had been occupied by the fortifications of the Spaniards to be searched, for he had left orders with them to bury all the gold that they might get. While this was being done, the admiral wished to examine a spot at about a league's distance, which seemed to be suitable for building a town, for there was yet time to do so;—and some of us went thither with him, making our observations of the land as we went along the coast, until we reached a village of seven or eight houses, which the Indians forsook when they saw us approach, carrying away what they could, and leaving the things which they could not remove, hidden amongst the grass, around the houses. These people are so degraded that they have not even the sense to select a fitting place to live in; those who dwell on the shore, build for themselves the most miserable hovels that can be imagined, and all the houses are so covered with grass and dampness, that I wonder how they can contrive to exist. In these houses we found many things belonging to the Spaniards, which it could not be supposed they would have bartered; such as a very handsome Moorish mantle, which had not been unfolded since it was brought from Spain, stockings and pieces of cloth, also an anchor belonging to the ship which the admiral had lost here on the previous voyage; with other articles, which the more confirmed our suspicions. On examining some things which had been very cautiously sewn up in a small basket, we found a man's head wrapped up with great care; this we judged might be the head of a father, or mother, or of some person whom they much regarded: I have since heard that many were found in the same state, which makes me believe that our first impression was the true one. After this we returned. We went on the same day to the site of the settlement; and when we arrived, we found many Indians, who had regained their courage, bartering gold with our men: they had bartered to the extent of a mark: we also learned that they had shown where the bodies of eleven of the dead Spaniards were laid, which were already covered with the grass that had grown over them; and they all with one voice asserted that Caonabó and Mayreni had killed them; but notwithstanding all this, we began to hear complaints that one of the Spaniards had taken three women to himself, and another four; from whence we drew the inference that jealousy was the cause of the misfortune that had occurred. On the next morning, as no spot in that vicinity appeared suitable for our making a settlement, the admiral ordered a caravel to go in one direction to look for a convenient locality, while some of us went with him another way.

Hernán Cortés (1485–1547)

The letters written by the conquistador Hernán Cortés to the King of Castile in the years 1519–1522 reveal the ferocious tenacity and audacity that characterized one of the most famous—and infamous—of the Spanish conquerors.

Born in Medellín, Spain, in 1485, Hernán Cortés was captivated as a youth by the explorations of Columbus. He immigrated to Hispaniola when he was eighteen. For his service in the conquest of Cuba in 1511, he received considerable land, slaves, and political power. In 1518, he seized an opportunity to lead an expedition to Mexico, ostensibly to assist Juan de Grijalva, who had been sent to exploit the riches of the mainland. Before Cortés could reach the Mexican coast, however, the governor of Cuba, Diego Velázquez, who had authorized the voyage, revoked the mission. The two had often quarreled, and Velázquez suspected (correctly) that Cortés meant to explore and eventually conquer Mexico himself. As Cortés explains in his first letter, he only disobeyed the governor's orders because he believed that Velázquez wanted to appropriate those riches for himself. In his efforts to legitimize his own renegade expedition, Cortés then summoned his men and "elected" a "town council," following a long-established Spanish rule that acknowledged the authority of town councils or *cabildos* before the king. Thus legitimized, Cortés could proceed with his expedition, while he awaited royal permission. Cortés's use of the *cabildos* in representing the power of the people would recur many times in Spanish America, becoming a decisive factor later on in the movement for independence (1808–1824).

Cortés's strategy, however, effectively produced two adversaries in his efforts to conquer Mexico—not just the Aztecs, whose capital city, Tenochtitlán, he had reached by November 1519, but also Velázquez, who sent troops under the direction of Pánfilo de Narváez to arrest his rival. In a risky and desperate move, Cortés left a small contingent in Tenochtitlán while he returned to defeat Narváez on the coast. In his absence, his men lost control of the Aztec capital. Returning with reinforcements from Narváez's troops, whose larger forces Cortés had improbably defeated and then recruited to his side, Cortés was nonetheless forced to flee the island of Tenochtitlán. When the Indians removed the bridges into the city, the Spanish horses were unable to jump the canals, trapping the men in Tenochtitlán and resulting in countless Spanish dead; the battle was remembered by the survivors as *la noche triste* (the night of sorrows).

Like his defeat of Narváez on the coast, Cortés's first conquest of Tenochtitlán was against great odds. Warnings by other peoples of Mexico, who were the enemies and victims of Moctezuma, as well as the small force Cortés commanded (only 600 soldiers), suggested that victory was unlikely.

But securing translators, including a native woman, Marina or Malinche (by whom he later had at least one child), and by exploiting the existing divisions in Moctezuma's empire, Cortés found allies, especially among the Tlaxcaltecan people, who helped him subdue the mighty Aztec empire.

In his second letter Cortés records his first encounter with Moctezuma in November 1519 and his description of the great city of Tenochtitlán, home to nearly 300,000 people. Welcoming Cortés as a guest, Moctezuma marked the occasion—as in many other initial encounters between native peoples and foreigners—with an exchange of gifts. The acknowledgment of the guest's higher position in effect placed Moctezuma at the mercy of the Spanish. Indeed, Cortés held the king captive for several months, using their relationship as a critical source of information about the political and economic systems of the Aztecs. For Moctezuma, that same captivity protected him from the growing rebellion by his people against the Spanish and against their own leader who had welcomed them so unwisely. The information Cortés acquired from the captive Aztec emperor was critical in securing the recognition and approval of Cortés's conquest as an official act by the King of Spain since his disobedience to Velázquez had put in jeopardy his status as conquistador, despite the authorizations of his "town council" in Veracruz.

Cortés narrates the splendid and orderly procession in which Moctezuma first appeared and how his attempt to embrace the king is stopped by the two principals at his sides. After exchanging necklaces and having everyone seated, Moctezuma then returns with other lavish gifts of gold for Cortés. Moctezuma's first speech proclaims the story of the Aztecs, noting that, according to their chronicles, neither he nor his people were actually native to these lands, but came from far away and now awaited the return of their natural lord from the East, from the direction of Cortés's entry. Though some historians question the authenticity of Moctezuma's speech, especially his linking of Cortés to the god Quetzalcóatl, certainly this familiar myth of Toltec culture might well have been used by Moctezuma to explain the Spanish presence. One way that a culture deals with the unfamiliar is to incorporate anomalies into more comprehensible contexts. Making Cortés part of the myth, to see him, at least at first, as a divinity and the ancestor who had promised to return from the East, was in some ways the best initial explanation for this unsettling invasion of very unusual beings.

Cortés's letter makes clear that he, too, is deeply impressed by the unfamiliar culture he has encountered. Moctezuma's political abilities as well as his luxurious and stately way of life seem admirable to the young conqueror, but he is also amazed by the Aztec empire, its productive agriculture, and especially the amazing variety of its huge markets. What struck Cortés was the splendor of an empire, reflected in its high degree of organization, encompassing details like specifying certain streets for the sale of specific products, as well as in the splendor of its houses, its lush gardens, and its rich variety of exotic foods. The letters reveal Cortés as a man in a new world, deeply impressed but also simply surprised by the series of events that have brought him here, to the brink of disaster many times, but according to him, events that, through God's favor, had nonetheless deposited him in this astonishing city.

The text is a selection from *Letters from Mexico*, translated and edited by Anthony Pagden, with an introduction by J. H. Elliot (New Haven: Yale University Press, 1986), 102–5. Copyright © 1971 by Anthony Pagden. Revised edition copyright © 1986 by Yale University.

From The Second Letter (1520)

Before I begin to describe this great city and the others which I mentioned earlier, it seems to me, so that they may be better understood, that I should say something of Mesyco, which is Mutezuma's principal domain and the place where this city and the others which I have mentioned are to be found.[3] This province is circular and encompassed by very high and very steep mountains, and the plain is some seventy leagues in circumference: in this plain there are two lakes which cover almost all of it, for a canoe may travel fifty leagues around the edges. One of these lakes is of fresh water and the other, which is larger, is of salt water.[4] A small chain of very high hills which cuts across the middle of the plain separates these two lakes. At the end of this chain a narrow channel which is no wider than a bowshot between these hills and the

---

3 On the eve of the conquest Motecuçoma's empire included the modern states of Puebla and Morelos, most of Guerrero, Mexico, Hidalgo and Veracruz, and a fair portion of Oaxaca. This "empire" was the creation of a Triple Alliance among the city-states of Tlacopan (Tacuba), Texcoco and Tenochtitlan, built around the Mexican valley lake system. The peoples who occupied these cities were respectively the Tepaneca, the Acolhua and the Mexica. By the time the Spaniards arrived, however, Tenochtitlan had wrested effective control of the empire from its neighbors. Cortés is here referring to Anahuac (*Atl-Nahuac* or "Near-the-Water"), a name which was originally given to the coastal regions and the lands around the lake system, but later seems to have become a metonym for all Mexico. (For the geography of the empire see Robert H. Barlow, *The Extent of the Empire of the Culhua Mexica*.) (All notes for this text are by Anthony Pagden.)

4 The lakes are Chalco, which is freshwater, and Texcoco, which is saltwater.

mountains joins the lakes. They travel between one lake and the other and between different settlements which are on the lakes in their canoes without needing to go by land. As the salt lake rises and falls with its tides as does the sea, whenever it rises, the salt water flows into the fresh as swiftly as a powerful river, and on the ebb the fresh water passes to the salt.

This great city of Temixtitan is built on the salt lake, and no matter by what road you travel there are two leagues from the main body of the city to the mainland. There are four artificial causeways leading to it, and each is as wide as two cavalry lances. The city itself is as big as Seville or Córdoba. The main streets are very wide and very straight; some of these are on the land, but the rest and all the smaller ones are half on land, half canals where they paddle their canoes. All the streets have openings in places so that the water may pass from one canal to another. Over all these openings, and some of them are very wide, there are bridges made of long and wide beams joined together very firmly and so well made that on some of them ten horsemen may ride abreast.

Seeing that if the inhabitants of this city wished to betray us they were very well equipped for it by the design of the city, for once the bridges had been removed they could starve us to death without our being able to reach the mainland, as soon as I entered the city I made great haste to build four brigantines, and completed them in a very short time. They were such as could carry three hundred men to the land and transport the horses whenever we might need them.

This city has many squares where trading is done and markets are held continuously. There is also one square twice as big as that of Salamanca,[5] with arcades all around, where more than sixty thousand people come each day to buy and sell, and where every kind of merchandise produced in these lands is found; provisions as well as ornaments of gold and silver, lead, brass, copper, tin, stones, shells, bones, and feathers. They also sell lime, hewn and unhewn stone, adobe bricks, tiles, and cut and uncut woods of various kinds. There is a street where they sell game and birds of every species found in this land: chickens, partridges and quails, wild ducks, flycatchers, widgeons, turtledoves, pigeons, cane birds, parrots, eagles and eagle owls, falcons, sparrow hawks and kestrels, and they sell the skins of some of these birds of prey with their feathers, heads and claws. They sell rabbits and hares, and stags and small gelded dogs which they breed for eating.[6]

---

5   This was the marketplace in Tlatelolco.

6   These were called *itzcuintlis*. They were an important article of trade sold mainly in Acolman. They appear frequently on pottery from western Mexico, and seem to have resembled the Chihuahua.

There are streets of herbalists where all the medicinal herbs and roots found in the land are sold. There are shops like apothecaries', where they sell ready-made medicines as well as liquid ointments and plasters. There are shops like barbers' where they have their hair washed and shaved, and shops where they sell food and drink. There are also men like porters to carry loads.[7] There is much firewood and charcoal, earthenware braziers and mats of various kinds like mattresses for beds, and other, finer ones, for seats and for covering rooms and hallways. There is every sort of vegetable, especially onions, leeks, garlic, common cress and watercress, borage, sorrel, teasels and artichokes; and there are many sorts of fruit, among which are cherries and plums like those in Spain.

They sell honey, wax, and a syrup made from maize canes, which is as sweet and syrupy as that made from the sugar cane. They also make syrup from a plant which in the islands is called *maguey*,[8] which is much better than most syrups, and from this plant they also make sugar and wine, which they likewise sell. There are many sorts of spun cotton, in hanks of every color, and it seems like the silk market at Granada, except here there is a much greater quantity. They sell as many colors for painters as may be found in Spain and all of excellent hues. They sell deerskins, with and without the hair, and some are dyed white or in various colors. They sell much earthenware, which for the most part is very good; there are both large and small pitchers, jugs, pots, tiles, and many other sorts of vessel, all of good clay and most of them glazed and painted. They sell maize both as grain and as bread and it is better both in appearance and in taste than any found in the islands or on the mainland. They sell chicken and fish pies, and much fresh and salted fish, as well as raw and cooked fish. They sell hen and goose eggs, and eggs of all the other birds I have mentioned, in great number, and they sell *tortillas* made from eggs.

Finally, besides those things which I have already mentioned, they sell in the market everything else to be found in this land, but they are so many and so varied that because of their great number and because I cannot remember many of them nor do I know what they are called I shall not mention them. Each kind of merchandise is sold in its own street without any mixture whatever; they are very particular in this. Everything is sold by number and size, and until now I have seen nothing sold by weight. There is in this great square a very large building like a courthouse, where ten or twelve persons sit as judges. They preside over all that happens in the markets, and sentence

---

7   Called *tameme* in Nahuatl. The amount they could carry and the distance they could travel was fixed by law.

8   The maguey (*metl* in Nahuatl) is the American aloe or *Agave americana*. The "wine" referred to here is pulque, a powerful syrupy liquor still popular today.

criminals. There are in this square other persons who walk among the people to see what they are selling and the measures they are using; and they have been seen to break some that were false.

In Context | Templo Mayor, Mexico City

After subjugating the Aztecs, Cortés made the critical decision to build the Spanish city—and future capital of the new territory—on top of the Indian city. The fact that Tenochtitlán was built on an island, in the middle of a lake that was divided into salty and fresh waters, was not clearly well understood by the Spaniards. Failing to comprehend the unique geography of the lake, they destroyed the dam that separated the different waters and thus provoked the first ecological disaster of the valley, not only by mixing the waters, but also by eliminating the city's natural flood protection. Cortés, committed to his original decision, ordered his men to build on top of the ancient city, just a bit higher, believing that this small change in elevation would avoid flooding. He was wrong, of course. Nevertheless, thanks to his determination, many important buildings of ancient Tenochtitlán, albeit in ruins, can still be seen in contemporary Mexico City.

Figure 2.1. Templo Mayor, Mexico City. Photograph by Diego Delso (2013). License CC BY-SA 3.0. By permission of the Instituto Nacional de Antropología e Historia.

Figure 2.2. Mestizaje: The Serpent Head. Museo de la Ciudad de México, Mexico City. Photograph by Jennifer Saracino.

In Context | Mestizaje: The Serpent Head

An actual ruin of an Aztec temple, this serpent head became the cornerstone of a colonial building, now on a busy street in the center of Mexico City. This particular architectural detail has enormous symbolic value. The results of the conquest are physically apparent: a whole civilization was suppressed and what remained was oppressed and impressed into service.

Fray Bartolomé de Las Casas (1474–1566)

Fray Bartolomé de Las Casas has always been a controversial figure, both during his life and in the four hundred years since his death. His first book, *A Short Account of the Destruction of the Indies* (1552), gave him a reputation as protector of the Indians and helped to create the "Black Legend" of Spanish America. Often promoted by Protestant colonizers eager to justify their own questionable behaviors, the "Black Legend" maintained that Spanish colonizers were particularly vicious in their treatment of native populations, a view that tainted colonial rule for centuries.

A merchant of Seville, Las Casas' father had accompanied Columbus on his second voyage, making him a very wealthy man. When his talented son declared his intention to become a priest, he could afford to send him to study at Spain's best university, Salamanca. At eighteen, Las Casas immigrated with his father to Hispaniola (presently Haiti and the Dominican Republic), arriving on April 15, 1502. The young man was granted an *encomienda* by the king—land and Indian laborers to work it. As an *encomendero*, Las Casas was expected to instruct his workers in Christianity, pay them a small wage, and offer them the nominal protection of the Crown. While managing his property, Las Casas also traveled as a provisioner with several military expeditions, witnessing massacres and the abject living conditions of the Taino throughout the island. In 1506, he went back to Spain and then to Rome, where he was ordained a priest. But after his return to Hispaniola, his conflicting status as *encomendero* and priest gradually became intolerable. Inspired by a fiery sermon by a Dominican priest, Antonio de Montesinos, in December of 1510, Las Casas publicly decried the maltreatment of the Indians; but it was not until 1514 that he actually renounced his own *encomienda* and began what became a lifelong campaign against the injustices and cruelty of the colonial system.

Las Casas engaged in a number of stratagems, both political and practical, to mitigate the harsh exploitation of the Indians; when those individual efforts failed, he joined the Dominican order in 1522. Traveling back and forth to Europe to argue in both the royal and papal courts for greater protection of the Indians—indeed for their humanity—Las Casas also served in various administrative capacities in the Americas, notably as vicar of Guatemala and later as bishop of Chiapas.

Though Las Casas wrote numerous works, *A Short Account of the Destruction of the Indies,* written in 1542 and published a decade later, is perhaps his most famous. As its title suggests, its intended audience is the King of Spain. Las Casas argues rather simply that if the goal of American conquest was Christianizing the Indians, the genocidal destruction perpetrated by the Spanish completely undermined that noble intent. The Spaniards themselves had become the devils, in thrall to the god of gold, for which they tortured, enslaved, and killed the native people. Las Casas exposes a depressing repetition of betrayal and brutality in the conquest of the Americas. According to Las Casas' eyewitness accounts, the abuse begins with an initial violation of trust: befriending the Indians, taking their leaders captive, and, then, after securing the gold the Spanish demanded, killing their victims or enslaving them. Such conquerors, Las Casas insists, hardly represent the teachings of Christ or even his Majesty, in whose name they conquer. The implicit argument is that the Indians are more Christian than the nominal Christians. In one of the selections here, for example, an Indian woman, having witnessed the atrocities around her, desperately chooses suicide and even tries to kill her infant son rather than suffer more at the hands of the Spanish. With death inevitable, suicide becomes an escape from a humiliating and painful demise—an ironic affirmation of life. Las Casas' repetitive descriptions of such cruel treatment throughout the region, in every encounter, without exception, emphasize his point. Recounting cases without including specific names and weaving horrendous atrocities with specific events make the relentless brutality even more alarming. That the Indians act more humanely and more like Christians than the Spanish reveals their subjugation to be wholly unjustified.

Las Casas' unyielding opposition to the *encomienda* system eventually achieved some success; in 1542, with Las Casas' help, the New Laws were passed, which, among other things, confirmed Indian freedom and prohibited the inheritance of *encomiendas*. But only three years later, yielding to the pressures of the colonists, this last provision was repealed by Charles V. Finally realizing that he could best defend the beleaguered Indians by remaining at court, Las Casas spent the rest of his long life in Spain, arguing for the rights of the Indians, sparring with his colonial enemies, and writing several major treatises, including his monumental *Historia de las Indias*, completed in 1561, but not published until 1875. He died in a Dominican convent in Madrid at the age of 92.

Even today, Las Casas remains the source of much debate in his role as "protector" and "defender" of the Indians, implying a patriarchal bias toward a lesser race. But in directly challenging the hierarchies that justified de facto slavery and the forced labor of captives, Las Casas also questioned the basic economic structure of the Americas—in itself a feat of no small significance.

The selection here is from *A Short Account of the Destruction of the Indies*, translated by Nigel Griffin (New York: Penguin Books, 1992), 71–74. Translation and notes copyright © Nigel Griffin, 1992. Introduction copyright © Anthony Pagden, 1992. All rights reserved. Reproduced by permission of Penguin Books Ltd.

From **The Kingdom of Yucatán (1552)**

The year of 1526 saw yet another thorough scoundrel elevated to a position of power, this time as governor of the kingdom of Yucatán.[9] As others seeking office in the New World had done before him, this man made false claims at court and made promises he had no intention of keeping in order to secure for himself a position and an authority which he then proceeded to use to feather his own nest at the expense of those he was appointed to govern. The kingdom of Yucatán was very densely populated, for it enjoys a healthy climate and produces foodstuffs in plenty, even more so than México province. This kingdom, some three hundred leagues in perimeter, is particularly well endowed with fruit of all kinds, and produces more honey and wax than has been discovered to date in any other part of the New World. The inhabitants stood out from all their neighbours not only on account of their virtue and their level of civilization but also because they were freer than any of their neighbours from the taint of sin and vice. Among all the peoples of the region they seemed the fittest to hear the word of God, and their territory the best suited by Nature to the establishment of towns and cities, where the local people might have lived side by side in peace and prosperity with the Spanish, who would then have found themselves, had they only proved worthy, in a paradise on earth. But the Spaniards were utterly unfit for such a future, their savage greed and manifest sinfulness rendering them as unworthy of such a paradise here as they had in every other region of the New World the Almighty had consented that the Spanish should discover. The poor innocent people of the area, who simply stayed in their homes and gave not the slightest indication of ill will towards the Spanish, found themselves attacked in the most vicious manner by this butcher and the three hundred men under his command, and many were killed. If there had been any gold in this province, the Spaniards would have finished off the local population by sending them down mines to dig it out of the earth; as it was, the only way they could realize a profit from the bodies and souls of these poor wretched for whom our Lord died on the Cross was to enslave all those whom they had not already murdered, and this they proceeded to do indiscriminately, bartering with the masters of the vessels that came in number to the region once it became known that slaves were to be had in exchange for goods. Natives were sold to buy wine, oil, and vinegar,

---

9 Francisco de Montejo (?1479–1553), who had been one of Cortés's companions in 1519 and conquered much of the Yucatán Peninsula between 1526 and 1537. His son, also named Francisco, founded the city of Mérida in 1542.

salt pork, items of clothing, a horse, or whatever else the butcher and his men imagined they might need. A man would be invited to choose from among fifty or a hundred young girls the one he most fancied, and she would then be handed over in exchange for an *arroba*[10] of wine or oil or vinegar, or for a side of salt pork. Two or three hundred young men would be lined up in similar fashion, the price being much the same. It happened that one young man, the son of a chief, was traded for a cheese; on another occasion a hundred natives were exchanged for a single horse. This went on for seven years, from 1526 until 1533, and during that time the whole region was devastated and the native population enslaved or massacred without quarter. In 1533, the people of the area were granted a short respite from this Hell, with the Spaniards leaving in response to news that great wealth was to be had in Peru; but it was not long before the commanders were back and the hellish round of atrocities, robberies and enslavement was once again in full swing. It still goes on today, and the whole region of three hundred leagues, once, as we have said, so full of bustle and life, is now almost entirely abandoned.

There is no way the written word can convey the full horror of the atrocities committed throughout this region; nor, even if it were to, would the reader credit the excesses that such an account would reveal. I shall accordingly give details of but two or three incidents. The wretched Spaniards actively pursued the locals, both men and women alike, using wild dogs to track them and hunt them down. One woman, who was indisposed at the time and so not able to make good her escape, determined that the dogs should not tear her to pieces as they had done her neighbors and, taking a rope, and tying her one-year-old child to her leg, hanged herself from a beam. Yet she was not in time to prevent the dogs from ripping the infant to pieces, even though a friar did arrive and baptize the infant before it died.

Bernardino de Sahagún (1499–1590)

In 1529, the Franciscan friar Bernardino de Sahagún arrived in the newly conquered territory of Mexico known as the Viceroyalty of New Spain. Sahagún was part of the second group of Franciscan missionaries dispatched from Spain. The first set had optimistically believed that they had converted millions of Indians to Christianity and were moving rapidly toward the

---

10 The *arroba*, in origin an Arabic term, was widely used throughout the Spanish empire as a measure, both of weight (roughly 25 pounds) and of dry capacity (roughly 15 liters), though its precise value varied regionally.

supposed goal of the conquest. But by the time Sahagún arrived, the Franciscans had begun to realize that most of these conversions had been purely formal, simply en masse baptisms without much concern for what the eager converts actually understood or believed about their new religion.

The new strategy for conversion would be different. Like careful doctors, the friars recognized that they had to understand their patients' illness before prescribing the proper remedy of Christianity. As a gifted linguist and dedicated missionary, Sahagún soon distinguished himself in developing this new method of conversion: knowing Indian religions and customs thoroughly in order to identify the sources of resistance as well as to recognize when and how idolatrous beliefs and practices survived.

In part, these different approaches to conversion reflected different understandings of what the discovery and conquest of these vast new territories meant. For the first group, the encounter with Native Americans was a millenarian sign; the conversion of these new peoples signaled the imminence of Christ's return. Such millennialist hopes had been greatly diminished by the time the second wave of missionaries arrived in Mexico, but the task of conversion generated other debates that persisted for the next three centuries of Spanish occupation. One important question was whether Christianity had come to the Americas with one of Christ's apostles. A rigorous view of scripture suggested a positive answer: Christ had ordered his apostles to spread the gospel all over the world, including this New World. But if that were so, where was the evidence of this original Christianity, the traces of that first conversion? Nearly every book written during the colonial period addressed this issue, noting the footprints of Saint Thomas left on a stone or demonstrating that the apostle's presence lay disguised in the myths of Nahuatl or Mayan or Incan gods.

Even more pressing, however, was the rationale for conversion itself. The legal basis for the conquest and possession of the Americas by Spain (and Portugal) derived from the Pope's explicit condition that the Indians be Christianized. If Saint Thomas had already converted the Americas, Spanish colonization was stripped of its primary justification. As late as the end of the eighteenth century, the controversy would continue in the debates over the origins of the miraculous image of the Virgin of Guadalupe, particularly in the works of FRAY SERVANDO TERESA DE MIER.

A native of Sahagún, Spain, Bernardino de Sahagún was educated at the great humanist university of Salamanca, where he joined the Franciscans and became a priest. Recruited by his superiors to help evangelize Mexico, Sahagún quickly became a student of Indian culture, learning the Nahua language and helping to found the Colegio de la Santa Cruz, in Tlatelolco, just north of the ancient city. There, Sahagún began teaching the children of Indian elites, recognizing that these young converts would be influential in spreading Christian doctrine and values.

In 1546, a devastating plague killed almost half of the native population. Believing that he was watching a culture disappear, Sahagún redoubled his efforts to gather material about native customs and histories. Over the next fifty years, he assembled an enormous quantity of drawings and manuscripts, in Nahuatl and in Spanish translations. A careful researcher, he developed methods to ensure the quality and accuracy of his findings, methods that centuries later became the basis of the modern sciences of anthropology, ethnography, and philology. Sahagún constructed questionnaires, conducted interviews, transcribed testimonies, and added linguistic commentaries to his investigations. Sahagún, along with many other early chroniclers and missionaries, thus pioneered the techniques and standards that produced modern historiography.

In 1577, the King asked that Sahagún send to Spain a version of his vast archival project. It is still unclear whether the King required the information or simply wished to destroy it, but the manuscript eventually made its way to a library in Florence and is known today as the *Florentine Codex*. Sahagún laid out his findings in two columns on each page, one in Nahuatl and the other translated into Spanish. Three years later, Sahagún also prepared a version entirely in Spanish, which was published in México in the 1830s as *Historia general de las cosas de la Nueva España* [General History of the Things of New Spain].

The excerpt here, describing the birth of HUITZILOPOCHTLI and the deaths of his sister COYOLXAUHQUI and his brothers, is from "Book III: The Origin of the Gods" in the *Florentine Codex: General History of the Things of New Spain*, translated from the Aztec into English by Arthur J. O. Anderson and Charles E. Dibble, eds. (Santa Fe, New Mexico: School of American Research and the University of Utah, 1952), 1–5. Reprinted by permission of the School for Advanced Research (SAR Press) from "Book III: The Origin of the Gods," number 14, part IV in *Florentine Codex: General History of the Things of New Spain* (Santa Fe, New Mexico, School of American Research, 1952). No part of this material may be printed, reproduced, transmitted, in any form or by any means, electronic or mechanical, including any information storage or retrieval system, without written permission from SAR Press.

From **Del Principio de los Dioses (1577) [The Origin of the Gods]**

HERE BEGINNETH THE THIRD BOOK

First Chapter, in which it is told how the gods had their beginning.

How the gods had their beginning and where they began is not well known. But this is plain, [that] there at Teotihuacan, as they say, in times past, when yet there was darkness, there all the gods gathered themselves together, and they debated who would bear the burden, who would carry on his back—would become—the sun. (This hath already been told elsewhere.) And when the sun came to arise, then all [the gods] died that the sun might come into being. None remained who had not perished (as hath been told). And thus the ancient ones thought it to be.

TO UITZILOPOCHTLI the Mexicans paid great honor.

The following they believed of his beginning, his origin. At Coatepec, near Tollan, there always had dwelt and lived a woman named Coatlicue, mother of Centzonuitznaua. And their elder sister was named Coyolxauhqui.

And this Coatlicue performed penances there; she swept; she was charged with the sweeping. Thus did she do penance at Coatepec. And once, as she swept, feathers, as it were, a ball of feathers, descended upon her. Then Coatlicue snatched it up and placed it in her bosom. And when she had swept, [when] she came to take the feather [ball] which she had placed in her bosom, she found nothing. Thereupon Coatlicue conceived.[11]

And when the Centzonuitznaua saw that their mother was already with child, they were very wrathful. They said: "Who brought this about? Who hath made her heavy with child? She hath dishonored and shamed us!"

And their elder sister, Coyolxauhqui, said to them: "My elder brothers, she hath affronted us; we must slay our mother, the wicked one who is already with child. Who is the cause of what is in her womb?"

And when Coatlicue learned of this, she was sorely afraid and deeply saddened. And her child, who was in her womb, comforted her. He spoke and said to her: "Have no fear; already I know [what I shall do]."

When Coatlicue heard the words of her son, she was much consoled by them and her heart was eased of what had so terrified her.

And upon this, when the Centzonuitznaua had assembled for their deliberations, when they had made up their minds that indeed they would slay their mother because verily she had brought dishonor, much did they harden themselves; they were exceeding wroth. As if bursting her heart, Coyolxauhqui

---

11 Coatlicue conceived Huitzilopochtli, tutelary god of the Aztecs. In some chronicles he is identified as Quetzalcóatl and in others Coatlicue is portrayed as conceiving Quetzalcóatl and Xolotl.

esto paue ser cosa muy buena, y
sabrosa, ya me sano, y quito la en
fermedad, ya estoy sano: y mas
otra uez le dixo el viejo. Señor,
beuedla otra vez, porque es muy
buena la medicina, y estareys
mas sano. y el dicho quetzalcoatl
beuio la otra uez de que se embo
rracho, y començo allorar triste
mente: y se le mouio, y ablan
do el coraçon, para yrse, y no se
le quito del pensamiento lo que
tenia, por el engaño, y burla,
que le hizo, el dicho nigromanti
co viejo. Y la medicina que be
uio, el dicho quetzalcoatl, era
vino blanco de la tierra: hecho
de magueyes, que se llaman teu
metl.

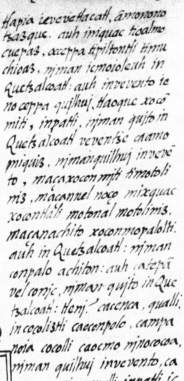

tlapia ieueueltlacatl, amonoio
tzazque. auh iniquac ticalmo
cuepas, accepa tipiltontli timu
chicaz. niman icmoioleuh in
Quetzalcoatl: auh invevento te
no ceppa quilhuj. tlaoque xoco
miti, inpatli, niman quito in
Quetzalcoatl veventze caamo
miquiz, nimanquilhuj inueve
to, macaxoconmiti timotoli
niz, macannel noço mixquac
xoconttlali motonal motolимis.
macanachito xoconmopalolti.
auh in Quetzalcoatl: niman
conpalo achiton: auh catepa
vel conie, niman quito inQue
tzalcoatl: tenj. cacenca, qualli.
in cocolistli caocenpolo, campa
noia cocolli caocmo ninococoa.
niman quilhuj invevento, ca
occe xoconj caqualli inpatli ic
chicaoaz inmonacaic, auh ni
man icicnoceppa ce conie, ni
man icivintie, niman ieic
choca velicllelquiça, icvpcan
moioleuh in Quetzalcoatl, vnca
tlapan iniollo. aocmocomilca
caoaia, caie inquimattinenca
inquimattinemia velquijolma

Figure 2.3. A page from the *Florentine Codex*. Reprinted by permission of the School for Advanced Research (SAR Press) from "Book III: The Origin of the Gods," number 14, part IV in *Florentine Codex: General History of the Things of New Spain*, translated from the Aztec into English by Arthur J. O. Anderson and Charles E. Dibble, eds. (Santa Fe, New Mexico: School of American Research, 1952), 38. No part of this material may be printed, reproduced, transmitted, in any form or by any means, electronic or mechanical, including any information storage or retrieval system, without written permission from the School for Advanced Research (SAR Press).

greatly incited and aroused the anger of her elder brothers, that they might slay their mother. And the Centzonuitznaua thereupon arrayed and prepared themselves for war.

And these Centzonuitznaua were like seasoned warriors. They wound and twisted [their hair]; they bound their hair about their heads [in warrior array].

And [there was] one named Quauitlicac, who was a traitor; that which the Centzonuitznaua said, he then told and brought as news to Uitzilopochtli.

And Uitzilopochtli said to Quauitlicac: "Watch well what they do, my dear uncle, and pay careful heed; for already I know [what I shall do]."

And finally, when [the Centzonuitznaua] were determined and of one mind in their deliberations that they would put to death and dispose of their mother, they thereupon set forth. Coyolxauhqui led them. Much did they exert and drive themselves. They were in war array, which was distributed [among them]; all put in place their paper array, the paper crowns, their nettles, painted paper streamers, and they bound bells to the calves of their legs. These bells were called *oyoalli*. And their darts [had] barbed points.

Thereupon they set forth; they went in order, in columns, in armed display, moving with deliberation. Coyolxauhqui led them.

And Quauitlicac thereupon hastened to run up [the hill] that he might warn Uitzilopochtli. He said: "Already they are coming."

Then Uitzilopochtli spoke: "Watch well where they come."

Thereupon Quauitlicac said to him: "Already they are at Tzompantitlan."

Again, Uitzilopochtli addressed him: "Where now do they come?"

Then [Quauitlicac] said to him: "Already they are at Coaxalpan."

Once more Uitzilopochtli called out to Quauitlicac: "See where they now come."

Then [this one] said to him: "Already they are at Apetlac."

Once again [Uitzilopochtli] spoke forth to him: "Where now do they come?"

Then Quauitlicac answered him: Already they have come half way[12] up the slope of the mountain."

And Uitzilopochtli again spoke forth to Quauitlicac; he said: "Watch where they now come."

Then Quauitlicac said unto him: "At last they are coming up here; at last they reach here. Coyolxauhqui cometh ahead of them."

And Uitzilopochtli then burst forth, born.

Then his array he brought forth with him—his shield [named] *teueuelli*, and his darts, and his dart thrower, all blue, named *xiuatlatl*. And in diagonal

---

12 In the original myth, possibly they were place names, which, in rituals, later came to be names of places around the Temple of Huitzilopochtli, used perhaps to recall the original account.

stripes was his face painted, with his child's offal, called his child's painting. He was pasted with feathers about his forehead and about his ears. And on his one thin foot, his left, he had the sole pasted with feathers, and he had stained both of his thighs with blue mineral earth, and both upper arms.

And one named Tochancalqui laid fire to the serpent *xiuhcoatl*[13] at the command of Uitzilopochtli.

Then with it he pierced Coyolxauhqui, and then he quickly struck off her head. It came to rest there on the slope of Coatepec. And her body went falling below; it went crashing in pieces; in various places her arms, her legs, and her body kept falling.

And Uitzilopochtli then arose and pursued the Centzonuitznaua, and went among them, and pounced upon them, and scattered them from the top of Coatepec.

And when he had pursued them to the base, the foot [of the mountain], he took after them and gave them chase around the skirts of Coatepec. Four times he pursued and followed them around. In vain they went about doing what they might against him; in vain they stood against him, striking about with their shields. No more could they do, no more could they achieve; neither could they take refuge. Uitzilopochtli quite overpowered them; he made them turn tail; he destroyed them in battle. He completely bested and ill-used them.

And not even now did he let them alone. He kept on. Much did they [then] importune him. They said to him: "Let this be enough!"

But Uitzilopochtli would not content himself with this. With force he hurled himself against them and took after them. And only very few fled his presence and escaped his hands. They went toward a haven to the south. For indeed to that place these Centzonuitznaua journeyed—the few who escaped the hands of Uitzilopochtli.

And when he had slain them, when he had spent his wrath, he took from them their vestments, their adornment, their paper crowns ornamented with feathers. He arrayed himself with these and took [them] for himself; he assumed [them] as his due, as if taking the insignia to himself.

And Uitzilopochtli was also known as an omen of evil; because from only a feather which fell, his mother Coatlicue conceived. For no one came forth as his father.

This one the Mexicans cherished, by making offerings to him, and by honoring and serving him. And Uitzilopochtli rewarded him [who did so]. And this

---

13 Corresponding Spanish text: "Una culebra, hecha de teas, que se llamaba xiuhcoatl."

veneration was taken from there, at Coatepec, just as had been done in days of yore.

Enough [of this].

"El Inca" Garcilaso de la Vega (1539–1616)

"El Inca" Garcilaso de la Vega was a first-generation *mestizo* born in Cuzco, Perú, with a privileged ancestry: he was the illegitimate son of a Spanish nobleman, while his mother was descended from Incan royalty. During one of the conquistadors' uprisings against the crown, Garcilaso's father saved the life of one of the rebellious leaders and lost the king's favor. In 1560, when El Inca Garcilaso traveled to Spain to finish his studies, one of his intentions was to clear his father's name from what he considered to be a libelous accusation. Though he never succeeded in that mission, his accomplishment in writing *The Royal Commentaries* far surpasses his original goal.

As early as the 1570s, El Inca Garcilaso seems to have considered writing a work that would both relate the history of his mother's culture and recount the conquest of Peru in a way that would exonerate his father's actions. However, the Spanish crown had by this time become particularly intolerant of the persistence of Indian religious rituals in its colony. The new viceroy, Francisco de Toledo, who arrived in Peru around 1569, launched an exceptionally violent campaign against such native practices, and Garcilaso's mother became one of its victims. Motivated by her death as well as by his personal dismay at the ignorant or prejudiced portrayals of Incan culture in most contemporary stories and chronicles, Garcilaso, who knew Quechua as well as Spanish, determined to write his own true history.

Better known than the rest of the text and much admired, *Part One of the Royal Commentaries* was published in 1609 and focuses on the Incan past. The second part, which traces the conquest of Peru, appeared posthumously in 1617. Among the many historiographies written on the conquest, Garcilaso's text is an acknowledged masterpiece. With a remarkably modern sensibility, Garcilaso offers unique observations about geography, religion, human psychology, and the cultural formation of society. Not limiting his account to the history of successive Incan rulers, Garcilaso provides a holistic vision of Incan civilization, including descriptions of temples, religious rites, the city of Cuzco and other important places, as well as agriculture and other industries; he even provides a critical explanation of the QUIPUS, the system of knots that was used to keep records. Though the text is not without its mistakes and exaggerations and an understandable partiality for Incas over other Andean peoples, it remains an indispensable source of information about many aspects of Inca culture that were either destroyed or erased by the conquest.

In addition to chronicling the native past and detailing its culture, El Inca also incorporated into his narrative an argument that the real purpose of this "gentile" civilization was to prepare the Andean peoples for the arrival of Christianity. El Inca Garcilaso argued that religious conversion would have been impossible without the Incan institutions established through-out the Andean chain. As evidence, El Inca notes the gradual disappearance of polytheism and idolatry in favor of a relatively concrete monotheism, as well as the development of various social institutions (such as secluded houses for women not unlike Christian convents) and the moral regime imposed by the kings. In his construction, then, the trajectory of Incan history was directed toward Christianity. Thus, when the Spanish missionaries arrived, the Incan people, together with the neighboring cultures that they had subdued, were positively ready for the true word of the Gospel.

As an apology for Incan culture, El Inca Garcilaso's work was not well received in Spain; indeed, after its publication in Lisbon, it was later suppressed as a dangerous text. But in the Americas, especially in the Andean region, it was widely read and continues to be appreciated as the best holistic description of an indigenous people in pre-Hispanic America. The *Royal Commentaries* also has exceptional literary value, in its lucid prose as well as in providing an early instance of the linguistic, historical, and cultural fusion that became a distinguishing mark of Spanish American culture. One aspect of that fusion appears in El Inca's signature consolidation of native and Christian theologies. Known as syncretism, such a blending of Christian, especially Catholic, religious practices with Indian traditions became common throughout Hispanic America. But El Inca Garcilaso may be the first writer who was so candidly syncretic in his worldview: proud to be a mestizo, he manifested that pride in his extraordinary work.

The selection is from part 1 of the *Royal Commentaries of the Incas and a General History of Peru*, translated by Harold V. Livermore (Austin: University of Texas Press, 1966), 40–43.

From The Royal Commentaries of the Incas (1609)

CHAPTER XV. The Origin of the Inca Kings of Peru

While these people were living or dying in the manner we have seen, it pleased our Lord God that from their midst there should appear a morning star to give them in the dense darkness in which they dwelt some glimmerings of natural law, of civilization, and of the respect men owe to one another. The descendants of this leader should thus tame those savages and convert them into men, made capable of reason and of receiving good doctrine, so that when God, who is the sun of justice, saw fit to send forth the light of His divine rays upon those idolaters, it might find them no longer in the first savagery, but rendered more docile to receive the Catholic faith and the teaching and doctrine of our Holy Mother the Roman Church, as indeed they have received it—all of which will be seen in the course of this history. It has been observed by clear experience how much prompter and quicker to receive the Gospel were the Indians subdued, governed, and taught by the Inca kings than the other neighboring peoples unreached by the Incas' teachings, many of which are still today as savage and brutish as before, despite the fact that the Spaniards have been in Peru seventy years. And since we stand on the threshold of this great maze, we had better enter and say what lay within.

After having prepared many schemes and taken many ways to begin to give an account of the origin and establishment of the native Inca kings of Peru, it seemed to me that the best scheme and simplest and easiest way was to recount what I often heard as a child from the lips of my mother and her brothers and uncles and other elders about these beginnings. For everything said about them from other sources comes down to the same story as we shall relate, and it will be better to have it as told in the very words of the Incas than in those of foreign authors. My mother dwelt in Cuzco, her native place, and was visited there every week by the few relatives, both male and female, who escaped the cruelty and tyranny of Atahuallpa (which we shall describe in our account of his life). On these visits the ordinary subject of conversation was always the origin of the Inca kings, their greatness, the grandeur of their empire, their deeds and conquests, their government in peace and war, and the laws they ordained so greatly to the advantage of their vassals. In short, there was nothing concerning the most flourishing period of their history that they did not bring up in their conversations.

From the greatness and prosperity of the past they turned to the present, mourning their dead kings, their lost empire, and their fallen state, etc. These and similar topics were broached by the Incas and Pallas on their visits, and on recalling their departed happiness, they always ended these conversations with tears and mourning, saying: "Our rule is turned to bondage" etc. During these talks, I, as a boy, often came in and went out of the place where they were, and I loved to hear them, as boys always do like to hear stories. Days, months, and years went by, until I was sixteen or seventeen. Then it happened that one day when my family was talking in this fashion about their kings and the olden times, I remarked to the senior of them, who usually related these things: "Inca, my uncle, though you have no writings to preserve the memory of past events, what information have you of the origin and beginnings of our kings? For the Spaniards and the other peoples who live on their borders have divine and human histories from which they know when their own kings and neighbors' kings began to reign and when one empire gave way to another. They even know how many thousand years it is since God created heaven and earth. All this and much more they know through their books. But you, who have no books, what memory have you preserved of your antiquity? Who was the first of our Incas? What was he called? What was the origin of his line? How did he begin to reign? With what men and arms did he conquer this great empire? How did our heroic deeds begin?"

The Inca was delighted to hear these questions, since it gave him great pleasure to reply to them, and turned to me (who had already often heard him tell the tale, but had never paid as much attention as then) saying:

"Nephew, I will tell you these things with pleasure: indeed it is right that you should hear them and keep them in your heart (this is their phrase for 'in the memory'). You should know that in olden times the whole of this region before you was covered with brush and heath, and people lived in those times like wild beasts, with no religion or government and no towns or houses, and without tilling or sowing the soil, or clothing or covering their flesh, for they did not know how to weave cotton or wool to make clothes. They lived in twos and threes as chance brought them together in caves and crannies in rocks and underground caverns. Like wild beasts they ate the herbs of the field and roots of trees and fruits growing wild and also human flesh. They covered their bodies with leaves and the bark of trees and animals' skins. Others went naked. In short, they lived like deer or other game, and even in their intercourse with women they behaved like beasts, for they knew nothing of having separate wives."

I must remark, in order to avoid many repetitions of the words "our father the Sun," that the phrase was used by the Incas to express respect whenever they mentioned the sun, for they boasted of descending from it, and none but

Incas were allowed to utter the words: it would have been blasphemy and the speaker would have been stoned. The Inca said:

"Our father the Sun, seeing men in the state I have mentioned, took pity and was sorry for them, and sent from heaven to earth a son and a daughter of his to indoctrinate them in the knowledge of our father the Sun that they might worship him and adopt him as their god, and to give them precepts and laws by which they would live as reasonable and civilized men, and dwell in houses and settled towns, and learn to till the soil, and grow plants and crops, and breed flocks, and use the fruits of the earth like rational beings and not like beasts. With this order and mandate our father the Sun set these two children of his in Lake Titicaca, eighty leagues from here, and bade them go where they would, and wherever they stopped to eat or sleep to try to thrust into the ground a golden wand half a yard long and two fingers in thickness which he gave them as a sign and token: when this wand should sink into the ground at a single thrust, there our father the Sun wished them to stop and set up their court.

"Finally he told them: 'When you have reduced these people to our service, you shall maintain them in reason and justice, showing mercy, clemency, and mildness, and always treating them as a merciful father treats his beloved and tender children. Imitate my example in this. I do good to all the world. I give them my light and brightness that they may see and go about their business; I warm them when they are cold; and I grow their pastures and crops; and bring fruit to their trees, and multiply their flocks. I bring rain and calm weather in turn, and I take care to go round the world once a day to observe the wants that exist in the world and to fill and supply them as the sustainer and benefactor of men. I wish you as children of mine to follow this example sent down to earth to teach and benefit those men who live like beasts. And henceforward I establish and nominate you as kings and lords over all the people you may thus instruct with your reason, government, and good works.'

"When our father the Sun had thus made manifest his will to his two children he bade them farewell. They left Titicaca and travelled northwards, and wherever they stopped on the way they thrust the golden wand into the earth, but it never sank in. Thus they reached a small inn or resthouse seven or eight leagues south of this city. Today it is called Pacárec Tampu, 'inn or resthouse of the dawn.' The Inca gave it this name because he set out from it about daybreak. It is one of the towns the prince later ordered to be founded, and its inhabitants to this day boast greatly of its name because our first Inca bestowed it. From this place he and his wife, our queen, reached the valley of Cuzco which was then a wilderness."

In Context | The Ceques of Cuzco

If in the Western world we like to say "all roads lead to Rome," then inhabitants of the Incan Empire might have said that all roads led to Cuzco. Called "ceques," there were at least forty or forty-one such roads, though archaeologists cannot agree on the exact number. Seen on a map, these roads all emerge from Cuzco at the center and extend like the rays of a star to cover the whole territory of the empire (fig. 2.4, 92). Indeed, even within Cuzco, the lines emanate from one specific place: the Temple of the Sun, the most sacred place of Inca civilization.

Felipe Guamán Poma de Ayala (1545?–after 1616)

Written at the turn of the sixteenth century into the seventeenth, *The First New Chronicle and Good Government* is certainly one of the most important sources for Andean perspectives on colonial society. The voluminous manuscript (about 800 pages), which was rediscovered in the Danish Royal Library in 1908, provides detailed information about the Andean past and its inhabitants together with a meticulous and sharply critical view of the colonial present. Divided into thematic sections, such as "Festivities," "Funerals," and "Government," the manuscript consists of numbered segments depicting topics and events both in text and in the splendid line drawings that probably helped to ensure the manuscript's preservation.

Little is known about Guamán Poma, though he was a native of central Perú and spent much of his life in the province of Huamanga, part of present-day Ayachuco. He seems to have worked closely with the Spanish colonial powers, serving as an interpreter and as a scribe for ecclesiastic inspectors, notably Cristóbal de Albornoz, who sought to eradicate idolatry in the Andes by destroying the *huacas*, objects and places sacred to the people. While Guamán Poma repeatedly notes his status as a convert to Christianity, his deep roots in Andean culture are obvious. A descendant of an ancient people, now bereft of power, Guamán Poma poses critical questions faced by all indigenous people as they confront a new religion and new ways of viewing the world. This condition of being between two worlds lies at the heart of this remarkable text, offering parallel views that shift with the reader's position and knowledge of Indian languages and cultures. On the one hand, Guamán Poma broadly affirms the dominant Christian view, proposing Genesis as the unique beginning of his narration of world history, but then he uses the values of Christianity to condemn

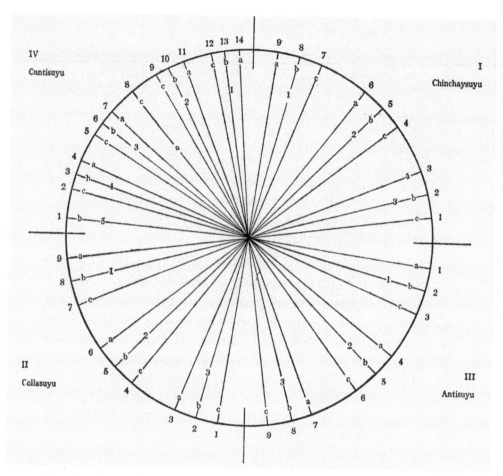

Figure 2.4. Ceques of Cuzco. The Arabic numerals outside the circle indicate the sequence of the ceque of each suyu, which the chronicler Bernabé Cobo follows in the enumeration in his *Relación de los ceques*. R. T. Zuidema, *The Ceque System of Cuzco: The Social Organization of the Inca* (Leiden, Netherlands: Brill, 1964), 2. By permission of Brill.

Andean society under Spanish rule, noting the current degradation from Incan morality and the social structures of the past.

The complexity of this dual view is exemplified in how Guamán Poma posits a biblical origin of Andean peoples, claiming their descent from one of Noah's sons, brought by God to the Americas. But Guamán Poma places this event in the Second Age of the World, an Andean division of time and place, or *pacha*. Incorporating Incan traditions into the frame of Western history, he manages both to refute the repeated claim that Indians are savages, outside the scope of the "civilized" world, and to demonstrate the congruence and persistence of Andean values within or even against those of the new regime. For example, Guamán Poma argues that in the Incan past, women were chaste and more faithful to their husbands than in the colonial present.

Such duality is particularly evident in the more than four hundred drawings, depicting Adam and Eve, for example, in a Peruvian landscape. Even more telling is the image "Pontifical mundo / Las Indias del Perú en lo alto de España / Castilla en lo abajo de las Indias" [Pontifical World: The Indies of Peru and the Kingdom of Castile] (fig. 2.5). In this drawing, the European kingdom is situated within the Andean spatial divisions of *hanan/urin* (high/low, right/left), with no concern for Western spatial realities, since Spain and America seem to occupy the same hemisphere. In Guamán Poma's portrayal, the world is structured only as high and low. Space has no separate empirical reality and cannot be recognized apart from this fundamental division. In fact, Western notions of space as autonomous only developed at the end of the seventeenth century, supported by Newton's scientific discoveries and the idea of "absolute space." Consistent with earlier Andean texts, however, Guamán Poma's images represent space as a continuum, a celestial sphere, where earth and sky mirror one another, unseparated as distinct physical bodies.

Guamán Poma also uses Andean notions by including a letter from his father in his introduction. After a rejection of legal claims to ancestral lands around 1600, followed by punishment and exile, Guamán Poma had turned to social activism and writing as a way of responding to colonial control. The composition of *The New Chronicle* was intended to propose to Philip III a synthesis of Andean and Spanish rule, and the text includes Guamán Poma's introductory letters to the Pope and the king. But the letter from Guamán Poma's father to the king serves another, less familiar purpose. Carefully stressing that the information of the *Chronicle* comes only from eyewitness accounts, from people who saw everything firsthand, this letter becomes a source of authority for writing, a critical feature of truth-telling in Andean culture. In Jaqi, Guamán Poma's native tongue, one cannot even speak without adding a linguistic suffix to every sentence, marking the source of one's information. The letter from his father, which confirms how and where the material of the *Chronicle* was obtained, thus establishes an Andean perspective at the very beginning of the narration and assures its truth. Though Philip III never actually received Guamán Poma's treatise, the *Chronicle* remains a uniquely valuable resource for understanding one of the Americas' richest cultures.

Figure 2.5. Peru over Spain from Felipe Guamán Poma de Ayala. *Nueva Corónica y Buen Gobierno,* transcription, prologue, chronological notes by Franklin Pease (Caracas, Venezuela: Biblioteca Ayacucho, 1980), 34.

The selection is from Felipe Guaman Poma de Ayala, *The First New Chronicle and Good Government, Abridged*, selected, translated, and annotated by David Frye (Indianapolis, Ind.: Hackett, 2006), 184–86. Copyright © 2006 by Hackett Publishing Company, Inc. Reprinted by permission of Hackett Publishing Company, Inc. All rights reserved.

From The First New Chronicle and Good Government

THE STEWARDS OF THE KINGDOM: THE ENCOMENDEROS
STEWARDS FOR COLLECTING TRIBUTE: THE STEWARDS OF
THE [SPANISH] RANCHES, FARMS, SUGAR PLANTATIONS,
TEXTILE MILLS, SUGAR MILLS, ORCHARDS, THE MINES
OF THE ANDES, AND COCA FARMS; HOUSE STEWARDS;
AND THE STEWARDS OF *CORREGIDORES*, PADRES,
AND OTHER RICH SPANIARDS

[*The next group to be criticized are the stewards or overseers* (mayordomos) *of Spanish estates and mines. These were administrators, (usually but not necessarily Spanish) who were hired by the owners of Spanish business undertakings, farms, and wealthy households in the Americas to handle their day-to-day operations.*] THESE STEWARDS are absolute despots. First, because they are never audited. Second, because they are never inspected. Third, because they are never punished. Therefore, they wrong the poor Indians who are going about their day labor, their chores, and their work.

If a laborer loses ten llamas, the steward makes him pay for twenty llamas. He takes away all his pay. He refuses to give him any food. He makes his wife and children work; he should have to pay each of them for their work day, but he even makes them work at night, and to keep from paying them, he hides their work, or hides other things that he has in his possession, and so he gets away with not paying them.

These stewards keep company with other Spanish stewards. They and their companions all have mistresses; they rob the Indians, and they have crowds of little mestizo sons and daughters. They deflower the maidens—the daughters of Indian herders, cattlemen, and servants. Aside from this, they have dozens of whores, in their kitchens and in their workers' huts. In order to do all these things, they bribe the *corregidores*, judges, and *doctrina* priests,[14] who therefore would indulge them even if they beat a poor Indian to death. There is no remedy: there is not even an inspector for these stewards in this kingdom.

The stewards make their own justice; they arrest, punish, and imprison Indian men and women in their storerooms and houses. A steward will also demand a half dozen men and a half dozen women to work for him as *mitayos*;[15] he will make them spin yarn, weave cloth, and work as bakers, *chicha*[16] vendors, and store keepers, and he will have lots of *yanaconas* [male servants] and *chinas* [female servants]—servant boys, cooks, maids, butlers, and much pomp and circumstance. This makes [his employer,] the *encomendero, corregidor*, or padre, very happy: indeed, [the employer] will take the Indian women into his own house, and so turn them into tremendous whores. That is why the Indians do not multiply, and there is not remedy in this kingdom.

It would be most just if all the fields, corrals, and pastures that have been sold in His Majesty's name were returned and restituted, because they cannot in good conscience be taken from the natives, the legitimate proprietors of these fields. One *hanegada* of land might have sold for ten silver pesos, another for twenty, depending on the result of the auctions, but even if they had been sold for one hundred pesos, the purchasers have been more than repaid in crops and cattle, and thus the Spaniards should return these fields, corrals, and pastures to the Indians.[17]

After the land is returned to the Indians, it will be worth much more to His Majesty, because the Indian man or woman to whom a field belonged, or the pueblo that has owned a communal field or pasture with proper titles since *ab initio*, since the time of Topa Inca Yupanqui, Wayna Capac Inca, and the Christian conquest, can let, lease, and rent the land to the Spaniards, mestizos,

---

14 Missionaries preaching the gospel.
15 Under Incan rule, subjects had to work part of the year in large public projects (warehouses, roads, temples) without compensation. This work was called the *mita* and the workers *mitayos*.
16 Alcoholic beverage made from fermented maize.
17 There had been a wave of land sales by the crown in the 1590s, to be followed by more in the 1620s and 1630s. (Technically, these were not land sales, but fees paid for legalized title to land, *composiciones de tierras*). The land affected was considered "idle," "vacant," or "abandoned," though the most frequently targeted fields were valuable ones lying close to Spanish markets in Lima, other Spanish towns, and the mines. A *hanegada* or *fanegada* is the amount of land that can be sown with a *fanega* (roughly 1.5 bushels) of grain, about seven or eight acres as figured in south-central Peru. See Stern, *Peru's Indian Peoples and the Challenge of Spanish Conquest*, p. 116.

mulattos, blacks, *cholos*,[18] *zambaigos*[19]—all those who are tending towards a new stock and generation—and to the Indians who inherited no land. They can rent it, and [the renters] can pay a certain amount to the land owner, and the land owner can pay the fifth[20] to His Majesty every year, in this kingdom. His Majesty should name a salaried general judge, who would reside in the city of Los Reyes de Lima. If an Indian did not rent out his land, he would not need to pay this tax.

Therefore, they should not sell these lands to the Spaniards, unless [the buyer and the owner] agree among themselves to sell and alienate a piece of land. In this way, neither the Indians nor the Spaniards will be wronged; God and His Majesty will be served; and His Majesty will not lose his royal fifth in this kingdom of the Indies of Peru.

Don Alonso de Ercilla y Zúñiga (1533–1594)

Seeking adventure, Don Alonso de Ercilla y Zúñiga came to the New World in 1555 to help subdue the Araucanians or Mapuche in Chile. The son of a Basque noble, Ercilla had become a page to the future king Phillip II, after his widowed mother joined the court as a lady-in-waiting. The young Alonso traveled extensively with the prince in Europe and was present when the news reached the new king's court of the revolt of the Araucanians and the death of Pedro de Valdivia, the first governor of the provinces of Chile. Of all the Spanish conquests, Chile had proved the most difficult, owing to renowned valor and fierce fighting capabilities of the Araucanians, qualities that Ercilla memorialized in his epic poem. By Ercilla's own account, *La Araucana* was composed during the military campaign against the Indians, led by García Hurtado de Mendoza, the newly appointed governor of Chile. With scarce supplies, Ercilla often used tree bark for paper, writing his poem during the short intervals of rest from battle.

---

18 *Cholo* can mean either a lower-class *mestizo* or an Indian who has adopted Western ways, usually in South America; in Central America and Mexico, a Westernized Indian is a *ladino*.

19 *Zambaigos* denotes a colonial social class; in some regions, referring to the offspring of Indian and Black parents, elsewhere, to that of Indians and Chinese.

20 The fifth (*el quinto*): As an incentive for returning land to its rightful Indian owners, Guamán Poma proposes an annual tax on land rental equivalent to the 20 percent royal tax on gold and silver ore mined in the Spanish realms.

During his relatively short stay in the Americas, Ercilla participated in at least seven battles against the Araucanians and in numerous lesser encounters. His field experience provided the historical framework for his epic, whose thirty-seven cantos were divided into three parts and then separately published—in 1569, 1578, and the last in 1589–1590. The form and values of the traditional epic poems of the Renaissance had reflected those of their classic models, particularly Virgil's *Aeneid*. While the Counter-Reformation shifted the form toward more somber concerns, such as religious history, Ercilla's epic, despite its lack of formal unity, reverts to the Virgilian mode. The verisimilitude of his poem also gives it a particular solidity, with a remarkable fidelity to events, native customs and local geography, even though Ercilla was also following the model of classic Italian romances, such as *Orlando Innamorato* (1495) by Boiardo and *Orlando Furioso* (1510–1532) by Ariosto. That influence is evident in several elements, including the celebrated love passages between Araucanian heroes, Caupolicán and Crepiano, and their female counterparts, Fresia and Tegualda.

Epic poetry has traditionally been distinguished by its affirmation of humanity's highest social and aesthetic ideals. But what is remarkable here is that Ercilla attributes those qualities to the Araucanians; the most intractable adversaries of the Spanish conquest become in these verses the most admirable. The Araucanians are represented as making the best tactical judgments, having an iron discipline, and possessing stellar beauty. In their physical and moral strength, they defy both the writer's skill and nature itself, becoming larger than life. Such amplification is reflected, for example, in a notable scene portraying the election of a leader by a competition to determine who can support a large tree trunk on his shoulders for the longest time. Caupolicán defeats all others by holding the giant trunk for more than two days. As the people then declare, "On such firm shoulders we unload the weight and seriousness of the task we undertake."

As these selections suggest, Ercilla creates his heroes by revealing how physical prowess signals moral strength and perseverance. Such ethical assertions make the epic poem itself a vehicle for strengthening social morality, a significant point at a moment when the value of imaginative literature was being questioned and when colonial power was eliciting some of the darkest aspects of human nature, as the writings of BARTOLOMÉ DE LAS CASAS all too keenly reveal.

Apart from its cultural implications, Ercilla's poem was an extraordinary literary achievement. Essentially a narrative, *La Aruacana* employs the *octava real* (the royal octet or ottava rima), a poetic stanza that is not particularly well suited to storytelling but is aesthetically quite beautiful. Consisting of eight lines of eleven syllables, the tight rhyme scheme alternates for the first six lines (ababab) and concludes with a couplet (cc). In Spanish, as well as in English, epic poetry more often employed couplets or romance or ballad stanzas because of their greater narrative flexibility. But Ercilla's inventive use of the *octava real* helped to make it an expressive vehicle for some of the finest poetry in Spanish in the next century, including Góngora's *Fábula de Polifemo y Galatea* [The fable of Poliphemus and Galatea] and *Vida de San Ignacio de Loyola* by HERNANDO DOMÍNGUEZ CAMARGO.

Influential in the Spanish literary tradition, Ercilla's poem assumed even greater significance in the nineteenth century when it became the basis for Chilean national ideology, creating—or inventing, some would say—a heroic past for a new nation. That legacy continues today, with a weekly Chilean journal called *Revista Ercilla*. Ercilla himself also found in the New World the adventures he sought, narrowly escaping execution after a quarrel in Chile and finally returning to Spain in 1562 where he married well, served at court, and completed his great epic poem.

The text is from *La Araucana: The Epic of Chile*, adapted from the Spanish and rendered into English verse by Walter Owen, illustrations by Carlos J. Vergottini (Buenos Aires: W. Owen, 1945), 9, 11, 15, 17, 33.

From **La Araucana, The Epic of Chile (1569)**

For lack of pilots, or some cause unknown,
Perchance of craft or reasons politic,
This secret path to rich untravelled lands,
To other nations known, from us was hid,
Rumoured alone in hearsay, and its site
Uncertain on the sphere; long time we sought.
Who knows the cause? Some say that in these seas
Great storms can change the coastline in a night.

Due North and South the Chilean coastline runs,
Fronting along the West the Southern Main;
Upon the East a range of cloud-capped peaks
Shuts in the plainlands for a thousand leagues;
Midway between the North and South is where

Our scene of war is set; here that fierce tribe
I speak of dwells; mild Venus here no part
Has in men's lives; but Mars alone is lord.

Stark-visaged War here all men's days employs,
And martial arts are all the cares of state;
In thirty-six degrees it lies; mark well the place
Where this ferocious and unbridled tribe
Spread fear and death, keeping all foes at bay,
And spilling out their own and other's blood;
Battle their sole delight, till far and wide
All Chile trembles at Arauco's name.

What need more words? Such was the hardy race
That o'er the greater part of Chilean soil
Held sway, pre-eminent in deeds and fame,
Whose high renown rang to her farthest bounds,
And that, as I shall tell, cost Spain so dear,
And for a season held her arms in check.
Full twenty leagues their boundaries contain,
And sixteen warrior chieftains hold the land.

Caciques these they call; these tribal lords
Each in his several portion[21] is supreme,
And each in valour and in thews the best
That ever yet barbarian mothers bore;
Refuge and champions of their teeming clans,
And equal each to each in government.
Others they have of chiefs and lesser braves,
But these sixteen above the rest excel.

To these alone the right of vassalage
And body service in their wars is due,
And every brave compelled by tribal law
When heralds bear the summons; they, no less,
Must teach them use of arms and martial skills,

---

21 Of Caribbean origin, "cacique" was adopted into Spanish to refer to the chief of a community who represented his people before Spanish authorities. "Portion" refers to a cacique's domain: there were sixteen portions—and caciques—in the Mapuche territory.

Order of battle, exercise of march,
And craft of ambush, siege, defence, attack,
Till each is perfect in his several part.

. . . .

The trained in arms, to warfare dedicate,
No daily tasks in house or field perform,
But all their needs, of every kind the best,
The women and the knavish sort provide;
They on their part by tribal rule compelled,
Fashion their arms and learn their use expert,
In mimic combat with their warrior peers
Ready for battle at the chieftain's call.

The weapons that these savage tribesmen use
Are chiefly these: the halberd, pike, and lance,
And blades of various shape enhafted fast,
Like to our glaives and guisarmes, pick and mace,
Axe, flail, and pole-axe, maul and javelin,
Longbow and arrows, ropes of platted reed
With running nooses—"lazos" these they call—,
Slung-shot as well, and slings for casting stones.

Some of these arms I name, this savage race
Of late has copied from the Christians' use,
And now in practice and proficiency
Improves from day to day; others themselves
By native wit had fashioned ere we came;
For, as the proverb holds, necessity
Is the quick mother of devices new,
And care the spur of ingenuity.

Corselets of double quilt their warriors wear,
Embracing back and breast, of body length,
And others too as gambesons that fall
To the mid-thigh, these are the later sort,
But most in use. Their limbs and heads they case
In greave and vambrace, casque and gorget-piece,

Jointed with art, of tanned and toughened hide
That can reject the best Toledo blade.

Each of these braves the single weapon wields
Best suited to his build and native bent,
And from his youth his daily exercise
Employs in this alone, till constant use
Makes man and weapon one. From this it comes
Each warrior of their host a master is
Of pike, or bow, javelin, or battle-axe,
And in the war a host of champions.

Their battle thus they dress: in order drawn,
Squadron by squadron, equal and complete,
A hundred men and more in rank abreast,
Of pikemen and of archers alternate;
Then as with quickening pace the squadron moves,
The bowmen at discretion loose their shafts,
Protected by the pikemen who press on,
Shoulder to shoulder till they close the foe.

. . . .

In sum, the lot and climate of this land,
If the true figure of her stars be cast,
Is conflict, fury, and discord and war,
To which alone her people are inclined;
Mars in her zenith burns for good or ill.
And all her brood delights in shedding blood,
Men quick to wrath, ferocious, desperate,
Born with the lust of conquest in their veins.

Robust and strong, hairless of lip and chin,
Well-grown and tall above the run of men,
Of ample shoulders and capacious breasts,
And brawny limbs thick-set with stubborn thews,
Ready and nimble and high spirited,
Haughty and daring, reckless in assault,

Hardy and tireless, bearing undismayed
Cold, hunger, heat, and all extremities.

Nor ever has a king by force subdued
This haughty people to his vassalage,
Nor has the foot of an invading foe
Left shameful print upon Arauco's soil,
Nor neighboring tribe so temerarious
To try the battle with their furious hosts.
Untamed and feared by all they live or die
With haughty neck unbowed to God or man.

Joan de Santa Cruz Pachacuti Yamqui Salcamaygua (1590?–1620?)

An Account of the Antiquities of Peru, written perhaps as early as 1613, is one of four key texts of the high Andes. It has immense ethnographic value, not only for its content but also for its authorship by a descendant of Inca chieftains, Joan de Santa Cruz Pachacuti Yamqui Salcamaygua. The other three texts are the MANUSCRIPT OF HUAROCHIRI, collected from the village of Huarochiri by Francisco de Ávila; the *Primer nueva corónica* [First New Chronicle] of Inca life composed by GUAMÁN POMA DE AYALA; and *Relación de la Conquista del Perú y hechos del Inca* [An Account of the Conquest of Peru and Deeds of the Inca] written by Diego de Castro Titu Cusi Yupanqui (1539–1571), who was himself a direct descendant of the royal Incan dynasty. Like the MANUSCRIPT OF HUAROCHIRI, Pachacuti's text was found archived with other Andean documents at the Biblioteca Nacional de Madrid. Both seemed to have belonged to Francisco de Ávila, the priest who collected the Huarochiri testimonies primarily to extirpate idolatry and recover the treasures buried with the *huacas* or idols. In fact, Ávila's connection to the Pachacuti text or its date of composition is still unclear.

What we know about Pachacuti is what he explains in the manuscript. He claims descent from the *curacas* (chieftains) from Guaygua Canchi, in the highlands south of Cuzco, the ancient capital city, and from the towns of Santiago of Anan Guaygua and Hurin Guaygua Canchi of Orcosuyu. He also states that one of his great-great-grandfathers was Don Gonzalo

Pizarro Tintaya, who had served one of the conquistadors, Gonzalo Pizarro, whose own brief rebellion occurred between 1544 and 1547.

Like Guamán Poma's chronicle, Pachacuti's account evokes the cultural richness of the Andean world, now divided from itself by colonization. The implications of that great gap persist today in the difficulties of interpreting the basic significance of this text: is it, as many believe, a relatively faithful representation of a forgotten Andean past? Or is it a projection of Christian ideology? In contrast to Guamán Poma's chronicle, which overwhelms the reader with detail, Pachacuti's text is fairly brief and presents Incan myth and history with an impressive talent for efficient narrative.

The selection here depicts how Inca Pachacuti (the great Incan ruler from the mid-fifteenth century) subjugates the region, finding "*huacas* and devils," interspersed with an account of the birth of his eldest son, Amaro Topa Inca. At that momentous event, according to the chronicler Pachacuti, all "the fiercest hidden animals were thrown out of Cuzco," thus linking the royal son's birth with the subjugation of dangerously concealed forces. This story of the wild animals (*khurus*) is echoed in the JALQ'A textile, exemplifying Andean narrative weaving. But by specifically describing these fierce creatures in Christian terms, calling them devils, Pachacuti imparts to the historic Incas a distinctly new role as extirpators of idolatry.

How the Incan past is filtered through the lens of Christianity is one of this text's most compelling features. Pachacuti repeatedly insists on his personal Christian identity (including his Christian surname, Santa Cruz, for example, among his many monikers), but he also asserts the merits of his native culture by demonstrating its congruity with universalized Christian values, present in the Andes for centuries. Like Guamán Poma, who declared that the peoples of the Andes descended from Noah after the flood, Pachacuti was making his own case for cultural survival within the dominating contexts of the colonial religion. The value of Pachacuti's text is that he achieves a double justification: claiming a place for himself and his culture within the new colonial order, and confirming the universality of Christianity, something much desired by Christian theologians because Christianity itself had been challenged by the discovery of the New World.

The text is taken from *Narratives of the Rites and Laws of the Yncas*, translated by Clements R. Markham (London: n.p., 1873). From the *Sacred Texts Internet Archive*, with additional edits by Josefa Salmón.

From An Account of the Antiquities of Peru (c. 1580)

He [Pachacuti Inca Yupanqui] next came to Huamañin/Guamañin, near Villcas, where he had first seen the seven evil *huacas* (deities). In Pomacocha,[22] a very hot place before coming to Villcas Huamán, his eldest legitimate son was born, named Amaro Yupanqui, and he rested there for some days. Here the news arrived of a miracle at Cuzco. A *yauirca* or *amaro* (snake), a ferocious creature, half a league long and two brazas and a half wide, with ears, eye-teeth, and a beard, had come forth from the mountain of Pachatusan, gone through Yuncaipampa and Sinca and then entered the lake of Quihuipay. Then two *sacacas* (comets) of fire came out of Ausangate, and went towards Arequipa; and another went towards some snowy mountains near Huamanga. They were described as animals with wings, ears, a tail, and four legs, with many spikes on their backs; and from a distance they appeared to be made of fire. So Pachacuti Inca Yupanqui set out for Cuzco, where he found that his father, Huiracochampa Incan Yupanqui, was now very old and sick.

Then were celebrated the festivals of his return, of the *Capac Raymi* and *Pacha Yachachi*, with great rejoicing. He introduces his son, his grandson, to his father. Then he celebrates the birth of his son and his name was Amaro Topa Inca, which means that at his birth, all of the most fierce hidden animals were thrown out of Cuzco. . . .

Afterwards Pachacuti undertook the conquest of the Condesuyos, and in the Collao he fell in with the Coles [Collas] and Camanchacas, who are great sorcerers. Thence he marched to Arequipa, Achacha [Chancha] and Hatun Conde, and to the Chumbivillcas, and thence to Parinacocha, returning to the city by the country of the Aymaras, Chillques, and Papres. [. . .] At that time they say that the Capacuyos sent a poor man with *ultis* (clay pots in which they keep *llipta* [lime]), who gave Pachacuti Inca a blow on the head with the intention of killing him. The man was tortured, and confessed that he was a *Cahuiña*[23] of the Quiquijanas, and that he had come to kill the Inca at the request of the Capacuyos. So the Inca ordered the province of the Cahuiñas to be laid waste; but they said that the fault was not theirs, but the Capacuyos, whose *curaca*

---

22 The deep valley of the river Pampas.

23 The Cahuiña believed that the souls of the dead went to a great lake, which they thought was the beginning of life and from which they would then enter the bodies of newborns. Their main *huaca* was Ausangate.

(chief) was Apo Lalama, Yamque Lalama of Hanan Sayas and Hurin Sayas, and who numbered near 20,000 men, besides women and children. They were all put to death. They say that they tried to murder the Inca, by advice of their *huaca*, Cáñacuay.[24]

---

24 Name of the mountain between Paucartampu and the eastern forests.

3

Colonization and the Expulsion of the Jesuits, 1640–1767

The physical subjugation of the Hispanic territories in America was largely complete by the middle of the seventeenth century. With the destruction of the great Indian empires and the demoralization of their people, significant military resistance became erratic within a few generations. But the work of colonization continued for two more centuries, largely focused on the exploitation of the region's vast natural resources, including human labor.

As from the beginning, the Catholic Church played a crucial role in transforming an array of native peoples into Spanish colonial subjects. One major force in these transformations was the religious orders, primarily Franciscans and Dominicans. But none after the end of the sixteenth century was more influential than the Society of Jesus, better known as the Jesuits.

Founded in 1541 by Ignatius of Loyola, a former Spanish soldier, the Society of Jesus quickly became a central participant in the great theological and philosophical debates of a tumultuous era. The Jesuits were in the forefront of the Counter-Reformation, challenging the rise of Protestantism throughout Europe and playing a critical role at the Council of Trent (1545–1563). During the next two centuries, the Society of Jesus was a leader in international missionary activity from California and Paraguay to China and India. Their direct allegiance to the Pope and their establishment of highly regarded schools and universities made them the most powerful and influential religious order in the Catholic world.

The Jesuits' broad range of missions, however, eventually resulted in the order's acquiring a contradictory and paradoxical character. For example, while the Dominicans were charged with implementing the Inquisition, the Jesuits became the most radical defenders of Counter-Reformation dogma; at the same time, their deep involvement in higher education kept them engaged with the profound philosophical, scientific, and ideological changes of the seventeenth and eighteenth centuries. The Jesuits thus included in their ranks some of the most conservative theologians together with the most sophisticated scientists, moralists who were among the most traditionally doctrinaire as well as the most heterodox. Some principled positions also led into dangerous political territory. Maintaining, for example, the medieval right to kill a tyrant, the Jesuits often came into direct conflict with modern monarchs who claimed absolute powers.

These intellectual variances inevitably produced major internal tensions, but the Ignatian commitment to brotherhood and obedience always prevailed. And even though the Society frequently challenged papal decrees, their loyalty to Rome never faltered. To maintain this delicate political and intellectual equilibrium, the Jesuits employed three primary tools: eclecticism, probabilism, and casuistry, all of which became targets of criticism.

Eclecticism was one of the ways the Jesuits resisted alignment with a specific philosophical system, insisting that no single school of thought could contain all truth beyond the fundamental dogmas of the Church. By freely selecting principles that suited current ideological needs, Jesuits could assert the truth of all theories, even contradictory ones, regarding a specific phenomenon, as there was always some truth in any perspective. However, in applying eclecticism to sacred texts or those with doctrinal authority, such as the writings of the Doctors of the Church (learned and sainted theologians), choices often had to be made. If there was any uncertainty among the options, between two interpretations of the notion of free will, for example, the Jesuits' solution was to choose the most convenient for the particular case under discussion, always trying to avoid conflict in order to conform to the dominant belief. By the early eighteenth century this second method, known as probabilism, was soundly condemned by the order's enemies, both within and outside the Church.

The third tool of Jesuit thought was casuistry, another oft-criticized technique. Using case histories to determine the morality of both particular and everyday behaviors, casuistry gave strong consideration to contexts. Often ignoring established and "universal" criteria, like the absolute dicta of the Ten Commandments, casuistry soon became accused of sanctioning lax conduct and existential decisions.

Despite widespread criticism of these intellectual techniques, what ultimately empowered the Jesuits over their rivals was the rigor of their educational system and their profound sense of corporatism. Their dominance endured until the mid-eighteenth century when political exigencies led

Louis XV to banish them from France. Portugal soon followed suit, expelling the order from all its territories. Finally, in 1767, Charles III banished them from Spain and Spanish America. Even Pope Clement XIV could not withstand the pressure of all three European crowns, and in 1773 he abolished the order that had represented his most loyal supporters. Still admired for their integrity and learning, many Jesuits found refuge in non-Catholic countries, in Russia, and in the United States. A majority found their way to the Papal States in the Italian Peninsula, and in 1815, at the end of the Napoleonic wars, Pope Pius VII finally reinstated the order.

Though the expulsion of the Jesuits from the colonies often had traumatic consequences, both for members of the order and for the institutions they supported, the order had a major impact on Spanish America. Throughout the continent, the Jesuits earnestly pursued their primary missions: evangelization and education. Indeed, as the missionary zeal of the first religious orders to come to America—the Franciscans and Dominicans—diminished, the Jesuits continued to open missions in remote and neglected areas, including Sonora and California in northern Mexico and in the South American interior. In the latter, they established an impressive chain of missions from Paraguay to Bolivia that doubled as a wall of defense against the Portuguese. In education, the Jesuits' primary role was to instruct the growing creole population, establishing schools and colleges throughout the Americas that were impressive rivals to both royal and Church-sponsored universities. The Jesuits also provided another, more material, legacy in their architecture. Their numerous churches, convents, and schools, constructed to support their educational and spiritual missions, typically embodied a Counter-Reformation aesthetic, with a proliferation of images and elaborately decorated façades and interiors. From Ecuador to Mexico, some of the region's most splendid architectural jewels are those built by the Jesuits.

Juan Espinosa Medrano (c. 1629–1688)

Cuzco, Perú, was the center of Juan Espinosa Medrano's life and work. Often assumed to be the son of Indian parents, Espinosa Medrano spent his life in that ancient city and, when he died in 1688, was widely mourned as a beloved native son. Little is known about his life before he entered the Dominican seminary in Cuzco in his teens. By then, he was composing music, learning languages, and writing allegorical religious plays in Spanish and in Quechua, mostly in a contemporary genre known as *auto sacramental,* most notably *El rapto de Proserpina* [The Rape of Proserpine]. Marked by a distinctive mole on his face, Espinosa Medrano was known throughout his life as "El Lunarejo," the one with a mole.

After graduating from the Jesuit University of San Ignacio de Loyola in 1654, Espinosa Medrano dedicated himself to his priestly duties, eventually becoming famous for sermons that attracted hundreds of listeners. Many of Espinosa's most notable compositions were, in fact, prayers and panegyric sermons, typically in praise of the Virgin Mary. But the text that remains most relevant was his treatise on the preeminent poet of the Spanish Baroque, Luis de Góngora. Written in response to an attack by a Portuguese critic and poet, Manuel de Faria e Sousa, the *Apologético en favor de don Luis de Góngora* [Apology in Defense of Don Luis de Góngora] first appeared in Lima in 1662.

Made up of an introduction and twelve parts (each including Faria's criticism and Espinosa Medrano's response), this text is remarkable on several counts. First, by employing a myriad of sources from the European tradition of letters—often with great rigor and deep familiarity—the *Defense* soundly refutes the notion that America (and Americans) were without cultural sophistication, isolated from European thought and traditions. The text itself, moreover, demonstrates an astonishing command of literary Spanish, including its tropes and classical roots. In these qualities, the *Defense* further proves false the assumption that natives were unable to assimilate European concepts and values. But most important, the *Defense* testifies to the deep roots that were being created in Latin America for *gongorismo*, the broad influence of Luis de Góngora himself (who had died only thirty-five years earlier in 1627) and the Baroque tradition that he defined.

For Espinosa Medrano—as for the Spanish Jesuit Baltazar Gracián whose *Agudeza y Arte del Ingenio* [Wit and the Art of Inventiveness] (1648) served as one of his models—*gongorismo* was not simply a virtuoso construction of figurative language and complex syntax. It was also the expression of intricate thought and subtle concepts. Accordingly, in defending Góngora's work, Espinosa Medrano not only addresses the poet's use of exotic figures like the hyperbaton (the alteration of the normal sentence order) but also how Góngora deploys such imagery and tropes to develop concepts that reveal deeply original thought.

In addition to exemplifying a sophisticated literary critique, the *Defense* sets forth the elements of the Baroque spirit that infuses the literary and cultural perspective of Spanish American colonies in this era. That spirit is largely an expression of two fundamental principles: first, that language is the vehicle by which the innermost processes of reason are unveiled; and second, that those processes themselves manifest the world's own intricate construction. The Baroque's convoluted display of abstract thought thus simply exposes the amazing construction of reality itself—a space of correspondences and invisible relations revealed through the imaginative uses of language. This implicit capacity for revelation and wonder often sets the Baroque apart from—if not in conflict with—the prevailing rationality of the political authorities. But the Baroque also draws its moral authority from the Catholic Church, whose own sacramental traditions privilege the material world even as it sanctions forms of mysticism and the miraculous. And finally, the Baroque expresses a deeply unorthodox pantheism, one consistent with the native traditions of the Americas.

Apologético en favor de D. Luis de Góngora is a principal pillar in an imposing colonnade of literary texts that support the Baroque vision that dominates the literature of Spanish America. Encouraged by the double vision of creoles and mestizos and Indians (like Espinosa Medrano), this perspective is echoed in at least four other major seventeenth-century works: *Grandeza Mexicana* [The Grandeur of Mexico] (1604) by Bernando de Balbuena; *San Ignacio de Loyola, Fundador de la Compañía de Jesús: Poema Heroico* [St. Ignatius of Loyola, Founder of the Society of Jesus: A Heroic Poem] (1666) by HERNANDO DOMÍNGUEZ CAMARGO; *Primavera Indiana* [Indian Spring] (1668) by CARLOS DE SIGÜENZA Y GÓNGORA; and *Primero Sueño* [First Dream] (1692)—and indeed, all of the poetry of SOR JUANA INÉS DE LA CRUZ.

The selection here focuses on a stylistic issue that, in fact, has important implications for linguistic theory. Góngora was often criticized for his use of "latinisms": "hispanicized" Latin words and Latinate grammar. One of these constructions, the hyperbaton, deliberately changes the "natural" order of the sentence. Influenced by the French, many Spanish grammarians considered the natural order to be subject-predicate. Within the predicate, the verb was followed by the accusative (direct object), the dative (indirect object), and the ablative (circumstantial object). Of course, there is nothing natural in that order, and Góngora freely changed those grammatical structures to suit his expressive intent, often producing some of the boldest constructions in Spanish literature. Espinosa Medrano argues that every use of the hyperbaton by Góngora is effective, purposeful, and creative.

The discussion of hyperbaton became significant a century later when theories about a "universal language" emerged. Against the notion that there was some implicit common grammar (presumably modeled by Hebrew), philosophers like Condillac argued that nothing proved the existence of a natural order and that the freedom of Latin syntax and the prevalence of inversions, such as the hyperbaton, demonstrated the flexibility of language. Figures of rhetoric were, accordingly, not simply flourishes but instruments of human expression, so that the same words could be used in a different order to express a different meaning. The point was not trivial, as the possibility of a flexible order within language indicated the power to express different points of view and, ultimately, different perspectives on the truth. Espinosa Medrano's text is thus an early precedent in the ongoing discussion of the relationship between language and thought—a topic central to current debates not only in linguistics but in philosophy and science as well.

The text is an original translation by Nathan Henne from Juan de Espinosa Medrano's *Apologético en favor de don Luis de Góngora* (Surquillo, Lima, Peru: Academia Peruana de la Lengua: Universidad de San Martín de Porres, Escuela Profesional de Ciencias de la Comunicación, 2005), 106–9.

From **Apologético en favor de don Luis de Góngora (1662) [A Defense of Don Luis de Góngora]**

Section XI

Add together all of his [Manuel de Faría y Sousa's] arguments and, in the end, they are easily refuted and dispelled. Let us see if by two reasoned arguments we can defeat all this opposition that has no rational argument behind it. *Caeterum ad haec, quae objectisis, numera, an binis verbis respondeam* [What's more, in answer to your objections, be assured that I don't answer you in doublespeak.[1]] Look at the brevity with which we respond [to each of the following objections]. *Góngora's writing is full of hyperbatons:* He is imitating the Latins. *The ancients used them:* No one uses them so gleefully. *He uses them too frequently:* He resembles those he imitates. *He takes away what is essentially Latin:* That takes great courage. *He uses obscure metaphors:* Nobody has questioned the ones that Virgil uses. *He shows very little judgment:* What poet does that? *He did not finish some of his works:* Those are even better than the finished works. *His "Poliphemus" lacks overarching design:* Homer's has even less design. *His writing is too audacious:* No one can be great without some

---

1   The Latin phrases in English reflect Espinoza's own translations of the Latin to Spanish. A direct translation of the Latin would be significantly different in some cases, and the intent is to reflect how Espinosa interpreted and used these texts, not an accurate translation of the Latin. [Trans. note]

audacity. *Some call him Homer:* That is not his fault. *Many do not understand him:* That does not matter if those who do not understand him are stupid. *His verses have no soul:* Do not allow envy to judge him; let truth judge him; put passion aside; let the cultured man read his poems, and allow the scholar to analyze them.

Section XII

121. Let the pen stop here; and let the denunciation of slandering cease; let us stop trying to persuade the slanderer to recant. Let the bitter truth be known: the serpent may have become the celebrated symbol of science because, while learning may lie wrapped unassumingly among innocent flowers, perhaps when it was trod upon by a cruel foot, it became an asp that ripples its scales, lets loose its hiss, flicks its tongue, sinks its fangs into flesh, and turns its antidotes into poisons. We do not wish to bring out the many mistakes in the works of Faria, which we certainly could, because it is beneath us to lie in wait and ambush other people's errors when such mistakes flow so abundantly among us mortals. If we have in fact mentioned a few of these errors above, it happened in spite of our modesty, in part because we learned this approach from Faria himself, and in part because truth, when provoked, often comes out acerbically. I say "in spite of our modesty" because, even in the case of one who so deserves the invective, there is no valor in bloodying one's wit; what would we stand to gain in the case of someone who, by contrast, deserves so many crowns, like Don Luis de Góngora? If the hyperbaton is indeed worthy of blame, then overlook it because of so many other delicacies in his work. Moreover, it is not a very noble achievement to insult great men and risk discrediting one's name and renown over a few irrelevant words or a banal oversight. *Illiberale facinus* (as Joseph Scaliger wisely says) *propter nescio quas verborum quisquilias aut propter errorem aliquem qui humanitus contigerit, tantorum hominum eruditionem, atque adeo, totum nomen, et famam in periculum vocare.* [I know not of a more shameful act than to cast doubt upon the wisdom, fame or renown of so many men because of a few inaccurate words or a purely human error.] The ones who do this are small men without discretion and foolish tact, who blunt what is sharp, wasting time spitting out words like thistles and burrs. *Hoc solent facere arguti homunciones, qui in jujus modi acanthologias totam aetatem contriverum.* [This is the kind of thing that small-minded charlatans tend to do, wasting their time on acanthology[2] like this.] What is more, who can tolerate these stinging nettles, these piercing brambles, that spread

---

2   Acanthology refers to the study of spines, as in sea urchins. Espinosa Medrano refers ironically and metaphorically to men who "spit out" words like spines.

their thin shoots out over the ground and glory in sprouting all those sharp thorns and flowering with satirical thistles? They think they rule over the incorruptible Lebanese cedars! *Quis ferat rhamnos illos humi repentes (says Matias Hauzer) et solis spinis ac aculeis satyricis gloriosos supra Cedros Libant regnare praesument?* [Who can stand those nettles that spread out along the ground with their thorns and satirical needles and dare to suppose they reign over the glorious cedars of Lebanon?]

122. All of these critics should take heed of that proverb of Apollo's, which the most discreet Trojano Bocalini[3] made famous, and which another critic, Sousa, the most vaunted Portuguese courtier, elegantly translated. One critic was punished by requiring him to remove the chaff[4] from the wheat and either sell the chaff to whoever would buy it or give it away free. The critic, desperate to be given his due credit, heard Apollo say: *The imperfections on which some people focus in what is otherwise good are not the merchandise of wise men, and wise men do not take advantage by either selling or giving them away; and he who acts this way should himself confess that he had been badly counseled when he undertook the indiscreet and impertinent job of forgetting the roses that he had found in the poem he censured and instead just gathered together and pointlessly saved all the thorns. In their studies of others' works, discreet and wise critics take their cue from the bees, who know how to extract honey from even the bitterest leaves; and not finding anything beneath the heavens that does not contain a mix of many imperfections, anyone might, curiously and carefully sift through the sieve of continuous study the writings of Homer, Virgil, Livius, Tacitus, and Hippocrates, who were the marvels of the world, and would not also fail to find in their writings a bit of chaff. And yet he would still be content and satisfied that the flour of their studious followers' writings would be worthy of sale in the market plaza; that the judicious and ingenious courtiers would cover up the defects of the wise and studious writers that others with bad intentions made public. Finally he would be satisfied to know that the profession of extracting only the imperfections in other writers' poems is solely the job of vile and foul-smelling beetles who delightfully entertain themselves with the disgusting excrement of others; and that the noble subjects who fruitfully nourish their spirits with honest and virtuous matters are far removed from this practice.* Truly, if a person has a brain at all, he should not slander men of don Luis' stature, but rather he should

---

3 Trojano Bocalini (1556–1613), Italian satirical writer, critic, and commentator and Tasso's advocate.

4 The reference is not actually to the seed-coverings of wheat, but to a valueless plant [*negilla* or angel-in-the-mist], that grows easily amidst wheat. Since the sense is separating the useful grain from the useless, I have substituted "chaff" as the more common English expression. [Trans. note]

exchange his censure for respect. That is the difference between great men and other men: those who get very few things right in their writing, clearly get the odd thing right only by mistake; but those who get many things right in their writing, allow us to see that they only got careless in spots just to ensure that we were paying attention, or that they left these minor errors in order to teach us that sublime spirits do not worry too much about small imperfections. Therefore, one who gets many things right in his writing should not be subject to diminished veneration just for slight stumbles, because perfection is impossible for humans; but just as the errors humans make are less admirable than what they get right, so good fortune only consists of making fewer mistakes than everyone else.

123. That is what our Faria should do (in those cases where hyperbatons are errors) and that is what our modern theologians should do, too, instead of wasting our paper, our time, and our lives with their disputes and their criticisms of other writers' oversights, all the while forgetting that, while they continue to fight, they have not taught us so much as one atom of truth or left us with one atom of patience.

124. Long live, then, the learned and vaunted Góngora! Long live Góngora in spite of the jealousies, *Pumpantur ut ilia Codro* [may Codro's guts burst (Virgil)]. Long live this rare bird, whose plumage, at his high level of flight, does not allow us to determine whether he is the swan of the Muses' harmony, or the eagle of all the lights of Apollo, or the Phoenix of all the aromas of erudition. The wise critic Gracián[5] said well when he said that he [Góngora] was all of these. *He, who was a swan on account of his melodiousness, was an eagle on account of his acuity, was a Phoenix on account of his precision.* He repeats the same thing in his Fifth Discourse. *This learned poet was a swan in his harmonies, an eagle in terms of his conceits, and in all kinds of eminent incisiveness.* Nor should we ignore another exaltation that Gracián affords him [Góngora] in terms of the sublime way that each poet exalted his language among the nations, saying: *I took the examples of the tongue in which I found them, whether the showy Latin of the relevant Floro, the Italian of the valiant Tasso, the Spanish of the learned Góngora or the Portuguese of the affectionate Camoens.* Long live, then, this man so deserving of eternal praise in the glorious realm of his erudition, whose merits could exhaust all the praises in the encyclopedia. *Ut sic meruit totius Encyclopedia laude unus nostro aevo clarissimus conciviset amicus noster Don Ludovico de Gongora* [So that in this way, in our time, may he

---

5   Baltasar Gracián (1601–1658), a Spanish Jesuit and moral philosopher, whose work *Agudeza y arte de ingenio* (1648) [Wit and the Art of Inventiveness] exemplifies the Baroque style in philosophy and literature.

be worthy of the praises of the whole Encyclopedia, this our illustrious countryman and friend: Don Luis de Góngora] says the erudite Villalpando in his *Magia*. Góngora is worthy of these tributes because of the honors that the Spanish language has achieved through his genius. Betis venerates him for his original and most illustrious glory:

> *Baetis oliviferi Góngora primus honor.*
> [Góngora, the most honorable son of Betis, the olive-producing region.]

From Góngora flows such brightness that these Andalusian accolades, even anointed with such brilliant praise, cannot fully encapsulate the value of his work. Góngora (as that most serious advocate says) is in fact the "second Pindar," though not even second to that first Pindar, the father of Spanish culture, the splendor of Cordoba, the ornament of Spain, and the portent of the whole heavenly orb. *Cui Allusit alter Pindarus, Crysis Pater, Cordubae decus, et ornamentum; totius Hesperiae, orbisque portentum Don Ludovicus a Góngora* [He whom I call The Other Pindar, father of Crysis, the honor and jewel of Cordoba, of all of Spain, and portent of the whole world: don Luis de Góngora].

May you prosper, you divine poet, you bizarre spirit, you sweet, sweet swan. May you thrive in spite of emulation; may you endure in spite of mortality. May the most beautiful lilies of Helicon crown the sacred marble of your ashes. *Manibus date lilia plenis* [Give lilies to his ashes.] May your glorious Manes[6] rest in peaceful serenity; may both peaks of Parnassus serve as a gravestone for your bones; may all the splendor of the heavenly bodies serve as your torches; may all the waves of Aganippe serve as your tears; may Fame serve as your epitaph; may the heavenly orb serve as your theater; may death serve as your triumph and eternity as your repose. *Dixi.* [I have spoken] *LAUS DEO* [Praise God]

In Context | Solomonic Columns

The Council of Trent (1545–1563) prepared the Roman Catholic Church to fight against the Reformation in all its manifestations. One of the Council's main recommendations was that Catholic ceremonies create a stronger appeal to the senses: making churches more elaborate in their interior and exterior decoration; proliferating images of the saints, of the Virgin Mary, and of Jesus Christ; introducing more music into the rituals. Which came first—this formal endorsement of the senses or the Baroque style

---

6   In Greek mythology, benevolent spirits of the underworld.

Figure 3.1. Solomonic columns. Church of the Compañía de Jesús, Quito, Ecuador. Photograph by Tohma (2008). License CC BY-SA 2.0.

that pervaded art and imbued everyday practices—may be impossible to determine. But Catholic churches soon became the primary setting for the development of Baroque art and architecture.

Looking at these columns can help one appreciate how the Baroque evolved. Classical columns derived from the ancient Greeks. They had a rigid structure, featuring a solid base, with fluting along their length, and capitals at the top. The Baroque gave movement to these classical columns. In designing the main altar of Saint Peter's Basilica in Rome, Gian Lorenzo Bernini (1598–1680) imagined that the columns of Solomon's Temple were originally "twisted" or coiled. From his masterpiece, the style of the "Solomonic" column traveled throughout Europe and the Americas. The simplicity of Bernini's columns was quickly forgotten as architects devised more and more elaborate and ornate versions of that basic Baroque form. Later, when columns were hollowed, these Solomonic columns achieved even greater fluidity. The elaborate façade of the Church of the Society of Jesus ("La Compañía") (1765) in Quito, Ecuador, demonstrates perfectly the culmination of the decorated Solomonic column.

Carlos de Sigüenza y Góngora (1648–1700)

As for a number of other writers in this era, the life and works of Carlos de Sigüenza y Góngora are an unambiguous refutation of the contemporary prejudice directed toward the creoles or *criollos* of the Americas. To their European counterparts, these American-born individuals of Spanish ancestry were at best ignorant, and generally incapable of higher thought or culture. While not many creoles had the erudition of a Sigüenza y Góngora, a majority were quite highly cultured people, supported by extensive libraries and well aware of the latest cultural and scientific developments in Europe—as well as in the Americas. The extent of cultural sophistication in Hispanic America is critical to the emergence of so many erudite authors in the colonial period.

The son of a tutor to the Spanish royal family, Sigüenza y Góngora was born in Mexico City, where his parents had emigrated. As a young man, he joined the Society of Jesus (the Jesuits), studying at Puebla until he was expelled from the order around 1667. He continued his clerical training at the Royal Pontifical University of Mexico and was ordained a priest in 1673. He served as chaplain to Amor de Dios Hospital and also became the chair of mathematics and sciences at the university, a position he held for twenty years, becoming quite famous for his scientific expertise. At his death in 1700, he donated his body to science and his library to the Jesuit College of Sts. Peter and Paul.

Carlos de Sigüenza y Góngora was a prodigious figure. In addition to teaching mathematics, he wrote several treatises in astronomy, was a consulting cartographer for the Viceroy, collected *antiguallas* (pre-Hispanic artifacts and codices), wrote poetry, adapted for publication a narrative of the fantastic adventures of a Puerto Rican sailor (*Los infortunios de Alonso Ramírez* [The Misfortunes of Alonso Ramirez] (1690), and was a noted historian and chronicler of current events.

While Carlos de Sigüenza y Góngora was an exceptional scholar, he was also a typical Mexican creole in his efforts to demonstrate the exceptionalism of New Spain to a disdainful mother country. One such effort—and one to which Sigüenza y Góngora directly contributed—was the emergence of Mexico's most famous icon: the Virgin of Guadalupe. Until shortly before

Sigüenza y Góngora's birth, the image was little known, venerated chiefly by Indians at Tepeyac, a small town north of Mexico City.

The exceptionalism of that now-famous image, painted in a conventional style of the period, has long invited speculation. Two basic explanations for the presumed uniqueness of that painting soon emerged. The first, arising around the beginning of the seventeenth century, simply declared the image a miracle: the Virgin had appeared to an Indian and impressed her image onto his cloak, made of a common cloth. In no previous apparition had the Virgin ever left a portrait of herself—only here in the village of Tepeyac in New Spain.

Even at the outset, this account met with serious objections: up close the cloth seemed only a painting. Soon a second theory emerged, connected to one of the most controversial ideas of the conquest, namely, that America had previously been converted to Christianity by one of Christ's disciples, Thomas. This new explanation held that the Virgin Mary had been painted inside St. Thomas's own cape and the current image was, therefore, a portrait of Christ's mother when *she was alive*—on fabric that had to be over 1,600 years old.

Whatever the explanation, the painting of the Virgin and the devotion it elicited were noteworthy. The fact that Mexico—or New Spain—was the place selected by the mother of God to manifest such a miracle was itself proof of the country's exceptionalism. For believers of the seventeenth century, and for Mexican creoles in particular, the Virgin's preference was more valuable than any other privilege—definitive evidence of the singularity of their new homeland.

Personally devoted to the Virgin of Guadalupe, Sigüenza y Góngora eventually came to believe in both explanations of the image. At first, he believed in the miracle of the apparitions, as reflected in his remarkable poem, *Primavera Indiana,* composed in the then-dominant "Gongorist" style. Later, having befriended various Indian and mestizo collectors of *antiguallas,* he became an ardent proponent of the notion that Quetzalcóatl was the Indian representation of St. Thomas, and that the painting of the Virgin Mary had been the Apostle's cape.

Though most creoles of New Spain were proud of living in a land where so many ancient cultures had once thrived, adorning their country with a plethora of splendid monuments (such as the Pyramids of Teotihuacán), few felt any attachment to the Indians in their midst. Indeed, creoles typically despised them and even considered the Indians as unworthy of Christianity. But they also harbored a guilty fear toward these native populations, constantly suspicious that the Indians might be planning a rebellion to exterminate all white people—creoles and Spaniards alike. Sigüenza y Góngora's chronicles of the corn riots of June 1692 reveals precisely these qualities of disdain and fear that creoles like him felt toward the native peoples of Mexico City.

Sigüenza y Góngora thus embodies the fundamental contradiction that has shaped Mexico's history since the colonial period, particularly after the largely creole seizure of power during the movement for independence: pride in an ancient Indian heritage and complete disdain for the actual descendants of the conquest. Even today, Mexico is a country proud of its Indian past and its dark-skinned Virgin of Guadalupe and yet still fundamentally racist in its treatment of living Indians.

Alboroto y motín de los indios de México [The Disturbances and Riots of the Indians of Mexico] is a key text in the representation of creole attitudes toward Indians even as it reveals an extraordinary sense of history and an impressive breadth of knowledge. An eyewitness to the events he describes, Sigüenza y Góngora explains how floods had ruined the corn harvest in a previous year, producing shortages that led to the riots in June. He includes descriptions of a plague whose sources he himself identified with his microscope, of an eclipse he saw through his telescope, and of his own efforts to save precious archival materials from a fire caused by the rioters. Sigüenza y Góngora thus compresses all the many facets of his knowledge and talents in his chronicle. But he also incorporates all of his prejudices: Indians are depicted in the worst possible light as conspiring, malicious, alcoholic, lazy, opportunistic—clearly a threat to his own privileged and precarious existence as a colonist of creole stock. At the same time, Sigüenza y Góngora reveals himself to be an observant historian, an outstanding scientist, a noteworthy poet, and a sincere devotee of the Virgin of Guadalupe: in other words, a typical creole.

Finally, this excerpt from Sigüenza y Góngora begins with an allusion to Nuestra Señora de los Remedios (Our Lady of Remedies). The cult of this image was associated with Cortés and the conquest, and so in a very Catholic and ironic way, this other revered icon, the official patroness of the Spanish in the Americas, was in effect a rival to the Virgin of Guadalupe.

The text, "Letter of Sigüenza y Góngora to Admiral Pez recounting the incidents of the corn riot in Mexico City, June 8, 1692," is a selection from Irving Albert Leonard, *Don Carlos de Sigüenza y Góngora, a Mexican Savant of the Seventeenth Century* (Berkeley: University of California Press, 1929), 242–48.

From **Alboroto y motín de los indios de México (1692) [Disturbances and Riots of the Indians of Mexico]**

Letter of Sigüenza y Góngora to Admiral Pez recounting the incidents of the corn riot in Mexico City, June 8, 1692

Another common cause for rejoicing on the part of everyone was the bring-ing of the Most Miraculous Image of Nuestra Señora de los Remedios to this city on the 24th of May of this present year. This was done, apparently, for no particular reason that would necessitate such a great event because there was still no lack of rain and the maladies afflicting the city were the usual ones and hence did not require such a great remedy. Since the love which all Mexico City has for this Venerable and Miraculous Figure is exceedingly warm and tender, the sight of the Image induced in their spirits and particularly in that of the populace, which is always delighted on such occasions, such a state of gratification that they forgot all about eating and hurried up to look at it.

THE POPULACE GROWS RESTLESS

On an occasion like this the populace behaved well and were happy but on the one that now followed, the departure of the Alguacil Mayor, Don Rodrigo de Rivera, for the city of Celaya, they became impatient and suspicious. With the authority and order of the Viceroy he went to safeguard the pack-trains that were transporting the corn from that city to the capital. It was said that these supplies were coming on His Excellency's own account; without any other basis than this rumor the multitude began to assume that he was tak-ing part in this business more for his own advantage than that of the general public. The following facts, which prove that what they so basely suspected was not true, carried no weight with them: first, the publicity with which it was done; second, that while the corn from Toluca and Chalco was being sold at six pesos a load and later at seven, the corn from Celaya was sold at four and five pesos because His Excellency had given the order that the latter should only be sold at cost and expenses; and, third, he had turned over to Don Francisco de Morales, Accountant of the Municipal Government, a current statement of this business matter and this was open to examination by anyone going into the office of the Accountant.

   These grumblings and suspicions had been very secret but on April 7th, the second day of Easter time, they became public. There was no other reason for this than the fact that on that day, in the presence of the Viceroy and all the court officials, a sermon was preached in the Cathedral which was not of a nature to comfort the people as it should in their adversity but, rather, to provoke them imprudently. This degraded audience responded to what the preacher was saying with benedictions and applause and with a noisy murmuring. And from that time on they considered their former suspicions as confirmed and now spoke with effrontery even in public places.

Those who most persisted in these complaints were the Indians, the most ungrateful, thankless, grumbling, and restless people that God ever created and the most favored with privileges in the abuse of which they cast themselves into all sorts of iniquities and senseless things and succeed in them. I do not wish to go on with all that sentiment dictates to me in this connection but, rather, I shall proceed remembering what I saw and what I heard from them on the night of the 8th of June. These Indians were the ones, as I have said, with the biggest complaints and the greatest impudence even though they had never experienced a better year in Mexico City than the present one. The proof of this last statement is plain. A very large number of Spaniards, the majority of the free Negroes and mulattoes, and the household servants, were eating tortillas. Neither the servants, nor the mulattoes, nor the Negroes, nor the Spaniards and their wives made these tortillas because they did not know how. Only the Indian women who were constantly selling them in heaps on the Plaza or in flocks on the street knew this art.

In order not to talk vaguely about what I wanted to tell, I dropped my pen and sent out to buy a *quartilla*[7] of corn which, at the rate of fifty-six reales silver per load, cost me seven. After giving this to an Indian woman to convert into tortillas she brought me back 350 of them. Disposed of at twelve per half-real, which was the price that I heard them selling for, they totaled 14 reales and a half and two were left over. What was spent in their manufacture was a real and a half, not taking into account the personal labor. I know positively that she lied a little. Then, if of every seven reales six at least were saved and, since the Indian women were the only ones who were making tortillas, how could they be perishing, as they kept shouting that they were, when what they were earning on the tortillas was not only more than enough for their sustenance (which costs them very little as everyone knows) but enough for them to lay by a store. And this does not take into consideration the steady income from their trades and the wages of their husbands. It was only this well known profit and not hunger that brought them to the Public Granary in such increasing numbers that they trampled upon one another in order to buy the corn. Therefore, no other year had been more favorable to them.

---

7   Quartilla: a measure of volume.

Pulque[8] was consumed in proportion to their surplus money and, in accordance with the abundance of this intoxicant in the city at that time, the Indians kept getting drunk. And, when the men learned from their wives that they were getting precedence in the purchasing of the corn even over the Spaniards, they began to boast in the *pulquerías* that such a circumstance resulted from our being afraid of them. At the same time they heard whole clauses of the recent sermon from those who were not Indians and, without the fact that the corn from Celaya was selling at five pesos and that of Chalco at seven making any impression upon them, they kept insisting that the Viceroy had something to do with it. From this notion that they persisted in, the matter of the sermon that they kept hearing, and the idea of our being afraid of them which they kept imagining, and all these discussed in the *pulquerías* where the police cannot enter on account of the iniquitous and ungodly stipulation to that effect granted to the contractor (*asentista*), what could result that would be useful to us? These *pulquerías* were not only frequented by the Indians as usual but also by the most contemptible of our infamous rabble which, upon listening to the Indians, made up its mind to scare off the Spaniards (as they say in their own language), burn the Royal Palace and, if they were able, kill the Viceroy and the Corregidor. And since, with this situation, others, who were present at these confabs and who were not Indians, would not lack an occasion to loot a great deal in such a conflict, I imagine (from what we saw afterwards) that they encouraged it.

That all this preceded the uprising is not merely probable to me but plain. I am not constrained to say this because one of those who were executed for this crime said so in his confession (he was known to everyone by the name of Rattón) but rather by what I saw with my own eyes and what I touched with my own hands. Quite a while before, when we were opening up the new canal which I told about before, an infinite number of tiny objects of superstition were taken out from beneath the Alvarado bridge. A great number of little pitchers and pots which smelled of *pulque*, and a still greater number of manikins or tiny figures of clay, were found. All of the latter represented Spaniards and all were either pierced by knives and lances formed by the same clay or had signs of blood on their throats as if they had been gashed.

It was on the occasion when the Viceroy came to inspect that canal that I showed them to him (and afterward to the archbishop in his palace). Both Princes questioned me as to their significance. I answered that it was proof

8   Pulque: an alcoholic beverage consumed since pre-Hispanic times and sold in *pulquerías*; it is made from the sap or *aguamiel* of the maguey plant.

positive of how utterly the Indians abominated us and an indication of what they earnestly desired for the Spaniards because, having defeated the Marqués del Valle [Hernán Cortés] on the night of the 10th of July, 1520, when he left México City they had, as their histories clearly indicate, consecrated this spot to their most important deity (which is the God of War) as a place of ill omen for us and propitious to them. And, since they had not forgotten their ancient superstitions even in these days, they throw there in effigy those whom they hate in order that the Spaniards, whom they now curse, may suffer the same fate as those of the earlier date who perished in the same canal. I inferred that this was the significance of those objects, judging by what I have read of their histories and by what they themselves told me when I was gathering them up. And now I add that, since the number of those figures was considerable and many of them had been thrown there recently, it was nothing less than to make manifest by that action the vicious state of mind that they were in and their desire to exterminate us all.

The Indians most earnest in these conversations were, as afterwards learned, those of Santiago, a barrio which now belongs to the City of Mexico and comprises half of it (with the name of Tlatelolco). In pagan times it had an overlord who governed the people and was distinct from the one in Mexico City (then called Tenochtitlán). If this is really so (as it assuredly is since in the thick of the riot they called each other by the name of santiagueños) this is not the first time that they have attempted to destroy Mexico City where we now live. Would that they had now done to each other as the Mexicans did against them and their overlord, Moquilhuix, when they were barbarians! Whether the santiagueños were the only ones who brought on the uprising by their talking I do not know for certain, I only know that all the Indian rabble of Mexico City, without any exception whatsoever, took part in it. And I also know that before it happened they got ready for it all by themselves.

The latter were not without some basis for their plans for they learned that, both on account of a shortage of corn from Celaya (on account of no mules being found to transport it), and because the corn that was coming from Chalco was so small in quantity that it made it necessary for Don Pedro de la Vastida to go to that Province to remedy the situation, there was also a shortage in the Public Granary at about six o'clock in the afternoon. [The officials] marveled at the racket and the uproar of the Indian women on this account and they wondered at the shameless, foul, and lewd words uttered, at the petty quarrels of the natives in which, however, they did not hurt each other but to which the men hurried up as if to make peace, thus giving rise to large groups of loungers. All these things seemed portents to them of an approaching disturbance. And those most closely associated with this matter saw that some of the very same women kept coming every day and even morning and afternoon to buy corn. Considering the great amount that some of the women were carrying off, they conjectured, as it never occurred to them that it was in order to resell the corn in the form of tortillas, that the women were doing this in order that there should be a shortage in the Public Granary and afford an opportunity for some commotion.

In Context | The Virgin of Guadalupe

The Virgin of Guadalupe (fig. 3.2, 126) is the most important image in the history of Mexico and among the most significant ones in the history of Catholicism. First of all, it is an image of the Virgin Mary with dark skin, venerated in a single place, Tepeyac, just north of Mexico City, in a church built (after the conquest) on the ruins of a temple dedicated to an Aztec goddess. This portrait of a dark-skinned virgin—that is, one with indigenous features—clearly exemplifies the intentions of the first missionaries: to use Christian images to substitute for Indian pagan gods. In this sense, it was an image created for the Indians.

Nevertheless, Spanish American creoles (born in Mexico to Spanish parents) soon developed a patriotic consciousness, the pride of being born in a dignified and valued city, as was their own metropolis. Subject to discrimination by more recent Spanish arrivals, these creoles adopted the Virgin of Guadalupe as their own, not just exclusively for Indians. They gave the object itself—the very cloth on which the virgin was painted—exceptional origins, the cloak of St. Thomas, as CARLOS DE SIGÜENZA Y GÓNGORA and others maintained.

By the eighteenth century, the Catholic Church had begun to uphold the miraculous account of the image: after appearing on several occasions to an Indian named Juan Diego, the Virgin had impressed her likeness onto his cloak. Pope John Paul II validated this version in 2002 when he visited Mexico City and canonized Juan Diego, confirming the apparitions on the supposedly historical reality of this devout Christian convert.

This centuries-old representation of the Virgin Mary, framed and protected by a special glass, is now on display for the many thousands of pilgrims and tourists who regularly visit the enormous Basilica of Guadalupe, just north of Mexico City. It is, according to official Catholic doctrine and the belief of millions of Mexicans, a miraculous image, unique in the world.

Figure 3.2. The Virgin of Guadalupe. Basílica de Guadalupe, Tepeyac, Mexico. By permission of the Instituto Nacional de Antropología e Historia.

Sor Juana Inés de la Cruz (1651–1695)

In her own time as well as in ours, Sor Juana Inés de la Cruz remains one of Latin America's most important thinkers and writers, most notably for her challenges to patriarchal authority in her life and in her remarkable writings. Born in Mexico (New Spain) as the illegitimate daughter of a largely absent Spanish father and a creole mother, Juana taught herself to read by the time she was three. When she was an adolescent, she acquired the patronage of Leonor Carreto, the wife of Mexico's new viceroy, Antonio Sebastián de Toledo, Marquis of Mancera (1664?–1673). Serving as a maid-in-waiting, Juana soon astonished court scholars with her intelligence and erudition. In 1667, she became a nun, a choice that was the only respectable alternative for women who did not—or could not—marry. By her own account, Sor Juana chose convent life in order to have more time to devote to her studies and to "know God." She was first a postulant in the Order of the Discalced (Barefoot) Carmelites, whose rigors were specified by the great Spanish reformer, Teresa of Ávila, but became ill after only a few months. She then entered the Convent of Santa Paula of the Order of St. Jerome, or the Hieronymites, where she remained cloistered for the rest of her life.

Over the next decade, Sor Juana continued to write occasional poetry and religious songs, but her work really flourished with the arrival in 1680 of a new viceregal couple, Tomás Antonio de la Cerda, Marquis de la Laguna, and his wife, María Luisa, Countess de Paredes, with whom Sor Juana became close friends. The countess actively encouraged the young nun's poetic vocation, and when María Luisa returned to Spain in 1688, she oversaw the publication of Sor Juana's writings. The first book of poetry, *Inundación Castálida de la única poetisa, musa dezima* [The Overflowing of the Castalian Spring by the Tenth Muse (of Mexico)], appeared in 1689 along with Sor Juana's finest sacred work, a sacramental play called *El divino Narciso* [The Divine Narcissus], as well as several secular plays, including *Los empeños de una casa* [The House of Trials], which had been performed in Mexico City as early as 1683.

During this active period, Sor Juana managed to pursue her own intellectual interests quite freely, transforming the convent itself into a respected site of teaching and learning. She studied science and astronomy, composed music, and wrote and performed plays and poetry. She became quite celebrated as a writer and a spirited participant in scholarly debates in both the court and in the church, along with CARLOS DE SIGÜENZA Y GÓNGORA, another towering intellectual. But as one of the first women in the

Americas to question—through her life and in her work—the social and ideological structures confining women, Sor Juana, of course, continues to be studied and translated, even becoming the subject of a film, *Yo, la peor de todas* (1990) [I, Worst of All], by the Argentinian María Luisa Bemberg.

Of course, even in her own time, challenges to patriarchy did not go unnoticed—or unpunished. In 1690, the bishop of Puebla, Manuel Fernández de Santa Cruz, published (without Sor Juana's knowledge) her critique of a sermon written forty years earlier by an eminent Portuguese Jesuit, Antonio Vieira. As a prologue to her *Carta atenagórica* [Letter Worthy of Athena], the bishop had attached a letter by one "Sor Filotea de la Cruz," who reprimanded "her sister" for her scholarly pursuits and advised her to dedicate herself instead to the salvation of her soul. Responding with her own missive, "Respuesta a sor Filotea" [Reply to Sor Philothea], Sor Juana set forth a series of brilliant arguments for maintaining her intellectual space. Recognizing that the ecclesial pressure to silence her stemmed from envy of her talents as much as religious dogma, she based her logic on two irrefutable principles already accepted by the Church: the authority of God over all creation (including women) and the notion that the laws of nature are intractable. Explaining that "God has implanted a natural impulse to know" and that "it is God who is directing this inclination toward learning," Sor Juana put her challengers in a difficult position since they could not refute God's authority. Prohibited from studying texts, she shows how observation, no less than books, was a source of knowledge. She recounts, for example, how she learned about optics by noting how some lines run straight but are not parallel; about physics by watching the spinning of a top; and about chemistry by noticing the differences between an egg that is fried and one that is saturated in syrup. But while Sor Juana's appeal to divine authority is consistent with contemporary beliefs, that authority remained the source of the gender and social categories that were being used to control her. Most explicitly here, but throughout her work, Sor Juana thus managed to transform into assets even her subjugated status as a woman and nun in a deeply hierarchical church and society.

Without royal allies, Sor Juana gradually succumbed to the increasing pressure of her male religious superiors. Though she never publicly renounced her work, by 1694 she had sold her enormous library of nearly four thousand books and all of her scientific and musical instruments to provide for the poor. The next year, while caring for her sisters, she contracted the plague and died at the age of forty-four.

Though Sor Juana is usually celebrated for her defiant spirit, she was also an exceptionally talented poet. She composed poems in a stunning range of genres, including sonnets, *redondillas* (rhymed quatrains) and *villancicos* (song lyrics for religious festivities). Not surprisingly, given her philosophical mind, argumentative logic is intrinsic to her compositions, reflected in the parallelism, *conceptismos* (conceits or witty metaphors), and antithesis that are characteristic of American Baroque. Perhaps the epitome of her poetic achievement is *Primero Sueño* (1692) [First Dream], in which a dream journey represents her quest for knowledge. Both poem and philosophical treatise, *Primero Sueño* posits material experience (the body and the poem) as well as the unconscious as valid sources of knowing. In so doing, Sor Juana radically expands the bases of truth and affirms the ways that not just abstract reason, but all creation provides access to an all-encompassing divinity.

The text is a selection from Sor Juana Inés de la Cruz, *A Sor Juana Anthology*, translated by Alan S. Trueblood, foreword by Octavio Paz (Cambridge, Mass.: Harvard University Press, 1988), 210–12, 224–26. Reprinted by permission of the publisher from *A Sor Juana Anthology*, trans. Alan S. Trueblood (Cambridge, Mass: Harvard University Press, 1988). Copyright © 1988 by the President and Fellows of Harvard College.

From Respuesta a sor Filotea (1690) [Reply to Sor Philothea]

My purpose in studying is not to write, much less to teach (this would be overbearing pride in my case), but simply to see whether studying makes me less ignorant. This is my reply and these are my feelings.

I have never written of my own accord, but only when pressured by others. I could truthfully say to them: *Vos me coegistis* ["You have compelled me" (2 Cor. 12:11)]. What is true and I will not deny (first because it is public knowledge and then—even if this counts against me—because God, in His goodness, has favored me with a great love of the truth) is that from my first glimmers of reason, my inclination to letters was of such power and vehemence, that neither the reprimands of others—and I have received many—nor my own considerations—and there have been not a few of these—have succeeded in making me abandon this natural impulse which God has implanted in me—only His Majesty knows why and wherefore and His Majesty also knows that, I have prayed to Him to extinguish the light of my mind, only leaving sufficient to keep His law, since any more is overmuch, so some say, in a woman, and there are even those who say it is harmful. His Majesty also knows that, not succeeding in this, I have tried to inter my name along with my mind and sacrifice it to Him alone who gave it to me; and that this was precisely my motivation in taking the veil, even though the exercise and shared life which a community entails were repellent to the independence and tranquility which my inclination to study needed. And once in the community, the Lord God knows and, in the world, he knows who alone had the right to know it, how hard I tried to conceal my name, and that he did not allow this, saying that it was temptation, which no doubt it was.[9] If I could repay you some part of what I owe you, my Lady, I think I would be paying you simply by relating this, for it has never escaped my lips before, except when addressed to one who had the right to know it. But I want you to know that, in throwing wide open to you the gates of my heart, exposing to your gaze its most tightly guarded secrets, my justification for the liberty I am taking is the great debt I owe to your venerable person and overly generous favors.

To go on with the account of this strong bent of mine, about which I want you to be fully informed, let me say that when I was not yet three, my mother sent a sister of mine, older than I, to learn to read in one of those establishments called Amigas [girls' elementary schools], at which point affection and mischievousness on my part led me to follow her. Seeing that she was being given lessons, I became so inflamed with the desire to learn to read, that I tricked the mistress—or so I thought—by telling her that my mother had directed her to give me lessons. This was not believable and she did not believe me, but falling in with my little trick, she did give me lessons. I continued attending and she went on teaching me, no longer as a joke, since the event opened her eyes. I learned to read in so short a time that I already knew how when my mother found out, for the mistress kept it from her in order to give her a pleasant surprise and receive her recompense all at one time. I kept still, since I thought I would be whipped for having acted on my own initiative. The person who taught me is still alive (may God preserve her) and can attest to this.

I remember that at this period, though I loved to eat, as children do at that age, I refrained from eating cheese, because someone had told me it made you stupid, and my urge to learn was stronger than my wish to eat, powerful as this is in children. Afterward, when I was six or seven and already knew how to read and write, along with all the sewing skills and needlework that women learn, I discovered that in the city of Mexico there was a university with schools where the different branches of learning could be studied, and as soon as I learned this I began to deluge my mother with urgent and insistent

9 A probable allusion to her confessor, Antonio Núñez de Miranda, S.J.

pleas to change my manner of dress and send me to stay with relatives in the City of México so that I might study and take courses at the university. She refused, and rightly so; nevertheless, I found a way to read many different books my grandfather owned, not withstanding the punishment and reproofs this entailed, so that when I went to the City of México people were astonished, not so much at my intelligence as at the memory and store of knowledge I had at an age at which it would seem I had scarcely had time to learn to speak.

I began to study Latin, in which I do not believe I had twenty lessons in all, and I was so intensely studious that despite the natural concern of a woman— especially in the flower of their youth—with dressing their hair, I used to cut four or five fingers' width from mine, keeping track of how far it had formerly reached, and making it my rule that if by the time it grew back to that point, I did not know such-and-such a thing which I had set out to learn as it grew, I would cut it again as penalty for my dullness. Thus it would happen that it would grow back, and I still would not know what I had set myself to learn, because my hair grew rapidly, whereas I was a slow learner, and I did indeed cut it as a punishment for my slowness for I did not consider it right that a head so bare of knowledge should be dressed with hair, knowledge being the more desirable ornament. I became a nun because, although I knew that that way of life involved much that was repellent to my nature—I refer to its incidental, not its central aspects—nevertheless, given my total disinclination to marriage, it was the least unreasonable and most becoming choice I could make to assure my ardently desired salvation. To which first consideration, as most important, all the other small frivolities of my nature yielded and gave way, such as my wish to live alone, to have no fixed occupation, which might curtail my freedom to study, nor the noise of a community to interfere with the tranquil stillness of my books. This made me hesitate a little before making up my mind, until, enlightened by learned persons that hesitation was temptation, I overcame it by the grace of God and entered upon the life I now pursue so unworthily. I thought I was escaping from myself, but, alas for me, I had brought myself along. In this propensity I brought my greatest enemy, given me by Heaven whether as a boon or a punishment I cannot decide, for far from dying out or being hindered by all the exercises religion entails, it exploded like gunpowder. *Privatio est causa appetitus* [Privation arouses the appetite] had its confirmation in me.

I went back (I misspeak: I had never stopped); I went on with the studious pursuit (in which I found relaxation during all the free time remaining from my obligations) of reading and more reading, study and more study, with no other teacher than books themselves. One can readily imagine how hard it is to study from those lifeless letters, lacking a teacher's live voice and explanations. Still, I happily put up with all those drawbacks, for the sheer love of learning. Oh, if it had only been for the love of God, which would have been the sound way, what merit would have been mine! I *will* say that I tried to uplift my study as much as I could and direct it to serving Him, since the goal I aspired to was the study of theology, it seeming to me a mean sort of ineptitude for a Catholic not to know all that can be found out in this life through natural means concerning divine mysteries. [. . .]

If I saw a figure, I at once fell to working out the relationship of its lines, measuring it with my mind and recasting it along different ones. Sometimes I would walk back and forth across the front of a sleeping-room of ours—a very large one—and observe how, though the lines of its two sides were parallel and its ceiling horizontal, one's vision made it appear as if the lines inclined toward each other and the ceiling were lower at the far end, from which I inferred that visual lines run straight but not parallel, tending rather toward a pyramidal figure. And I asked myself whether this could be the reason the ancients questioned whether the world was spherical or not. Because, although it appears to be, this could be an optical illusion, and show concavities where there might in fact be none. [. . .]

This turn, or habit, of mind is so strong that I can look upon nothing without reflecting on it. Two little girls were playing with a top in my presence. The moment I saw its movement and form, I began, in my crazy way, to consider the easy motion of the spherical form, and how, the impulse once given, it continued independently of its cause, since at a distance from the girl's hand, which originated the motion, the top went on dancing. Nor was this enough for me. I had flour brought and sifted, so as to tell, when the top danced over it, whether the circles its motion described were perfect or not. I discovered that they were simply spirals which moved farther and farther from the circular in proportion as the impulse wore down. Other girls were playing with pins—childhood's most frivolous game. I would approach and observe the shapes the pins took, and on noticing that three chanced to form a triangle, I would set about actually connecting them, recalling that this was the shape the mysterious ring of Solomon was said to have taken—that ring on which there were distant glimmerings and depictions of the Most Holy Trinity, by virtue of which it worked such prodigious and marvelous things.[10] This was also

---

10   No such ring is mentioned in the Bible. An occult tradition is perhaps being invoked here.

said to be the shape of David's harp, for which reason Saul was said to have been cured by its sound. The harps of our day have retained the same shape.

What could I not tell you, my Lady, of the secrets of Nature which I have discovered in cooking! That an egg hangs together and fries in fat or oil, and that, on the contrary, it disintegrates in syrup. That, to keep sugar liquid, it suffices to add the tiniest part of water in which a quince or some other tart fruit has been. That the yolk and white of the same egg are so different in nature, that when eggs are used with sugar, the yolks must be used separately from the whites, never together with them. I do not wish to tire you with such trivia, which I relate only to give you a full picture of my native turn of mind, which will, no doubt, make you laugh. But, Madam, what is there for us women to know, if not bits of kitchen philosophy? As Lupercio Leonardo said: One can perfectly well philosophize while cooking supper.[11] And I am always saying, when I observe these small details: If Aristotle had been a cook, he would have written much more.

Hernando Domínguez Camargo (1606–1659)

San Ignacio de Loyola: Poema Heroico is not only one of the longest poems in Spanish, but it is also one of the most beautiful. Like ERCILLA in *La Araucana*, Domínguez Camargo uses the *octava real*, one of the preferred forms for long poems during the sixteenth and seventeenth centuries—a difficult eight-line stanza with eleven-syllable lines (the other preferred one was the *silva*). The five books of *San Ignacio* are divided into numerous cantos describing the life of the Spanish founder of the Society of Jesus, the religious order to which the poet himself briefly belonged.

Given its massive length (1,116 royal octaves or 8,928 lines of poetry), the poem can be read both as a single work of many parts (not all equally successful) or 1,116 poems with different clusters of themes. Both assessments are justified: *San Ignacio* is both a sweeping epic account and a collection of some of the best poems in Spanish. The man from Nueva Granada (modern Colombia) exhibits a stunning command of vocabulary, metaphor, and syntax. He takes the Spanish language to levels rarely achieved by any poet. Like his contemporary, SOR JUANA INÉS DE LA CRUZ, Domínguez Camargo was deeply influenced by the Spanish Baroque poet, Góngora

---

11 The Aragonese poet Bartolomé Leonardo de Argensola (1562–1631), not his brother Lupercio, is the source of the saying ("First Satire," lines 143–44).

(1561–1627). But while many poets imitated Góngora's manner, these two Spanish American poets made Gongorism their own, creating in their best work distinctive poetic voices and styles.

Though *San Ignacio* was published posthumously in Madrid in 1666, it demonstrates the profound appropriateness of the Baroque for the Spanish American worldview. While Góngora represented only one aspect of Spain's complex body of poetic and ideological practices, the Baroque was the dominant poetic style in Spanish America, ideal for conveying a distinctively American perspective.

Two aspects of the Spanish American Baroque stand out: the high regard for the senses that virtually excludes transcendental religious concepts, and the conviction that this world has no substance, being merely a product of our beliefs. These qualities underlie the constant beauty of Domínguez Camargo's descriptions, revealing how everything can be aestheticized, that the empirical and spiritual worlds are known only through our senses. The Baroque, particularly in this poem, anticipates Goethe's observation a century and a half later that "everything can be poetic."

Ostensibly a work of hagiography replete with sincere Catholic devotion (which remarkably never contradicts its lack of transcendence), *San Ignacio* is foremost an act of the imagination, exploiting any occasion or object to exercise the powers of metaphor. While describing a battle, for instance, the poet pauses to recall when shields and spears and battering rams were the weapons of war, contrasting that moment with the present, when gunpowder, rifles, and cannons generate an awesome lethality (book 1, canto 2, octaves CXXVII–CXXX). Elsewhere, Domínguez Camargo details the beauty of quite minor characters, like the lovesick "garçon" Julio. The poet's evident delight in describing the boy's unnamed beloved consumes five royal octaves, often considered as a set piece one of the most dazzling love poems in Spanish (book 4, canto 6, octaves CCXXVII–CCXXXII).

Everything in this world seems created or invented to serve Domínguez Camargo's metaphors, hyperbaton, and ellipses; everything exists to convey the purely sensual meaning of the world. The miracles of Ignatius's life, the person of Christ, even the most ethereal concepts are subject to an overpowering materiality. This deep embedment in the sensual does not preclude religious dogma, such as the immortality of the soul or God's final judgment. But the juxtaposition of such extreme materiality with Christian orthodoxy does generate a sharp and sometimes grotesque awareness of the fragility of life. To the Baroque sensibility, death is always nearby. At the end of book 4, for example, there is an unusual allegory, in which the bones of the body write letters about the passage of time, suggesting that the body is only the "library" wherein the text of death is written (book 4, canto 6, octave CCLXXIII).

Domínguez Camargo himself was as contradictory as the Baroque itself. Born in Bogotá, he was educated at the Jesuit College in Quito and joined the Society in 1623. Living in Cartagena in New Granada at the height of the slave trade, he worked alongside his fellow Jesuit, the saintly Pedro Claver (1581–1654), who spent over forty years ministering to enslaved Africans. (Peter Claver was canonized by Pope Pius IX in 1888.) Despite this ministry, Domínguez Camargo himself never mentions Indian culture or even the existence of blacks in his writings. Though his own religious views were fairly unorthodox, he also functioned as an official of the Inquisition; and while he served in poor Indian parishes, he evidently owned a good deal of lavish clothing. Even after he was expelled from the Society of Jesus in 1636 for "grave faults," he continued writing his heroic poem in honor of Saint Ignatius and, at his death, left his library to the Society. After his dismissal from the Jesuits, Domínguez Camargo became a secular priest, serving in various isolated towns of Nueva Granada, until finally settling among his relatives in the city of Tunja. Continuing his contradictory life, he became a businessman: buying houses, lending money with interest (a practice forbidden by the Church), becoming an associate of a merchant from Cartagena—and serving as the parish priest of the cathedral.

Apart from *San Ignacio*, Domínguez Camargo only wrote a handful of other poems and a prose satire, *Invectiva apologetica* (1652) [Ire and Vindication], before his death in 1659. Despite the many contradictions of his personal life, Domínguez Camargo is one of the century's most talented poets and the author of one of its most engaging and complex poems. However, his achievement had been largely unappreciated and his great epic almost forgotten until the middle of the twentieth century, when scholars began recovering many lost authors and texts. The moment coincided with a general critical reevaluation of the Baroque and the revitalization of *gongorismo* by writers and poets like Alfonso Reyes, MARTÍN ADÁN, JOSÉ LEZAMA LIMA, and José Gorostiza. The recovery of Domínguez Camargo was particularly fortuitous, highlighting the continuing importance of the Baroque as a critical feature of Latin American identity and expression.

The text is an original translation by Henry Sullivan of stanzas CXXVII– CXXX, CCXXVIII–CCXXXII, CCLXXIII of *San Ignacio de Loyola, fundador de la Compañía de Jesús. Poema heroico* in *Obras: Edición a cargo de Rafael Torres Quintero; con estudios de Alfonso Mendez Plancarte, Joaquin Antonio Peñalosa, Guillermo Hernandez de Alba* (Bogotá: Instituto Caro y Cuervo, 1960), 78–79, 304–5, 315.

From **San Ignacio de Loyola (1666) [St. Ignatius of Loyola]**

CXXVII

Oh gunpowder! Invention of a human viper!
Oh German alchemist, what a mortal foe
To life! Thou by whose hand was shaped and hewn,
In paltry powder, centuries of punishment
Against the noblest actions, because its grains
Are shelter after which the coward seeks,
Where craft imperiously doth coerce by fire
And pare down lightning flashes to a closure!

CXXVIII

And thou hast pierced through wounded arteries
With spark-besprinkled blood from flint,
Thou hast composed of charcoal and saltpeter
A brief inferno of tempestuous sands;
Thou hast chained up such deadly thunderbolts—
Crumbling in yon fine and tiny powders—,
That they are atoms of the fire or, against the crag,
Demolished eyes of basilisks as cannon.

CXXIX

With raging anger shortened into minutes
And—into granules—impatience of the flame,
Gunpowder is mustard, in smoke so absolute,
It irritates high peaks of greatest fame;
And also—of the ages—sauce, that twixt the brutish
Ridges spills itself with famine such,
It crams its maw in quick and hurried bursts
With what it could not listless eat a hundred years.

CXXX

Before thou sprangst to life, the big and hefty
Giants of the earth were feared; the soldier
Prized the protection of his buckler dear;
An arrow from the bowstring was dispatched
Against the deadly viper; a rude battering-ram
Caused high-raised ramparts to disintegrate;
Born to the cannon now, thy anger found—
Against lives far away—a telescopic sight.

. . . .

CCXXVIII

Not even gold were gold in her fair hair,
Nor mother-of-pearl were nacre on her brow,
Nor upon either leaf of her full comely lips
Would ruby waste its price so radiant;
Snow would besmirch that alabaster neck,
And pearls would stain her incandescent teeth,
A rose would cast a shadow on her cheek,
A feather's touch would make her flesh grow hard.

CCXXIX

Be there a Phoenix of loveliness in Araby,
She either matches it or doubles it;
If ostentatious peacock in America,
Its plume-tailed eyes are sealed within her eyes;
If swan of lamentation on the foam,
Her whiteness makes fair feathers seem as bronze;
If e'er there were lilies white amid the snow,
Her hand would taint them violet shades of black.

CCXXX

If his bow lends splendor to the arm of Cupid,
It will have been copied in her eyebrows twain,
And if a second mine of Potosí were found,
It will have been shared between her silver breasts,
If ever Pontus heard its mermaids sing,
Their sweetness will reach the Straits between that mouth,

If suns have cradles, and the stars an urn,
Hers is the dimple on her lovely chin.

CCXXXI

Her tiny mouth—as workplace—shall anoint
The sea with amber: then from there, her breath
The wind would nurture—to spice and season tides—
From tooth to tooth, just like from rock to rock;
Indeed, her perfumes thus articulated, summon
The trilling of the matutinal birds;
Because—from what her lips exhale and tresses gild—
They swear she is the rising of their dawn.

CCXXXII

This right beauteous, then, if populous
Regal metropolis of loveliness,
For Julio was his galley of affection,
Wherein, in chains so sweetly onerous,
His foot became licentiously involved
When Cupid's concupiscent bowstring coarse,
Wounding his shoulder-blades—by oar-strokes—lashed
The harpoons in his quiver to his arm.

. . . .

CCLXXIII

"Oh, rummage in the history of past days,
Through weighty volumes of a sepulcher obscure;
And read the letters which, in ashes cold,
These bones—those skeletons unclean—write down;
In numerous of these Libraries of Death,
Julio heeds, all ill at ease, cadavers of
Those bones—and in their writing—is admonished
They are the very alphabets of death!"

In Context | Churriguera Style

Many of the architects and interior designers of churches throughout Spain and Hispanic America originally worked in the theater business, building scenographies. Such was the case of the individuals who designed the façade of the Biblioteca Miguel Lerdo de Tejada in Mexico City.

After the Baroque "twisting" of the columns, another step in making decoration more elaborate was the *estípite*, in which the cylindrical body

Figure 3.3. Churriguera style. Biblioteca Miguel Lerdo de Tejada, Mexico City, Mexico. Photograph by Ismael Villafranco (2012). License CC BY-SA 2.0.

Figure 3.4. Jesuit missions. Main front of the Cathedral of Concepción with its imposing bell tower. Santa Cruz, Bolivia, part of the "Jesuit Missions of the Chiquitos World Heritage Site" by Bamse (2008) CC BY-SA 3.0.

of the column became an inverted triangle (sometimes called a square column), and the classical capital disappeared. Associated with the Spanish artist José Benito Churriguera, this style became known as *churrigueresco*. In fact, José Benito belonged to a family of architects and sculptors, many of whom contributed to this stylistic shift. These changes occurred gradually, however, and many scholars maintain that the most radical designers and sculptors of altarpieces in this period (from the end of seventeenth century through the first half of the eighteenth) were not the Churriguera family. In any case, as the style evolved, *estípites* began to be fused to the façades, blending in with the rest of the ornamentation. This fusion of the column with the façade marks a final step in the Baroque before the eighteenth-century return of the Greek and Roman classical styles.

In Context | Jesuit Missions and Their Legacies

At the end of the sixteenth century, when the first wave of colonial evangelization faltered, the Society of Jesus was ready to take on the missionary efforts begun by Franciscans and Dominicans and other orders. The Jesuits dispersed to regions ignored by earlier missionaries—to the north of New

Spain (present-day Mexico), to Sonora and California, and to the center of South America, from present-day Paraguay to Bolivia—where this splendid example of Jesuit architecture (fig. 3.4) was built in 1753–1756 in the town of Concepción.

In this new missionary era, as the competition between the old powers—landowners and the Spanish crown—intensified, the Jesuits sought to protect "their" Indians by establishing "missions" or religious outposts. While these closed communities certainly benefited the Society, the missions also prevented the Indians from falling under the direct control of the crown and from being exploited by landowners who coveted their cheap labor. An overall map of the missions' locations reveals another intent—creating a wall against the intrusions of Portuguese-dominated Brazil, a nation that never ceased in its attempts to expand into Spanish and Indian territories.

While the value of the missions for Indians remains a matter of intense debate, in Paraguay, at least, the social integration that followed independence in 1811 was not coincidental or unrelated to the legacy of the missions. An ultimately unsuccessful experiment in social cooperation was initiated by Paraguay's controversial and dictatorial leader, José Gaspar Rodríguez de Francia. Inspired by the principles of the French Revolution and committed to defending the lower classes, Dr. Francia—as he was known—was promptly demonized abroad, particularly by the English, the Brazilians, and the oligarchies of Bolivia and Argentina. Dr. Francia's Rousseauian social and economic policies posed a direct and dangerous challenge to the "free market" and the creation of vast land holdings that were configuring the rest of the Americas.

Two decades after Francia's death in 1840, the War of the Triple Alliance (1865–1870) finally brought an end to his efforts. Instigated and supported by the English banks and implemented by Argentina, Brazil, and Uruguay, the war was one of the most devastating events of the nineteenth century; SARMIENTO, as president of Argentina and one of the leaders of the Triple Alliance, once boasted that the war had eliminated the entire male population of Paraguay between the ages of fifteen and fifty-five.

In Context | Iturbide's Palace

Iturbide's Palace, a once-grand residence in Mexico City, exemplifies civil architecture during the first two centuries of colonial rule. One basic material of the era was *tezontle*, the petrified foam of volcanic lava. Porous, and therefore very light, the red *tezontle* provided a strong decorative contrast

Figure 3.5. Iturbide's Palace, Mexico City, Mexico. Photograph by Jennifer Saracino.

with the gray stones. The Spaniards borrowed the use of *tezontle* from the Aztecs, who understood perfectly well that heavy buildings would sink in a land that was practically floating on water. The lightweight and durable *tezontle* supplied the perfect building material for the ancient city of Tenochtitlán—as well as for colonial Mexico.

4

The Wars of Independence, 1767–1824

The expulsion of the Jesuits from all Spanish territories by King Charles III in 1767 marked a decisive moment in the history of Spanish America. The primary objections to the Society of Jesus were its unconditional loyalty to the Pope and its concomitant (if counterintuitive) resistance to absolute monarchy, regarded as a secular challenge to divine authority. But the politics of the Enlightenment that eliminated the Jesuits also set in motion an irreversible process that led toward independence for the colonies.

One reason for the Jesuit expulsion was the effort to restrict the influence of the Pope and the Church, whose growing power in the colonies had increasingly limited the profits of the Spanish crown. Intending a more efficient process for collecting the riches of the Americas, Charles III ordered other reforms: he established new territorial borders; he created a new viceroyalty (the Rio de la Plata); he changed the methods of tax collection; and he sharply curbed church authority in the colonies.

Some of these efficiencies had unexpectedly far-reaching outcomes. Most notably, improving colonial administration (including better organization of local militia) and relaxing many onerous commercial and social restrictions made colonists more acutely aware of their dependent status. The contexts of change and uncertainty also encouraged some of the most radical Indian rebellions of the eighteenth century, particularly in the Andean region, with successive uprisings led by Tupac Amaru and Tupac Katari.

The Enlightenment that was sweeping Europe also seemed to reaffirm the "black legend" of Spain—the view that Spain had never contributed anything positive to the scientific and cultural development of Europe. Spanish history, at least since the explorations of the fifteenth century, was widely regarded as a series of reactions arising from fanaticism, obscurantism, and rigid religious orthodoxy. While many mainland Spanish thinkers sought to refute this view, a similar reassessment of the Hispanic legacy was emerging in the colonies. Using the same rationalism that undermined Spain's tenuous claims to modernity, the creoles of the Americas were reasserting the validity of their own traditions and perspectives. That process was significantly assisted by the Jesuit exiles in Italy, who were composing the first "national" histories of their former homes—including Mexico, Chile, Ecuador, and Argentina.

The Jesuits' influence on the independence movements actually extended well beyond these early histories, which often included strong defenses of the virtues of these distinctly American societies. The educational institutions that the Jesuits had founded, even after coming under the control of other religious orders, continued to disseminate the Jesuits' progressive ideological, political, and social teachings to prominent young men across the Americas, many of whom became leaders in the movements for independence. Some of the Jesuits even developed specific proposals for independence, like Juan Pablo Viscardo's famous "Letter to Spanish Americans" (1792), which later inspired the Venezuelan revolutionary Francisco Miranda, who included Viscardo's stirring words in his own proclamation for independence in 1806.

Despite the efforts at reform by Charles III, the corruption and incompetence of his son, Charles IV, along with the turmoil created by the French Revolution, soon ended that endeavor. By the end of the eighteenth century, Spain's long and uneasy alliance with France had deepened into political and economic disaster. One notable contributor to the economic collapse in Spain was, in fact, a royal reform, one that contributed decisively, if inadvertently, to the rise of the independence movements. In 1804, the bankrupt Spanish crown decided to consolidate its royal promissory notes in the colonies, with disastrous financial results in the Americas. By the late eighteenth century, the Catholic Church had accrued considerable wealth, through its many land concessions and forced Indian labor, as well as through donations from the faithful for masses and various spiritual favors. Enriched with all this capital, the Church became the primary bank in the colonial economy, offering loans to the largely creole population of hacienda owners, merchants, and mining operators. Forbidden by canon law to charge interest, the Church secured these loans with property, further increasing its real estate holdings in the cities and the rural areas when owners defaulted. The imposition of *vales reales* by Charles IV meant that all debts owed to the Church were immediately due to the king. Many creoles who did not have the money were forced to sell their properties at a loss, and while the measure was revoked only four years later in 1808, many creoles were financially ruined. Moreover, in that same year, Napoleon's troops invaded Spain and precipitated an internal crisis. Charles IV wanted to flee to the Americas, but supporters of his son, Fernando VII, detained him. Charles eventually abdicated in his son's favor, but within a few months, Napoleon took both men prisoners and installed his brother, Joseph Bonaparte, as king of Spain.

The wars of independence that followed in the wake of the Napoleonic invasion of Spain were not simply Americans against Spaniards. Instead, the various struggles, beginning in Quito in 1808 and ending with the battle of Ayachuco in Peru in 1824, exposed and exacerbated any number of political, economic, geographic, and racial divisions that existed throughout the colonies. The higher levels of the Royal Army, for example, were occupied by creoles and *peninsulares*, with the lower ranks filled by Indians, blacks, and mestizos, the mixed-race people who constituted the majority in most Hispanic-American countries. Racial tensions, crisscrossed by differing political and economic goals, often generated bitter civil wars, which in some territories virtually destroyed the entire social and economic fabric. Central Mexico and the Andes were caught up in such conflicts for many years, while Argentina, especially around Buenos Aires and Córdoba, suffered relatively minor disruptions.

One of the great military figures of the wars of independence was SIMÓN BOLÍVAR. At the beginning of 1813, shortly after being defeated in Venezuela, Bolívar fought his way back to his native country and then took the struggle west through Colombia to Ecuador, Peru, and the Alto Peru, a region later named in his honor: Bolivia. Known as the Liberator, Bolívar's military leadership was crucial to achieving independence. However, the most important political factor was probably the short-lived Constitution of Cádiz, proclaimed in 1812 and revoked just two years later. Though its intent was not particularly radical, the Constitution embodied many liberal ideals, including universal male suffrage, limited government, and regional sovereignty; it later became a model for many post-revolutionary constitutions in Europe as well as in the Americas. In its unprecedented redefinition of the political relationship between Spain and its colonies, the Constitution played a decisive role in the independence movements—and often created ironic allegiances. For example, after the constitution was restored in Mexico in 1820, a faction of the military who were fighting against the independence forces also opposed the reinstatement of the constitutional reforms. Rather than submit to the constitution, the group preferred an alliance with the enemy—those who were fighting for independence.

The final battle for independence in South America occurred in November 1824, at Ayacucho, when Antonio José de Sucre, one of Bolívar's most trusted generals, defeated a large force of the Royal Army, capturing several Spanish generals along with the last regional viceroy of Peru, José de la Serna. The victory ensured the independence of Peru—and that of all Spanish America.

But while independence from Europe was a landmark event in the Americas, one of its most lasting consequences had been foretold by Bolívar himself in his "Letter from Jamaica" in 1815. Bolívar warned that while slavery had been abolished and Indians were already free from many colonial obligations, the creoles, who remained in power throughout most former Spanish colonies, would not readily relinquish their authority. Bolívar was right; the only real movement toward equality occurred in Paraguay, where Dr. José Gaspar Rodríguez de Francia instituted a regime of land distribution among peasants and middle-class laborers, though closely controlled by the state. Class and racial conflict would continue to shadow the new American nations long after independence.

Francisco Javier Alegre (1729–1788)

Francisco Javier Alegre was born in the province of Veracruz, New Spain, in 1729. Having studied law and philosophy in Puebla and Mexico City, Alegre entered the Society of Jesus in 1747, a community that proved capable of satisfying both his religious devotion and his intellectual ambition. Master of several languages, including Nahuatl, Alegre served as a teacher of grammar, theology, and philosophy at several locations, including Mexico City, Puebla, Merida, and even Havana, Cuba. As both teacher and preacher, he was notably supportive of fair treatment for Indians and African slaves.

Like FRANCISCO JAVIER CLAVIJERO and other Jesuits, Alegre was committed to scholasticism[1] as the primary mode of Catholic dogma, but he also produced commentaries on several contemporary philosophical doctrines prohibited by the Church, particularly the scientific discoveries that were changing Western thought, from the heliocentric understanding of the solar system to the law of gravity and the circulation of blood in the human body. Fearing that these radically new ideas would undermine

---

1 Scholasticism refers to the philosophic system that combined Aristotelian principles (especially logic) with Church doctrine. Originating in the late Middle Ages, scholasticism remained influential well into the nineteenth century.

biblical truth and Catholic orthodoxy, the Church tried to repress such teachings. However, the Jesuits, though unconditional in their support of the papacy, recognized that the suppression of science would ultimately decrease the relevance of Catholicism in a world that was undergoing rapid, multifaceted change. They evolved an approach of philosophical eclecticism, which combined the scholastic principles of deductive reasoning with modern experimentalism, allowing a selective and relatively open examination of new ideas while maintaining the integrity of basic church dogma. When extended to moral issues, eclecticism became casuistry, a process that allowed Jesuits to seek shades of meaning and to identify exceptions in dealing with supposedly fixed biblical beliefs and tenets. Morality became subject to interpretation, as each and every deed was analyzed to determine the circumstances that might render it morally acceptable.

Eclecticism required an enormous amount of knowledge—of theology, philosophy, science, and culture. In the Americas, where most Jesuits were themselves creoles and serving populations with large numbers of Indians, understanding non-European cultures was vital to their mission and teaching. Alegre—like fellow Mexican Jesuit FRANCISCO JAVIER CLAVIJERO—exemplified this kind of breadth, embracing both the erudition of Spain and Europe as well as firsthand experience of creole and native cultures. This comprehensive perspective was not always appreciated, in the mainland or in the colonies. But that view is central to Alegre's best-known text, *Historia de la Compañía de Jesús en Nueva España* [The History of the Society of Jesus in New Spain], which includes valuable details of daily life and culture in the Americas. Alegre had nearly finished this massive work in 1767, when the Jesuits were expelled from the Americas, and he was forced to leave his manuscript and notes behind. With the help of CLAVIJERO, Alegre later reconstructed his account from memory in Bologna, Italy, where he lived in exile until his death in 1788.

But Alegre also made a significant contribution to the Hispanic Baroque. Though this Counter-Reformation style was expressed differently by each European tradition, in Spain the Baroque drew on the paradox of a nation at once the richest in Europe—its wealth derived from reaping American treasure—and the poorest—as a result of continuing religious wars with the Netherlands and the Ottoman Empire, along with the failure to modernize its economy. Perfectly suited to that historic moment in Spanish culture, the Baroque combined splendor with deeply pessimistic attitudes, coupling the poignancy of life's ephemerality with an enthusiastic pleasure in the senses. The Spanish Baroque profoundly affected the arts in the Americas, an influence intensified in its adaptation by many Jesuits, whose institutional appreciation of paradox allowed writers like Alegre, HERNANDO DOMINGUEZ CAMARGO, JUAN DE ESPINOSA MEDRANO, CARLOS DE SIGÜENZA Y GÓNGORA, and Bernardo de Balbuena to excel in the style.

Though Alegre published several literary texts, including a short epic poem and a Latin translation of the *Iliad*, his primary contribution to the development of the Baroque was his translation of an influential poem by the French writer Nicholas Boileau. When the Bourbons came to power in Spain in 1700, neoclassicism was at its height, especially in France, where, as the Baroque influence waned, a revindication of classic (Greek and Roman) aesthetic principles began to dominate European art and thought. French neoclassical rhetoric was notorious for its rigor, and French standards were soon being applied to Spanish literature. Even revered authors like Lope de Vega, Góngora, and Cervantes were devalued as insufficiently classicist. But it was Boileau who most clearly articulated the strict notion of the French neoclassical in *L'Art poétique* [The Art of Poetry], published in 1674. Drawing on the classical models of Aristotle and Horace, Boileau's verse cantos established the rules for poetry that became admired and imitated by writers throughout Europe.

In 1737, Ignacio Luzán (1702–1754) developed standards for Spanish literature that were even more stringent than Boileau's. Disdainful of most writers of the Golden Age, Luzán was especially scornful of Góngora, whom he accused of having disfigured the national language. Though Luzán's *Poética* [Poetics] was very influential, Alegre viewed Luzán as an insensitive critic, rendering judgments that functioned to censor poetry rather than enrich it. To refute him, Alegre undertook his own translation of the first three cantos of Boileau's poem. Alegre actually adapts Boileau with the same freedom that the French poet employed in adapting Horace: using his own insights and considerable learning to transform Boileau's notions into an original poetics of his own. One of Alegre's most telling changes is the omission of Boileau's examples, often substituting Spanish texts instead. Alegre also adds to his "translated" text extensive footnotes, which frequently occupy more space than the original poem and allow Alegre to expand his reflections on the appropriate qualities of literary art.

Alegre thus poses an exceptional challenge to the tenets of French neoclassicism that dominated European aesthetics. In citing Góngora as an extraordinary lyric poet, perhaps the best in Spanish, Alegre further underlines the continuing relevance of the Baroque in Spanish America.

Surviving not merely as a style, but also as a mode of feeling and thought, a way of looking at the world, the Baroque persisted for the next two centuries, emerging most vividly in the twentieth-century revivals by JOSÉ LEZAMA LIMA and MARTÍN ADÁN.

The selection is from "Arte Poética de Boileau" in *Opúsculos inéditos latinos y castellanos del Padre Francisco Xavier Alegre* [Unpublished Latin and Castilian Novels of Father Francisco Xavier Alegre], edited by Joaquín García Icazbalceta (Mexico City: Imprenta de Francisco Díaz de León, 1889), 5–6. Rare Book collection, Latin American Library, Tulane University. Poem translated by Henry Sullivan; notes translated by Isabel Bastos and Marvin Liberman.

From Arte Poética de Boileau [Poetic Art by Boileau], translated by Francisco Javier Alegre (1774)

Canto I

To reach the verdant summit of Mt. Helicon
A foolhardy author does aspire in vain,
And does in vain lay claim
To gird his brow with crown of lushest laurel,
Despite the fact a kindly planet,
By imponderable influence,
From birth chose not to make a poet of him.
Captive and lonely in his limitations,
Pegasus for him is always tardy coming,
Apollo is always deaf to his imploring.
And Ye, therefore, whose hearts Apollo sets aflame,
Glorious darlings of the elusive Muses
And of an ageless fame,
Do not—taking your desire to be divinity—
Shackle yourselves down with such a perilous endeavor.
Consult your forces first
In very gradual fashion, and what your genius
May bear—be that waggish, grave or stern,
Tender, shy, austere or amorous.
The wise and sapient Author of all Nature,
With art and by design,
Distributes—without rancor—

Talents among the different writers.
Let Villegas paint an amorous flame;
Let jester Quevedo hone an epigram;
Let Garcilaso describe the shepherds,
The fountains and the meadows;
Of warlike arms and fame-reported lords
Let Camões sing, the Virgil of Portugal;
And as a rival of the Roman
Swan, among the nightingales of Andalusia,
Let Góngora praise the ruling might of Spain
From the French Pyrenees (note 7) to Atlantis of the Moors.

Note 7 (by Alegre)

This is Don Luis de Góngora's verse contained in the song to the Spanish Armada that the King Don Philip II sent against England, which starts like this:

Levanta, España, tu famosa diestra.
[Raise up O Spain, your splendid right hand.]

You will be surprised, no doubt, that I here call Góngora a rival of Horace and that I place his poetry as the exemplary Spanish lyric verse: the same Góngora who so many times you might have heard me say is one of the men with the worst taste [ever] produced by Spain. All of this is true. There is nothing more beautiful and sublime than Góngora when he is sensible in his writing, which occurs only rarely. There is nothing more chaotic, overblown and tiresome than Góngora when he is enraptured and vomits unrestrainedly:

The pride of heaven, seems
Upon the stars in sapphire fields to graze
. . .
Or sucks the effluence of the sky, or sips
Saliva from the silent stars that drips

—and a thousand other expressions that he is full of. The most famous of his works are the worst; I mean to say *The Solitudes*, *Galatea* and his seven comedies, a poetic genre in which he is completely hopeless. In *The Solitudes* he sought obscurity in the most trivial of things, using expressions like the ones I have just quoted—pompous and sonorous yet without substance; as Sophocles said about someone else, he is like a man who opens his big mouth and stupidly inflates his cheeks only to blow into a tiny fife. *Galatea* is a little more moderate, but he still errs a lot. He has hundreds of sonnets, love and heroic songs, ballads and burlesque *letrillas*.[2] All of them are full of bad things. Nevertheless, six or eight of his sonnets, two or three of his songs and some felicitous expressions here and there in his very numerous works reveal a sublime ingenuity parallel with or even superior to what we find in this genre by the Greek and Latin poets [. . .] I could mention a hundred of these places in which this Cordovan poet infinitely exceeded the ancients. [. . .] Some ponder that to be a poet is to say things in a way that is not understandable. If this were so, Homer and Virgil would be the most unfortunate poets in the world. Poetic enthusiasm is not a disorder, but an elevation of fantasy.

Francisco Javier Clavijero (1731–1787)

Francisco Javier Clavijero was born in Veracruz, the main port of New Spain, in 1731. The son of a Spanish official and a creole mother, he became familiar with several native cultures of Mexico, as the family moved around the region. He joined the Jesuits in 1748 and, at the seminary in Mexico City, became a classmate of FRANCISCO JAVIER ALEGRE. After his ordination, Clavijero taught at the School of San Gregorio, an institution that was dedicated to the education of Indians. He also began to study pre-Hispanic cultures, especially fascinated by the codices collected by CARLOS DE SIGÜENZA Y GÓNGORA. Clavijero's work was facilitated by his fluency in Nahuatl, the native tongue in the Valley of Mexico and throughout the pre-conquest period of Aztec expansionism. Clavijero's superiors, evidently displeased by his dedication to these early texts, transferred him in 1764 to Puebla, where he continued to teach and work with the native peoples of the region. After three years, Clavijero was sent to act as substitute teacher in the city of Valladolid (present-day Morelia) and then to Guadalajara. Unsatisfied with all these assignments, he eventually asked to be sent back to Mexico City; but in 1767 the Jesuits were expelled from all the territories ruled by the King of Spain.

The order for the expulsion was carried out with great swiftness. The Jesuits were not granted time or permission to take personal items into exile, much less books or manuscripts. Like his comrade, ALEGRE, whose collected materials on the history of the Jesuits were left behind, Clavijero was forced to abandon much of the research and manuscripts he

---

2   Letrillas are poetic compositions composed of short verses. [Trans. note.]

had accumulated, especially during his stay at the School of San Gregorio. But also like ALEGRE, Clavijero eventually managed a painstaking reconstruction of that research in order to write his most important book, *Historia antigua de México* [The History of Mexico]. Written in Spanish and then translated into Italian, the ten-volume history was published in 1780 in Italy, where Clavijero died seven years later.

While in exile, many had to take refuge in the Pontifical States (present-day central Italy); most Jesuits received a meager pension from the king, barely sufficient for their needs. But in spite of having to work to support themselves, these men often had time to miss the nations they had left behind, places made more precious by distance and the impossibility of returning. Even after the Society of Jesus was suppressed in 1773, its members could, of course, become secular priests and return home, but very few did so; indeed, most Jesuits remained faithful to the Society even after it ceased to exist in any official sense.

Nostalgia was not, however, the sole stimulus for the astonishing wealth of intellectual work carried out by the Jesuits in Italy. One incentive was the cold reception they received from their Italian colleagues and the general prejudice against the exiled Jesuits. Associated with Spain, a country generally regarded as backward throughout Europe, and in exile from—and often natives of—Hispanic America, a region considered synonymous with barbarism and ignorance, the Hispanic Jesuits were perceived to be unsophisticated as individuals and inferior as scholars. The outpouring of manuscripts by these exiles was in many ways a deliberate effort to contradict such negative images, both of themselves personally and of Hispanic culture in general.

Translated from the Italian by Charles Cullen, Clavijero's *The History of Mexico* is emblematic of this larger Jesuit effort to vindicate their native region and its culture, but it also underlines the shift to an emergent nationalism. Clavijero provides valuable details about the history and civilization of the Aztecs, which he generally views quite positively. Clavijero wanted to write a balanced account, validating the contributions of both indigenous groups and the Spanish in the creation of new countries like the viceroyalty of New Spain. But in his support of native peoples, Clavijero was departing significantly from contemporary creole perspectives on the history of New Spain and thus—albeit unconsciously—laying the groundwork for the emergent Mexican nation. For while creoles in the era of independence certainly appreciated the achievements of their pre-Hispanic ancestors and even venerated historic figures like Moctezuma or Cuauhtemoc, they rarely viewed the living heirs of those remarkable people with anything but contempt. In many other writers, such as SIGÜENZA Y GÓNGORA, the creole paradox of marveling at the cultures of the past while despising their descendants is evident. But Clavijero's work subtly challenges that paradox even as it illuminates its sources.

The selection is from *The History of Mexico. Collected from Spanish and Mexican Historians, from Manuscripts, and Ancient Paintings of the Indians. Illustrated by Charts, and other Copper Plates. To which are added, Critical Dissertations on the Land, the Animals, and Inhabitants of México.* Translated from the original Italian by Charles Cullen, Esq., 2 volumes (London: Printed for G. G. Robinson, 1787), 83, 172. Special Collections and Archives, J. Edgar and Louise S. Monroe Library, Loyola University New Orleans.

From **The History of Mexico (1787)**

Book II

Of the Toltecas, Chechemecas, Acolhuas, Olmecas, and other Nations that inhabited the Country of Anahuac before the Mexicans. The expedition of the Aztecas, or Mexicans, from their Native Country of Aztlan. The Events of their Journey into the Country of Anahuac; and their Settlements in Chapoltepec and Colhuacan. The Foundation of Mexico and Tlatelolco. Inhuman Sacrifice of a Colhuan Girl.

Section II. The great civilization of the Toltecas

The Toltecas were the most celebrated people of Anahuac, for their superior civilization, and skill in the arts; whence, in after ages, it has been common to distinguish the most remarkable artists, in an honourable manner, by the appellation of Toltecas. They always lived in society, collected into cities, under the government of kings, and regular laws. They were not very warlike, and less turned to the exercise of arms than to the cultivation of the arts. The nations that have succeeded them, have acknowledged themselves indebted to the Toltecas for their knowledge of the culture of grain, cotton, pepper, and other most useful fruits. Nor did they only practice those arts which are dictated by necessity, but those also which minister to luxury. They had the art of casting gold and silver, and melting them in whatever forms they pleased, and acquired the greatest reputation from the cutting of all kinds of gems: but nothing, to us, raises their character so high as their having been the inventors, or at least the reformers of that system of the arrangement of time, which was adopted by all the civilized nations of Anahuac; and which, as we shall see afterwards, implies numerous observations, and a wonderfully correct astronomy.

Cav. Boturini,[3] upon the faith of the ancient histories of the Toltecas, says, that observing in their own country of *Huehuetlapallan,* how the solar year exceeded the civil one by which they reckoned, about six hours, they regulated it by interposing the intercalary day once in the four years; which they did, more than one hundred years before the Christian era. He says besides, that in the year 660 under the reign of *Ixtlalcuechahuac,* in Tula, a celebrated astronomer called *Huematzin,* assembled, by the king's consent, all the wise men of the nation; and with them painted that famous book called *Teoamoxtli* or Divine Book, in which were represented, in very plain figures, the origin of the Indians, their dispersion after the confusion of tongues at Babel, their journey in Asia, their first settlements upon the Continent of America, the founding of the kingdom of Tula, and their progress till that time. There were described the heavens, the planets, the constellations, the Toltecan calendar with its cycles, the mythological transformations, in which were included their moral philosophy, and the mysteries of their deities concealed by hieroglyphics from common understandings, together with all that appertained to their religion and manners. The above mentioned author adds, that that eclipse of the sun which happened at the death of our Saviour, was marked in their paintings, in the *year Seven Tochtli;*[4] and that some learned Spaniards, well acquainted with the history of the paintings of the Toltecas, having compared their chronology with ours, found that they reckoned from the creation of the world to the birth of Christ, five thousand one hundred and ninety-nine years, which is exactly the computation of the Roman calendar.

Whatever may be in these things mentioned by Boturini, upon which I leave the prudent reader to form his own judgment, there cannot be a doubt, with those who have studied the history of that people, that the Toltecas had a clear and distinct knowledge of the universal deluge, of the confusion of tongues, and of the dispersion of the people; and even pretended to give the

---

3   Lorenzo Boturini (1702–1753) was an Italian nobleman who lived eight years in New Spain, collecting documents of indigenous cultures and becoming a devotee of the Virgin of Guadalupe. After his arrest by the authorities, his valuable collections were scattered. His *Sketch of a general History of New Spain, founded upon a great Number of Figures, Symbols, Characters, Hieroglyphics, Hymns, and Manuscripts of Indian Authors, lately discovered* was published in Madrid in 1746.

4   All those who have studied carefully the history of the nations of Anahuac, know very well that those people were accustomed to mark eclipses, comets, and other phenomena of the heavens, in their paintings. Upon reading Boturini I set about comparing the Toltecan years with ours, and I found the 34th year of Christ, or 30th of our era but I did this merely to satisfy my own curiosity, and I do not mean either to confirm or give credit to the things told us by that author. [Original note.]

names of their first ancestors who were divided from the rest of the families upon that universal dispersion. It is equally certain as we shall show in another place, however incredible it may appear to the critics of Europe, who are accustomed to look upon the Americans as all equally barbarous, that the Mexicans and all the other civilized nations of Anahuac regulated their civil year according to the solar, by means of intercalary days, in the same manner as the Romans did after the Julian arrangement; and that this accuracy was owing to the skill of the Toltecas. Their religion was idolatrous, and they appear by their history to have been the inventors of the greatest part of the mythology of the Mexicans, but we do not know that they practiced those barbarous and bloody sacrifices which became afterwards so common among the other nations. [...]

*   *   *

Book IV

Acts of the King Nezahualcóyotl, Marriage of Nezahualcóyotl with a princess of Tacuba, Inundation of Mexico

Section IV. Judicious Regulations of King Nezahualcóyotl

The kingdom of Acolhuacan was not then in such good order and regulation as Techotlala had left it. The dominion of the Tepanecas, and the revolutions which had happened in the last twenty years had changed the government of the people, weakened the force of the laws, and caused a number of their customs to fall into disuse. Nezahualcóyotl,[5] who, besides the attachment which he had to his nation was gifted with uncommon prudence, made such regulations and changes in the state, that in a little time it became more flourishing than it had ever been under any of his predecessors. He gave a new form to the councils which had been established by his grandfather. He conferred offices on persons the fittest for them. One council determined causes purely civil, in which, among others, five lords who had proved constantly faithful to him in his adversity, assisted. Another council judge of criminal causes, at which the two princes his brothers, men of high integrity, presided. The council of war was composed of the most distinguished military characters, among whom Icotihuacan, son-in-law to the king and also one of the thirteen nobles of the kingdom, had the first rank. The treasury-board consisted of the king's majordomos, and the first merchants of the court. The principal majordomos who took charge of the tributes and other parts of the royal income, were three in number. Societies similar to academies were instituted for poetry,

---

5   Nezahualcóyotl (c. 1431–1472), poet and philosopher, was king of Texcoco, located east of the Aztec city of Tenochtitlán (present-day Mexico City).

astronomy, music, painting, history, and the art of divination, and he invited the most celebrated professors of his kingdom to his court, who met on certain days to communicate their discoveries and inventions; and for each of these arts and sciences, although little advanced, schools were appropriated. To accommodate the mechanic branches, he divided the city of Texcoco into thirty odd divisions, and to every branch assigned a district; so that the goldsmiths inhabited one division, the sculptors another, the weavers another, &c. To cherish religion he raised new temples, created ministers for the worship of their gods, gave them houses, and appointed them revenues for their support, and the expences which were necessary at festivals and sacrifices. To augment the splendor of his court he constructed noble edifices both within and without the city, and planted new gardens and woods, which were in preservations many years after the conquest, and show still some traces of former magnificence.

Juan Benito Díaz de Gamarra y Dávalos (1745–1783)

After the expulsion of the Jesuits from Spain and its overseas territories in 1767, many less prominent religious orders quickly took over their role in higher education, often adopting as their own the Jesuits' pedagogical methods and the principles for which they were best known—and most often criticized. At the end of the eighteenth century, eclecticism, casuistry, and probabilism dominated thought and education in Hispanic America as much as if the Jesuits had never left. This lingering influence in the colonies has often been considered to have had a reactionary effect on Spanish American thought, particularly with respect to the development of independence. But as in the case of the Jesuit Juan Pablo Viscardo's revolutionary letter written in England or the work of the Mexican scholar and priest Juan Benito Díaz de Gamarra, the relationship proves to have been more complicated.

Not a Jesuit himself, Gamarra was born in Zamora, present-day Michoacán, and studied in Mexico City, where he joined the Oratorians of Saint Philip Neri in 1764. He quickly rose to prominence in the order and earned a doctorate at the University of Pisa before returning to teach at the university in San Miguel el Grande (San Miguel de Allende). His best-known work, *On the Elements of Modern Philosophy* (1774), was originally written in Latin as a compendium for his students. In this and in his other works, Gamarra became an influential figure in advancing enlightenment ideas throughout New Spain.

The excerpt here demonstrates how Gamarra deals with one of the defining debates of the scientific revolution: whether the universe was geocentric or heliocentric. As a guardian of scripture, the Catholic Church was deeply invested in these deliberations. Beginning in the sixteenth century, the Office of the Index prohibited any uncensored publication defending heliocentrism. Of course, many Catholic thinkers were convinced that the new theory offered a better explanation of planetary phenomena than the Ptolemaic account, and many believers faced an intellectual conflict. The astronomer Tycho Brahe tried to reconcile these theories, proposing that all planets circled the sun, except the earth, which was at the center of the sun's orbit. Though Brahe's ingenious explanation made many astronomic phenomena more comprehensible, it also posited an absurd composition of the planetary system.

For the Jesuits, who controlled much of the educational system, such absurdities and contradictions were actually irrelevant, because all theories were simply hypothetical. Since none of these systems could be proven and no probabilistic solution applied, an eclectic position could be adopted, allowing all these varied hypotheses to be considered as intellectual possibilities. The Church remained officially entrenched in its antiscientific posture, but, despite such unconventional teachings, the Jesuits' general resistance to liberalism sufficiently confirmed their orthodoxy. By Gamarra's time—the 1780s—books that defended heliocentrism were at least no longer listed in the official *Index of Prohibited Books*, although Copernicus's revolutionary text of 1543 and earlier arguments for heliocentrism remained forbidden until 1835.

Gamarra's presentation of these theories—and much of his work as an educator and philosopher—reveals quite clearly the persistence of Jesuit ideas in Spanish America. Considered the first Mexican philosopher of enlightened rationality, Gamarra incorporates a fundamentally Jesuit approach in his explanations, particularly in applying eclecticism in his efforts to reconcile a Catholic orthodoxy with the tenets of modern science. Moreover, by articulating what is essentially an independent Spanish American/ Mexican philosophical perspective, Gamarra builds an intellectual framework for the movements toward political independence that soon followed.

Implicit in that independent perspective is another legacy of the Jesuits, their support for the rights of the people. Despite their allegiance to traditional hierarchies, the Jesuits consistently defended the principle that royal power depended on the consent of its subjects; kings could not even abdicate (as Carlos IV and Fernando VII had done) without the permission of the people or the courts. The Jesuits' steady support of the rights of creoles and mestizos and Indians thus helped to shape a specifically Spanish American perspective on independence, one that also drew on Enlightenment principles that were being promoted by Gamarra and others. Gamarra's writings thus constitute a significant bridge between the resilient traditions of Jesuit education and thought and the radical ideas of political independence that were finally about to be put into practice throughout Spanish America. Not coincidentally, it was precisely where Gamarra taught (San Miguel and its environs) that the movement for New Spain's independence began in 1810.

The selection is from *Elementos de filosofía moderna: Presentación, traducción y notas de Bernabé Navarro*, in *Filósofos mexicanos del siglo XVIII*, edited by Mauricio Beuchot; translated by Nathan Henne (Mexico: UNAM, 1995), 179–83.

From Elementos de filosofía moderna (1774) [On the Elements of Modern Philosophy], sections 732–741

On the Composition of the World

Briefly Expounding on World Systems[6]

732. To philosophers, the term "system" here refers to the order or arrangement of the universe and its principal parts as a way of explaining celestial movements and phenomena. Over the years, in both astronomy and physics, three such systems have been promulgated and they are still in vogue today. Consequently, I shall now expound briefly on each of these three systems.

733. I. The Ptolemaic system is named after Claudius Ptolemy. His system places the Earth at the center of the universe with everything revolving around it: first the air, then fire, and then he posits seven solid heavens—one for each of the

---

6 "Mundo" or "world" in this context is not simply the earth and its atmosphere. Rather, for Gamarra, "mundo" refers to the solar system and its outer galaxies, imagined from an earth-centered perspective. The Ptolemaic universe is not, of course, a solar system but a "World System"— a phrase commonly used in contemporary economic theory, where it has a completely different meaning. [Trans. note.]

planets—in concentric rings around the Earth. Saturn moves in the concentric ring farthest from the earth, Jupiter in the second farthest, Mars in the third, the Sun in the fourth, Venus in the fifth, Mercury in the sixth, and the Moon in the seventh (or that closest to the Earth). Finally, above all of these circles he places the firmament containing the fixed stars, which he called *primer móvil*, (first mover) because he believed that, when this firmament moved, the orbits of the inferior planets were dragged along with it in the space of 23 hours, 56 minutes, and 4 seconds.

734. II. The Tychonic system was constructed by Tycho Brahe. He leaves the Earth at the center of the universe, encircled by its immobile atmosphere; but, around this atmosphere, he situates first the Moon, then the Sun; next, closer to the Sun, which he considers the center of the remaining planets, he puts Mercury, Venus, Mars, and then Jupiter with its four satellites, discovered by Galileo, and finally Saturn with its two satellites; above all these, he added the firmament, which is also concentric to the Earth.

735. III. The Copernican system derived its name from Nicolas Copernicus, who spent thirty years figuring out how to illustrate his hypothesis. According to him, the sun is located—immobile—in the center of the system, around which moves Mercury, then Venus; he maintains that these two planets are followed by the Earth, which also orbits around the Sun while the Moon spins around the Earth; then comes Mars, then Jupiter, and finally Saturn; but beyond all of the planets, and also at a nearly incalculable distance, he puts the sphere of the fixed stars, absolutely deprived of any movement whatsoever. He adds to each of the planets—excluding the Sun, which effectively removes it from the category of planets altogether—a periodic movement governed by the Zodiac, so that the planets pass through each of its signs.

736. To the Earth, Copernicus assigns a triple movement: first is its rotation around its own axis, from the west to the east, which, for Copernicans, explains the succession of night and day, since, given this motion, the Sun appears to move from the east to the west, while the Earth always presents a different part of its surface to the Sun to be illuminated. Copernicus called this movement diurnal because it is completed in the interval of one day. The second movement of the Earth is its huge orbit around the Sun within the ecliptic, which Copernicus calls periodic; following this path the Earth moves through each sign of the Zodiac so that the Sun seems to us to be located in the sign that it covers, explaining how, when the Earth is actually located in the boreal signs, the Sun appears to be located in the austral signs, and vice versa; he calls this motion *annual* because it occurs in the space of one year.

737. Copernicus also adds a third motion, the parallel movement, by which the Earth's own axis, as it revolves around the Sun, appears to be parallel to the axis of the solar system at one point but at other points appears to be parallel only to its own axis; through this motion, the Copernicans explain the phenomena of the succession of the seasons. However, to explain this fact they also posit an inclination of the Earth's axis in relation to the plane of the ecliptic, in relation to which it forms an angle of 66 degrees and 30 minutes. "In this age of ours [says the illustrious theologian Jacinto Serry] many gentlemen who are renowned for their piety and religiosity, even some who are eminent cardinals, permit themselves to believe along the liberal lines of Galileo and Copernicus, as long as they do not assert that it is a certain and indubitable system, but rather a hypothesis, which they consider appropriate for use in astronomy, as was put forth in the Decree of the Sacred Congregation of the Inquisition in the year 1620." [And this is where Copernicus left it.]

Critical Analysis of [These Explanations] of the Solar System

738. This is what I believe: the Copernican Solar System, seen simply as a hypothesis to explain the movements and phenomena of the stars, seems to me more adequate than either the Ptolemaic or the Tychonic one. First, let's demonstrate this in general terms. In effect, Copernicus' hypothesis does not run counter to either physics or astronomy as the Ptolemaic system does. After all, in the Ptolemaic system, who could possibly understand how the outer ring of the firmament would drag all the inferior spheres from the East to the West, while at the same time, these spheres appear to move in the opposite direction every day, from the West to the East, through the signs of the Zodiac? In fact, if the surfaces that touch each other where these different spheres meet—that is, the convex surface of the inferior sphere and the concave surface of the superior sphere—are smooth, then the superior sphere will not cause the inferior one to move, at least to the degree that the inferior one would spin without simply being dragged along with it; on the other hand, if these surfaces are rough and the particles that stick out interlock, then clearly they would all produce one and the same motion, which would apply to both the superior spheres and the inferior ones, as Gassendi rightly argues.

739. That the Ptolemaic system coincides even less with astronomical observations is demonstrated quite clearly by the related phenomena. It has been confirmed that Mercury and Venus sometimes appear to the side of the Sun and sometimes they appear above it. Now, according to Ptolemy's hypothesis, these planets should always appear beneath the Sun and closer to

it. Moreover, Ptolemy's placement of the fixed stars is disproportionate, with all of them attached to only one surface, when it is clear to astronomers that the stars are situated on different planes, some farther away than others.

740. Second: The Copernican hypothesis is more orderly [than the other two systems] and ties together both the place and the order of the heavenly bodies in a more harmonious way; in the Copernican system none of the primary planets cuts through the orbit of another, as happens in Tycho's system; what's more, the Copernican system requires that all the planets orbit around the same center, that is, the Sun, another point that differs from the Tychonic system. In addition, Copernicus' hypothesis, by attributing movement to the Earth, while the Sun and the fixed stars stay in place, is much simpler, explaining the cyclic phenomena with fewer principles than the Tychonic hypothesis: in the Tychonic system, all of the heavenly bodies in the skies, except the Earth, are all put into motion, which, incidentally, would mean that each one carries out its revolution around the Earth in 24 hours, such that they would be moving at an almost unbelievable speed. Given these points, the Copernican hypothesis is preferable.

741. For these reasons, the Copernican system is much easier and much more useful for carrying out astronomical observations and demonstrations than the Tychonian one: in fact, even Tychonian astronomers borrow the Copernican hypothesis to carry out their own observations and to put together their charts. Furthermore, as the illustrious Serry observes, the Copernican system was even used by the Church itself at one point as the basis for correcting the Roman calendar.

In Context | Mexico City: The Venice of the New World

"By comparison with the major cities of Europe, the status enjoyed by Mexico City—the capital of the Kingdom of New Spain—is a matter of common knowledge; and if in sheer size the great metropolises may have an advantage over Mexico City, it is fair to say that—in beauty, symmetry, geographical location and wealth—they do not outstrip her and that there are few cities which can even come close." (See map 4.1, 162–63.) Only a year after this map was printed in Madrid, the famous Spanish traveler Antonio de Ulloa visited Mexico City (in 1777) and provided this appreciative assessment. For many, Mexico City—despite repeated flooding—remained the "Venice of the New World," a moniker it has retained since the beginning of the seventeenth century.

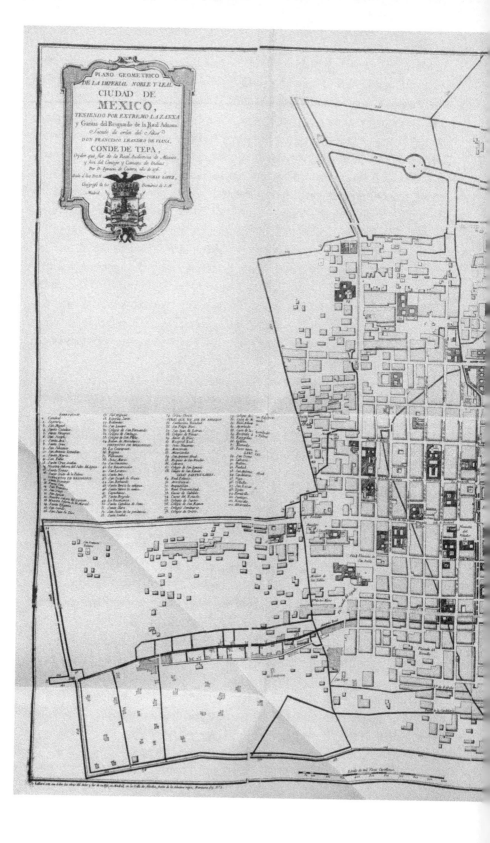

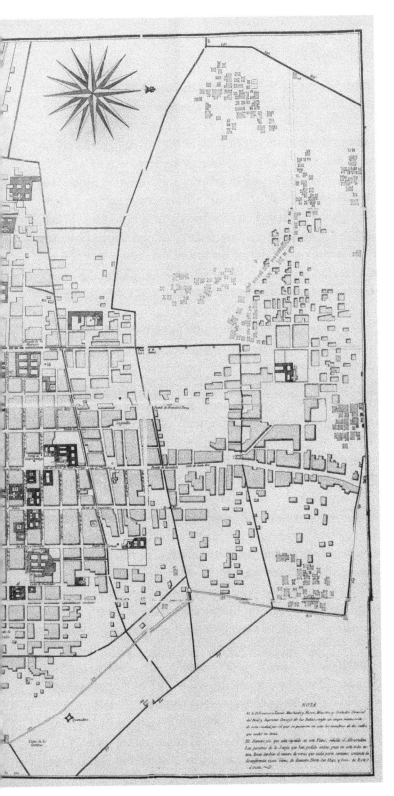

Map 4.1. Map of Mexico City in 1776. From Francisco De Solano, *La ciudad de México en el año de 1777: Según el testimonio inédito de Antonio de Ulloa* (Mexico City: Centro de Estudios de Historia de México, 1980), appendix.

Juan de Velasco (1727–1792)

Born in Riobamba in present-day Ecuador on January 6, 1727, Juan de Velasco was a man whose life and work were essentially indistinguishable. Velasco entered the Society of Jesus at sixteen and was ordained a priest in 1753 in Quito. Trained in the humanities, he taught throughout Ecuador and Colombia and, since he spoke Quechua, often acted as confessor to the Indians. During his travels, he began gathering information for a book commissioned by his superiors, which became his magnum opus: a history of the Kingdom of Quito—today's Ecuador and parts of Colombia. When the Jesuits were exiled from the Americas in 1767, Velasco went to Faenza, Italy, where he spent the remainder of his life painstakingly completing his three-part masterpiece: *Historia Natural; Historia Antigua*; and *Historia Moderna*. The first two volumes were published in 1789, but Velasco died in 1792 before the final volume could be approved.

The History of the Kingdom of Quito was only published in Ecuador for the first time in 1841, but its timely appearance made it seminal for the emergent new nation, representing an early articulation of the country's historic integrity. Velasco's text also represents a pioneering achievement in establishing the connections between natural and social history, a link made more famous by the botanist and explorer, Alexander von Humboldt (1769–1859), after his five-year exploration (1799–1804) of parts of Hispanic America. Velasco published several other notable works, including a chronicle of the Jesuits in Quito and a vocabulary of Peruvian and Incan languages.

The tripartite division of Velasco's *Kingdom of Quito* actually belies the complex correlations that inform its intent. Part 1 describes the natural and physical aspects of the region; part 2 traces the history of the Shyris, the kings of Quito before their conquest by the Incas, to the death of Atahualpa in 1533; and part 3 recounts the history of the Spanish conquest and its government. Anticipating Humboldt's arguments by nearly fifteen years, Velasco recognized that the descriptions of the natural environment were intrinsic to understanding the territory's different cultures. For early Andean peoples particularly, human history remains inextricably related to natural history—indeed, they are one and the same. Such interrelationships between natural and social history characterize these texts as well.

The selection here, from part 3, highlights another aspect of Velasco's sense of historiography, its dependence on narration rather than chronology. For Velasco, particular events cannot be understood without an appreciation for the totality of history (time) and space as well as their relationships to and among each other. Accordingly, he chooses to relate particularly notable events; keenly aware of the limits of mere chronology, he also provides narrative themes that assist the reader in grasping the complex totality of history that he wants to convey. As he observes near the end of his prologue, readers must not misinterpret as dogmatic truth "the Venerable [. . .] miracles, revelations, prophecies, sainthood, martyrdom, and other such things" that he includes with various historic episodes and physical details. Obedient to the rules of the Inquisition, Velasco reminds us that he is simply reporting the rich composite of human facts that constitute the full history of this remarkable kingdom.

In conceiving of the Kingdom of Quito, his place of origin, his "mother land," as a distinctive social and political entity, Velasco makes a significant contribution to the development of nationhood in the Americas. As a creole aristocrat, he continued to perceive that new nation in the context of the Spanish empire, not as an independent country. And though Velasco died in exile, far away from the Kingdom of Quito, his life's work was, in fact, to make that kingdom a reality.

The selection is from *Historia del Reino de Quito en la América meridional* (Caracas, Venezuela: Biblioteca Ayacucho, 1981), volume 3 [1789], 247–48, 254. Translated by Nathan Henne. [The capitalization patterns of the archaic Spanish in the original are followed in the text. Trans. note.]

From Historia del Reino de Quito en la América Meridional (1789) [The History of the Kingdom of Quito]

Prologue and Presuppositions for This Last Volume of History

1. More than two and a half centuries ago the emerald, formerly the ancient insignia of the Kings of Quito, first added its precious luster to the Spanish Crown. The first eighteen years after the Spanish conquered this kingdom, that is, from 1533 to 1550, are already included in the Ancient History. The events that followed, from 1551 up until the present time, are the subject of its Modern History. It would require many volumes, after stirring up and shaking off the dust from the archives of the Kingdom, to write about a period as long as these 238 years and cover it completely: a task that would be impossible on the one hand, and of very little interest on the other. My intent here will be to put down only the principal, and most notable, acts and events that I can describe. The hardest part in achieving this task is not [*as one might imagine] figuring out how to boil these events and acts down to a succinct account,

but rather figuring out how to make them less tiresome for the reader. If all of the diverse events that happened at the same time are separated out from each other, it becomes very confusing, and the chronology of the relationship among these events is lost; it would then become necessary to repeat the same thing many times, which is remarkably tedious. If, on the other hand, a rigorous general chronology of events is used to structure the account, the narrative themes themselves are interrupted at every step, causing perhaps even more annoyance on the reader's part.

2. Since both of these obstacles are inevitable in the expansive seas of History, and since, moreover, it is necessary here to provide a brief description of the Provinces of the Kingdom in their present form, I have decided not to follow a strict overarching order, but rather to organize the narrative according to the internal chronology of the particular province being described. In this way, I will relate the main events that happened in each of the provinces according to that province's particular chronology, to the degree that this is possible. This is the only way that the reader will be able to see clearly how each of these provinces was at the beginning, in the times between, and at present, without suffering tedious interruptions. What is more, when I say "at the present time," I do not mean right up to the year I am writing this account but only up to 1767, which is the year I left that Kingdom; the truth is that since then, I have been able to secure only little isolated bits of news, and even these only rarely. So from here forth, the Modern History of Quito, as covered in this the third and final part, is reduced to a succinct historical, geographical, political, and ecclesiastical description of each of its Provinces, from 1551 up to recent times. In order to best understand these descriptions, it will be necessary for the reader to make some presuppositions about more general points.

I

3. Concerning the political and ecclesiastical divisions of government that have been in effect and continue to be in effect in the Kingdoms of Peru: Almost all of southern America which is under the dominion of Spain has been broadly, and somewhat improperly, called the Kingdoms of Peru, excepting only the Islands of Barlovento [the Antilles]. Since these islands were the first ones conquered, they have kept their own names and their separate governance both politically and ecclesiastically. Politically, they are governed by the Royal Audience of Santo Domingo, whose president is the Governor and the Captain General of all those islands. Ecclesiastically, they are governed by the Archbishop of that same island, Santo Domingo, who is called the Primate of all America, and who has three Bishops under his authority: the Bishop of

the Island of Cuba, the Bishop of the Island of Puerto Rico, and the Bishop of Caracas on the coast of the continent's mainland.

4. All of the other Kingdoms, such as the Kingdom of Tierra Firme, the New Kingdom of Granada, Quito, the New Kingdom of Castilla, the New Kingdom of Toledo, Tucumán, Paraguay, Buenos Aires and Chile were called—some properly and others improperly—the Kingdoms of Perú because they fell under the higher governance of one Viceroy, who was called the Viceroy of Peru and who resided in Lima, which was the Capital of the New Kingdom of Granada for 185 years following the Conquest. The difficulty of one person's being responsible for such a vast dominion, especially during times of war with foreign powers, made it necessary to create another Viceroyalty in the New Kingdom of Granada, whose new Viceroy resided in the Capital City of Santa Fe. However, since this new Kingdom, due to its poverty, was unable to contribute the necessary financial resources for the subsistence of a Viceroy, the Court ordered, as a corrective measure, the dissolution of the Royal Audiences of Quito and of Panama, which were judged to be less necessary, in order to allocate the financial resources of their Colonial Judges to the Viceroy of Santa Fe. This plan was put into effect in 1718, and the seat of the Viceroyalty was filled by the Honorable Sr. D. Jorge de Villalouga, who had been the Governor of what was then the province of Callao in Lima and who had also been the General of the armies of Peru up until that time.

*   *   *

VII

21. One clarification I must make about this part of this History: There are times when one is recording a history like this that it is necessary to grant certain people the title of "the Venerable" and at other times it may be necessary to speak of miracles, revelations, prophecies, sainthood, martyrdom, and other such matters, I need to clarify, in order to comply with the Decrees of the Holy Papal Apostolate, that I myself do not put my faith in, nor should anyone else put any more faith in these events than are merited by a strictly human, always fallible faith in the truth of whatever I have written in this work concerning such matters; in all these things I submit myself in complete obedience to the Decrees of Pope Urban VIII and the rest of the other Holy Popes, to the Office of the Holy Inquisition, and to correction of the one and only Holy Roman Catholic Church, as her true son.

Eugenio de Santa Cruz y Espejo (1747–1795)

Eugenio de Santa Cruz y Espejo was a native of Quito, born to a Quechua father and mixed-race mother. Though not technically a creole, Espejo exemplifies the intellectual and cultural contradictions that shaped creole culture, particularly at the end of the eighteenth century when the desire for independence from Spain became increasingly vehement.

Espejo's early training was from his father, a medical assistant at the hospital in Quito. Medicine was not a particularly prestigious profession in this era, but Espejo studied the most recent methods available and received degrees in both medicine and law in 1772. He was especially concerned about issues of public health and sought to promote his own sophisticated understanding of hygiene to combat smallpox and other diseases. But Espejo's greatest contribution to Spanish American thought was his critique of contemporary education and its debilitating effects on the citizenry. Two of his most important works, *El Nuevo Luciano de Quito* (1779) [The New Lucian of Quito] and *Marco Porcio Catón* (1780), sharply condemned the Jesuit legacy of an outmoded pedagogy and thought.

Though Espejo himself had received a Jesuit education, he came to believe that the Jesuits' teaching methods and their reliance on scholasticism resulted in knowledge that was both shallow and useless in the modern world of the Enlightenment. But while Espejo adopted a contemporary rationalist stance, he employed very conservative and orthodox Catholic arguments to critique the Jesuit concepts of eclecticism, probabilism, and casuistry. By quoting the *Lettres provinciales* (1656–57) [Provincial Letters] of Blaise Pascal, for example, Espejo praised the Jansenists,[7] a group condemned by the Pope as heretical for their extreme orthodoxy. Urging reforms and more enlightened perspectives, Espejo thus ironically employed deeply conservative arguments to undermine the Jesuit practices he considered unsuited to modern education.

Like GAMARRA's in New Spain, Espejo's work testifies to the continuing influence of Jesuit education in Latin America, even after the expulsion and suppression of the Order. But his writings also manifest how resistance to the Jesuits could lead to positions and ideas that advanced the cause of independence. Though Espejo died in 1795, many of his friends played

---

7   Jansenism was a theological movement within the Catholic Church that opposed free will and argued that salvation was entirely dependent on divine grace. The proximity of these doctrines to Calvinism made them inimical to the Jesuits. At the beginning of the eighteenth century, the Jansenists were condemned by the Catholic Church but survived clandestinely.

key roles in the struggles for independence in Nueva Granada (today's Colombia) as well as in Quito just a decade later.

Espejo himself was deeply committed to improving the lives of his countrymen, working for economic as well as educational reforms and recommending public sanitation to combat disease. As a member of Quito's Sociedad Patriótica (Patriotic Society), an international association formed to promote intellectual and economic development, Espejo helped to found the city's first newspaper. After the group was dissolved by the king, Espejo was arrested in 1795, accused of conspiring against Spanish authority and of having praised the French Revolution as "being in accord with God's law and with natural reason." He died within the year from the dysentery he acquired in prison.

A figure of contradiction—religiously conservative and intellectually progressive, a native of the Americas with European ideas—as well as a man of great accomplishment, Espejo is remembered for his profound sense of irony as well as for his talent for "Platonic dialogue" as a rhetorical technique. His most important works use this mode, allowing ideas to confront each other, refuting or confirming themselves.

In Espejo's dedication to the ideals of freedom and contentment for his people, his work can be compared (likely to his great annoyance) to many Jesuit projects in the Americas, such as the efforts of Juan Pablo Viscardo y Guzmán, who worked in London in the 1790s, trying to convince the British to assist South American movements toward independence. The similarity of the political and social goals of these men and their very different methods and moral positions underline the many conflicting threads that defined Hispanic culture at the end of the eighteenth century. The selection is from *Obra Educativa: El nuevo Luciano de Quito* (1779), edited by Philip L. Astuto (Caracas, Venezuela: Biblioteca Ayacucho, 1981), 96–99. Translated by Isabel Bastos and Marvin Liberman.

From Obra Educativa: El nuevo Luciano de Quito (1779) [Works on Education: The New Lucian of Quito]

Dr. Mera.—Very well, I have caught you there. Your honor has judged the rule of fasting satisfied after contenting the belly with that noblest and most nutritious concoction, which is chocolate.

Dr. Murillo.—I'm appalled that your honor would talk like this, having belonged to the Society of Jesus, where there was great fondness for this magnificent beverage, and where it was endorsed by all the most learned individuals, the greatest moralists in the entire world, who added that it was lawful to take it *toties quoties* [as many times as one would wish].

Dr. Mera.—Precisely because I was a Jesuit, I learned about Jesuit morals, and today it is a salutary disappointment [to recognize] that [Jesuit morals] were and are extremely lax and thus dangerous for one's salvation. I avoid adapting to them myself, knowing how pliable they are.

Dr. Murillo.—So that's it! Now I see that there aren't enough words within my sphere of moral language. Yes, your honor is a great follower of the latest fashion, undeniably a soldier who has deserted the Society and gone under the flag of Captain Concina. [Daniel Concina, 1687–1756, controversial Italian theologian who wrote the most acerbic criticism of probabilism]

Dr. Mera.—The truth is that having observed my fellow brothers' outrageous opinions, I have become a turncoat. [An idiom referring to someone who has changed his opinion]

Dr. Murillo.—I have to confess that your honor is the first person I have met who has abandoned the doctrine one learned at school. All the rest who call themselves expelled from the Society seem determined to defend their Jesuit opinions. Your honor, rather than docile, must be very fickle.

Dr. Mera.—Dear Doctor, my ingenuous attitude does not warrant this interpretation or treatment. My desire to insure my salvation through wholesome doctrines should not be attributed to instability. And if your honor recollects the moral treatises that he studied in his four years of Theology, I have no doubt that you'll be shocked at the repugnance of these opinions.

Dr. Murillo.—Truthfully, after all the light your honor has imparted in our previous conversations, the only thing that I can honestly recall is that in these treatises we encountered many such subtle questions, and reduced them with much liveliness and wit to classroom debates: for example (something very close to what your honor referred to when speaking about *Peccatis* [sins]), on the topic of *de Conscientia*, [individual conscience] we began with the variety of views by several authors and we debated whether conscience was something that belonged to will, which is what Enríquez [Enríque Henríquez, Portuguese Jesuit theologian] said; and since Enríquez was in my youth a famous author, we then examined different opinions of the Doctors regarding Enriquez' explanations; because some said that he [Enriquez] understood how [conscience] belonged to the will, [given] the will's inclinations and its proclivity towards a particular good, according to the dictates of reason. Scotus says . . .

Dr. Mera.—My dear Doctor, would your honor be good enough to stop here, otherwise we will go back to the tiring prattle of those same old conversations. I already understand what your honor wants to say. And no doubt this was the method used in our Society when dealing with these moral issues that were debated in the classroom.

Dr. Murillo.—Well, if that is the same method, allow me to repeat it, or would your honor please explain it to me, as you have known and considered it very intuitively. The truth is that I cannot recall those atrocious opinions that make my hair stand on end every time you mention them.

Dr. Mera.—Having mentioned the pointless and ridiculous scholasticism of those classroom treatises, I would say that we used to regard them as fine for speculation and debate, and thus we defended the world's greatest monstrosities, aided by the quibbling little distinction: *Assequibilis sen defensabílis speculative; non vero reduciblis ad praxim in muñere conffesarii exercendo* [So that it can be understood and defended speculatively, although its truth cannot become a guide for the confessor in his duties]. Instead, to be competent to hear confession and assist with interior acts [in Thomistic theory, the interior act is one's intention while the exterior act is what one does by choice or command], our Father Professor, or more properly, our Father who resolved our dilemmas, turned, according to his temperament or inclination, to [Hermann] Busembaum, [Claudius] Lacroix (who was the Holy Father of Morals), [Michelangelo] Tamburini, [Juan] Azor, the famous Amadeo 'Guimenius' or in truth Father Moya[8] [Mateo Giménez de Moya],—even though this was quite rigorously prohibited by the Papal Bull of Innocent XI, but with all that, we had him [his book] hidden and we referred to it without mentioning him, because we appreciated it as a wonderful and valuable moral gem.

Dr. Murillo.—Don't tell me, your honor, that this Father [Moya] is banned, since the Jesuit's expulsion I have just bought his book, and it appeared to me that it contained moral theology's *non plus ultra*, especially knowing that the book came right from the Society as the bookseller assured me.

Dr. Mera.—Then, you'll have to turn it over to the Inquisitor right away. I made this same warning to someone else who had also been sold a copy from the Society, and I threatened to denounce him to the Inquisition if he didn't hand it over.

---

8   "Amadeo Guimenius" was the pseudonym of Mateo de Moya, who published a "brief moral treatise" in 1664, arguing that casuist theories predated the Jesuits. Hermann Busembaum was a German Jesuit, whose own tract on morality was later expanded by Claudius Lacroix, a fellow German Jesuit theologian. Juan Azor was a Spanish Jesuit, while Michelangelo Tamburini was General Supervisor of the Society of Jesus from 1706 until his death in 1730.

Dr. Murillo.—Well, I'll go immediately, although it's painful to lose such a wealth of opinions, both for and against, which is such a consolation.

Dr. Mera.—Really, what a deplorable and pernicious moral skepticism! This is what the world has lost. But more or less of the same caliber as Father Mora, are those others that I mentioned, and even better than all the rest is our Father [Antonio] Escobar,⁹ who should have been called the hero of morality, the most distinguished of our Society.

Dr. Murillo.—Who is this Escobar? Is he by chance Zámbiza's priest, my dear Doctor Don Sancho and our preacher who has given us both matter and motive to talk so much without contempt, or is he Don Claudio de Escobar, the Doctor from Ambato?

Dr. Mera.—None of these. Escobar, a moralist author, is a Jesuit who wrote a *Moral Theology* in the last century, drawn from the works of twenty-four of our Fathers, and for this reason, in the Preface, he allegorizes this book with Revelations, which was stamped with seven seals, adding that Jesus Christ likewise offers this stamped [volume] to the four beasts, [namely] Francisco Suárez, Vázquez, Molina and [Gregorio] Valencia,¹⁰ in the presence of 24 Jesuits who represented the 24 elders. The allegory is even more detailed in order to display the excellence of the book; and there can be no doubt that Father Antonio de Escobar presents in his six volumes of *Moral Theology* (look here, my dear Doctor Murillo), first, the commonly held or true opinions and then the problematic ones. He says *it is* with [these] twelve elders: *it is not* with those other twelve, and so on with all the rest. Your honor, as I turn the pages, you'll quickly see. Here it says: *sufficit et non sufficit* [It suffices and it does not suffice]. Further on: *potest et non potest* [It is possible and it is not possible].

Dr. Murillo.—My God! What a prodigy! This author is such a man, what can I say? He's an angel. Turn more pages, your honor, more and more. Oh, what a good thing! *Excusat et non excusat* [It's excused and it's not excused]. Here, *infert et non infert* [it's concluded and it's not concluded].

Dr. Mera.—As your honor has already taken a look at his method for resolving

---

9 Bartolomé de Escobar (1560–1625) was born in Spain and became a Jesuit in Peru, where he rewrote the *Crónica de Chile* by Pedro Mariño de Lobera; he was also known as an expert on liturgy and theology. According to Espejo, Escobar seems to have simplified the rule for compulsory fasting during Lent.

10 Luis de Molina (1535–1600) was a Jesuit theologian who defended free will against contemporary determinists. Franciso Suárez (1548–1617) was a Spanish Jesuit and a major figure in Neo-Scholasticism, the official philosophical doctrine of the Catholic Church. The Spanish Jesuits Gregorio Valencia and Gabriel Vázquez were also renowned theologians of the sixteenth century.

things in general, now consider, your honor, something in particular. What would you like to see?

Dr. Murillo.—I want to see that I'm not obliged to fast, as fasting tires me.

Dr. Mera.—Let's go to the first treatise, Ex. 13, Num. 67.

Dr. Murillo.—Never mind sir, don't make a big deal of it, it was a stupid joke of mine. But—how is Father Escobar to release me from fasting, or all the Escobarean lawyers with all their books?

Dr. Mera.—Wait a little, your honor, and tell me: does your honor sleep badly when you fast?

Dr. Murillo.—I certainly don't have a very good night when I don't have dinner.

Dr. Mera.—Then your honor can stop fasting. Look at this resolution, your honor: *Dormire quis nequit, nisi sumpta vesperi cena; teneturne ieiunare? Minime* [One cannot sleep if one has skipped dinner; is one obliged to fast? Not at all]. Is your honor happy?

Dr. Murillo.—I'm not happy or very satisfied, because in this case, I could fast at midday, taking a light meal, and have dinner at night.

Dr. Mera.—I tell your honor the truth: a stupid man who doesn't open books observes God's laws better than the ignoramus who reads the casuists.

In Context | Caste System in the Americas: The Mestizo Is Born of a Spaniard and an Indian Woman

Colonial society in Hispanic America was a conglomerate of castes. Race was a key component of an individual's social ranking, providing access to different legal rights. Everyone needed to know what "stage" or "position" he or she occupied in the maze of blood crossings. "*Casta* paintings" were made to illustrate the range of possibilities, with the primary goal of marking how close any individual was to Spanish descent (fig. 4.1, 174). These were often huge boards divided into squares, each containing three figures—the father, the mother, and the child—the whole painting thus representing a racial code, a linguistic system of racial composition.

The presence of such codes suggests the internal contradictions of colonial Hispanic society. It was fundamentally racist, giving and depriving rights according to one's racial heritage. But these paintings and the codes they represent also testify to the reality of—and tolerance for—interracial relationships. The physical results could be codified, but mixed-race couples were free to marry and live together openly.

An eighteenth-century saying depicts the most basic instance of racial mixing: "The mestizo [mixed-blood] who is usually humble, tranquil and

Figure 4.1. José Joaquín Magón, *Del español y la india nace el mestizo, por lo común, humilde, quieto y sencillo* [The Mestizo Is Born of a Spaniard and an Indian Woman], example of a *casta* painting, Mexico, eighteenth century. Oil on canvas, 100.5 × 136.5 cm. Coleccion Particular, Monterrey, N.L. In Guadalupe Jimenez Codinach, *México su tiempo de nacer 1750–1821* (Mexico City:Fomento Cultural Banamex, A.C., 1997), 284.

simple is the offspring of a Spaniard [father] and an Indian [mother]." The text indicates the moral function of these paintings, codifying racial classifications as well as the appropriate morality for one's status. A tag above the illustration reads: "In the Americas, people of different colors, customs, character and languages are born." This example shows the child holding a card that reads: *Parco*—sober, temperate.

Servando Teresa de Mier (1765–1827)

Servando Teresa de Mier is a decisive figure in the development of Mexican nationalism and in the struggle for independence. But his role in that struggle was shaped by a single determining event. On the feast of the Virgin of Guadalupe, December 12, 1794, the young Dominican priest, already well known for his oratory, preached a sermon at the Basílica de Guadalupe in the presence of the highest authorities of the viceroyalty. Nothing in his life would ever be the same.

Mier had taken a side in a volatile controversy. Two versions of the origins of the image of the Virgin of Guadalupe circulated throughout New Spain: one claimed that the image had been printed miraculously on the cloak of an Indian in 1532, while the other insisted that the image was a portrait from life transported to the Americas on the cape of the missionary apostle, Thomas. Each view had serious political and theological implications. The idea of an initial conversion in the Americas during apostolic times, for example, would support the Christian origin of many Indian customs and increase the status of the native population. But if conversion had preceded the conquest, a principal legal underpinning of the Spanish occupation of the Americas would be lost—since colonization was explicitly justified by the missionary role entrusted by the Pope to Spain. Not surprisingly, then, by the end of the eighteenth century, the more acceptable—and official, from the point of view of the Spanish authorities—version was that the image had miraculously appeared after the conquest. Unfortunately, Mier defended the alternative account on that day in 1794. Less than a week later he was arrested and sent to Spain to serve a ten-year prison sentence at a Dominican convent.

Mier did not return to New Spain until 1817, when he boarded a ship from England as part of an expedition intent on securing independence. During his twenty-two years in exile, Mier had wandered Europe as a fugitive, frequently escaping from prisons (at least seven times over the course of his life), often engaging with the authorities to exonerate himself, and ultimately encountering a number of people and events that would contribute significantly to independence in the Americas. In this way, Mier's life connects many of the disparate elements that finally led to self-rule in Spanish America.

On his first trip to France, for example, he met SIMÓN RODRÍGUEZ (a.k.a. Samuel Robinson), SIMÓN BOLÍVAR's former tutor who had left Venezuela in 1797. In 1802, Mier traveled to Rome to request secularization to free himself of the obligations of Dominican life. Fleeing arrest, he was in Portugal when Napoleon invaded Spain in 1808 and joined the battalion of Valencia to fight the French. After participating in several battles, Mier found himself in Cádiz where he was an active spectator of—though not a participant in—the Constitutional Assembly of 1812. Harassed by the authorities, he fled to London where he met many of the era's most prominent conspirators for South American independence: Vicente Rocafuerte, ANDRÉS BELLO, José de San Martín, and Carlos María Alvear.[11]

In 1813, under the name José Guerra, Mier published perhaps his most influential book, *Historia de la Revolución de Nueva España* [History of the Revolution of New Spain], in which he establishes the reasons for independence in New Spain, offering details, documents, and extraordinary analysis.

Although Bolívar only makes a brief mention of Mier in his LETTER FROM JAMAICA (1815), he used Mier's book extensively in constructing his own arguments for independence. Unfortunately, Mier's involvement in the actual battle for independence was short-lived. The expedition in 1817 led by Francisco Javier Mina ended in failure and Mier was once again imprisoned. After many vicissitudes, including an escape to Havana and a brief residence in Philadelphia, Mier finally returned to his native New Spain when it had become the nation of Mexico, in time to participate in the creation of its new government. Shortly before his death in 1827, Mier gathered his friends in Mexico City to offer a justification of his life and work, including his lasting commitment to the apostolic origins of the image of the Virgin of Guadalupe. He is remembered today as one of the founders of Mexican independence.

Written while imprisoned, Mier's *Memoirs* cover events between 1795 and 1805, including his meeting with SIMÓN RODRÍGUEZ in 1801. Neither man had the least idea that their encounter was historic. That the Venezuelan had tutored an adolescent named SIMÓN BOLÍVAR or that Mier's fateful sermon had been momentous beyond his personal life probably did not occur to them. But while their meeting was not particularly significant at the time, for later generations, it represents the convergence of

---

11 Vicente Rocafuerte (d. 1847) was a tenacious supporter of Spanish American Independence. He helped form the first independent Mexican government and later returned to his native Ecuador where he served as president from 1834 to 1839. José de San Martín and Carlos María de Alvear were two leading military men in Argentina's war of independence; but while San Martín is considered one of the nation's founders, Alvear's role has been subject to question.

two men who had a definitive impact on the independence of Mexico and much of Latin America.

The Napoleonic Wars essentially brought these men together, but Mier and Rodríguez are also connected by their relationship to romanticism, specifically to one of the first romantic novels, René Chateaubriand's *Atala* (1801), which recounts the tragic love of two Indians in Louisiana. Though romanticism was not yet defined as a movement in France, *Atala* attracted the attention of both Mier and Rodríguez because it took place in America. Mier later claimed to have translated the novel, though research has shown that both deserve that credit. And while both men were certainly prone to exaggeration about their achievements—Mier more than Rodríguez—it would be difficult to underestimate the stature of these two men who helped to establish model republics in Spanish America.

The selection is from *The Memoirs of Fray Servando Teresa de Mier*, edited by Susana Rotker, translated by Helen Lane (New York: Oxford University Press, 1998), 12–14, 19–21. Reprinted by permission of Oxford University Press.

From **The Memoirs of Fray Servando Teresa de Mier** (1813)

The next day, in order to enter Bayonne [France], which is a walled city, the muleteer had me dismount and enter the town by mingling with the people on the public promenade, where for the first time I saw carriages drawn by oxen. This precaution was of no avail, for the guard's suspicion was aroused because of the way I was dressed and because I was wearing boots and was covered from head to foot with dust from the road. He took me to the city hall, where I presented my Mexican passport, and since no one could understand it, they gave me my entry card, or safe-conduct pass. All this was quite necessary at that time because of the disturbances, which still had not died down altogether, in the Republic. It was still a republic, though governed by consuls, with Bonaparte as First Consul. The day was Good Friday of the year 1801.

What to do to make a living, especially since I was possessed of a strong sense of pride, as befitted my highborn station, and incapable not only of begging, but of allowing my poverty to show? I went through some terrible experiences, and would never have survived them had I been a libertine. By sheer chance, I unwittingly entered the Jewish synagogue in the Sancti-Spiritus quarter. The psalms were being sung in Spanish, and the sermon was preached in Spanish. All the Jews in France, and in almost all of Europe, save for Germany, are Spanish by descent and many by birth; because I saw them as they came to Bayonne to be circumcised; all of them speak Spanish, men and women alike; their Bibles, all their prayers are in Spanish, and above all they observe conventions such that, when a German Jew who didn't understand Spanish was married in Bayonne, even though the marriage contract was also written in Hebrew so that he would understand it, it was first read to him in Castilian, and this was the one he signed. And they still follow Spanish customs, and are also the ones who carry on the principal commercial dealings with Spain, which they all have visited. The reason behind this stubborn insistence on preserving all things Spanish is their claim that those who came to Spain because they were sent there by the emperor Hadrian belong to the tribe of Judah.

I entered the synagogue the very next day after I arrived, and that day was none other than the Passover of unleavened bread and lamb. The rabbi preached, proving, as is always done on Passover, that the Messiah had not yet come, because the sins of Israel are holding him back. As I left the synagogue, everyone flocked about me to find out what I had thought of the sermon. They had been surprised to see me, because I was wearing a clerical collar, and because I removed my hat, whereas all of them had kept theirs on inside the synagogue, and the rabbis who were officiating were wearing a prayer shawl over their heads as well. The greatest mark of respect in the Orient is to cover one's head. Only at Kaddish, or the ceremony in commemoration of the dead, which is always recited by an orphan, do worshippers bare their heads in the synagogue. And the way they have of telling whether a person is Jewish is to ask him in Hebrew: "What is your name?" In a moment's time I demolished all the arguments of the rabbi who preached the sermon, and they challenged me to a public debate. I agreed, and since I had at my fingertips Bishop Huet's evangelical proof, I made such an impression at the debate that they offered me in marriage a beautiful, wealthy young maiden named Rachel, whose name in French was Fineta, because all of them use two names, one for among themselves and another for outsiders; and they even went so far as to offer to pay for my journey to Holland to marry there, if I did not care to do so in France.

I naturally refused their offer, but from that day on I enjoyed such a credit among them that they called me Japá, that is to say, learned one; I was the first one invited to all their ceremonies; the rabbis came to consult me about their sermons, to have me correct their Castilian, and made me a new habit. When out of curiosity I went to the synagogue like other Spaniards, the rabbis bade me seat myself on their dais or in their pulpit. And once the ceremony had ended at nightfall, I remained behind by myself with the officiating rabbi, watching him as he studied what was to be read the following day. He then brought out the law of Moses, which when the congregation is present is brought out with great ceremony and reverence, as everyone bows before it. It is written on scrolls, without accent marks for the vowels, with only the consonants, and the rabbi would study it, as meanwhile I read it in the Bible with accent marks. And then I would snuff out the candles of the votive lamps, because they are forbidden to do so, nor are they permitted to light a fire to cook or to warm themselves on the Sabbath. They use Christian maidservants to do all this, and I told them that for that reason their religion was incapable of being a universal one.

Since I was still good-looking, I did not lack for young Christian ladies seeking to marry me either, none of whom found it difficult to explain what they had in mind, and when I answered that I was a priest, they would say that that was no obstacle if I were willing to abandon my calling. The horde of priests who contracted a marriage out of terror of the revolution, which forced them to marry, had left them without scruples. In Bayonne and all of the administrative district of the Lower Pyrenees as far north as Dax the women are fair-skinned and pretty, particularly the Basque ones; but I was never more aware of the influence of climate than when I began journeying on foot to Paris, because I saw, quite evidently, all the way from Montmarsan, some eight or ten leagues from Bayonne, to Paris, men and women who were dark-skinned, and the latter were ugly. French women as a general rule are ugly, and physically resemble frogs. Misshapen, short and squat, big-mouthed and slant-eyed. As one goes farther north in France, they get better-looking. [. . .]

Shortly after I reached Paris, Simón Rodríguez arrived there, a native of Caracas who, under the name of Samuel Robinson, taught English, French and Spanish in Bayonne when I was there; this latter language was also taught by a discalced Trinitarian friar, named Gutiérrez, an apostate and a libertine, who later was the author of the little Spanish gazette of Bayonne, and was ultimately executed in Seville by order of the Central Junta, because he often went to Spain, by order of Napoleon, to conspire with Ferdinand VII's Lord Privy Seal. Robinson came to live with me in Paris and encouraged me to set up a school with him to teach Spanish, which was very much in vogue.

The reason for this popularity was the fact that Spain had just ceded to Napoleon the island of Santo Domingo (three-quarters of which, the most productive regions, belonged to us), and Louisiana, without specifying the terms of the cession, or realizing that it was ceding a territory as large as the whole of

New Spain—all this in exchange for tiny Tuscany, so as to crown the Prince of Parma king of Etruria. Godoy[12] had previously offered Louisiana to Napoleon, simply to win his favor; neither he nor Spain remembered, however, that the king, according to the Laws of the Indies, cannot transfer ownership of even the smallest part of America, and if he cedes it, the cession is null and void.

This cession took place during the brief interval of peace between Napoleon and England, called the peace of Amiens, the city where the peace treaty was signed. The war then went on; and before the English could take over Louisiana and before Spain could cede it to him, Napoleon sold it to the United States for thirteen million pesos or dollars, even though it is claimed that Spain had ceded it to him under the terms of a pact that guaranteed it the right to buy it back. What is certain is that the English in America have taken over territory extending as far as Eastern Florida, the capital of which is Saint Augustine, and have located their Fort Clayborne only sixty leagues away from our settlements in Texas. It will not be long before they take over the eastern provinces in the interior and extend their territory as far as México, as only stands to reason; for through commerce, industry and freedom, the welcome that they extend to all foreigners and the land that they distribute to all families that emigrate from Europe, whom they themselves bring over, they have adopted every possible means of multiplying their numbers, and in forty years they have increased their population to nine million, from the two and a half million it numbered at the time of the insurrection. We, on the other hand, numbered a hundred million at the time of the Conquest, and today there are barely nine million of us, including the kingdom of Guatemala, because we have adopted every possible means of hindering the growth of the population and diminishing it. Among them are the impediment to marriage occasioned by the excessive fees owed priests, the imaginary division of the population into castes, the continual levies of men (on one pretext or another) for the Philippines, Havana, Puerto Rico, for the royal fleet, and for the presidios on the deadly coasts, in addition to the general oppression, the lack of free trade, industry and agriculture, and excommunication from the human species in which we live. Not to mention the butchery of revolution, in which no quarter is given and which has already cost us a million men, and the cruel, perfidious and incessant war waged against the nomad [Indian] nations, with whom the North Americans live in peace and treat as brothers. Spain's own policy will cause it to lose its American territories if it does not change its Machiavellian system.

---

12 Manuel Godoy was the Prime Minister to King Carlos IV, from 1792 to 1798 and again from 1801 to 1808 as de facto Prime Minister.

As for the Spanish language school that Robinson and I decided to set up in Paris, he encouraged me to translate, in order to serve as proof of our ability, the little novel or poem by Monsieur Chateaubriand entitled *Atala*, set in America and enjoying great popularity, which he was about to have printed thanks to the recommendations he had brought with him. I translated it, though I did so almost word for word, so that it could be used as a text for our pupils, and it cost me more than a little effort, since there was no botanical dictionary in Spanish and the poem is full of the proper names of many exotic plants that grow in Canada, and so on, which it was necessary to Hispanicize.

The translation was printed under the name of Robinson, because this is a sacrifice demanded of poor authors by those who pay the costs of having their works printed. Hence the Barcelonan don Juan Pla is the author of Cormón's *Gramática* and *Diccionario*, since Cormón, who did not know Spanish, paid the printing costs. Alvarez, who didn't know Spanish well either, passed himself off as the author of [Antonio] Capmany's *Diccionario*, which he had reprinted in Paris, with an additional second part, in other words the part from Spanish to French, compiled by some Spaniards who lived in Paris. Ródenas wagered in Valencia that he could translate *Atala* into Castilian in three days, and all he did was reprint my translation, omitting the prologue in which Chateaubriand explained the sources he had used for all the characters in the story, though he reprinted even the notes that I had added.

Simón Bolívar (1783–1830)

Born to a wealthy Venezuelan family, Simón Bolívar had lost both parents by the time he was nine. Instilled with deep commitment to liberal ideals by prominent teachers, including SIMÓN RODRÍGUEZ and ANDRÉS BELLO, Bolívar studied briefly in Europe as a young man and married a Spanish woman, who died after their return to the Americas. Joining the military in 1811, Bolívar committed himself to the liberation of his native land. Though he fought alongside various factions as issues and enemies changed, he soon became a leader in the republican forces. Despite his early success, an alliance between the royalists and the *llaneros* dealt Bolívar a major defeat in 1814, ending the Second Republic of Venezuela. The *llaneros* were fierce opponents, cowboys from the rural south, who were suspicious of the republicans as simply another version of creole and urban domination. Soon after the defeat, Bolívar withdrew to Nueva Granada (present-day Colombia).

By the time of Bolívar's first exile, the wars of independence had begun to attract the notice of Europe. After the downfall of Napoleon in 1814, several European monarchs had formed an alliance to suppress the liberalism that had led to the French Revolution. After Ferdinand was restored to the monarchy, one of his first acts was the revocation of the Constitution of Cádiz, which had established the principles of colonial autonomy—though not independence—and had also revived rebellious actions in the Americas. Supported by Spanish loyalists as well as by the European "Holy Alliance," Ferdinand then launched a force of ten thousand soldiers to pacify the province of Rio de la Plata and Montevideo. The violence in Venezuela had intensified, however, so the strategy changed and the troops were directed to Nueva Granada. Bolívar was among the republican forces that encountered the Spanish expedition at Cartagena, but he proved unable to rally the deeply divided factions. Suffering a decisive defeat in May 1815, he again departed for exile, this time to Jamaica.

In September of that year, Bolívar composed his famous "Letter from Jamaica." Nominally addressed to Henry Cullen, a British resident, the letter is both a manifesto about the failures of the republican cause in Venezuela and a plea to England to assist in the fight for independence in the Americas. Bolívar incorporates into epistolary form a detailed and extensive history of the complicated regional wars as well as an argument for the legitimacy of the rebellion against Spain. But its enduring interest proceeds from its pointed descriptions of American societies and its perceptive analysis of the contemporary problems that would bedevil those societies for decades.

Two of those analyses proved particularly prescient. The first derives from Bolívar's bitter complaints against the condescending Spanish attitudes and policies directed toward the creoles. Noting that creoles were directly descended from the conquerors or children of Spaniards born in the Americas, Bolívar observes that such policies had kept creoles from taking positions of power or responsibility in colonial society. Faced with the prospect of independence, these individuals had no experience in politics or in government. Consequently, they did not know how to govern themselves, a fact that would undermine national stability for the next century. Bolívar had previously addressed this problem in another document, the *Manifiesto de Cartagena* (December 1812).

The second problem Bolívar identifies is related, though it signals an even gloomier future for Spanish American nations. Creoles knew, better than most, that the lands they owned and exploited were not really theirs. The descendants of the original inhabitants of the Americas remained very visible, comprising a large segment of most colonial populations.

But despite the uneasiness of their claims, the creoles continued to refuse giving any power to the Indians, even suffrage. Bolívar's unusually candid confession implies the lack of legitimacy that the creoles now faced in forming independent governments. Indeed, Bolívar identifies what emerges as one of the deepest and most destructive tensions in Spanish American societies: racial conflict. Only rarely in the nineteenth century were these issues addressed with so much clarity. This fact alone gives the "Letter from Jamaica" a unique value in Spanish American history.

Bolívar himself spent the remainder of his life dedicated to achieving independence in the region, initially as the commander of revolutionary forces, helping to liberate all or parts of today's Venezuela, Colombia, Ecuador, Peru, Panama, and Bolivia—the latter one of the world's few countries named for an individual. Later, Bolívar served as the first president of the huge state of *Gran Colombia* (then composed of Venezuela, Colombia and Ecuador), established in 1821. Eventually disillusioned by his failure to unite the new independent nations of the southern hemisphere, he resigned his presidency in April 1830 and determined to go again into exile. Before he could depart, he died of tuberculosis in December 1830 in Santa Marta on the coast of present-day Colombia.

The selection is from *Selected Writings*, compiled by Vicente Lecuna, edited by Harold A. Blerck Jr., translated by Lewis Bertrand (New York: Colonial Press, Banco de Venezuela, 1951), 109–12.

From **Carta de Jamaica (1815) [Letter from Jamaica]**

It is even more difficult to foresee the future fate of the New World, to set down its political principles, or to prophesy what manner of government it will adopt. Every conjecture relative to America's future is, I feel, pure speculation. When mankind was in its infancy, steeped in uncertainty, ignorance, and error, was it possible to foresee what system it would adopt for its preservation? Who could venture to say that a certain nation would be a republic or a monarchy; this nation great, that nation small? To my way of thinking, such is our own situation. We are a young people. We inhabit a world apart, separated by broad seas. We are young in the ways of almost all the arts and sciences, although, in a certain manner, we are old in the ways of civilized society. I look upon the present state of America as similar to that of Rome after its fall. Each part of Rome adopted a political system conforming to its interest and situation or was led by the individual ambitions of certain chiefs, dynasties, or associations. But this important difference exists: those dispersed parts later reestablished their ancient nations, subject to the changes imposed by circumstances or events. But we scarcely retain a vestige of what once was; we are, moreover, neither Indian nor European, but a species midway between the legitimate proprietors of this country and the Spanish usurpers. In short, though Americans by birth we derive our rights from Europe, and we have to assert these rights against the rights of the natives, and at the same time we must defend ourselves against the invaders. This places us in a most extraordinary and involved situation. Notwithstanding that it is a type of divination to predict the result of the political course which America is pursuing, I shall venture some conjectures which, of course, are colored by my enthusiasm and dictated by rational desires rather than by reasoned calculations.

The role of the inhabitants of the American hemisphere has for centuries been purely passive. Politically they were non-existent. We are still in a position lower than slavery, and therefore it is more difficult for us to rise to the enjoyment of freedom. Permit me these transgressions in order to establish the issue. States are slaves because of either the nature or the misuse of their constitutions; a people is therefore enslaved when the government, by its nature or its vices, infringes on and usurps the rights of the citizen or subject. Applying these principles, we find that America was denied not only its freedom but even an active and effective tyranny. Let me explain. Under absolutism there are no recognized limits to the exercise of governmental powers. The will of the great sultan, khan, bey, and other despotic rulers is the supreme law, carried out more or less arbitrarily by the lesser pashas, khans, and satraps of Turkey and Persia, who have an organized system of oppression in which inferiors participate according to the authority vested in them. To them is entrusted the administration of civil, military, political, religious, and tax matters. But, after all is said and done, the rulers of Ispahan are Persians; the viziers of the Grand Turk are Turks; and the sultans of Tartary are Tartars. China does not bring its military leaders and scholars from the land of Genghis Khan, her conqueror, notwithstanding that the Chinese of today are the lineal descendants of those who were reduced to subjection by the ancestors of the present-day Tartars.

How different is our situation! We have been harassed by a conduct which has not only deprived us of our rights but has kept us in a sort of permanent infancy with regard to public affairs. If we could at least have managed our domestic affairs and our internal administration, we could have acquainted ourselves with the processes and mechanics of public affairs. We should also have enjoyed a personal consideration, thereby commanding a certain unconscious respect from the people, which is so necessary to preserve amidst revolutions. That is why I say we have been deprived of an active tyranny, since we have not been permitted to exercise its functions.

Americans today, and perhaps to a greater extent than ever before, who live within the Spanish system occupy a position in society no better than that of serfs destined for labor, or at best they have no more status than that of mere consumers. Yet even this status is surrounded with galling restrictions, such as being forbidden to grow European crops, or to store products which are royal monopolies, or to establish factories of a type the Peninsula itself does not possess. To this add the exclusive trading privileges, even in articles of prime necessity, and the barriers between American provinces, designed to prevent all exchange of trade, traffic, and understanding. In short, do you wish to know what our future held?—simply the cultivation of the fields of indigo, grain, coffee, sugar cane, cacao, and cotton; cattle raising on the broad plains; hunting wild game in the jungles; digging in the earth to mine its gold—but even these limitations could never satisfy the greed of Spain.

So negative was our existence that I can find nothing comparable in any other civilized society, examine as I may the entire history of time and the politics of all nations. Is it not an outrage and a violation of human rights to expect a land so splendidly endowed, so vast, rich, and populous, to remain merely passive?

As I have just explained, we were cut off and, as it were, removed from the world in relation to the science of government and administration of the state. We were never viceroys or governors, save in the rarest of instances; seldom archbishops and bishops; diplomats never; as military men, only subordinates; as nobles, without royal privileges. In brief, we were neither magistrates nor financiers and seldom merchants—all in flagrant contradiction to our institutions.

In Context | Humboldt and Chimborazo

In 1802, Alexander Von Humboldt (1769–1859) and Aimé Bonpland (1783–1858), along with indigenous guides, climbed the Chimborazo near Quito. They knew they could not reach the summit but wanted to attain the highest possible point so that Humboldt could carry out his scientific measurements of atmospheric pressure, air composition, and the vegetation line (fig. 4.2, 186). His subsequent, monumental works on the geography of plants reflected his lifelong efforts to understand nature holistically, as an interrelated system. Though Humboldt himself never claimed to have reached the crest of Chimborazo, the legend persisted for decades.

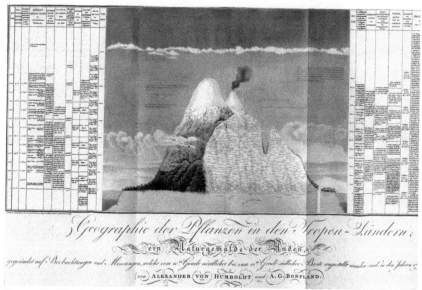

Figure 4.2. Humboldt and Chimborazo, 1802. Humboldt's illustration of the distribution of plants. *Geographie der Pflanzen in den Tropen-Ländern*, Louis Bouquet after Alexander von Humboldt, Schönberger, and Turpin (1807). Wikimedia Commons, public domain.

José María Heredia (1803–1839)

In the summer of 1824 José María Heredia visited Niagara Falls on the border between the United States and Canada—an experience that inspired the most famous lyric of Cuba's finest Romantic poet. Born in Santiago de Cuba, Heredia actually spent his early years in Pensacola, Florida, where his father was an official of the Spanish government. The family was then transferred to Venezuela, during some of the fiercest fighting of the Wars of Independence (1812–1817), and later to Mexico, where his father died. Heredia returned to Cuba to finish studying law, but his involvement with revolutionary groups caused his exile. He fled to the United States in 1823, where he published his first volume of poetry in New York City. He negotiated political asylum in Mexico and lived there from 1825 until his death from tuberculosis in 1839. He returned only once to his native Cuba, visiting his mother by special permission in 1837. He died at Toluca, outside Mexico City, two years later.

In Mexico, Heredia practiced law, held political office, and, more important, published several literary journals, translated and staged numerous European dramas, and wrote poetry that made him famous throughout the Americas. Ironically, Heredia's most intense and long-lasting poem,

"Niagara" ("Niágara" in Spanish) had been composed during his brief residence in the United States. The poem is technically a *silva* (a lyric form consisting mostly of eleven- and seven-syllable lines); it is remarkable for its profound tribute to nature, the massive Falls of Niagara, and its poignant expression of Heredia's discomfort as an exile, facing an uncertain future, away from his loved ones and native land.

Bearing traces of Neoclassicism and Baroque prosody, "Niagara" is the first poem in both Spanish and Latin American literature to reflect the distinctive spiritual attitudes and themes of Romanticism: the sympathetic relationship between nature and the poet's inner reality, the experience of the sublime—detached from religious enthusiasm—and the deliberate intent to make language express emotional states.

Romanticism was rooted in the mid-eighteenth century discovery of the sublime—the ways that natural entities, like the grand peaks of the Alps or the vast and ever-changing expanses of the ocean, can overwhelm the senses. As the magnitudes of nature exceed the capacities of the human eye and ear, a sense of terror and awe is evoked. Perhaps not coincidentally, the very moment that such experiences were revealing the plummetless mysteries of nature, the deliberate application of reason was offering human beings the opportunity to subdue that astounding power. Indeed, by 1824, three generations of European writers had largely exhausted the terror implicit in a transcendent nature, and poets were turning to manufactured objects to experience the sublime: panoramas and dioramas or the views from balloons. Niagara Falls and the staggering scenery of the western territories nonetheless remained an evocative presence in the Americas. Their unexplored unfamiliarity could still provoke awe, as Heredia suggests in the opening lines of "Niagara."

Heredia also brings to that grand scenery another great Romantic theme, the notion that nature itself reflects the spiritual state of those who contemplate it deeply. For Heredia, what the chaos and turmoil of the great falls elicit are the young Cuban poet's own confusion and despair at a moment of personal transition and profound uncertainty. The real achievement of the poem lies in Heredia's skill in finding the precise poetic language to reflect that identity and that despair—manifesting at only twenty-one the technical proficiency of an accomplished poet. The poem's unusual enjambments, for example, express the abrupt changes in the river's rapids as they fall into the void, while sound effects, like double sibilants (the double "rr" in *terribly, terrors, torren*t), reproduce the resonant shudder of the thundering falls.

The identification of language and poetic object make "Niagara" a seminal poem in nineteenth-century Spanish American literature. Only the Cuban JOSÉ MARTÍ in the 1870s and the Nicaraguan RUBÉN DARÍO in the 1890s handled poetic language with such expressive dexterity. And while several Latin American poets followed in Heredia's footsteps to Niagara Falls—including Cuban poet GERTRUDIS GÓMEZ DE AVELLANEDA, the Colombian Rafael Pombo, and the Venezuelan Juan Antonio Pérez Bonalde—none of their poetic tributes has ever matched the intensity and lucidity of "Niagara."

The selection is from Alfred Coester, *The Literary History of Spanish America* (Norwood, Mass.: MacMillan, 1928), 94–98.

Niagara (1824)

My lyre! Give me my lyre! My bosom feels,
The glow of inspiration. O, how long
Have I been left in darkness, since this light
Last visited my brow! Niagara!
Thou with thy rushing waters dost restore
The heavenly gift that sorrow took away.

Tremendous torrent! For an instant hush
The terrors of thy voice, and cast aside
Those wide-involving shadows, that my eyes
May see the fearful beauty of thy face!
I am not all unworthy of thy sight,
For from my very boyhood have I loved,
Shunning the meaner track of common minds,
To look on nature in her loftier moods.
At the fierce rushing of the hurricane,
At the near bursting of the thunderbolt,
I have been touched with joy; and when the sea
Lashed by the wind hath rocked my bark, and showed
Its yawning caves beneath me, I have loved
Its dangers and the wrath of elements.
But never yet the madness of the sea
Hath moved me as thy grandeur moves me now.

Thou flowest on in quiet, till thy waves
Grow broken 'midst the rocks; thy current then
Shoots onward like the irresistible course
Of Destiny. Ah, terribly they rage,—
The hoarse and rapid whirlpools there! My brain
Grows wild, my senses wander, as I gaze
Upon the hurrying waters, and my sight,
Vainly would follow, as toward the verge
Sweeps the wide torrent. Waves innumerable
Meet there and madden,—waves innumerable
Urge on and overtake the waves before,
And disappear in thunder and in foam.

They reach, they leap the barrier,—the abyss
Swallows insatiable the sinking waves.
A thousand rainbows arch them, and woods
Are deafened with the roar. The violent shock
Shatters to vapor the descending sheets.
A cloudy whirlwind fills the gulf, and heaves
The mighty pyramid of circling mist
To heaven. The solitary hunter near
Pauses with terror in the forest shades.

What seeks my restless eye? Why are not here,
About the jaws of this abyss, the palms—
Ah, the delicious palms,—that on the plains
Of my own native Cuba spring and spread
Their thickly foliaged summits to the sun,
And, in the breathings of the ocean air,
Wave soft beneath the heaven's unspotted blue?

But no, Niagara,—thy forest pines
Are fitter coronal for thee. The palm,
The effeminate myrtle, and frail rose may grow
In gardens, and give out their fragrance there,
Unmanning him who breathes it. Thine it is
To do a nobler office. Generous minds
Behold thee, and are moved, and learn to rise

Above earth's frivolous pleasures; they partake
Thy grandeur, at the utterance of thy name.

God of all truth! in other lands I've seen
Lying philosophers, blaspheming men,
Questioners of thy mysteries, that draw
Their fellows deep into impiety;
And therefore doth my spirit seek thy face
In earth's majestic solitudes. Even here
My heart doth open all itself to thee.
In this immensity of loneliness,
I feel thy hand upon me. To my ear
The eternal thunder of the cataract brings
Thy voice, and I am humbled as I hear.

Dread torrent, that with wonder and with fear
Dost overwhelm the soul of him that looks
Upon thee, and dost bear it from itself,—
Whence hast thou thy beginning? Who supplies,
Age after age, thy unexhausted springs?
What power hath ordered, that when all thy weight
Descends into the deep, the swollen waves
Rise not and roll to overwhelm the earth?

The Lord has opened his omnipotent hand,
Covered thy face with clouds, and given voice
To thy down-rushing waters; he hath girt
Thy terrible forehead with his radiant bow.
I see thy never-resting waters run,
And I bethink me how the tide of time
Sweeps to eternity. So pass of man—
Pass, like a noonday dream—the blossoming days
And he awakes to sorrow. I, alas!
Feel that my youth is withered, and my brow
Ploughed early with the lines of grief and care.

Never have I so deeply felt as now
The hopeless solitude, the abandonment,

The anguish of a loveless life. Alas!
How can the impassioned, the unfrozen heart
Be happy without love? I would that one
Beautiful, worthy to be loved and joined
In love with me, now shared my lonely walk
On this tremendous brink. 'Twere sweet to see
Her sweet face touched with paleness, and become
More beautiful from fear, and overspread
With a faint smile while clinging to my side.
Dreams,—dreams! I am an exile, and for me
There is no country and there is no love.

　Hear, dread Niagara, my latest voice!
Yet a few years, and the cold earth shall close
Over the bones of him who sings thee now
Thus feelingly. Would that this, my humble verse,
Might be, like thee, immortal! I, meanwhile,
Cheerfully passing to the appointed rest,
Might raise my radiant forehead in the clouds
To listen to the echoes of my fame.

In Context | Niagara Falls

By the mid-nineteenth century, these falls—long an inspiration to American painters—had become one of the most visited tourist sites in the entire United States (fig. 4.3, 192). And while a number of other Latin American poets found in these majestic cataracts inspiration for poems about the power of nature, nearly all of these texts would also recall that Heredia had been there first.

In Context | *Woman with a Cigarette*

This anonymous painting from nineteenth-century Mexico (fig. 4.4.,192) suggests the widespread social tolerance for tobacco. Tobacco was strictly controlled by a state monopoly, as were sugar and any kind of gambling activity, including cards and dice. But the act of smoking tobacco was not under such control, nor was it restricted to men. In fact, many descriptions from the eighteenth and nineteenth centuries attest to the fact that smoking was very common among women and did not violate any social proprieties.

Figure 4.3. Thomas Cole, *Distant View of Niagara Falls*, 1830. Oil on panel, 47.9 × 60.6 cm (18⅞" × 23⅞"). Art Institute of Chicago, Friends of American Art Collection, 1946. By permission of the Art Institute of Chicago.

Figure 4.4. Anonymous, *Woman with a Cigarette*, nineteenth century, Mexico, *Señora con cigarro*. Oil on canvas, 25.5 × 20.2 cm. Coleción Fomento Cultural Banamex, A.C. Mexico, D.F. Photograph by Michel Zabé. In Guadalupe Jiménez Codinach, *México su tiempo de nacer 1750–1821* (México: Fomento Cultural Banamex, A.C., 1997), 87.

In Context | Josefa Ortiz de Domínguez

As in many other areas, women's contributions to the historical movements and events of Hispanic America have yet to be adequately assessed and evaluated. Josefa Ortiz de Domínguez was one of those women who played a pivotal role during the early struggles for Mexican independence, allowing insurgents to gather in her house to plan the revolution. While Ortiz de Domínguez's contribution has always been recognized, many such women remain unacknowledged for their deeds. Fortunately, research in the past few decades has done much to ameliorate that lack of information about the part that women played in the wars of independence. Much more work remains to be done, reexamining women's activities across the whole range of historical periods and social conditions. This illustration is a very rare artifact: a wax portrait of Josefa Ortiz de Domínguez fashioned in the nineteenth century.

Figure 4.5. Anonymous, *Josefa Ortiz de Domínguez*, nineteenth century, Mexico. Wax 11 × 9 cm. Colección Museo Nacional de las Intervenciones, INAH, Mexico City. In Guadalupe Jiménez Codinach, *México su tiempo de nacer 1750–1821* (Mexico City: Fomento Cultural Banamex, A.C., 1997), 164. By permission of the Instituto Nacional de Antropología e Historia.

5

The Civil Wars, 1824–1870

Many of the campaigns for independence were civil wars from the outset, but the decades that followed often intensified the internal conflicts. Most historians identify the main factions as the liberals, who wished to modernize their new countries, and the conservatives, who sought to maintain colonial institutions and social structures. Such a view oversimplifies the unique situations faced by each country and deemphasizes the extended duration of hostilities, in which the issues as well as the participants gradually changed. At least three different generations took turns occupying center stage during this era, each bringing different political premises, different strategies and different goals. Moreover, the social, political, economic, and geographical conditions varied immensely across the continent, making generalizations difficult.

In Argentina, for example, the main issue during this period was federation versus centralization. Located near the mouth of the Río de la Plata, Buenos Aires was the country's sole port and only point of contact with European markets. The city and the province thus sought a centralized system that would enable them to control the lucrative profits from their commerce. The interior provinces wanted a federal government, so that the income from customs and duties collected at the country's bustling port would be more equitably distributed. These political positions were not peacefully resolved; rather, this disagreement marked the start of a long civil war in Argentina. Although the federalists theoretically favored an equitable distribution among all the provinces, under the rule of Juan Manuel de Rosas (1829–1852), the federalist government consistently favored Buenos Aires to the detriment of the other provinces. In his classic work, *Civilización y barbarie: Vida de Juan Facundo Quiroga* (1845), DOMINGO FAUSTINO SARMIENTO artfully exposes these contradictory policies.

There was a similar debate over federalism and centralization in Mexico. However, what overshadowed every issue was the legitimacy of power: who could rule with lawful authority? With this question unanswered, internal controversies constantly led to whole new governments, with the sudden shifts in leadership frequently accompanied by violence. Mexico remained in nearly perpetual crisis from 1821 until 1847, when losing the war against the United States dramatically reduced its northern territories. This disheartening defeat eventually led to a period called *la Reforma*, spearheaded by a new generation of Mexican politicians, including most prominently Benito Juárez, the leader of the most radical liberals.

In both Argentina and Mexico, the failure to resolve such basic issues began to render the factions fighting for and against independence irrelevant. In both countries, the next generation criticized and rejected both sides of the struggle, which created essentially three groups with conflicting agendas. Throughout the 1830s, the two groups who had sought independence also clashed with a younger generation that repudiated them both.

Another fundamental problem that plagued the entire continent during this time was the creation of constitutional republics. While most new countries believed that a republican government was preferable to a monarchy or an empire, the character of their constitutions—the way these legal documents addressed the distribution of power, their definitions of suffrage (particularly for the large populations of Indians, blacks, and mestizos), and their guarantees of property rights—was much in dispute. While constitutions often had very short lifespans, in Argentina the Federalist dictator, Juan Manuel de Rosas, successfully opposed the creation of a constitution throughout his two-decade rule. When he was finally driven into exile in 1852, the first task faced by the victors was that of establishing a constitutional assembly.

In some countries, the presence and power of the Church created quandaries for nascent governments. Catholicism was often, in law and in practice, the only recognized religion, and the church and the state constantly wrangled for control of each other's domains. One solution to the continuing tensions was the widespread adaptation of the Jesuit principle of eclecticism. With this approach, states could impose whatever laws and institutions they chose, as long as the principles of Catholicism were not attacked. That notion allowed church and state to coexist, even as Spanish American societies became increasingly secularized throughout the nineteenth century. By the second half of the century, the philosophical rationale for the coexistence of church and state had gradually shifted from the Jesuit legacy of ideological rationalism to a more aggressive positivism. Closely associated with the work of Auguste Comte (1798–1857), positivism had emerged from the domination of Newtonian principles throughout the sciences. Comte, who had trained at the Ecole Polytechnique in Paris, believed that basic laws could be identified for every kind of reality, including society. The discovery of such principles would bring an end to conflict, since societies would follow indisputable laws rather than unproven authorities or contested opinions.

As the reading from GABINO BARREDA indicates, positivism was a perfect tool to accommodate these dissenting national views as well as the conflicting projects for economic and political development. Positivism came to be interpreted throughout the region as a doctrine of the *fait accompli*, a sort of realism in which historical events were accepted as inevitable. But positivism also served Latin America in the second cycle of capitalist development, as its nations became the key providers of raw materials for U.S. and European industries. This economic boom, along with the pragmatic political perspectives of positivism, helped to mitigate many social and political rivalries in this era, even as other, more enduring, conflicts were emerging in the social underground.

Simón Rodríguez (1769–1854)

Simón Rodríguez is perhaps best known as SIMÓN BOLÍVAR's mentor—but many of his original ideas have had an even more significant impact. Born in Caracas, Venezuela, Rodríguez became a teacher in 1791, but his political involvements forced him to flee the country in 1797, initially to Jamaica, where he changed his name to Samuel Robinson. After traveling to the United States and then to France in 1801, he encountered his former student again in 1804, and together they visited France, Switzerland, and Italy. Before parting in Rome in 1805, Rodríguez urged the young Bolívar to pronounce his famous oath that he would spend his life fighting for the independence of the Spanish American nations. Rodríguez himself only returned to Spanish America in 1823, two decades later, undoubtedly heartened by the victories that his disciple had achieved throughout the region.

Bolívar's devotion to his teacher is evident in his published correspondence. In a letter of May 6, 1824, sent from Ecuador to Bogotá, he states: "On my behalf, give money to Don Simón Rodríguez. I will pay for everything so that he can come to see me. I love that man in a crazy way. He was my teacher, my travel companion, and he is a genius, a vessel of grace and talent for the one who can discover it and value it." Rodríguez tried to join

Bolívar but by the time he had arrived in Guayaquil, Bolívar was already in Peru. On January 7, 1825, Rodríguez wrote back to his former student, praising his success: "Friend: I did not come to America because I was born here but because now they treat its inhabitants in a manner that pleases me and it does so because it is good. It is now the appropriate place for discussion and implementation because it is you who has initiated and upheld that idea."

Following Rodríguez's return to Spanish America, he assisted the independence movement in several countries, from Colombia and Venezuela to Ecuador, Peru, and Bolivia, but education was always his priority. However, few of his reformist projects were successful, especially after Bolívar's death in 1830, when there was no longer anyone to "discover and appreciate" his talent or support his monumental plans for improving education.

One of Rodríguez's most lasting ideas was formulated in 1834: *O inventamos o erramos* [Either we invent or we err.] It was only many years later that JOSÉ MARTÍ fully articulated what Rodríguez meant. In an essay, "Our America," Martí explicitly indicts Spanish America for imitating Europe instead of developing its own human and historic potential. Rodríguez was convinced that European models were inadequate for America, and he believed that Bolívar's project was precisely to found a truly American society. In fact, that project was never realized—by Bolívar or Martí—though the idea of American originality remains a fertile one even today.

Many of Rodríguez's notions were unappreciated by his contemporaries. His introduction to *Las sociedades americanas en 1828* [American Societies in 1828] was vehemently criticized, for example, and Rodríguez then tried to defend himself in *Luces y virtudes sociales* (1834) [Lights and Social Virtues]. *Lights and Social Virtues* became Rodríguez's masterpiece—a revolutionary appraisal of the role of education in a progressive society. The title encapsulates his basic point. By *luces* (lights), he means all of the new data, theories, discoveries, technology, and information that were associated with the Enlightenment, the dominant philosophical movement of the eighteenth and early nineteenth centuries—known in Spanish as *el siglo de las luces* [the century of lights]. True "enlightenment" consisted of acquiring and transmitting knowledge, or education. But the second term—*virtudes* (virtues)—suggests Rodríguez's most original idea: that the purpose of "light" was the social good. For Rodríguez, education must support the good of the whole and become the basis for the new American societies. Applying knowledge for the common good was one's duty, the constant responsibility of each individual to ensure that his or her actions would benefit the collective. Rodríguez was adamant: only if everyone worked in this way, could we create truly new nations and societies.

Such concepts were profoundly revolutionary, and few really understood what Rodríguez was proposing. One of his most radical ideas was that the state should educate all citizens *from birth*. In Spanish America, where the Catholic Church controlled education and where paternal authority determined the destiny of most children, that notion was almost unthinkable. Moreover, current immigration policies favored adult European populations, and Rodríguez believed that his program of enlightened education would only be effective for children—that is, people not yet contaminated by false principles. Appreciating that his was a unique historical moment, Rodríguez understood better than most of his countrymen that innovation rather than imitation was critical; that European social, economic, and political forms, considered superior just because they were European, would not suffice in the New World—and that education was the key to that revolution.

Wary of his critics in the government and in the church, Rodríguez limited himself to veiled expressions of these notions in *Lights and Social Virtues*. The church was clearly unwilling to relinquish its role in educating the young, and political leaders were understandably reluctant to undertake the immense responsibilities that Rodríguez's reforms required. Opposing authoritarianism in every form, Rodríguez believed that true liberty consisted in the individual's ability to think independently. But it remained to successors, like the Chilean FRANCISCO BILBAO, to promote such ideas more openly.

Rodríguez's radical perspective is apparent in the presentation of his writing on the physical page, anticipating many of the techniques of avant-garde poetry a century later. Using different font types and brackets and other typographical variants, Rodríguez sought to make his thought *visible*. The path of his thought becomes palpable in print. Footnotes are integrated into the body of the text, making digressions, caveats, or immediate reflections available to the reader along with the unfolding of his argument.

Simón Rodríguez died in 1854 in a small town in northern Peru, where he had been chased—once again—by creditors, upset over the failure of his most recent enterprises. Prophetic in many ways, Rodríguez's vision of a new America based on a genuinely public education remains potent if still largely resisted. A man ahead of his time, he becomes more and more a man of our time.

The selection is from Rodríguez's 1834 *Luces y virtudes sociales* in *Escritos de Simón Rodríguez*, compiled by Pedro Grases (Caracas: Imprenta Nacional, 1954), 153–55. Translated by Isabel Bastos and Marvin Liberman.

From Luces y virtudes sociales (1834) [Lights and Social Virtues]

INTRODUCTION

The objective of the author, as it pertains to American
Societies is
POPULAR EDUCATION
And by
POPULAR . . . I mean . . . WIDESPREAD
TO INSTRUCT is not TO EDUCATE
Nor is *Instruction* equivalent to *Education*
However, *Instructing* may *Educate*
To demonstrate that the accumulation of knowledge, which is extraneous to
the art of living, has done nothing to shape social conduct—look at the many
badly-raised learned men that populate the world of the sciences. While a philosopher can speak appropriately about strategy, in the end he is not a soldier.
Neither can the ways of GENERALIZING knowledge
Become a substitute for
The continuous acts of PUBLICATION that are
Being taught in *Schools, High Schools* and *Universities,*
Nor those acts of DISSEMINATION
That are produced by the press
what is not WIDESPREAD
without exception
is not truly PUBLIC
and
what is not PUBLIC is not SOCIAL,
that is, everything DISCLOSED among *ordinary people*
by means of *proclamations, posters* or *newspapers*
but nothing can become widespread if it is not conveyed
THROUGH ART so that it reaches WITHOUT EXCEPTION
To all individuals of a social body
To convey through art will be, not only to make
EVERYONE

know what is available
but to provide
GENERALLY
Effective ways of making that knowledge available
And still, it will be necessary to declare that
The possession of the means
Imposes the obligation to make use of them.

All Governments know (when they want to) how to *make general* what is, or what appears to them, appropriate; but only an ENLIGHTENED Government can make Instruction general . . . furthermore. . . . they must; because enlightenment obliges them to undertake the work of enlightening others—and it strengthens them in opposing the resistance raised against them by the protectors of the old customs.

Rousseau disapproved of *general* instruction because he feared its effects: he was not wrong:—To *Instruct* is not to *Educate* (as has been said): knowledge is a *weapon* that, as a rule, can be used against a society without its being aware of it: and even the best man in the world can do harm . . . or even offend . . . through ignorance: evil men do it all the time, on behalf of bad institutions.

With all the knowledge transmitted up to now, Usurpers, Fraudsters, Monopolists and Stockpilers, have managed to act legally—knowing how to create accounts and document them—bringing lawsuits—winning and avoiding punishments—in the end, they abuse good faith with impunity, and they make fun of magistrates. Since the knowledge of chemistry and the art of engraving have become available, there is no adequate control to stop the counterfeiting of money, whether metal or paper: let such skills on which advanced nations base their priorities be extended a little further, and the swindlers will just keep two versions of their accounting books.

Only in the hope of achieving what is thought of as PEOPLES' EDUCATION can WIDESPREAD INSTRUCTION be defended. . . . and one must defend it, because the time has come to teach people how to live, so that they can do *well* what otherwise they are bound to do *badly,* beyond any possibility of repair. Before, people let themselves be governed because they believed that their only mission in this world was to obey: now they no longer believe this, and their aspirations cannot be denied, nor (. . . what would be worse . . .) can they be kept from helping others to achieve those aspirations.

PUBLIC ORDER
IS THE ISSUE OF THE DAY
In America there are many castes

If it were possible to keep. . . . not the majority of men but . . . EVERYONE in a state of ignorance, which now passes for innocence—if it were possible to strip them of the means of resistance that they have acquired . . . simple and defenseless, the most capable, or the least weak, would rise up and rule over them without any problem; but it is not permitted to appeal to those desires.

For lost INNOCENCE must be substituted REASON
(which is not formed in ignorance)
WEAKNESS must encounter ART
(all interests must submit to a single
Well-understood interest . . . that of good harmony)

People cannot stop learning, nor stop feeling their power: very soon, among the people, the principal engine for all actions will be widespread, that being the following:
Material power is in the MASSES
and the * *moral power* * in the MOVEMENT
Even to pull out a single hair, such reasoning is necessary: everyone decides to act according to this principle, although they do not realize it; but . . . necessity determines the kind of action, and circumstances assert the necessity.

In Context | Simón Rodríguez and the Printing of Thought

Simón Rodríguez left Venezuela to what might have been a lifelong exile had not his disciple, SIMÓN BOLÍVAR, won his campaigns for South American independence. Little is known about Rodríguez's exile, lasting twenty-two years (1797–1823), though its high point was certainly his encounter with Bolívar in 1804, when they journeyed to Rome together and Bolívar swore to free the American countries from Spanish domination. There are few other details, but Rodríguez also apparently worked for a time at a print shop in Baltimore.

What is better known is Rodríguez's encyclopedic reading. He read passionately the works of Rousseau, Diderot, and Voltaire, as well as lesser (but perhaps more influential) authors like Condillac, Destutt de Tracy, Saint Simon, and Pestalozzi. Rodríguez also read widely in the fields of chemistry, physics, and botany and studied new industrial techniques.

His knowledge of printing, his interest in education, and his philosophical readings led him to conclude that it was not enough to teach facts; it was necessary to educate with a new authentically republican sense of

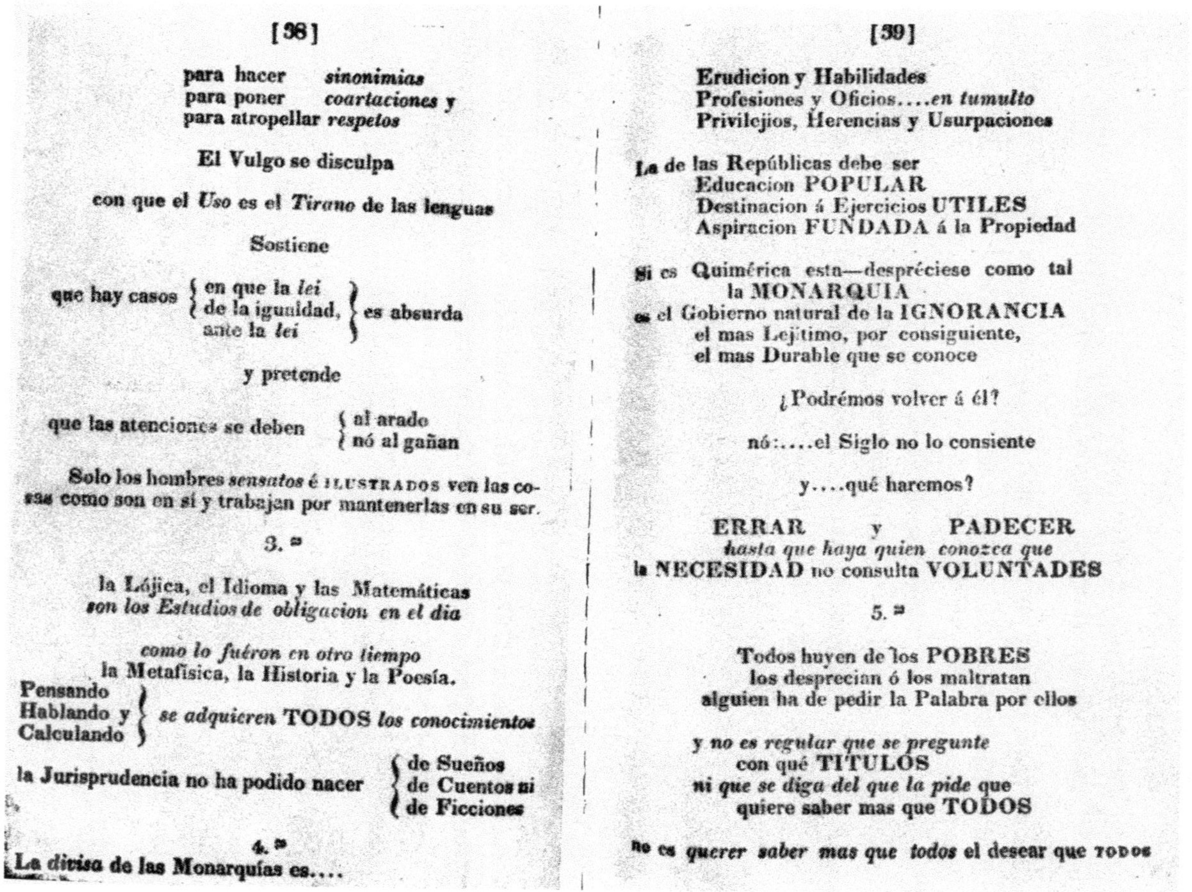

Figure 5.1. A page from Simón Rodríguez's *Luces y virtudes sociales*. In *Escritos de Simón Rodríguez*, comp. Pedro Grases, vol. 2 (Caracas: Imprenta Nacional, 1954), 190–91.

[38]

para hacer *sinonimias*
para poner *coartaciones* y
para atropellar *respetos*

El Vulgo se disculpa

con que el *Uso* es el *Tirano* de las lenguas

Sostiene

que hay casos { en que la *lei* } es absurda
{ de la igualdad, }
{ ante la *lei* }

y pretende

que las atenciones se deben { al arado
{ nó al gañan

Solo los hombres *sensatos* é ILUSTRADOS ven las cosas como son en sí y trabajan por mantenerlas en su ser.

3.ª

la Lójica, el Idioma y las Matemáticas *son los Estudios de obligacion en el dia*

Pensando
Hablando y } *se adquieren* TODOS *los conocimientos*
Calculando }

como lo fuéron en otro tiempo
la Metafisica, la Historia y la Poesía.

la Jurisprudencia no ha podido nacer { de Sueños
{ de Cuentos ni
{ de Ficciones

4.ª

La divisa de las Monarquías es....

[39]

Erudicion y Habilidades
Profesiones y Oficios....*en tumulto*
Privilejios, Herencias y Usurpaciones

La de las Repúblicas debe ser
Educacion POPULAR
Destinacion á Ejercicios UTILES
Aspiracion FUNDADA á la Propiedad

Si es Quimérica esta—despréciese como tal
la MONARQUIA
el Gobierno natural de la IGNORANCIA
el mas Lejítimo, por consiguiente,
el mas Durable que se conoce

¿ Podrémos volver á él?

nó....el Siglo no lo consiente

y....qué harémos?

ERRAR y PADECER
hasta que haya quien conozca que
la NECESIDAD no consulta VOLUNTADES

5.ª

Todos huyen de los POBRES
los desprecian ó los maltratan
alguien ha de pedir la Palabra por ellos

y no es regular que se pregunte
con qué TITULOS
ni *que se diga del que la pide que* TODOS
quiere saber mas que TODOS

no es querer saber mas que todos el desear que TODOS

social responsibility. One of Rodríguez's principal insights continues to be overlooked: to educate and to be educated one must know how to think— one must know the mechanics of thought. Rodríguez's typography—revolutionary even today—is a response to his discovery that thought is not sequential like writing, but panoramic. Ideas and logical processes appear in the mind all at once and can be deconstructed like chemical formulas.

Although Simón Rodríguez certainly owes much to the popular ideologues of his time (Destutt de Tracy and De Gerando, for example), he does not owe to anyone his decision to print on the page the complex process of thought.

Andrés Bello (1781–1865)

Andrés Bello was born in Caracas, Venezuela, the eldest son of cultivated parents who were descendants of Canary Islanders. Exceptionally bright, Bello was briefly with the German Alexander Humboldt when he explored Mount Ávila, fostering a lifelong interest in the natural sciences. He completed his baccalaureate at the University of Caracas and became one of SIMÓN BOLÍVAR's teachers, even though he was only two years his senior. Like many other precocious creoles, Bello found little opportunity to exercise his talents in Spanish America. As SIMÓN RODRÍGUEZ repeatedly argued, neither society nor the state provided the institutional supports that would make an education useful. One of the principal complaints of the era was that the policies of the Spanish crown systematically denied creoles the positions of responsibility that would have allowed their brightest to flourish—a point that BOLÍVAR reiterates in his LETTER FROM JAMAICA.

Like his countryman Rodríguez before him, Bello departed Venezuela (in 1810) never to return. Only after independence did either man come back to the Americas, bringing with them major intellectual projects that they would implement in the new nations. While Rodríguez sought to transform the education system with modern pedagogies, Bello, after spending nineteen years in England, brought his talents to bear in several fields. Originally a government employee, Bello often struggled to support himself and his family in London as a translator. He also began to write poetry, including "Alocución a la poesía," 1823 [Invocation to Poetry] and "Silva a la agricultura de la zona tórrida," 1826 [An Ode to Agriculture in the Torrid Zone], published as *Silvas Americanas* and intended to be part of a larger poem, *América*, which he never finished.

Invited in 1829 to serve in the Chilean ministry of foreign affairs, Bello moved to Santiago with his second wife, an Irish Catholic, and soon became deeply involved in the development of this new country. He helped to found the University of Chile in 1843 and served as its rector until his death; he authored Chile's Civil Code, enacted in 1855; he edited an influential newspaper, *El araucano* [The Araucanian], encouraged the development of theater in Santiago, and published essays on philology, jurisprudence, and aesthetics. But Bello's most significant intellectual achievement in this period was the publication in 1847 of his seminal text, *Gramática de la lengua castellana destinada al uso de los americanos* [Spanish Language Grammar for Spanish Americans].

Until 2009, when the Royal Spanish Academy and the Association of Spanish Language Academies published the *Nueva gramática de la lengua española* [New Spanish Language Grammar], Bello's work remained unchallenged as the authoritative Spanish grammar—for over 150 years. One testament to his amazing accomplishment is the fact that only the collaborative effort of hundreds of linguists finally superseded his work. But Bello's prologue, along with the less-known body of his text, continues to be an invaluable resource in modern linguistic thought in Hispanic studies.

Bello asserts that the main purpose of his treatise was to foster unity in language, preserving Spanish as a communal instrument, avoiding the diversification of dialects across the Americas and steering clear of neologisms. In articulating these goals, Bello reveals his intention to lay out a proper grammar in a precise historical moment. Instead of outlining a Latinized grammatical system, like that developed by the Royal Spanish Academy (in Madrid), or proposing a general grammar, as was the vogue in the mid-nineteenth century, Bello accepts the historicity of language—and consequently its rules—as engendered within a community. Such an idea seemed paradoxical even to later philologists, like Rufino José Cuervo (1844–1911), who developed a comparative dictionary for Spanish and other languages and another on Spanish syntax. Cuervo predicted that Spanish, like Latin, would simply fragment into the different languages of its different nations. But history has proven Cuervo wrong: Spanish did not split into "Spanish" and "Mexican" and "Argentinian" and "Venezuelan" and "Cuban." Instead, the language has preserved its essential unity while actively tolerating all the inevitable differences that emerge across countries, regions, and social classes.

Bello's perspective—no less than his grammar—contributed decisively to this outcome. The notion that language could retain its internal identity even as it served as a flexible instrument of social communication, changing with time and circumstance, was significant. Twentieth-century scholars like Enrique Anderson Imbert and Amado Alonso have both observed that Bello probably first encountered this concept in the work of Wilhelm Humboldt, Alexander's brother, when the latter visited Caracas in 1800. By the end of the eighteenth century, Wilhelm Humboldt was already developing his theories of how language structures thought through its grammar, the details of which were laid out in his posthumous publication: *On Language: On the Diversity of Human Language Construction and Its Influence on the Mental Development of the Human Species* (1836–1839). But another source might also have been the very similar theories of the Spanish Jesuit Lorenzo Hervás y Panduro, whose *Catálogo de lenguas de las naciones conocidas, y numeración, división, y clases de éstas según la diversidad de sus idiomas y dialectos* [Language Catalogue of Known Nations, Their Classification, Division, and Types according to the Different Languages and Dialects] was published in six volumes between 1800 and 1805. Humboldt himself met Hervás y Panduro while serving as Prussian envoy to the Vatican, and between 1803 and 1808, Humboldt consulted—perhaps even copied—all the American grammatical archives used by Hervás y Panduro to compile his catalogue. And Bello certainly knew Hervás y Panduro's work, encountering it while he lived in London, if not before.

Perhaps the most striking confluence of purpose, however, may be between Bello's effort to create an instrument of American identity and the educational enterprise of SIMÓN RODRÍGUEZ, who had also sought to promote American intellectual development. Both Bello and Rodríguez shared a relationship as teachers to SIMÓN BOLÍVAR, and the two men knew each other fairly well, both in Venezuela in the 1790s and again at the end of the 1830s when both were living in Chile. Certainly all three men were committed to advancing the singularity of American culture.

Though finally superseded, Bello's grammar remains a singular document of linguistic and philosophical thought in Spanish. Its prologue, presented here, endures as one of the most lucid reflections on the historical condition of language. The selection is from *Selected Writings of Andrés Bello*, edited by Ivan Jaksic and translated by Frances M. Lopez-Morillas (New York, Oxford: Oxford University Press, 1997), 96–99. Reprinted by permission of Oxford University Press.

From **Gramática de la lengua castellana (1847) [Grammar of the Spanish Language]**

Prologue

Although in this grammar I would have preferred not to depart from the usual nomenclature and explanations, there are points on which I felt that the practices of the Spanish language could be represented in a more complete and exact manner. Some readers will no doubt call arbitrary the alterations I have introduced on these points, or will attribute them to an exaggerated desire to say new things; the reasons that I adduce will at least provide that I have adopted them only after mature consideration. But the most negative prejudice, because of the hold that it possesses over even quite well-educated persons, is the prejudice of those who believe that in grammar there is no harm in inadequate definitions, badly made classifications, and false concepts, if only, on the other hand, the rules of good usage are carefully set forth. However, I believe that these things cannot be reconciled, that usage cannot be correctly and faithfully explained except by analyzing it, by uncovering the true principles that govern it. I believe that strict logic is an indispensable requisite for all teaching, and that in the first test of the awakening intellect it is most important not to let it be satisfied with mere words.

The speech of a people is an artificial system of signs, which in many respects differs from other systems of the same kind; it follows from this that each language has its own particular theory, its grammar. Hence we must not apply indiscriminately to one language the principles, terms, and analogies into which, more or less successfully, the practices of another are resolved. The very word idiom (in Greek, particularity or characteristic), tells us that each language has its genius, its physiognomy, its turns of phrase. The grammarian would do his office badly if, when explaining his own language, he were to limit himself to what it had in common with another, or (worse still) to assume resemblances where only differences existed—and important, radical differences at that. General grammar is one thing and the grammar of a given language another; it is one thing to compare two languages and another to consider a language as it is in itself. Are we dealing with the conjugation of the Spanish verb? We must enumerate the forms it assumes, and the meanings and uses of each form, as if there were no other language in the world but Spanish. It is a necessary position with regard to the child, who is taught the rules of the only language within his grasp, his native tongue. This is the viewpoint in which I have tried to place myself, a viewpoint in which I beg intelligent persons, to whose judgment I submit my work, to place themselves as well, laying aside most particularly any reminiscences of the Latin language.

In Spain as in other European countries, an excessive admiration for the language and literature of the Romans placed a Latin stamp on almost all productions of the mind. This was a natural tendency of men's spirits in the period when letters were being restored. Pagan mythology continued to supply the poet with images and symbols, and the Ciceronian period was the model of elocution for elegant writers. Hence it was not strange that the nomenclature and grammatical canons of our Romance tongue should be taken from Latin.

* * *

Signs of thought doubtless obey certain general laws which, derived from those laws which regulate thought itself, govern all languages and constitute a universal grammar. But if we except the resolution of thought into clauses; and the clause into subject and attribute; the existence of the noun to express objects directly; that of the verb to indicate attributes; and that of the other words that modify and determine nouns and verbs in such a way that, with a limited number of both, all possible objects, real as well as intellectual, can be designated (as well as all the attributes that we can perceive or imagine in them), then I see nothing that we are obliged to recognize as a universal law from which no language can be exempt. The number of parts of speech can be larger or smaller than it is in Latin or the Romance tongues. The verb might conceivably have genders and the noun tenses. What is more natural than the agreement of the verb with the subject? Well, in Greek it was not only allowed but customary to make the plural of neuter nouns agree with the singular form of verbs. To the intellect, two negatives must necessarily cancel each other out, and this is almost always the case in speech; but it does not alter the fact that in Spanish there are circumstances in which two negatives do not make a positive. Therefore we must not transfer lightly the effects of ideas to the accidents of words. Philosophy has erred no little in assuming that language is a faithful copy of thought; and this same exaggerated supposition has caused grammar to stray in the opposite direction. Some argued from the copy to the original, others from the original to the copy. In language, conventional and arbitrary factors include a great deal more than is commonly thought. Beliefs, whims of the imagination, and myriad casual associations cannot fail to produce an enormous discrepancy in the means that languages use to make manifest what is taking place in the soul. It is a discrepancy that becomes greater and greater the farther they depart from their common origin.

I am willing to listen patiently to the objections that may be made about what seem to be the new features of this grammar, though on careful examination it will be found that on those very points I sometimes do not innovate but restore. The idea, for example, that I present of the cases in declension is the old and genuine one, and in attributing to the infinitive the nature of a noun I am merely bringing back an idea that is perfectly set forth in the Priscian: "... *uim nominis [rei ipsius] habet verbum infinitum ... dico enim 'bonum est legere,' ut si dicam 'bona est lectio.'*" [The infinitive (of the action itself) has the force of a noun. I say "To read is good" as if I should say "Reading is good."] On the other hand I have not wanted to depend on "authorities," for to me the ultimate authority with regard to a language is the language itself. I do not feel that I am entitled to divide what language constantly unites, nor to forcibly unite what it separates. I regard analogies with other languages as no more than accessory proofs. I accept practices as language presents them, without imaginary ellipses, without other explanations than those that illustrate usage by means of usage.

*   *   *

I do not claim to write for Spaniards. My lessons are aimed at my brothers, the inhabitants of Spanish America. I believe that the preservation of our forefathers' tongue in all possible purity is important, as a providential means of communication and a fraternal link among the various nations of Spanish origin scattered over the two continents. But what I presume to recommend to them is not a superstitious purism. The prodigious advances of all sciences and arts, the diffusion of intellectual culture and political revolutions, daily require new signs to express new ideas; and the introduction of novel words, taken from ancient and foreign languages, no longer offends unless they are manifestly unnecessary, or unless they reveal the affectation and poor taste of those who think that by using them they are embellishing what they write. There is another and worse vice, which is to give new meanings to known words and phrases, thus multiplying the ambiguities that arise out of the variety of meanings from which all languages suffer more or less, and perhaps even more so those most often studied, owing to the almost infinite number of ideas to which a necessarily limited number of signs must be accommodated. But the greatest evil of all, and one which, if it is not controlled, will deprive us of the precious advantages of a common language, is the torrent of grammatical neologisms which inundate and render obscure much of what is written in America, and which by altering the structure of the language tend to change it into a multitude of irregular, undisciplined, and barbaric dialects; embryos of future languages which, during a long development, would reproduce in America what happened in Europe during the dark period of the corruption of Latin. Chile, Peru, Buenos Aires, Mexico, would each speak their own language, or, to express it better, a number of languages, as happens in Spain, Italy, and France, where certain provincial languages predominate but a number of others exist beside them, hampering the spread of enlightenment, the execution of laws, the administration of the State, and national unity. A language is like a living body: its vitality does not depend on the constant identity of elements, but on the regularity of the functions that those elements perform, and from which arise the form and nature that distinguish the whole.

Whether or not I exaggerate the danger, it has been the chief reason that has led me to compose this book, so superior to my powers in so many ways. Intelligent readers who honor me by reading it with some attention will observe how much care I have exercised in marking out, so to speak, the boundaries that good usage in our language respects, amid the looseness and freedom of its turns of phrase; and in pointing out the corruptions most widespread today and showing the essential difference that exists between Spanish constructions and foreign ones that resemble them up to a point, which we tend to imitate without exercising the discernment we ought to employ.

Let no one believe that, by recommending the preservation of Castilian Spanish, I intend to accuse as harmful and spurious everything peculiar to American speech. Very correct locutions exist which are considered outdated in the Peninsula, but which persist in Spanish America. Why outlaw them? If according to general practice among Americans the conjugation of some verb is more logical, why should we prefer the one that has prevailed more or less by chance in Castile? If we have formed new words from Spanish roots according to the ordinary rules of derivation that the Spanish language recognizes, and which have been used and are still being used to increase its capacity, why should we be ashamed of using them? Chile and Venezuela have as much right as Aragon and Andalusia to have their occasional divergences tolerated, when they are supported by the universal and authentic usage of educated persons. These differences are much less damaging to purity and correctness of language than are those Frenchified usages that are sprinkled today through even the most admired of Peninsular writers.

Esteban Echeverría (1805–1851)

Known as the first writer of a distinctly Argentine literature, Esteban Echeverría was born in Buenos Aires, Argentina, on September 2, 1805. He spent several formative years between 1825 and 1830 studying in Paris, where he witnessed two major events that profoundly shaped his impact on the culture of Argentina: the emergence of Romanticism in France and the formation of the Saint-Simonian Society in Paris. When he returned to Buenos Aires in 1830, Echeverría brought with him radical ideas that profoundly influenced a generation of young men—including Juan Bautista Alberdi, Juan María Gutiérrez, and Miguel Cané (the Elder)—who shaped the education, culture, and politics of Argentina, especially after the fall from power in 1852 of Juan Manuel de Rosas, dictator of the Argentine Federation.

As a Romantic poet in his own right, Echeverría's literary reputation rests in substantial part on a long narrative poem, "La cautiva" [The Captive], which recounts the capture of a white frontier couple by Indians. Drawing on both the British poet Lord Byron and Victor Hugo (whose *Les orientales* appeared in Paris in 1829), "La cautiva" was included in Echeverría's book of poetry, *Rimas* (1837) and came to be one of the most influential poems in Argentinian literature. Echeverría's poem appeared at the very moment that Juan Bautista Alberdi was publishing *La moda*, a journal that Echeverría helped to develop into an influential vehicle not only for the principles of French Romanticism but also for the progressive ideas of Saint-Simon.

A group of restless young intellectuals, yearning to affect contemporary politics, soon gathered around Echeverría. They organized themselves as the Asociación de Mayo [Association of May] and later as La Joven Argentina [Young Argentina], both names revealing their political goals. The former appropriates a month associated with Argentine independence, largely accomplished by the previous generation, while the latter echoes The Young Italy, a European group that likewise sought radical political change. These newcomers believed that history had assigned them the role of taking charge of the country, but first there had to be a nation. The continuing civil wars only demonstrated the country's lack of unity, with the Federalists defending the independence of the provinces and the Unitarians trying to preserve a centralized power in Buenos Aires. Such struggles laid bare the failure of the previous generation to produce a stable nation—and sharpened the goal of the next generation to create a new and stronger state.

Saint-Simon's writings had suggested to Echeverría the practical root of the problem: before any governmental model could be established, whether centralized or federalist, a cohesive society with healthy and effective institutions had to exist. Even the title of the manifesto of the Asociación de Mayo came directly from Saint-Simon: *Socialist Dogma*. It is a "dogma" because it contains undeniable truths, requiring faith in their affirmation. It is "socialist" in Saint-Simon's terms, stressing "union" and "association" between and among groups; in this way it differs significantly from Rousseau's notion of a social contract between the extremes of the individual citizen and the general will—without any other mediation.

For Saint-Simon, cooperation among three basic groups was critical: the industrialists, the scientists or knowers, and the artists. By industrialists, Saint-Simon meant all workers, whether peasants, artisans, laborers, bureaucrats, or even managers. People who did not work, in fact, posed the worst menace to society, and among them Saint-Simon included traditional aristocrats as well as the expanding number of idle capitalists. The second group included the scientists, whose knowledge would guide industry to progress, while the third group consisted of the artists, without whom the association itself could not be conscious of itself. At a moment when science and rationalism were deepening their challenges to the authority of Christianity in Europe, what Saint-Simon offered was a novel form of union, a new religion of cooperation and justice based in labor. Radical in its consistency, his system even called for equality between men and women.

Echeverría's *Socialist Dogma* only incorporated selected concepts from Saint-Simon, those most congenial to the new liberalism of Spanish America. Primary among them were the cooperation between different social classes and social equality (though not between genders). But even the term "association" was applied in a limited way, since Echeverría had no intention of including all the lower classes, such as blacks, whom he thought to be intrinsically lazy. Echeverría's goal was basically to create a society in which the political and social interests of industrialists, scientists, and artists would simply fuse, without any specific regulation of their relationships.

As might be expected, Juan Manuel de Rosas, the Federalist leader, did not view such radical theories with much pleasure, and Echeverría, along with many other members of the Association, was forced to emigrate to Montevideo in 1840. In exile, Echeverría continued to agitate against the Argentine Federation and to promote a national literature. He also wrote some of his best poetry, including "La guitarra" (The Guitar) and "El ángel caído" (The Fallen Angel), though "La cautiva" remains his most significant poem. Echeverría died in 1851 in Montevideo, just a few months before Rosas' downfall.

Only with the publication of Echeverría's complete works in 1871 by fellow poet Juan María Gutiérrez did the great Argentine's masterful short story "El matadero" [The Slaughterhouse], written in 1839, come to light. Set in a Buenos Aires slaughterhouse, the tale is a political allegory depicting the Federalist enforcers as violent butchers and the Unitarian opposition as helpless animals—the young men who had sought to transform Argentine society, sacrificial victims of the barbarism represented by Rosas and all those who obstructed a progressive and civilized future for the nation.

"La cautiva," "El matadero," and *Dogma socialista* remain the best accomplishments of Echeverría as an artist and as a political thinker. This passage on the critical concept of association is from Esteban Echeverría, *Dogma socialista* (1837) in *Obras escogidas* (Caracas, Venezuela: Ayacucho, 1991), translated by Charles Becker.

From **Dogma socialista (1837) [Socialist Dogma]**

1. Association

Society is a fact stamped upon the pages of history and the necessary education that Providence imposed upon man to exercise the free and full development of his faculties, when he was given the Universe for his heritage. It [Society] is the vast theater where his power grows, his intelligence is nourished, and the successive fruits of his relentless labors are born.

Without association there is no progress; rather, it is the requisite condition of any civilization or progress.

To work to propagate and spread the spirit of association within every social class is to become engaged in the great task that is the progress and civilization of our nation.

True association can only exist among equals. Inequality engenders hatreds and passions that stifle fraternity and strain social ties.

To extend the sphere of association, and invigorate and deepen it, social individualities need to be evened out or must commit to making equality a reality.

For association to be meaningful to its purposes, it must be organized and formed in a way that neither collides with nor mutually damages social and individual interests, or must combine these two elements: the social element and the individual element, the nation and the citizen's independence. The entire issue of social science arises from the alliance and harmony of these two principles.

The rights of man and the right of association are equally legitimate.

Politics must aim through association to ensure the freedom and individuality of each citizen.

Society must place the independence of every one of its individuals under its wing, just as every individuality is required to marshal its strengths for the benefit of the nation.

Society must not swallow the citizen or demand the absolute sacrifice of his individuality. Nor will social interest admit the exclusive predominance of individual interests; otherwise society would dissolve, leaving its members with no bond in common.

The will of a people or of a majority may not establish a predatory right over the right of an individual, because there is no absolute authority on the face of the earth, because no authority is an infallible agency of supreme justice, and because the law of conscience and reason prevails over human laws.

No legitimate authority can ever rule except on behalf of the law, justice, and truth. The national will, the true public conscience, must be interpreted and determined with great care as to what is right, what is true, what is compulsory—this is the realm of positive law. But beyond this law, on a higher sphere, are the rights of man, which as the foundation and essential condition of social order come above that law and hold sway over it.

No majority, no party or assembly is entitled to establish laws that attack natural laws and the principles that conserve society and which place at the whim of one man the security, freedom, and life of everyone.

The people who commit this assault are senseless or, at a minimum, stupid; because they use a right that does not belong to them, because they sell what is not theirs—the freedom of others; because they sell themselves without being able to do so; and they become slaves, when by the law of God and nature they are free.

The will of the people can never sanction as just what is essentially unjust.

To use reasons of state to justify the violation of these rights is to launch Machiavellianism and subject people, de facto, to the disastrous rule of force and arbitrariness.

The health of the people arises from nothing other than the religious and inviolable respect for the rights of each and every one of the members who constitute it.

To exercise rights over its members, society owes all of them justice, equal protection, and laws that safeguard their person, their property, and their freedom. This requires society to protect them from injustice and violence; to keep them in line, so that their reciprocal passions will not be harmed; to provide them with the means to work, without trace of disturbance, for their own welfare without infringement of others' welfare; to place each *one* under the safeguard of *all,* so that he may peacefully enjoy what he possesses or has acquired through his work, industry, or talents.

Social authority that fails to do this—that instead of fraternizing, divides; that sows distrust and anger; that incites partisan spirit and vengeance; that encourages disloyalty, espionage, and betrayal of trust, and that tends to convert society into a swarm of informants, executioners, and victims—is heinous, immoral, and abominable.

The institution of government is not useful, moral, or necessary, except to the degree that it is committed to ensuring every citizen of his everlasting rights and mainly his freedom.

The optimal condition of this association lies in the proposition of freedom for one and for all. To achieve this, fraternity, generosity, and mutual sacrifice among members of the same family must be encouraged. Efforts are needed so that all individual strengths, far from isolating themselves and focusing on their own selfishness, join together simultaneously and collectively in a single goal: in the progress and prominence of the nation.

We are lost in the overwhelming sway of our individualism. Selfish passions have sown anarchy in the fields of freedom and brought forth barren fruits. As a result, social ties have been strained; selfishness has seeped into our very hearts and everywhere displays its deformed and ominous nature; hearts do not beat to the same words or to the sight of the same symbols; our minds do not meet in a shared belief in the nation, in equality, in fraternity, and in liberty.

How can a society in dissolution be revived? How can the sociable element of the human heart be made to predominate, and the nation and civilization saved? The remedy is found only in the spirit of association.

Association, progress, freedom, equality, fraternity—correlative terms from the great social and humanitarian synthesis—divine symbols of the fortuitous destiny of peoples and humanity.

Freedom cannot be achieved except through equality, nor can equality without the aid of association or the concurrence of all individual strengths aimed at a single objective, an indefinite one,—*continuous progress*—; the fundamental formula of nineteenth-century philosophy.

The social organization that will be the most perfect is the one that offers the best safeguards to develop equality and freedom, and the broadest space for the free and harmonious exercise of human faculties. The best government will be the one that most closely reflects our customs and our social conditions.

The road to freedom is equality; equality and freedom are the only progenitors of democracy.

Thus, democracy is the regime that suits us, the only one within our grasp.

To prepare the elements to organize and constitute the democracy whose germ exists in our society is also our mission.

The association of the Young Argentine Generation represents in its provisional organization the future of the Argentine nation. Its mission is essentially organizational. It shall manage to spread its spirit and its doctrine, to extend the circle of its progressive tendencies, to draw in spirit toward one great national association by reconciling opinions and focusing them on the nation and on the principles of the equality, liberty, and fraternity of all men.

*   *   *

In its definitive organization, it shall discover how to reconcile the two fundamental ideas of these times—*nationhood and humanity*—and make the progressive movement of the nation advance with the progressive movement of the great humanitarian association.

Gertrudis Gómez de Avellaneda (1814–1873)

Gertrudis Gómez de Avellaneda was born in Puerto Príncipe, present-day Camagüey, Cuba. The author of novels, plays, poetry, and short stories, she also edited a ground-breaking journal for women, *Álbum Cubano*. But her most memorable work, published in Spain in 1841, was her novel, *Sab*, which is distinguished for its fresh style and flawless structure, no less than for its radical resistance to slavery—a theme with international resonance in the mid-nineteenth century.

Gómez de Avellaneda moved with her family to Spain in 1836, initially to Seville, where she produced her first successful play *Leoncia* (1840), and then to Madrid. As with her older and more famous French contemporary George Sand (the pseudonym of Amantine-Lucile-Aurore Dupin [1804–1876]), Gómez de Avellaneda resisted traditional roles for women in her life as well as in her writings. After several public affairs and her rejection by the Royal Spanish Academy because of her gender, she married a fellow native of Cuba and returned there in 1859. Though welcomed as a national heroine, Gómez de Avellaneda went back to Spain in 1865 after her husband's death. She occupied herself editing her *Complete Works* until her own demise from diabetes in Seville in 1873.

Writing an antislavery novel in the 1830s and 1840s was hardly unusual. In Cuba there were several antislavery associations, reflecting various motives for abolition. The most familiar was simply the rejection of an inhuman and exploitative labor system that contradicted basic Christian principles. But another argument was driven by the fear that slaves would become a majority and would annihilate Hispanic—if not all Western—culture on the island. Indeed, by the 1840s, enslaved people and freed Afro-Cubans numbered over 600,000—45 percent of the total population. Both of these abolitionist positions were linked to Cuba's political status. Some antislavery groups simply favored independence, while others supported Cuba's annexation to Spain, following the reforms of the Cádiz Constitution of 1812. Spanish authorities rejected both positions, preferring to maintain the island as a colony, and the leaders of both antislavery movements were persecuted with a vigor that varied with the political winds of the moment.

Among those whose abolitionist politics were closely linked to literary activity was the circle of Domingo del Monte in Havana. Some of the most important writers and thinkers of the period gathered around him, including several whose fictions about slavery and the color line influenced Gómez de Avellaneda's masterpiece. One of the first was Anselmo Suárez y Romero's antislavery novel *Francisco*, published in 1838, the same year that Francisco Manzano wrote his justly famous *Autobiografía de un esclavo* [Autobiography of a Slave]. With the support of del Monte and his literary circle, Manzano's book was translated and published in London. The following year Cirilo Villaverde published his short story about a mulatta in love with her white half-brother. Revised and expanded, its plot served as the core for Cuba's best-known nineteenth-century novel, *Cecilia Valdés*, published in New York in 1882.

Though published in Spain, Gómez de Avellaneda's *Sab* played a critical role in the antislavery debates. Echoing Villaverde and Manzano, her protagonist, Sab, is a person of mixed race. A freed slave, Sab is in love with Carlota, whom he only later learns is his first cousin. But this latent possibility of incest never really interferes with the plot, which focuses instead on the even greater taboo of a relationship between a mixed-race man and a white woman. When Sab dies, he leaves a letter to Teresa, Carlota's cousin, revealing his undeclared and forbidden passion.

Sab's letter to Teresa is one of the most notable texts of the nineteenth century in its refutation of numerous contemporary testimonies about the bestiality, stupidity, irrationality, and cruelty of enslaved blacks. The contradictory arguments employed in these texts to disguise slavery's crass economic motives are evident. To reject the inhumanity of enslavement, blacks were claimed to be less than human—animals. But to justify the severity of their ill-treatment, slaveholders had to argue that blacks were clever schemers and pagans who required stiff discipline if rebellion was to be avoided. Such arguments were also promoted as well-intended warnings to freedmen, whose mere existence posed a grave threat to white society.

Sab's letter to Teresa reveals the profound hypocrisy in these arguments simply by representing Sab as an honest, sensitive human being, perfectly capable of a coherent and intelligent statement. Gómez de Avellaneda's novel and particularly Sab's eloquent letter constitute critical denunciations of slavery for the era. Like Harriet Beecher Stowe's North American novel, *Uncle Tom's Cabin* (1852), *Sab* reflects the power of writing in opposing social evil. Sab does not have to fight directly against slavery but only to represent with his intelligence and eloquence the absurdity of its premises.

But Sab's letter, beneath its fairly moderate response to a profound injustice, also reveals another voice—that of Gertrudis Gómez de Avellaneda herself. Recalling that Sab's claims originate from a young Cuban woman barely in her twenties, the antislavery arguments achieve even greater resonance, echoing a familiar trope among nineteenth-century women writers: that women were themselves enslaved. Gómez de Avellaneda is explicit: at the end of Sab's letter, women are described as even less free than slaves, since enslaved persons can at least buy their freedom, while women, after they marry, cannot. The letter reflects sentiments that Carlota might express after experiencing the disillusionments of marriage or what Teresa might herself have written if she had not retired to a convent.

In this classic antislavery narrative, Gertrudis Gómez de Avellaneda fashions a forceful metaphor about the condition of women and a sharp critique of marriage, which earned her vigorous criticism from many of her contemporaries. She also becomes one of the first voices in Spanish America to denounce the subservient status of slaves and women as sharing a similar destiny. If Sab recognizes his own situation—"You are a mulatto and a slave"—he also articulates Gómez de Avellaneda's insight about Carlota—and most women: "You are a woman and a wife."

The selection is from the 1841 version of *Sab*, translated by Nina M. Scott in *"Sab" and "Autobiography"* (Austin: University of Texas Press, 1993),

From **Letter to Teresa, in** *Sab* (1841)

And yet, my God, I accept this new test and, with no sign of aversion, will empty the last drop of gall which You have poured into the bitter chalice of my life.

I am dying, Teresa, and I want to bid you farewell. Haven't I told you this before? I believe I have.

I want to bid you farewell and thank you for your friendship and for having shown me generosity, selflessness, and heroism. Teresa: you are a sublime woman, and I have tried to imitate you—but can the dove soar like the eagle? You rise great and strong, ennobled by sacrifices while I fall back broken. When the hurricane launches its chariot of fire across the land, the *ceiba* tree remains upright, its victorious crown illuminated by the halo which its enemy bestows on it, while the bush, which has vainly attempted to survive in the same way, is left only to attest to the force which has destroyed it. The sun comes out, and the *ceiba* greets it by saying "Here I am," while the bush exhibits only scattered leaves and broken branches.

And yet, you are a weak woman: what is this strength which sustains you and for which I vainly ask my virile heart? Is it virtue which gives it to you? I have thought a great deal about this: during my wakeful nights I have invoked that great word—Virtue! But what is virtue? Of what does it consist? I have wanted to understand it, but in vain I have asked men for the truth. I remember that when my master sent me to confess my sins at the feet of a priest, I asked God's minister what I should do in order to attain virtue. The virtue of the slave, he replied, is to obey and be silent, serve his lawful masters with humility and resignation, and never to judge them.

The explanation did not satisfy me. Well then, I thought, can virtue be relative? Is virtue not one and the same for all men? Has the supreme head of this great human family perhaps established different laws for those who are born with white skin and those with black? Don't all have the same needs, the same passions, the same flaws? Why, then, do some have the right to enslave and others the duty to obey? God, Whose supreme hand has evenly distributed His benefits among all the countries of this earth, Who makes the sun come up for all of His great family scattered all over the world, Who has written the great dogma of equality on the grave, could God sanction the iniquitous laws on which one man bases his right to buy and sell another, and can His spokesman on earth tell a slave "Your duty is to suffer: the virtue of the slave is to forget that he is a man, to renounce the gifts God gave him, to give up the dignity with which He has endowed him, and to kiss the hand that brands him with the seal of infamy"? No, men lie: virtue does not exist among them.

Many times, Teresa, in the solitude of the fields and in the silence of night have I thought about this great word: Virtue. But for me Virtue is like Providence: an unknown need, a mysterious power which I can imagine but which I don't know. In vain have I looked for it among men. I have always observed that the strong man oppressed the weak one, that the clever cheated the ignorant, and that the rich disdained the poor. Among men I have failed to find the great harmony that God has established in nature.

I have never been able to understand these things, Teresa, as much as I have questioned the sun, the moon, and the stars, the roaring winds of the hurricane, and the gentle breezes of the night. To my sorrow the thick clouds of my ignorance obscured the flashes of my intelligence; and when I ask you now if you owe your strength to virtue, I have yet a new doubt and wonder if strength is based not on virtue but on pride. Because pride is the greatest and most beautiful thing I know, and the only source from which I have seen men's noble and brilliant actions emanate. Tell me, Teresa, the greatness and selflessness of your soul, isn't it only pride? And what if it is? Whatever the name of the feeling which calls forth noble actions, it must be respected. But what do I lack that I cannot compare myself with you? Is it a lack of pride? . . . Is it that this great feeling cannot exist in the soul of a man who has been a slave? Nonetheless, although a slave, I have loved everything beautiful and great, and I have felt my soul rise above my destiny. Oh, yes! I have possessed great and beautiful pride: the slave has let his faculty of thought range freely, and his ideas have soared higher than the clouds which bear the lightning. Then what is the difference which exists between your moral order and mine? I will tell you, I will tell you what I think. It is that within me there is an immense ability to love: you have the courage to resist, and I the energy to act; you are upheld by reason, and I am devoured by emotion. Your heart is of the purest gold, mine of fire.

I was born with a rich store of interests. When, in my early youth, Carlota would read aloud to me the ballads, novels, and histories which she liked best, I listened to her breathlessly and imagined a multitude of ideas, and a new world would evolve before my eyes. I found the destiny of those men who fought and died for their country very beautiful. Like a charger who hears the sound of the trumpet, I quivered with a savage zeal at great words like "country" and "liberty": my heart swelled, my nostrils flared, my hand groped intuitively and eagerly for a sword, and Carlota's sweet voice was barely able to wrest me from my trance. At the same time as the beloved voice, I thought I heard martial music, shouts of triumph, and songs of victory, and my spirit soared toward the magnificent destiny until a sudden and devastating reminder came to whisper in my ear: "You are a mulatto and a slave." Then a dark rage would constrict my breast, and my heart's blood coursed like poison through my swollen veins. How many times did the novels which Carlota read refer to the mad love which a vassal felt for his queen or a humble man for some illustrious and proud lady! . . . Then I listened with a violent trembling, and my eyes devoured the book; but oh! the vassal or the plebeian were free, and their faces did not bear the brand of disfavor. To them Heaven opened the gates of fortune, and courage and ambition came to love's aid. But what could the slave do, to whom destiny opened no path, to whom the world conceded no rights? His color was the mark of an eternal fate, a sentence of moral death.

*　　*　　*

Teresa, how many thoughts oppress me! Death, which already chills my hands, has not yet reached my head and my heart. My eyes, however, grow dim . . . I think I see visions before me. Don't you see? It is she, it is Carlota, with her wedding ring and virgin's crown . . . but a hateful, squalid band follows her! They are Disillusionment, Tedium, Regret and behind them a monster with sepulchral voice and head of iron: the Inevitable! Oh, women! Poor, blind victims! Like slaves, they patiently drag their chains and bow their heads under the yoke of human laws. With no other guide than an untutored and trusting heart, they choose a master for life. The slave can at least change masters, can even hope to buy his freedom some day if he can save enough money, but a woman, when she lifts her careworn hands and mistreated brow to beg for release, hears the monstrous, deathly voice which cries out to her: "In the grave." Don't you hear a voice, Teresa? It is that of the strong who say to the weak: obedience, humility, resignation . . . that is virtue. Oh, I feel sorry for you, Carlota, I feel sorry for you although you are happy and I lie dying, although you fall asleep in the arms of pleasure and I in those of death. Your destiny is a sad one, poor angel, but never turn against God, nor confuse His holy laws with those of men. God never shuts the doors on repentance. God does not accept impossible vows. God is the God of the weak as well as the strong and never asks more of a man than what He has given him.

Oh, what anguish! It is not death, it is not ordinary jealousy which torments me, but the thought, the foreboding of Carlota's destiny . . . to see her profaned! She, Carlota, a dawn flower who had never yet been touched except by the breezes of Heaven! And the solution is impossible! Impossible—what an iron word! And these are men's laws, and Heaven is silent . . . and God allows them! Oh, let us worship his inscrutable judgment! Who can understand it? But no, You will not always be silent. God of all justice! *Error, Ignorance, and absurd prejudice: you will not always rule in the world: your decrepitude foretells your ruin. The word of salvation will resound over all the earth: old idols will topple from their profound altars, and the throne of justice will rise brilliantly over the ruins of old societies.* Yes, a heavenly voice tells me this. In vain, it tells me, in vain will the old elements of the moral sphere fight against the regenerative principle: in vain will there be days of darkness and hours of discouragement in that terrible battle . . . the day of truth will dawn clear and brilliant. God made His chosen people wait forty years for the promised land, and those who doubted were punished by never setting foot therein; but their children saw it. Yes, the sun of justice is not far off. The world waits for it in order to rejuvenate in its light: men will bear a divine mark, and the angel of poetry will shine its rays over the new kingdom of the intellect.

Teresa! Teresa! The light which has shone in my eyes has blinded them . . . I cannot see what I am writing any more . . . the visions have disappeared . . . the divine voice is silent . . . a deep darkness surrounds me . . . a silence . . . No, it is interrupted by the death rattle of someone who is dying and by the moans that a nightmare wrenches from an old woman who sleeps! I want to see them for the last time . . . but I cannot see any longer! I want to embrace them . . . my feet are leaden! Oh, death! Death is a cold and heavy thing like—like what? With what can death be compared?

Carlota . . . perhaps at this very moment . . . let me die first. My God . . . my soul wings to You . . . farewell, Teresa . . . the pen falls from my hand . . . farewell! I have loved, I have lived . . . I no longer live . . . yet I still love.

Domingo Faustino Sarmiento (1811–1888)

Domingo Faustino Sarmiento was a man of many talents: journalist, educator, essayist, polemicist, soldier, governor, diplomat—and president of the Argentine Republic (1868–1874). Together with ESTEBAN ECHEVERRÍA, he was part of the "Generation of 1837," young men who helped to define both the politics and literature of Argentina by resisting the Federalist regime of Juan Manuel de Rosas and by fostering Romanticism in their writings and perspectives. Sarmiento himself became a champion of education and modernization as well as the author of one of Argentina's founding texts, *Facundo: Civilization and Barbarism* or in its full title: *Civilización y barbarie: Vida de Juan Facundo Quiroga* (1845) [Civilization and Barbarism: The Life of Juan Facundo Quiroga].

Sarmiento was the child of a former soldier in the wars for independence and of a deeply religious mother from San Juan, near the Chilean border. The only surviving son of fifteen children, Sarmiento received a good basic education but soon found himself caught up in the ongoing civil wars. At sixteen, he witnessed the invasion of San Juan by the Federalist gaucho, Facundo Quiroga, an event that solidified his commitment to Unitarian goals and to active resistance. Though he fought alongside the Unitarian militia, Sarmiento was eventually forced into exile in 1831. In Chile's relatively liberal environment, he became a teacher, founding a school and writing political commentary. When Quiroga was assassinated in 1835, Sarmiento returned to Argentina to continue his labors. He was soon associated with other activists who opposed Juan Manuel de Rosas' regime, including the circle of Buenos Aires, known as the Generation of 1837.

By 1840, Sarmiento was once again exiled to Chile. He settled in Valparaíso, again working as a journalist and teacher. In 1845, he founded his own newspaper, *El Progreso* and began the serial publication of his semi-fictionalized account, *Facundo*. By that point, the Argentine government was pressuring Chile to extradite Sarmiento and other refugees, and he had to work quickly. He later explained how that rush into print resulted in numerous inaccuracies, but while later editions incorporated his notion of changing politics, Sarmiento rarely made any other corrections. Despite this raw quality, *Facundo* remains a key text in understanding Argentine history. In one sense, *Facundo* is not simply a book but an event, a historical text-fact. Originally composed as a weapon in the fight against Rosas, the despised governor of the province of Buenos Aires, *Facundo* has consistently served as a point of reference in defining social, historical, and even psychological alternatives for Argentina.

Beginning with its dichotomy between civilization (the cities) and barbarism (the countryside or the pampa), *Facundo* became as early as the 1850s the hinge upon which all thinking about Argentine nationality turned: for or against those opposing terms. Others would refine or even invert Sarmiento's priorities, but the tension remained intact. Juan Bautista Alberdi, for example, whose book *Bases y puntos de partida para la organización política de la Republica Argentina* partly inspired the 1853 constitution, criticized Sarmiento for equating the cities with civilization.

For Alberdi, it was the city that produced the barbarism (including Rosas' primary supporters), while the countryside—the pampa—was the real source of Argentine civilization, generating wool, cattle, and other agricultural products that supported the nation's wealth.

Despite its hasty composition, Sarmiento's book has a clear tripartite structure. In the first section, the Argentine nation is defined through its geographical, historical, and social characteristics; the second part details the history of the independent nation up to the death of Facundo Quiroga, whose biography is the focus of the narrative; and finally, the third portion analyzes Argentine politics from Rosas' dictatorship to 1845. Such a clear structure, however, does not preclude the text's many contradictory judgments that challenge any coherent summation—nor its oddity as history, since it lacks crucial dates. However, the force of Sarmiento's arguments suggests that he was analyzing a profoundly contradictory situation.

From the many paradoxes embodied in this critical text, at least three are noteworthy. First, Sarmiento insists that Rosas' gravest mistake was to base his power in groups that responded primarily to barbarism: gauchos, Indians, blacks, and the common people. Such reliance, in his view, weakened the civilizing force of the cities. Of course, Sarmiento believed that some cities, like Córdoba, exuded Catholic backwardness, and he seemed to overlook the fact that a majority of Rosas' supporters were city-dwellers. But Sarmiento ultimately relies on a paradox: while Rosas self-identified as a Federalist—upholding the relative independence of the provinces—his immense power inevitably made Buenos Aires critical to his dictatorial control, in effect, realizing the goals of his enemies, by making Buenos Aires the seat of a centralized government.

Another paradoxical point derives from Sarmiento's critique of Rosas' opposition to writing a constitution. A constitution imposes a general law, whose legitimacy resides in the power of the state and excludes other legal regimes, including local or private regulations, canon law, or custom. But in the very first section of *Facundo*, Sarmiento specifically describes the country's juridical relationships that correspond to specific social sectors and that depend on a particular kind of sociability to function. Of course, Sarmiento assumes that such a legal framework must be fundamentally rural and scattered throughout the country, that sociability cannot be urban or concentrated in a city. In the end, though, the legal system Sarmiento defends is not based in the written language of a constitution (which the Federalists fiercely opposed), but in custom and tradition.

Finally, *Facundo* is shaped by widespread nineteenth-century theories of the hero, an individual whose actions became determinant in their respective nations and in human history as a whole. Napoleon remained, of course, the paradigmatic European hero, despite his death some twenty-four years earlier. For Sarmiento, such a heroic and dominating influence in Spanish America was embodied in the *caudillo*, a local chieftain or warlord. Sarmiento's portrait of Facundo Quiroga unconsciously mythologizes that figure, highlighting his special knowledge and his intimate understanding of the psychology of his soldiers. Of course, Sarmiento also hated the *caudillos*, holding them responsible for all the evils of the republic, even as he made Facundo a romanticized model of the Spanish American hero.

The opening narration of the life of Facundo Quiroga is a masterful piece of writing, in which Sarmiento musters a variety of literary resources to reveal the *caudillo*'s character. Facundo is initially portrayed as an ordinary anonymous bandit, pursued by a wild beast that chases him ignominiously up a tree. But the vivid details of this adventure also identify the fierce general Facundo Quiroga himself, who, after all and against the odds, comprehends both fear and vengeance.

Sarmiento was a prolific author, whose complete works consist of many volumes. Among the most notable are an early autobiography called *Recuerdos de provincia* (1850) [Recollections of a Provincial Past] and *Viajes por África, Europa y América* (1849) [Travels in Africa, Europe and America], which recounted his travels between 1845 and 1847, studying educational systems. After 1855, Sarmiento became active in the politics of Buenos Aires, serving as governor in his home province and an emissary to the United States in 1865, where he was impressed by the ideals of Lincoln and certain aspects of North American democracy. Even after his term as president of Argentina, Sarmiento continued to be embroiled in political struggles and to work to improve education, one of his most enduring achievements. In 1888, Sarmiento died of a heart attack in his villa in Paraguay in the presence of his daughter and companion. His body was returned to Buenos Aires for burial.

Despite his progressive views and his efforts to modernize education, Sarmiento embodies paradox in nearly every dimension of his life and work. One of his last books, for example, was *Conflicto y armonías de las razas en América* (1883) [Conflict and Harmonies between the Races in America]. Envisioned as a sequel to *Facundo*, the work remains a controversial reflection of the racist views that continue to affect the political and social experience of all the Americas.

The selection is from the translation of Kathleen Ross, *Facundo: Civili-*

zation and Barbarism (Berkeley and Los Angeles: University of California Press, 2003), 91–94. Reproduced with permission of University of California Press via Copyright Clearance Center.

From Civilización y barbarie: Vida de Juan Facundo Quiroga (1845) [Facundo: Civilization and Barbarism]

Chapter 5: Life of Juan Facundo Quiroga

Au surplus, ces traits appartiennent au caractère original du genre humain. L'homme de la nature, et qui n'a pas encore appris à contenir or déguiser ses passions, les montre dans toute leur énergie, et se livre à toute leur impétuosité. [Moreover these traits belong to the original character of the human race. The natural man who has not yet learned to restrain or disguise his passions displays them in all their energy and gives himself up to their impetuosity.]

Alix, *Histoire de L'Empire Ottoman*

Childhood and Youth

Between the cities of San Luis and San Juan there lies a vast desert, which because of its complete lack of water is given the name *travesía*. In general, those solitudes have a sad and abandoned aspect, and no traveler coming from the east passes the last reservoir or cistern of the countryside without supplying his *chifles* with a sufficient quantity of water. In this *travesía*, there once took place the following strange scene. The knife fights so common among our gauchos had forced one of them to abandon the city of San Luis precipitously and to gain the *travesía* on foot, with his saddle over his shoulder, in order to escape the pursuit of the law. Two companions were to catch up with him as soon as they could rob horses for all three.

At that time, hunger and thirst were not the only dangers awaiting him in that desert, where a "ravening" tiger had been roaming for a year, following travelers' tracks, and by then more than eight were those who had become victims to his predilection for human flesh. It sometimes happens, in those areas where man and beast dispute the dominance of nature, that the former falls beneath the bloody claw of the latter; then the tiger begins to prefer the taste of his flesh, and is called *cebado* when it is given to this new sort of hunt, the manhunt. The country judge of the area immediate to the scene of this devastation summons able men to the chase, and under his authority and direction they pursue the *cebado* tiger, who rarely escapes the sentence that declares it outside the law.

When our fugitive had walked some six leagues, he thought he heard the tiger roar in the distance, and his fibers shuddered. The tiger's roar is a grunt like that of a hog, but sharp, prolonged, strident, and even with no reason to fear, it causes an involuntary shaking of the nerves, as if the flesh all by itself were trembling at the announcement of death.

Some minutes later, he heard the roar more distinctly and more near; the tiger was on his track now, and only at a great distance could he sight a small carob tree. He needed to hurry his pace, even to run, because the roars were following each other with increasing frequency, and each was more distinct, more vibrant than the last.

Finally, throwing his saddle down by the side of the road, the gaucho headed for the tree he had sighted, and despite its weak trunk, luckily quite a tall one, he was able to climb up to the top and sway continuously, half-hidden among the branches. From there, he could observe the scene taking place on the road. The tiger marched at a hurried pace, sniffing the ground and roaring more frequently as it sensed the proximity of its prey. It passed the point where the latter had left the road and lost the track; the tiger became infuriated, whirled around until it sighted the saddle, which it tore to pieces with a slap of the paw, scattering all the gear in the air. Irritated all the more by this disappointment, it went back to search for the track, finally finding the direction in which it went, and lifting its gaze, perceived its prey using his weight to keep the little carob tree swaying, as does the fragile reed when birds perch on its tip.

From that moment, the tiger roared no more: it bounded over, and in the blink of an eye its enormous paws were bearing on the slender trunk two yards above the ground, sending it a convulsive tremor that worked its way into the nerves of the badly secured gaucho. The beast tried to make a leap, in vain; it took a turn around the tree, measuring its height with eyes reddened by the thirst for blood, and finally, roaring with rage, lay down on the ground, ceaselessly switching its tail, eyes fixed on its prey, mouth partly open and parched. This horrible scene had now lasted two deadly hours; the strained pose of the gaucho and the terrifying fascination exerted over him by the bloody, immobile gaze of the tiger—from which, owing to an invincible force of attraction, he could not avert his eyes—had begun to weaken his strength, and he could feel the moment coming in which his exhausted body would fall into the tiger's wide mouth, when the far-off sound of galloping horses gave him hope for salvation.

In fact, his friends had seen the tiger's tracks and had raced forward with no hope of saving him. The scattered saddle gear showed them the place, and to fly there, unroll their lassos, throw them over the tiger, heels dug in and blind with fury, was but the work of a moment. The beast, stretched between two ropes, could not escape the repeated blows of the knife with which, in vengeance for his prolonged agony, the one who would have been its victim ran it through. "That was when I found out what being afraid means," General Juan Facundo Quiroga used to say, telling a group of officers this story.

He too was called the "Tiger of the Plains," and in truth, the designation was not a bad fit. Phrenology and comparative anatomy have, in fact, demonstrated the relationship that exists between external form and moral disposition, between the physiognomy of man and that of some animals similar to him in character. Facundo—because that was what the people of the interior provinces long had called him; General Don Facundo Quiroga, most excellent Brigadier General Don Juan Facundo Quiroga, all of that came later, when he was received in the bosom of society and crowned with the laurels of victory—Facundo, then, was of short and well-built stature; his broad shoulders supported, on a short neck, a well-formed head covered with very thick, black, and curly hair. His face, slightly oval-shaped, was sunk in the middle of a forest of hair, matched by an equally thick, equally curly and black beard that went up to his rather pronounced cheekbones, to disclose a firm, tenacious will.

His black eyes, full of fire and shadowed by heavy eyebrows, caused an involuntary feeling of terror in those on whom, at some moment, they fixed; because Facundo never looked straight ahead, and by habit, by design, because of a wish to make himself always fearsome, he ordinarily had his head down and looked up through his eyebrows, like the Ali Pasha of Monvoisin. The Cain represented on stage by the famous Ravel Company reminds me of the image of Quiroga, except for the artistic, statue like positions that don't fit him. In other ways his physiognomy was normal, and his slightly dark complexion went well with the thick shadows among which it was enclosed.

The structure of his head, however, revealed beneath this jungle-like covering, the privileged order of men born to lead. Quiroga possessed those natural qualities that made a Brienne student into the genius of France, and an obscure Mameluke who fought the French at the Pyramids into the viceroy of Egypt. The society into which they are born gives these characters their particular manifestation: noble, one could say classic, they lead civilized humanity in some places; terrible, bloody, and evil, they are in others their stain, their shame.

Facundo Quiroga was the son of a San Juan native of humble origins, who, settled in the Llanos of La Rioja, had acquired a moderate fortune from pasturage. In 1799, Facundo was sent to his father's hometown to receive the limited education that could be had in its schools: reading and writing. When a man comes to fill the hundred trumpets of fame with the noise of his deeds, curiosity or an investigative spirit will track down even his insignificant childhood, in order to tie it to the hero's biography; and more than a few times, among the fables invented by adulation, the germ of the historical personage's characteristic features can already be found there.

In Context | The Gauchos

While the origin of the word "gauchos" remains unknown, the identity of these men is not: they were the inhabitants of South America's vast rural territories—nomadic wanderers on horseback, typically surviving by raising cattle or sheep. The gauchos were often racially mixed, living in the vast pampas and open territory of what is now Argentina, still largely populated by indigenous people. Few individuals of European origin lived in the countryside, and the gauchos generally maintained peaceful relations with the natives, as long as territorial boundaries were respected.

By contrast, the cities—like Buenos Aires, Córdoba, Rosario, and Santa Fe—were inhabited by people of European descent and enslaved people of African heritage. Urban survival depended on commerce with Alto Perú (present-day Bolivia) and the circulation of contraband throughout the maritime ports. By forbidding commercial transactions between colonies or with foreign territories (like nearby Brazil), the Spanish crown had actually encouraged such illegal enterprise and made it profitable.

Allied with these urban areas, Sarmiento wrote *Facundo* to challenge the *caudillos* or leaders of the gauchos (although not all of them were themselves gauchos), who often joined forces to defend their basic civil rights. For Sarmiento, the gauchos had several qualities that made them unsuited for the newly independent nation: dispersed across the pampas, they lacked an appropriate social core; they rejected commerce and the acquisition of wealth that was necessary for the accumulation of capital; and they were racially impure, with either African or Indian blood.

The gauchos persisted for many decades—so long as cattle ranches had no fences and the herds could graze freely as the property of whoever could find or slaughter them to survive. By the middle of the nineteenth century, however, as landholdings were fenced and cattle became the private

Figure 5.2. Gaucho of the Argentine Republic. Photographed in Lima, Peru, in 1867 by Courret Brothers. Library of Congress.

property of the landowners, the gauchos' options became more limited. New laws created in the cities soon converted their traditional ways into theft, and the gauchos were reduced to becoming cattle rustlers or farmhands. Their gradual disappearance by the end of the nineteenth century—except as icon and legend—was guaranteed.

In Context | Paraguay's War (1864–1870)

Paraguay's War, or the Great War (as it was called in Paraguay), is also known as the War of the Triple Alliance: Brazil, Argentina, and Uruguay united against Paraguay. One of the reasons for the alliance was Paraguay's development of a system of landownership that eliminated large landholdings and redistributed property more equally, albeit with strong state supervision. The Paraguayan government had also stimulated the creation of small industries, allowing its people to choose to decline the products that the British wanted to impose on the markets of the new Hispanic American nations. For many, Paraguay's rejection of modern liberalism was tantamount to barbarism.

The pretexts for this costly war were some of the dirtiest in the diplomatic and political history of the nineteenth century, all driven by the interests of wealthy ranchers and farmers, British banks, Argentine and Uruguayan oligarchs, and Brazilian slave owners. One of the ironies of the war, in fact,

Figure 5.3. Paraguay's War (1864–1870), "Inroad of the Cavalry" (engraving) in "The War in Paraguay," *Harper's New Monthly Magazine*, vol. 40 (1869–1870): 638. Wikimedia Commons, public domain.

was British support for Brazil. While England had officially denounced the slave trade in 1807, Brazil's continuing acceptance of slavery proved no real obstacle to collaboration. The hypocrisy of English liberalism—proclaiming the civilizing importance of slavery's abolition—was blatant. Not for the first or last time in history, the priority of commercial interests made it more important to destroy a country like Paraguay that resisted market demands than to defend the principled liberation of enslaved people.

Numerous testimonies confirm the unpopularity of the war in the Argentine provinces and in Uruguay; both governments eventually had to use force to "recruit" the army to fight the Paraguayans. Notable are the many documents that recount payments to blacksmiths for making chains for the so-called volunteers who were drafted for this dismal war.

Francisco Bilbao (1823–1865)

The intellectual work of Francisco Bilbao resembles that of a secular missionary. A single problem propels his thought, from his first book, *La sociabilidad chilena* (1844) [Chilean Society], to his last, *El evangelio Americano* (1864) [The American Gospel]: How can a free individual be created in Spanish-American societies?

The son of a member of Chile's constituent Congress (1828), Francisco Bilbao was born in Santiago, though when the boy was five, his father's political troubles sent the family to Lima until 1839. Bilbao then returned to study law in Santiago and at the age of twenty-one published *La sociabilidad chilena*, which resulted in a trial, a fine, and, to avoid prison, Bilbao's departure to France in 1845. But it was there that he encountered his most influential teachers, historians Edgar Quinet and Jules Michelet, along with former priest and Christian radical, Felicité Robert de Lamennais. Today, Quinet's accomplishments are largely eclipsed by that of his friend and collaborator, Jules Michelet. But both men were fiercely anticlerical and sought to renew Christianity by returning to its earliest meanings: love of one's neighbor and solidarity with invalids, with the oppressed, and with the poor.

Bilbao readily adopted their essentially Romantic positions, recognizing as principal enemies any institution opposed to authentically charitable republics. Chief among those institutions was the Catholic Church and particularly the Jesuits, whom Michelet and Quinet also sought to expel from France. Bilbao's anticlericalism was actually a function of his fanatical anti-Catholicism, since he believed that Catholicism was a major source of oppression; but he never rejected religion or the spiritual vitality that also enlivened the thought of his mentors. Thus among his writings is a beautiful biography of the young Peruvian mystic, Saint Rosa of Lima, whom Bilbao admires—without any self-contradiction—for the passion and intensity that characterize any remarkable individual.

For Bilbao, the fundamental element of an authentic republic is the self-sufficient, autonomous individual, one who makes his or her own rules and lives by a personal code. But how could such individuals form a social body if making one's own rules precludes even the possibility of assembly and collective action? Bilbao devoted immense energy to understanding this paradox: that a true republic demands autonomous individuals, but to generate such independent individuals an autonomous republic must be in place.

Central to this paradox (or vicious circle) was, for most nineteenth-century thinkers, the issue of faith. Like others in this era, Bilbao's philosophical scheme posited the lack of faith as the root of contemporary problems. For Bilbao, of course, this faith was not transcendental but the internal relationship between the individual and society. The individual and the social body are inseparable, as inconceivable without each other as a living organ is to the body as a whole. But while neither could be comprehended or function independently, how could an individual behave as an organ or a society act as a body? Bilbao identified the solution as faith—a spiritual conviction that this paradox could be realized. To carry through with one's individual convictions, one must examine the self and confront one's inward reality as a genuinely free individual. That inner freedom then allows one to recognize one's basic obligation, one's primary duty: to understand one's personal liberty as inherent in the liberty of all.

If Bilbao's argument seems faintly Cartesian, that is hardly a surprise, given Descartes's powerful influence on nineteenth-century French thinkers like Quinet. What distinguishes their thought is the lack of separation between the individual and society, or the subject from the objective forms. For Bilbao, society, like a living organism, nourishes and perpetuates itself according to its own rules. And the paradox is thus resolved: the rules made up by the individual are, in fact, the rules imposed by the social organism, but individuals exercise their liberty by freely applying that law to themselves. Bilbao's thought was often misunderstood, since most contemporary thinkers were more concerned with how to consolidate state power or merely how to acquire more power. But Bilbao was trying to understand how to create and consolidate the social fabric of a nation, or what he named in his first book—sociability.

Bilbao returned to Chile in 1849 and together with other youths of his generation established the Society for Equality (Sociedad de la Igualdad). Comprising budding intellectuals and groups of artisans and workers, the Society became allied with a liberal movement opposing the election of the conservative Manuel Montt, who counted among his advisors the Argentine DOMINGO FAUSTINO SARMIENTO. When the liberals were defeated, Bilbao again fled into exile, first to Peru in 1855, and later to Brussels, where he was disappointed to find his beloved teacher, Quinet, likewise in exile from a much-changed France.

Two years later, Bilbao left Europe to settle in Buenos Aires, where he remained politically active, engaging in Freemasonry, publishing several books and newspaper articles, and again confronting his old rival, Sarmiento. One of his last books, *La América en peligro* [America in Danger], was written in response to the French invasion of Mexico in 1862. In 1863, Bilbao married the daughter of an Argentine revolutionary, though he survived the death of their infant son in 1864 by only a few weeks. Bilbao's final work *El evangelio americano,* which appeared posthumously, reiterates the Chilean's enduring belief in freedom as the linchpin not only of human dignity, but of the American character.

The selection is from *El evangelio americano* [*The American Gospel*], translated by Charles Becker (Caracas: Ayacucho, 1988).

From El evangelio americano (1864) [The American Gospel]

First Part: The Sovereign, Section II

American Man, your honor is to be republican, your glory is having conquered the Republic, your right to govern yourself is the Republic, and your duty is to remain so forever. Never allow another government or authority over yourself other than the proper authority of conscience, the proper and personal government of individual reason, that is the Republic, that is democracy, that is autonomy, that is what is known as *Self-Government.*

And there is no other true government.

Why? Because man is sovereign.

If man is sovereign, there can be no other legitimate form of government than that which the sovereignty of man enshrines and institutes and creates.

If man is not sovereign, any form of tyranny or despotism is not only possible but just, whether it be monarchy, empire, theocracy, aristocracy, feudalism, or castes of priests, soldiers, or landowners.

Whether in metaphysics, theology, morality, religion, policy, administration, or an economic system of property, labor, finance, production, distribution, or consumption of wealth, all must resolve the issue in the same way: either to acknowledge man's sovereignty or to deny it.

A metaphysics or theology that denies freedom is the root of slavery.

A morality or religion that denies freedom is a morality or religion of slaves. A policy or administration that denies the right of all to government and administration is a policy or administration of exploitation and privilege. A distribution of property, organization of labor, or distribution of products that denies the freedom and right of everyone to credit is feudalism, proletarianism, despotism, and misery.

Sovereignty is, thus, the criterion of all social sciences.

Let us examine what sovereignty is. Let us see whether by its essence it is the first human principle. Let us demonstrate the axiom if possible.

Man is an individual. As an individual he is himself and no one else. As an individual he is indivisible. Individuality is a fundamental condition of his existence.

What is it that constitutes man's individuality? His thinking, his consciousness, his reasoning, his will.

An individual whose essential attributes are reason and will is a person. His personal character is his consciousness of his own individuality.

I know I am myself through my own thinking. If another thought for me, I would not be myself, rather I would be another or part of another; and it is proven that I am indivisible, and *inseparable*.

I know I am myself and not another by my consciousness of my own will. If another will were to operate in me, I would not be myself, but rather an instrument of another, I would be someone else's thing, which is what is known as slavery.

If I am an individual, a person, a conscious property of myself, I am because I am the one who thinks, the one who performs the actions of my personal character, *I am sovereign*.

That is, I am free. Freedom is my sovereignty. Sovereignty is thus one's own authority. I command myself, I govern myself. True government of man is thus man's sovereignty. False government is that which denies or fails to recognize equality in all that is sovereign.

The *bedrock*, the essence of true government, thus is freedom. The *form*, the organization, the manifestation of true government is equality.

Freedom without equality is privilege.

Equality without freedom is the leveling of the slaves. Freedom is the force, the fundamental and indestructible element of association. Freedom is the right of the individual.

Freedom, as a force, needs direction; that is, it has a law over its action or movement.

Equality is the law or determination of this force. The law of freedom may be formulated as follows:

Be free in every man. I am the man, every man. My freedom is the freedom of everyone.

If to be free is my right, to be free in everyone is what is called my DUTY.

Positive aspect: Practical consciousness, development, free and integral life of the personality: full, perfectible enjoyment of rights. Absolute dominion of myself.

Negative aspect: Deprivation or denial of anything that would divide my individuality, appropriate my individuality, hold in submission the intrinsic independence of my own thinking. Denial of all public or individual authority, of all domestic or foreign government that would usurp my own stake in my own government.

Legal aspect: Government of each: Independence of each citizen. Personal status of every man. Individual reason above all else. This is the right, that has no right to suicide. It is the basis of the basis of all constitutions. This is the dogma that no man, no party, no people, no clergy, nor government can deny.

Sovereignty. This is man's truth, by which man exists. If humanity conspired to negate it, this negation would be proof of the blasphemy and lie and cowardice of the human species; because *by denying sovereignty* it would be saying that humanity debased itself through an act of sovereignty in order to negate sovereignty; just as the man who denies thought by denying that he thinks is *proving* that he thinks.

And since this individuality, this individual status and character, this sovereignty over one's self, this right of man, this self-government, this freedom achieved in my consciousness, in my will, and in the exterior that surrounds me, depends on my individual reason, on my own thought, on my consciousness, which is aware of the truth that presides over its determinations, it is evident that rights, freedom, and sovereignty depend on our own free personal exercise of individual reason in each of us. If I believe because someone else believes, I am not sovereign.

If I believe, if I think what I've been made to think, without judgment of my own, I am not sovereign. What lies in the independence of your judgment, in your free thought, in pure reason, is the essence of your sovereignty. The sovereign is a *Free Thinker*. Do not forget this.

And do not forget that the condition for free thought is to judge by our own reason what we should believe, what we are told to believe, and in not performing any act without the consciousness of what we believe to be true and authentic.

This also means that being by *essence* sovereign, God has constituted man's reason with necessary principles that no one invents, that are born with man. These principles form sovereignty, and they make us judges of all ideas, knowledge, and principles that others would want to teach us.

For example: If they say to you, you poor, ignorant plebeian, and they would have it believed that Peter, John, or this or that saint has visited and has been seen at the same time at the same instant in Buenos Aires and in Santiago de Chile, you will say that this is impossible, and you would say so correctly.

You have judged, you have performed an act of free thought, an act of sovereignty, and you have stated the undeniable truth that it is *impossible*.

By virtue of what principle have you said it is impossible that a man is both here and there at the same time?

By virtue of the innate, inherent principle that comes with your reasoning, even if you may not be able to explain it, a principle formulated in the following way: one thing cannot occupy two spaces at the same time; what is here is not there; or put another way, all movement is verified in time, *what is before cannot be now, nor after*; all movement supposes past present and future; all movement supposes position, that is, a period of time. Thus it is impossible that an object, even if it is light itself, passes through two points at a single time. You will not be aware of these principles but these principles are what make you judge and reason and govern yourself at the same time.

Now then: Imagine that you will not judge, that you will not think. Then I can make you believe what I want. And if I govern your thought, will you be able to govern yourself? Impossible. He who does not think has to be a slave. To be free and sovereign it thus is necessary that one think for one's self, because by thinking for ourselves, we judge by the eternal principles of truth and justice that constitute man's reason. By thinking, you govern yourself and you are free.

By not thinking, they govern you and you are a servant to alien interest or thought. This is why justice, freedom, and law constitute self-government, the individual sovereignty of each person.

Self-government thus is the government of truth in each person. And since the truth is the law, by thinking and governing ourselves, the law governs. *Self-government* could be called MONOCRACY.

Now do you understand why all religious and political despotism condemns and persecutes free thought?

Now do you understand that there can be no law, right, or justice, without absolute freedom of one's own thought and that freedom of thought and conscience is the basis for all freedom?

Now do you understand that by thinking for one's self and having the right to govern yourself by your own reason, you will judge whether there is justice in press-ganging you into becoming a soldier, in making you work whether from need or by force without fair compensation from your wages; you will judge whether it is right for your work to enrich the wealthiest, caring for his cattle in all weather, working the earth, felling forests, digging up rocks from mines, without your being able to accumulate what is necessary to support your family and not to live as a slave to man.

Then you will comprehend that you, just as the rich man, the powerful one, the wise man in the right of sovereignty, should concern yourself with, take interest in everything having to do with the exercise of citizen rights. You have the right to vote. With your vote you may appoint the one whom you know to be honest to represent you to make law. This is why you should vote with your own thought, because otherwise, it will be *another* who will make the law that will make you the soldier, that will impose taxes, that will do justice or injustice. Today you have your vote to appoint men to represent you, but do not forget that you should aspire to be represented by yourself, that you are the one who some day must become the legislator.

These examples will make you comprehend the importance of the right to think. There are men of religion who will tell you that you must believe *without reasoning*. These are your principal enemies. Why do they so fear that you might think? Because you will not be governed, nor exploited, nor abused, nor humiliated; because you will not be the tool of anyone else, rather a true sovereign. So detest falsehood, as it should be detested, detest that doctrine called *blind obedience*. *Blind obedience* is the decapitation of freedom.

To be sovereign is thus the law of your human essence, it is your right.

There is no sovereign unless you think freely for yourself.

There is no sovereign unless you are governed by your own thought.

Your own thought is the revelation or vision of truth that God incarnated in every man.

To abdicate your thought is to abdicate your sovereignty.

Accordingly, your self-government is the government of truth and of law.

And since this law shines in everyone, everyone is a sovereign. This is what is known as EQUALITY. To attack other's sovereignty is to violate the law by which you are sovereign. To respect the sovereignty of your fellows is your DUTY.

And as you love yourself, likewise should you love men, because they are like you, sovereigns and brothers. Sons of the same Father, illuminated by the same law, men must love one another just as the good and beauty in one's own existence are loved. Fraternity is the complement of rights and duties, the crown of the blessing that the Eternal One has placed over the brow of humanity.

You know the law. There is no happiness without laws, rather degradation. Wealth without possession of that law is rot. Life, without the law of sovereignty living in everyone is debasement. To be a serf due to ignorance is excusable, but do not absolve yourself of negligence for failing to think, for the abandonment of native dignity.

To be a voluntary slave is to deserve being a prisoner. To be a slave and to legitimize your own slavery with sophistry, cowardly excuses, or lies is to make yourself worthy of being a beast.

Thus, my brother, do not forget your sovereignty, do not crush yourself under the weight of all the conspiring interests of evil ones. Your cause is that of God who made you sovereign. Your sovereignty is the sacrosanct religion, which makes you worthy of compensations or punishments, of glory or ignominy, of being an agent and collaborator of the Supreme Being for the happiness of the earth, or an agent and collaborator of the evil ones for the degradation and enslavement of the human race. And one day you will have to answer to Justice eternal for the use of your sovereignty. And that Justice will judge you with the law of its own thought and say: you, the free one, you who have suffered for freedom, to my right! And be the blessed of the Father. You, the slaves, instruments of all tyranny, to my left! And receive the punishment of purgatory.

Juana Manuela Gorriti (1818–1892)

At the beginning of *Peregrinaciones de una alma triste* [Wanderings of a Sad Soul] a young woman from Lima accidentally hears that a man has been cured of tuberculosis by traveling. Having been declared terminally ill with the same disease, the young woman seeks the same remedy: she embarks on a trip that begins in the port of El Callao and is directed on her journey only by chance, with its single purpose being the recovery of her health.

Thus commences one of Spanish America's most surprising nineteenth-century novels, published by Juana Manuela Gorriti in 1876 in Buenos Aires as part of her collection titled *Panoramas de la vida* [Landscapes of Life]. The novel's surprises begin immediately, when the traveler decides to return to her native land by crossing the Andes, thus revealing that she is not from Lima, but (like the author) was born in Salta, Argentina. From that point until the novel's conclusion, the narrative unfolds on two levels: the self-discovery of the young woman and the varied social contexts revealed through her adventures.

The young woman's return to Salta evokes nostalgic memories of her childhood, but these are interrupted by sudden violent attacks from a band of *montoneros*. After this incident, she receives an invitation from her brother, who owns a ranch in the province (both facts that the reader is surprised to learn) and who invites her to stay. En route, there is a lively story about the narrator's grandfather, but immediately after her arrival at her brother's house, he decides he must rescue his wife's parents from Paraguay. Leaving his wife to care for the couple's children, the brother sets out with his sister (the narrator) for an exciting river journey to Asunción. The allusions to a devastating war offer one of the novel's few points of chronological reference, indicating that the siblings arrive in Asunción around 1870, at the end of the War of the Triple Alliance against Paraguay.

When the narrator is about to return to Argentina with her brother, she receives a letter from her husband telling her to meet him at a remote location in the Amazon. The startling news that the woman is married hardly fazes the attentive reader, now accustomed to the novel's penchant for unexpected revelations. The protagonist embarks on her perilous way from Asunción to Rio de Janeiro, and then up the Amazon River to the mysterious location where her husband presumably awaits—except he has had to leave. Without warning, the reader now discovers that her husband has another wife who has retrieved him first. We also learn at this point that the absent husband is European, maybe Austro-Hungarian. After miraculously saving herself from dastardly rogues who attack her house at night, the narrator returns to Lima. Only at this point does the narration proper begin. All these adventures have been, it appears, reported to a friend after the protagonist's return to the city. Restored to health by her travels, the young woman lingers in Lima, but when tuberculosis again threatens, she sets out once more, now recording her journey in the letters that make up the rest of the novel.

Such an anecdotal summary, of course, renders these extraordinary events absurd, especially if strict realism is the measure of credibility. In fact, the apparently unexpected disclosures of the plot reflect the deep energy of the protagonist in following her destiny, a destiny inherent in the narrative itself. Whenever her travels take a predictable or even sedentary path, an element emerges that pushes the protagonist toward an alternate route with unpredictable consequences, but one that nonetheless leads steadily to an affirmation of a healthy life. Generated by a diagnosis of illness, the narrative reveals that well-being has its own principle of integrity: simply following one's immediate impulses and deepest convictions. At the novel's conclusion, the protagonist writes to her friend that she has received another letter from her husband, now imprisoned in Austria, instructing her to meet him. She announces that she will join him, and here the narrative suddenly ceases. Gorriti simply never finished her story.

This remarkable novel emerges in the context of several Spanish American women writers of the nineteenth century, including Gorriti's contemporaries, GERTRUDIS GÓMEZ DE AVELLANEDA and Eduarda Mansilla de García (1834–1892), author of the extraordinary *Lucía Miranda* (1860), along with several Peruvian writers, notably Clorinda Matto de Turner (1852–1909), famous for her novel *Aves sin nido* (1889) [Birds without a Nest] and *Tradiciones cuzqueñas* (1884) [Cuzco Traditions], itself a deeply original transformation of a genre originated by RICARDO PALMA.

Gorriti's own life was shaped by historical, political, social and literary events that were inextricably linked, and her experience teemed with the same accidents, relocations, travels, and tragedies that later filled her fiction. The daughter of prominent Unitarians, Gorriti and her family fled from the attacks of Federalists into Bolivia, where at thirteen she married Isidoro Belzu, a young army officer. Though he later became president of Bolivia (1848–1855), he abandoned his wife and daughters after nine years, and Gorriti left La Paz for Lima in 1846. During her long residence, she founded a school and two influential journals; she also began to write, hosting *tertulias*, or literary discussion groups, that inspired two generations of Peruvians, including RICARDO PALMA, Clorinda Matto de Turner, Mercedes Cabello de Carbonera (1845–1909), and the Ecuadorian poet Numa Pompilio Llona (1832–1907).

Gorriti wrote several biographies and novels in addition to *Wanderings of a Sad Soul* and some memorable short stories, including "El guante negro"

(1852) [The Black Glove]. She was also versatile—editing a celebrated cookbook, *La cocina ecléctica* (1890) [The Eclectic Kitchen]—and enterprising, becoming one of the first individuals to write fiction for commercial purposes, producing her short story "Oasis en la vida" (1888) [Oasis in Life] as advertising for a life insurance company.

Though *Peregrinaciones de una alma triste* includes events in Buenos Aires, Gorriti did not visit that city until 1875, and only returned to Salta, her birthplace, years later, when she was sixty-eight. Gorriti eventually wrote about her reacquaintance with Salta in *La tierra natal* (1889) [The Native Land], but her native land was never again hers. Proudly proclaimed as Argentina's best nineteenth-century woman writer, Juana Manuela Gorriti died in 1892 in Buenos Aires, a city she hardly knew, far from Lima, where her writing had first flourished, making her one of the best narrative authors in all of Spanish America.

The selection comprises parts I and II of *Peregrinaciones de una alma triste* (1876), translated by Charles Becker.

From **Peregrinaciones de una alma triste (1876) [Wanderings of a Sad Soul]**

I. An Unexpected Visit

One day, upon entering my room I found a beautiful young woman waiting for me, who no sooner than she saw me threw herself silently into my arms.

The spontaneous familiarity of that action, along with something in her winning features, revealed to me a person I knew and loved; but where? When? I couldn't recall.

—What!—she exclaimed at my bewilderment—Has my suffering so changed me that you no longer recognize me?

—Laura! Oh my dear, you are not the same, and you've lost your accent...

—Our blessed accent! It reminds me of the forgetful heart of my friends.

—But you have turned into a real beauty, my sweet dear! How could I recognize that pale, emaciated invalid, with her hunched back and lifeless gaze in this vivid, striking woman right here in front of me? Slender as a palm tree with eyes that...

—What a flatterer! I'd have to be sorely vain to believe what you're saying.

—Liar! Every day the mirror says the same thing to you. But tell me, what became of you? All of a sudden you disappeared. And even more important, how did you regain your health and beauty?

—Wandering all over the place [and absorbing the winds]. It's a long story . . . but there are people there who want to talk to you and are coming to interrupt us. I'd better leave you now.

—Leave? No, my dear, not until you've told me of your strange disappearance.

—Please! From what I can see, you don't have an hour for yourself. By day, you are absorbed in teaching; and nighttime . . .

—Is all mine.

—You spend it in the midst of loud talk.

—Yes. To forget painful thoughts.

—Ah, my tale is a sad one, and it will bring you more sorrow.

—Perhaps I'll find points in common that will smooth it out.

—Impossible. You've surrendered your soul to it and, as would a drunk with drink, you attribute all sorts of virtues to it.

—There you are: I have further reasons to hear your story.

—Fine, then. If that's what you want to hear . . . But I forgot that you have half a dozen visitors waiting for you . . . I'm sleepy, I just came ashore, and the last day on the ship left me exhausted. I'll leave you. Good bye.

—No, you don't. I've already told you: you're being held. Don't you wish to come join me in my soirée? I've got another bed right by mine. You lie down there and I shall spend the night listening to the story of this impenetrable cloud over your life.

—Like in *The Thousand and One Nights*?

—Precisely, although with a small change, enormous for you, of course, and that is that the offended sultan is far away from his beloved queen.

Laura let out a deep sigh. Was it the memory of delight in reading children's stories or was it the absent owner of her destiny?

II. The flight

—Are you sleepy, lovely Scheherazade?—I asked Laura when I calculated she had slept six hours—Well, if you are awake, tell me, I beg you, this intriguing story.

—My dear Dinazard—she answered while yawning—you're a wag, and you will tell everybody.

—No, I won't. I promise, not a peep.

—Thanks to the Abbot L'Epée the mute knows how to write.

—Oh, most beautiful pearl of the harem, grant me this favor for the love of your sultan. Would you like an epigraph? There, here is the one from . . .

—Chapter One. "On how the moribund Laura regained her health and beauty thanks to the marvelous science of a homeopathic physician."

—Not so, I cured myself. The doctor was useless.

—How quick to cast blame! How can you speak like that about a man whose merits are so well known?

—Really? In my case he squandered them sorely. And yet, it was a warning from him that saved me. One day, one of my worst days of sickness, in the midst of his endless prattle about the great benefits of homeopathy, he recalled the notorious escapade of a young customer of his, already in the third-stage of tuberculosis, who abandoned the doctor's prescribed treatment and exposed his ravaged lungs to the fatigue of endless journeys. "And a freak of nature it was," the doctor added, "that protracted trembling, that prolonged fatigue, they saved him, he recovered . . . But these are isolated, exceptional cases that don't happen more than once. You try that cure here, when it's no longer any use, and in the initial stage, it will all be over." And with his big claws he lifted my emaciated body and let it fall onto the bed, causing me insufferable pains. "Nevertheless, my dear," he continued with an emphatic smile, "from this day forward you shall begin to take the cure that to others brings death: arsenic. Arsenic in the morning, arsenic after noon, arsenic at night . . . Horrible, is it not? Huh, huh, huh. Have you read *Germana*?" "Yes, doctor." "Well, become one with that lovely child; surrender your soul to faith, and abandon your body to the mysterious action of that terrible, specific, active poison, and as such, sometimes, a miraculous remedy."

Speaking thus, he removed from his vest pocket a carefully folded piece of paper, emptied its content into the bottom of a glass, made a potion, and directed me to drink it. I hesitated, looking at it against the light. "I understand"—the doctor said, seeing my bewilderment—"This is one of those girls who won't eat just to avoid being seen with their mouths open. Well, drink up." And he turned away. Then, quickly pouring the liquid into my handkerchief, I exclaimed with an air of disgust: "Done, doctor, that medicine tastes so bad." "Medicine, in the end, even if it were nectar, will always taste bad to one's palate. Double dose tomorrow, triple the day after; and so on, and very soon, those eyes now dull shall shine; those pale lips shall regain their red color; this flesh, its health, too, and *voilà* another fine young woman in the world will say: 'Here I am.'" He gazed at me, smiling; patted my cheek softly, he believed, and went off, rubbing his hands together with a triumphant air.

That night I could not sleep, but my insomnia, although exhausting, was filled with welcoming visions. The image of the young TB sufferer restored to good health thanks to long journeys, went to and fro before me, smiling a smile full of life, and extending his arm to show me faraway horizons of purest blue whence hope beckoned to me. I told myself: "As in me, so too in him, the sickness of the soul produced that of the body. So it was logical that the doctor, who attacked the illness without concern for the cause, resorted to the only remedy that could defeat both of them: variation of landscapes for one's life and change of air for one's lungs."

Let us do as the sick man did: let us tear ourselves from the grip of this physician, who seeks to fill me up with poison; let us change our existence down to the last detail; let us flee from beautiful Lima, where every inch of land holds a sorrowful memory, and let us seek in other spheres the air that this delicious and lethal atmosphere denies me. Let us go!

Go! But how? I've got here the dear mother who keeps watch beside me, and wants to protect me from even the slightest effort; then there are my brothers, who won't leave me by the wayside, and carry me in their arms so I'll avoid the effort of walking; I've got here the whole medical establishment that declares me to be incapable of withstanding a trip to the mountains.

How then even to suggest my decision, without their deeming it completely insane? Nevertheless, I'm dying and I want to live! Live for my mother, live for my brothers, for this world of beauty, so full of promise when we are twenty years old! My gaze is overcast, and I want my eyes, like the doctor says, to shine; my lips to regain their color; my flesh, its freshness. I want to rediscover my health and beauty. I'm still too young to die. Let us go!

And taking hold of life with the strength of an infinite longing, I decided, whatever might happen, to flout attentive watch all around me and depart without delay.

Gabino Barreda (1818–1881)

A native of Puebla, Gabino Barreda was a physician and philosopher who is remembered today as the architect of a revolution in the Mexican educational system, the *Preparatoria* (preuniversity study or high school), one of the most enduring institutions in Mexico's state structure. In fact, for many historians, Mexico's educational history is divided into two periods: before and after the *Preparatoria* of Gabino Barreda, which went into effect in 1868.

After studying at both the College of San Ildefonso and the School of Mines, Barreda served as a surgeon in the Mexican-American War. Between 1848 and 1851, he continued his medical studies in Paris, where he first encountered the philosophy of Auguste Comte (1798–1857), particularly the *Cours de Philosophie Positive* [Course in Positive Philosophy]

(1830–1842). When Barreda returned to Mexico, Comte's positivist stance, with its reliance on science and logic, informed Barreda's approach to both education and history.

Invited by the new government of Benito Juárez to develop a system of education for the republic, Barreda used Comte's positivist approach to organize preuniversity instruction. First, the scientific disciplines were privileged over the humanities. Second, the sciences were hierarchically ordered according to the degree their laws could be verified: astronomy, physics, chemistry, biology, psychology, and lastly sociology—a discipline invented by Comte. Finally, the cohesive element of all teaching was to be logic and mathematics. By teaching everyone to think rationally, to follow logical and objective processes, Comte (and Barreda) believed that dissent would cease. The *Preparatoria* would also address the phenomenon that SIMÓN RODRÍGUEZ yearned to remedy: the absence of strong educational structures to nurture bright individuals in Spanish America.

Barreda had been teaching at the national School of Medicine when the French invasions forced him to retreat to Guanajuato in 1863. It was there that Barreda wrote his remarkable essay, "La oración cívica" [The Civic Prayer], which was intended to provide a logical account of Mexican history, using the same rationality that would shape the *Preparatoria*. When "The Civic Prayer" was read in Guanajuato on the day of independence, September 16, 1867, only two months and ten days had passed after the June execution of Maximilian, the French emperor of Mexico who had been imposed with the support of the Catholic Church and ultraconservative Mexicans. While most Mexicans favored President Benito Juárez's decision to carry out the death sentence, a vocal domestic minority (and many outside the country) condemned the government for refusing to grant clemency, calling the action "barbaric"—as if the invasion itself had been a civilized act. Most Mexicans remembered all too well the bloody consequences of the edict by Napoleon III and Maximilian, sentencing to death, without trial or appeal, any captured and armed Mexican. Even against strong international public opinion, these rulers refused to consider members of the Mexican resistance as combatant enemies, but treated them simply as outlaws.

Barreda was trying to make sense of these and other recent traumas in Mexican history, which over the past three decades had included not only the French invasion of 1862 and the installation of Maximilian, but also the war with the United States in 1847, resulting in the forfeiture of more than half of Mexican territory, preceded by the devastating loss of Texas in

1836. Comte gave Barreda a framework for his reinterpretation. According to Comte, events must be judged by a nation's own specific contexts. And thus while nations evolved in three stages—theological, philosophical, and positivist—these stages were experienced unevenly and asynchronously across regions and societies. For Comte, comparing stages of development between nations was a pointless exercise, especially since the progression between stages was itself irregular and overlapping, even within a single nation. Mexican history had to be understood on its own terms. Intending to end all dissent about the direction of Mexican history since 1810, Barreda used Comte's thought to explain events as evolving in these fundamental areas—the scientific, the religious, and the political.

Unfortunately, while Barreda's explanation is brilliant, it does not necessarily demonstrate a scientific evolution in Mexican politics. In fact, by dismissing anomalous events as treason or aberration, Barreda seems to have also adopted a Hegelian perspective, permitting "the cunning of reason" to account for chance in the understanding of history. What Barreda does explain with great clarity is that the execution of Emperor Maximilian was a political necessity, though his arguments are based more on "reasons of state" than on scientific or historical law. While science had indeed seeped into politics, making some events foreseeable, only one event was reliably predicted: the consolidation of the Mexican state. And even that consolidation only lasted forty years; after the start of the Mexican Revolution in 1910, the state was destroyed and rebuilt several times.

Continuing to champion rationalist education as the first director of the National Preparatory School, Barreda served in the Mexican Congress and was also appointed ambassador to Germany in 1878. He died in Mexico City.

The selection is from "The Civic Prayer," in *Pensamiento positivista latinoamericano*, edited by Leopoldo Zea (Caracas: Ayacucho, 1980), translated by Isabel Bastos and Marvin Liberman.

From Oración cívica (1867) [The Civic Prayer]

After three centuries of peaceful domination by a system perfectly suited to prolong endlessly a situation that sought to maintain itself everywhere unchanged, making education, religious beliefs, politics and government converge toward the same clear and well-defined outcome: perpetual domination and continuing exploitation; when everything was ready so that it was impossible to penetrate this system from without, nor even to germinate from within any new idea without passing through the sieve formed by the tight mesh of the secular and regular clergy, adroitly stretched across the entire country—clergy who were completely devoted to the service of the metropolis, where most of them were from, and securely bound by the inducement of considerable benefits and critical immunities and privileges, which placed them well above the rest of the population, especially its Creoles; when that clergy, armed both with heaven's lightning and earth's sorrows, serving as the supreme head of all education, when they had occupied every avenue that the enemy might penetrate, and had every means to exterminate any adversary that might appear; after three centuries, I repeat, in this situation, it seems impossible that suddenly, by following an obscure and hapless parish priest [Miguel Hidalgo y Costilla, who declared independence from the Spanish Crown in the parish church of Dolores], the people [of Mexico], formerly submissive and lethargic, have risen up as if propelled by a wellspring, without organization or arms, without clothes or resources, pitting themselves against a courageous and disciplined army, attaining victory with no more tactics than just baring their naked breasts to the lead and steel of their fearsome foes, who once had vanquished them just with their gaze.

If such a crucial event had not been preceded by a combination of slow and silent—though real and powerful—forces, it would be completely inexplicable, and it would not now be an historical fact but only a fabulous tale; it would not have been achieved by heroism but by a miracle, and would remain outside our perspective, which—coinciding with the precepts of true philosophical science, whose objective is always predictability—has to set aside all supernatural influence, which, not subject to constant laws, cannot be the foundation for rational explanations or predictions.

What, then, were those invisible influences whose accumulated effects over the course of time could, in an opportune moment, first struggle against and later emerge victorious over resistances that had seemed insurmountable? All can be reduced to a single, yet formidable and decisive cause: intellectual emancipation, characterized by the gradual decay of old doctrines, and their progressive replacement by modern ones; a decline and substitution that, proceeding unceasingly and steadily, finally produced a complete transformation before its advances were even noticed.

Scientific emancipation, religious emancipation, political emancipation: these were the triple branches of that powerful torrent that has been growing day by day, increasing its strength as it encountered resistances, obstacles that sometimes blocked it temporarily, but which always were swept away completely, attaining nothing more than prolonging the malaise and increasing the ruin inherent in a destruction so fundamental and so inevitable.

*   *   *

One could say that the triple evolution—scientific, political and religious—that necessarily precipitated the terrible crisis we have been through was not only imminent, but was basically accomplished during that time by that Catholic clergy who, having given birth to the conversation, were later determined to suffocate it; one can say that the clergy recognized the costs of their ambitious claims. But thanks to the fortunately irresistible appeal of the true and useful, of the good and beautiful, they were seduced—against their own counsel—not to follow their own interests, and, like Cerberus of the fable, were dazed by the charm of these new ideas and allowing the enemy they were supposed to repel to penetrate their closely-controlled territory.

However, once that first step was taken, the rest had to follow, and all the resistance that might be amassed, could only delay and disguise the final result, which was both fatal and inevitable. Science, developing and growing like a weak child, had first to test and increase its strength on level paths without any obstacles; little by little, as its strength increased, science could enter into combat against fears and superstition, finally emerging triumphant and victorious after a dreadful, but decisive, struggle.

*   *   *

Fellow Citizens: remember today how the sun that shone on the corpse of Napoleon I on the 5th of May [in 1821] also shone on the humiliating defeat of Napoleon III [in the battle of Puebla on May 5, 1862]. Keep in mind that, on that same glorious day, the name of [Ignacio] Zaragoza, the Mexican Themistocles, was linked forever with the ideas of independence, civilization, liberty and progress, not only for his own country, but for all humanity. You know that the *genízaros* [the Algerian Zouaves, who had fought with the French army in Puebla] of Napoleon III were forced to bite the dust on that day, those Persians from the banks of the Seine more bold and blind than their precursors on the Euphrates, those who tried to destroy the autonomy of an entire continent and reestablish on the classic ground of liberty, in the world of Columbus, the theocratic principle of castes and hereditary rule; that defeat of that reactionary crusade by the soldiers of the Republic in Puebla, I repeat, saved the future of the world, just like the Greek soldiers in Salamina, by preserving the republican principle, which is the modern standard of humanity. You surely know that the battle of the 5th of May was the glorious prelude to a bloody and formidable struggle that endured five years, but whose final result was already determined that day. Those who achieved that first victory had to win the last! And those who crept, without honor, across the mountains of Acultzingo had to retreat ingloriously through the port of Veracruz!

In Context | The Translucent Air of the Valley of Mexico

During his stay in Mexico City in 1803, Alexander von Humboldt verified a quality that made the valley of Mexico famous: the clarity of its atmosphere. Although Humboldt did no scientific investigations on this topic, he did claim that the city's atmosphere represented a unique natural phenomenon, generating the description of Mexico City as having the world's most transparent air. It was soon discovered that the quality of this air depended on several conditions: the city's altitude, at nearly 8,000 feet; that the site is not a valley, but a basin where several rivers empty into lakes; and the character of the lakes themselves. At certain temperatures, a unique vaporization occurs that created this remarkable clarity of the air.

Figure 5.4. José María Velasco, *The Valley of Mexico*. Oil on canvas, 54.13" × 88.98". Museo Nacional de Arte. Photograph by Alejandro Linares García. © D.R. Museo Nacional de Arte / Instituto Nacional de Bellas Artes y Literatura, 2016. Reproducción autorizada.

Many painters tried to capture that special translucence, but the one who did so best was the Mexican painter Velasco. Unfortunately, he would also be the last, as the basin's critical lakes continued to be desiccated, both deliberately and thoughtlessly. What had been an island—Tenochtitlán—and later the famed "Venice of the New World" (see map 4.1) would soon be transformed into a dusty city requiring its water to be transported from outside the basin or from artesian wells that were then drilled by the thousands in the nineteenth century. Soon enough, the fauna and flora disappeared together with the water from Mexico City. Velasco's work remains a faithful testimonial to the valley that was once regarded as one of the most beautiful places on earth.

6

Consolidation and Crisis of Liberalism,
1870–1930

While the new nations of Spanish America struggled to consolidate the consequences of their independence, the rest of the Western world was becoming engaged in another kind of revolution: the Industrial Revolution. The first industrial revolution, engendered by the shift to steam power, did little to transform the economies of the continent; however, the second industrial revolution, based on new energy sources including gas and electricity, had profound results and ushered many of the nations of Spanish America abruptly into modernity.

The second industrial revolution, which occurred in the last third of the nineteenth century, produced uneven but consequential effects for the balance of economic and political power across the world. For already industrialized countries like England and France, the transition from steam to electricity and petroleum was not smooth. With substantial investments in older technologies, these countries also had established labor forces rooted in a steam-driven economy and were thus less agile in adapting to new configurations of production. But for countries still on the verge of industrialization, such as the United States and Germany, the shift to the new technologies was rapid and profound. Indeed, by the beginning of the twentieth century, the second industrial revolution was transforming the United States into a world power.

These technological shifts were also transforming the economics of capitalism. Companies began to centralize production and management, creating new efficiencies and often eradicating any competition. These monopolies then began to seek ever-larger markets for their products across the globe. That search spawned a second quest: to look for the natural resources to supply them. In Europe, governments assisted these enterprises by overseeing the violent colonization of other continents, particularly

Africa. Spanish America was not exploited so directly; nevertheless, the effort to include the region in this new capitalist system with global ambitions was resolute. Latin America, as these countries were starting to be called, was about to be recolonized.

The internal conflicts that had wracked most Latin American nations after independence began to temper, as competing oligarchies tacitly adopted a political commitment to national autonomy. The opposing factions did not, however, renounce their autocratic principles; instead, they shifted their shared opposition to what might be called a technological and financial neocolonialism, one that originated outside their borders. Indeed, by the end of the nineteenth century, an unforeseen status quo was taking shape in many countries. Liberals were adopting many conservative principles while conservatives assumed many of the gestures and ideals that characterized liberalism. This unlikely truce did not solve the fundamental problems of governmental stability, but it did allow most countries of Latin America to embrace the mirage that they had entered called modernity.

The nations of Latin America thus began a process of forming national identities and economies that were sometimes congruent but often contradictory. The writers in this section offer a panoramic view of this shifting political landscape. Perhaps no one saw this process and its implications more clearly than JOSÉ MARTÍ. He understood all too well that the nationalist fervor uniting the factious oligarchies was simply another way for the American creoles to continue to exploit their economic and social power. Rather than being motivated by the welfare of the nation, these dominant groups were simply adapting to the values and ambitions of foreign interests. Nationalism offered them another avenue to consolidate and secure their social power in the face of a transforming global economy. What forged their political truce with one another was their recognition that any version of national stability would allow creoles—liberal and conservative alike—to make handsome profits, as they shared in the new wealth circulating through Latin America, wealth that resulted from the international demand for its rich natural resources. But as the dawn of the twentieth century loomed on the horizon, bringing centennial celebrations of independence, the mask of that truce could not conceal the fundamentally unsolved problems that continued to plague this recolonized Latin America. The writers and thinkers of this era bring those contradictions into sharp relief.

Ricardo Palma (1833–1919)

Ricardo Palma was a poet, historian, playwright, journalist, politician, anthologist—and director of the National Library of Peru. But above all, he was a master storyteller, perhaps the best of the nineteenth century—challenged only by JUANA MANUELA GORRITI. Others wrote narrative masterpieces in this era, including Mexicans Manuel Payno (1810–1894), *Los bandidos de Río Frío* (1889–1891) [The Bandits of Rio Frio] and Luis G. Inclán (1816–1875), *Astucia: El jefe de los hermanos de la hoja o los charros contrabandistas de la rama* (1865–1866) [The Chief of the Tobacco Brothers or the Smugglers of Tobacco], and the Argentinian ESTEBAN ECHEVER-RÍA, "El Matadero" (1839/1871) [The Slaughterhouse]. But Palma stands alone in having produced such an extensive body of narrative whose influence and popularity have endured.

Palma's parents separated when he was young, and he was raised by his mestizo mother in Lima. Educated in Jesuit schools, he served for six years in the Peruvian Navy. His literary career began as a poet around 1848, when he helped to form a bohemian group, imitating the youth of Paris. Though he wrote a few plays, his interest in the colonial archives turned his literary ambition to prose and ultimately to the genre for which he is now most famous. The genre of the *tradiciones*, a blend of history and fiction, was well known in Spanish America, though Palma gave the form its distinctive identity. His first *tradición* was published in 1854, followed by a collection in 1872. These vignettes were admired and imitated throughout Spanish America, but few others matched Palma's achievement, with the possible exception of fellow Peruvian Clorinda Matto de Turner (1852–1909) in her *Tradiciones cuzqueñas* (1884).

Part of what distinguishes Palma's work in the genre was his conviction that authentic narration is based on complete freedom: the ability of the narrative to proceed unimpeded by previous models or formal constraints. Like JORGE LUIS BORGES a few decades later, Palma resisted conventional structures in the creation of his intense and imaginative tales. One of Palma's techniques was achieving a careful balance between the oral and written idiom. Palma's stories have the rhythm of a conversation, but he skillfully embeds passages that could only be expressed in writing. "Saint Thomas's Sandal" brings together a typical mélange of styles—colloquial, historical, and narrative. Similarly, Palma incorporates material from historians and chroniclers without ever privileging their authority over the popular voice.

The structure of the anecdote is also inventive. Typically, Palma's *tradiciones* begin with a proverb or a popular phrase, whose origins must then be pursued. Often the topic generates the subject with scant justification. In "Saint Thomas's Sandal," the apostle's presence in America begins with the testimony of Brazilian authors and then languidly moves on to other allusions. The narrator seems led by the story's own associations, giving way to digressions, asides, clarifications, or information about precedents. The narration implies a state of anxiety: readers do not know where the *tradición* will go—or when it will end. Only the conciseness of the form alleviates that anxiety: the endings are always in sight, precise and indispensable. "Saint Thomas's Sandal" exemplifies another common element of Palma's *tradiciones*: irony. As Palma ostentatiously insists, he never takes sides—"God did not create me to be an instructor or trial judge." But that critical distance opens a space for many implausible versions of events about Thomas's "sandal," improbabilities that Palma often highlights and exaggerates—presenting himself as a mere reporter, impartial about the bizarre truths that others have proposed.

Palma's *tradiciones* often achieve an essential ambiguity about narrative control: does it reside in the author or in the narrative itself? As in "Saint Thomas's Sandal," no distinction is made between what is true and what is not, what is historical or legendary, real or fantastical. By simply including the voice of the "other" (of tradition, of legend) without questioning its truthfulness, Palma seems to anticipate the twentieth century's magical realism. Like Gabriel García Márquez, Palma does not question what characters say or believe, or critique the traditions that live in people's memory.

Though Palma published a series of *Peruvian Tradiciones* between 1872 and 1910, their popularity was attributed to their brevity and the curiosity of their subject matter rather than Palma's literary talents. Moreover, Palma's fame was always constrained by his rivalry with MANUEL GONZÁLEZ PRADA. González Prada actively opposed the hegemony of the Peruvian oligarchy, which had lost the War of the Pacific with Chile (1879–1882) and squandered the country's vast guano revenues. A powerful fertilizer, guano was much coveted in Europe between 1840 and 1870. In 1888, at a fundraiser to rescue the provinces captured by Chile, González Prada publicly attacked the oligarchy and its cultural symbols, including its colonial nostalgia and pining for the purity of Spanish. The speech was also a direct affront to Palma, whose *tradiciones* had become identified with an ideology of nostalgia, an imagined past devoid of social conflict, oppression, racial discrimination, or religious fanaticism.

The continuing rivalry between Palma and González Prada was reflective of Peru's political realities. The ambition of the oligarchy, the exploitation of the Indians, racial discrimination and the church's relentless dominance were largely responsible for Peru's failure to take advantage of the economic opportunities offered by its guano and saltpeter. And the loss of territory in the War of the Pacific was a direct consequence of the incompetence and irresponsibility of that powerful minority. González Prada's critique was well justified. But even if Palma's idyllic stories fail to confront the problems of the colonial era, his work does convey the creole mindset, one that persisted even after independence and one whose strengths and weaknesses BOLÍVAR had described in his "Letter from Jamaica." The *tradiciones* construct a world that doesn't even have a language of its own, only references to others' realities; nonetheless, it maintains that world by a deliberate oblivion with respect to contemporary conflicts, a feigned ignorance that allowed the creoles to preserve their unquestionable domination. To creole society, Indian rebellions or even the War of the Pacific existed somewhere else. Palma himself, writing in 1909, commented that "Up until 1850, Lima lived in its Colonial past, as in the days of Viceroys Abascal and Pezuela. Nothing changed in my city except for its titles: the 'his Excellency, Mister Viceroy' was replaced by 'his Excellency, Mister President.' Socially, the aristocracy of scrolls and blue blood still prevailed."

Such blindness affected the entire Peruvian aristocracy, enabled by their seamless political, social, and economic sovereignty. But if Palma's *tradiciones* provide some insight into this closed creole worldview, they also introduce a paradoxical possibility: the freedom with which this unconscious social class is described also presents a narrative model that other writers soon adopted to denounce these unjust, unequal, and anachronistic social structures.

In addition to his literary legacy, Palma contributed significantly to the preservation of Peru's bibliographical heritage. Appointed as director of the National Library in 1883, following the Chilean troops' destruction of both the national library and his personal collections, Palma worked tirelessly to restore the library to its former state. After his nemesis González Prada was named his successor in 1912, Palma retired with his family to Miraflores, a suburb of Lima, where he died in 1919.

The selection is from *Peruvian Traditions*, translated by Helen Lane and edited by Christopher Conway (New York: Oxford University Press, 2004), 137–39. Reprinted by permission of Oxford University Press.

Saint Thomas's Sandal (1872)

If you take to reading Brazilian chroniclers and historians, you can't help firmly believing that Saint Thomas traveled all over South America preaching the gospel. The facts and documents on which these gentlemen base their belief are so authentic that there is no weak point into which to sink one's teeth.

In Ceará, in San Luis de Maranhao in Pernambuco, and in other provinces of the empire next to us a number of proofs of the apostolic visit exist.

In Belén del Pará the one who is writing these lines was shown a boulder, highly venerated, on which the disciple of Christ had stood. Whether this is true or not requires verification that I want nothing to do with, for God did not make me to be an investigating magistrate.

The matter, moreover, is not a dogma to be taken on faith nor has anyone put my neck in a noose to make me believe or burst.

We the people could not be left behind when it came to the evangelical visit. It would have been all we needed if, had Saint Thomas attended a social gathering in the vicinity, he had turned up his nose or had he been so finicky about coming to party with us here in Peru where his house is.

In Calango, 16 leagues from Lima and near Mala, there exists on a hillside a very smooth, polished white boulder. I have not laid eyes on it, but someone who has seen it and run his hand over it told me about it. On it, as though imprinted in soft wax, there can be seen the outline of a size 14 foot, and around it Greek and Hebrew characters. In his *Crónica Agustina,* Father Calancha[1] says that he examined this rock in 1615, and that ten years later the bachelor-of-law Duarte Fernández, touring the diocese on a mission from the Archbishop don Gonzalo de Ocampo, ordered the letters destroyed, because the idolatrous Indians attributed a diabolical meaning to them. A great shame, say I!

Since it is but a short distance from Calango to Lima and the road not at all rough, it is safe to say that one day we had as our guest who drank water from the Rimac[2] one of the 12 beloved disciples of the Savior. And if this is not a great honor for Lima, as were the recent visits of the duke of Genoa and don Carlos de Borbón, never mind.

"But, Señor collector of traditions, how did Saint Thomas get from Galilee to Lima?"

---

1   Friar Antonio de Calancha (1584–1654) was born in Chuquisaca (Bolivia) and wrote the *Crónica moralizada del Orden de San Agustín en el Perú, con sucesos egemplares en esta Monarquía* (1638) [A Moralized History of the Augustianians in Peru with Exemplary Incidents from the Present Monarchy].

2   The river that traverses Lima.

"How should I know? Go to heaven and ask him. It might have been by hot air balloon, by swimming, or *pedibus andando*.[3] What I assert, and along with my eminent writers, both sacred and profane, is that His Grace turned up in these parts. That's all there is to it, and there's no use pestering me with impertinent questions."

But there is something more to say. Other towns in Peru lay claim to the same good fortune.

In Frías, in the district of Piura, there is a rock on which there is preserved the outline of the apostle's foot. In Cajatambo another like it can be seen, and when Saint Toribio visited Chachapoyas His Grace granted indulgences to those who prayed before a certain boulder, for he was convinced that this distinguished personage had stood on top of it to preach.

Many people marveled at how gigantic the footprint was, for the foot of the sinning sons of Adam isn't 14 inches long or, in other words, a size 14. But a religious chronicler sententiously replies that a size 14 isn't all that large for such a great man.

I'll be damned! And what a foot!

But since the apostle left traces even in Bolivia and Tucumán, as is proved by a book in which there is a lengthy discussion of the cross of Carbuco venerated as an object belonging to the blessed traveler, we Peruvians wanted something more; and when the volcano of Omate or Huaina-Putina felt like playing one of its tricks, the Dominican fathers of a monastery in Parinacochas found, among the ashes or lava, nothing less than one of Saint Thomas's sandals.

The chronicles did not say whether it was for a right foot or a left, an unforgivable oversight on the part of such intelligent writers.

The sandal was made of a material never used by either Indians or Spaniards, which proves that it came directly from the shop of Ashaverus or Juan Waiting-for-God (the Wandering Jew), a famous shoemaker in Jerusalem, the Fasinetti of our day, so to speak.

Friar Alonso de Ovalle, the superior of the monastery, placed it with great ceremony in a rosewood box with gold fittings, and around the year 1603, approximately, brought it to Lima, where it was received in procession beneath a canopy and with great festivities attended by the Viceroy Marqués de Salinas.

Erudite authors of that century say that the blessed sandal wrought many, a great many, miracles in Lima, and that it was highly revered by the Dominicans.

---

3   By walking [Latin]. [Trans. note.]

Calancha states that, once the curiosity of the inhabitants was satisfied, Father Ovalle returned to Parinochas with the relic, but others maintain that the sandal never left Lima.

The truth remains in the place where it belongs. I neither add nor subtract, neither alter nor comment, neither deny or assert.

I simply note down the tradition, taking the matter under advisement, with some saying white and others red.

Manuel González Prada (1844–1918)

Manuel González Prada was born in Lima to a family of wealthy landowners. Despite his elite origins, González Prada became an articulate spokesperson against oppression and consistently manifested a brave determination to face reality regardless of its consequences. That oppositional quality was a family tradition: in protest against the government of General Ramón Castilla, González Prada's father uprooted his entire family into self-imposed exile in Valparaíso, Chile. There González Prada attended an English school with excellent teachers, from whom he learned English, French, and German, acquiring a solid and diversified education. Upon returning to Peru, González Prada refused to study at the Catholic seminary and enrolled himself at a secular school, exhibiting a determination to pursue the truth that later caused members of his class to view him as traitorous.

In the 1870s, González Prada helped to found the Literary Club of Lima and became a keen observer of Peruvian society and government. He was critical of the oligarchy's imprudent waste of income generated by guano, a valuable and nonrenewable natural resource, and he also challenged the regressive influences of the Catholic Church. But it was the War of the Pacific (1879–1884) that radicalized González Prada. He was outraged at the Peruvian army's incompetence and its division along class and racial lines, where the commanders were members of the oligarchy and the soldiers were Indians and peasants. When he met Peruvian soldiers who were so ill-informed that they thought they were fighting for "General Peru" against "General Chile," he was incensed, confronted by the depths of poverty and ignorance that the oligarchy's appropriation of the nation's wealth had created.

But even as González Prada blamed his class for the calamities of the war, he took the Chilean occupation personally and refused to leave his house for three years to avoid any encounter with the enemy. Afterward,

González Prada became increasingly vocal in his opposition to the government. In 1888, he delivered two famous speeches, one at the Politeama Theatre and the other at the Olimpo, in which he publicly declared his dismay at the wasteful legacies of the Peruvian leadership, their refusal to create an inclusive nation, and the colonial nostalgia reflected in their art and culture, a criticism clearly directed at RICARDO PALMA's romanticized *tradiciones*. When the government tried to subdue González Prada by offering him official posts, he declared he was not for hire.

The new Literary Circle that González Prada had helped create in 1886 led to the organization of an opposition party, Partido de Unión Nacional (National Union Party). However, when he was encouraged to become its leader, he and his French-born wife, Adriana Verneuil, boarded a ship to Europe, determined to avoid the political *caudillismo* or cronyism that so afflicted his country. His self-imposed exile lasted seven years, mostly in Paris where he attended the lectures of the anticlerical progressive Ernest Renan at the Collège de France. When Renan died in 1892, González Prada composed a moving account of his funeral, celebrating him as a major force for modernity. Two years later, González Prada published his first book, *Páginas libres* [Pages of a Free Man] (1894), a collection of essays that included his speeches at the Politeama and Olimpo in Lima.

It was González Prada's visit to Barcelona, however, that introduced him to anarchism, whose antistatist principles he readily embraced. In Spain González Prada met Rubén Darío and many individuals who were to become part of the Generation of '98, a group responding to the traumatic loss of the Spanish War of 1898 against the United States. That same year, González Prada and his family returned to Lima, where he founded several anarchist newspapers and contributed essays to the anarchist journal *Los Parias*, writings that were later collected as *Anarquía*. He also published his first book of poetry, titled *Minúsculas* (1901).

In 1904, González Prada composed his most fiery defense of indigenous people, "Nuestros indios" (Our Indians). According to his son, because the essay was unfinished, it was not included in the first edition of *Horas de lucha* [Times of Struggle] (1908), though it did appear in a second, posthumous, edition in 1924. *Horas de lucha* was itself a radical example of González Prada's unflinching honesty and courage in his speeches and essays. The first half focuses on intellectual issues, comparing mental and manual work, or women and the Catholic Church, while the second part addresses in very frank terms the social, political, economic, and intellectual corruption of the Peruvian oligarchy. "Our Indians" exhibits a blunt candor that is unusual in Spanish America. No writer before González Prada had ever dared to speak so clearly and so vehemently about the condition of the Indians. And no one else had ever concluded that the solution to their oppression was an armed movement. Of course, there had already been any number of armed rebellions by Indians, and González Prada's call to arms is not, in that context, as subversive or as irresponsible as it might seem. But the essay is both a powerful cry to terminate, once and for all, the ill-treatment of the Indians and also an act of solidarity with Indian resistance—the occasion of so many deaths past and future.

González Prada succeeded RICARDO PALMA as director of the National Library in 1912, serving two terms, 1912–1914 and 1916–1918. He died in 1918 of a heart attack in Lima. González Prada's influence extended for several generations. One important group was associated with the journal *Colónida* and included publisher and writer Alfredo González Prada (1891–1943)—Manuel's only son—and the avant-garde poet, Abraham Valdelomar (1888–1919). Later writers and thinkers, such as the influential poet César Vallejo (1892–1938) and JOSÉ CARLOS MARIÁTEGUI, also deeply admired González Prada and helped to establish a radical strain in Peruvian thought that persisted well into the next century.

The selection "Nuestros indios" by González Prada (1904) is from *Horas de Lucha* [Hours of Battle] (1908), Marxist Internet Archive. The excerpt is translated by Sarah Taylor Cook.

From Nuestros indios (1904) [Our Indians]

III

Does the Indian suffer less under the Republic than under Spanish domination? Even though there are no longer tax collectors and law enforcers or the *encomienda* system, there is still forced labor and the press-gang. What we make the Indians suffer ought to insult our own humanity. It is we who preserve this state of ignorance and enslavement. We debase them in the quarters where they are confined. We coarsen them with liquor. We throw them into battle against their brothers, and sometimes we have even hunted and massacred them, as we have done in Amantani, Ilave and Huanta. (A trustworthy and well-informed individual offers the following details: "The Amantani Massacre: Not long after the first Piérola dictatorship had begun, the Indians of Amantani, from the island of Titicaca, lynched a foreman who had made the mistake of trying to require them to do military exercises. The response was to dispatch from Puno two warships that ferociously bombed the island from six in the morning until six at night. The killing was horrible, without distinction of age or gender, and even today the number of Indians who perished is unknown. All that is left are the bleaching skeletons, corpses stuck in crevices of boulders, as if they were seeking refuge."The massacres of Ilave and Huanta occurred during the second presidency of Piérola) [between 1895 and 1899].

One can see in practice everywhere the unwritten axiom that the Indian has no rights, only obligations. When it comes to the Indian, any complaint is taken as insubordination, while a collective complaint is seen as an uprising. The pragmatic Spaniards killed any Indian that tried to break free of the conquerors' yoke. We, patriotic Republicans, massacre them when they protest burdensome taxes or when they tire of bearing in silence the iniquities of the local satrap.

Our form of government is reduced to a colossal lie, since we cannot claim to be a democratic republic when two or three million individuals live unprotected by the law. If on the nation's coasts one can at least glimpse the guarantees that might exist for everyone in this parody of a republic, in the interior, one can feel directly the violation of every right under a truly feudal regime. There is no rule of Law, no tribunal of justice. Landowners and bosses settle all questions, arrogating to themselves the roles of judge and executioner. Political authorities, far from assisting the weak and the poor, almost always help the rich and powerful. In these regions, justices of the peace and governors are at the service of the hacienda. What governor, what manager—not to mention what deputy—would dare go face-to-face against a landowner?

A hacienda is formed by amassing small lots, ripped from the hands of their legitimate owners, and a master exercising the authority of a Norman lord over his peons. Not only does the master handpick governors, mayors and judges, but he oversees marriages and designates inheritances, insuring that the son must assume his father's debts, condemning children to a servitude that lasts their whole lives. He metes out cruel punishments—shackles, whippings, the pillory or execution—and imposes ridiculous sentences—shaving heads or compelling cold-water enemas. For these men, who have no respect for life or property, it would take a miracle for them to treat Indian women with honor or courtesy. Any Indian woman, whether single or married, can become the target of the brutal desires of the "lord." Kidnapping, rape, or molestation mean nothing when Indian women are subject to absolute power. And in spite of it all, the Indian must not speak to the master without kneeling and kissing his hand. One cannot just claim that these landowners act this way because they are an ignorant or uncultured lot. The sons of these landowners leave for Europe as children, to be educated in France and England, returning to Peru with every appearance of civilized individuals, but as soon as they return to the confines of their haciendas, they lose their European veneer and act with even more inhumanity and violence than their parents. Dressed up in a hat, a poncho and spurs, the beast returns. In sum: the haciendas constitute kingdoms at the heart of the Republic; the landowners play the role of autocrats in the center of a democracy.

IV

The Indian question is not just a matter of education; it is economic; it is social. How can we address this issue? Not long ago a German came up with the idea of restoring the Empire of the Incas. He learned Quechua, he went into the Cuzco Indian territory, he began to amass followers, and he might even have started a revolt if death had not caught up with him after returning from a trip to Europe. But is such a restoration even possible today? To try it, to attempt to make it happen, we would only achieve a diminished imitation of past greatness.

The Indians' condition can only improve by two paths: either the heart of the oppressor, softened to an extreme degree, begins to recognize the rights of the oppressed; or the spirit of the oppressed acquires enough strength to teach the oppressor a lesson. If the Indian would buy rifles and bullets with the money he wastes on alcohol and carousing; if in the corner of his shack or in the crevices of a rock, he would hide a weapon—then his condition would change. He would force people to respect him and his property. Violence must be met with violence. Teach a lesson to the master who steals his wool, to the soldier who conscripts him in the name of the government, to the armed bandit who seizes his livestock and his pack animals.

One should not preach humility and resignation to the Indian, but rather pride and rebellion. What has been gained by compliance and patience over these last three hundred, four hundred years? As long as the authorities suffer no consequences, they will continue to inflict more pain. There is one telling fact: a greater state of well-being exists in the regions farthest away from the great haciendas; people enjoy more order and tranquility in the towns least frequented by the authorities.

To conclude: the Indian will be saved by the grace of his own efforts, not by the humanization of his oppressors. Every target is, more or less, a Pizarro, a Valverde or an Areche.

In Context | The Inventive Photography of Juan Manuel Figueroa Aznar (1878–1951)

This photo might well have been taken in Paucartambo (Peru), probably between 1915 and 1920, since many of Figueroa's photos belong to this period. The old man, possibly hauling water to a well, seems to be carrying too much weight for his age, but the photo captures both his strength and his vulnerability, as well as the poverty indicated by his worn clothes and makeshift shoes.

Figueroa thought of himself primarily as a painter though he was later recognized as a major figure in the Cuzco School of Photography. Part of an influential artistic movement in the first half of the twentieth century, the group included Pablo Veramendi, the Cabrera brothers, Horacio Ochoa, José Gabriel González, and César Meza.

Figure 6.1. Juan Manuel Figueroa Aznar (1878–1951), *Cargador*. Courtesy of Fernando Figueroa.

Figueroa's photography followed two distinct approaches, a realist one as in the photo here and a more innovative technique, mixing photographs with oil paintings. In blending his photographic and painterly talents, Figueroa often invented new backgrounds for his portraits and photographs. He is one of the first artists in Cuzco to have depicted Indians—including some models who posed as Indians. Figueroa's work often has a dramatic edge, as in one of his photographic collages, illustrating the progressive stages of a man drinking until he had almost collapsed.

José Martí (1853–1895)

The life and works of José Martí are virtually seamless, his action and thought intersecting at every point. Exceptional in the range of his achievements, literary and political, Martí spent his life fighting for his political beliefs and died defending them. With a journalist's eye, his writing vividly and insightfully chronicles the events and daily life of his times. In addition, he was a gifted poet, whose poems are emotionally exact and technically sophisticated; an effective narrator of complex situations; an inventive commentator on politics and literature; a skilled translator, professor, and editor. But he is best remembered for his tireless defense of individual liberty and the freedom of his native land, Cuba.

Born in Havana to a middle-class family, Martí was a precocious adolescent. He attended a variety of schools, believing at one point that he might become an artist. But his early passion for justice soon intervened. On October 10, 1868, sparked by a Puerto Rican rebellion known as the Grito de Lares, (The Proclamation of Lares) a movement for Cuban independence began—the Grito de Yara, named for the town where the revolution began. At the onset of what was to become the Ten Years' War, the fifteen-year-old Martí published a patriotic play and a sonnet "10 de octubre" about these events. Soon after, he was arrested for his letter to a classmate, criticizing him for enlisting in the Spanish army. Despite the efforts of his family, Martí was condemned to six years of forced labor. When the privations of imprisonment seriously weakened his health, he was exiled to Spain.

From this point, Martí became a man in motion. Though he studied canon and civil law in Spain, with the intention of settling in Mexico, he continued to be involved with other Cuban exiles, writing for progressive newspapers and journals. He traveled to Mexico in 1875, and after a failed attempt to immigrate to Cuba, settled in Guatemala where he taught at the university and continued his activism. With the end of the Ten Years' War in 1878, Martí was allowed to return to Cuba but not permitted to practice law. Now married—to Carmen Zayas Bazán—and with a young son, Martí was soon in trouble again for his political activities. Exiled to Spain, he presently moved to New York City and then to Venezuela; disappointed by its authoritarian regime, he returned to the United States in 1881 and rededicated himself to the struggle for Cuban independence.

Martí remained in the United States for fourteen years, working tirelessly to organize Cuban immigrants in New York and in Florida in the effort to free their country. Martí himself was employed as a translator and journalist, becoming a highly regarded interpreter of Latin American politics and events. The emergence of the telegraph, uniting continents and hemispheres, was at that moment transforming journalism, giving more immediate access to world news and strengthening the interpretive role of the reporter. Martí understood acutely the profound and irreversible changes that were affecting Spanish America, but he also appreciated the corrosive spirit that accompanied these transformations. The social solidarity and strong community spirit that had once bound people together were being replaced by the raw competition for power and wealth.

Martí was not beguiled by the so-called benefits of progress. Rapid technological development, internationalized markets, the global exploitation of natural resources, not to mention the partition of Africa among the European powers—these were for Martí signs of decadence in the Western and Christian spirit. The consolidation of social power was diminishing the value of personal authenticity as control shifted into the hands of crass military leaders and wealthy monopolists like Andrew Carnegie and John D. Rockefeller in the United States and Werner von Siemens in Germany. For Martí, a better and alternative model was New York native Walt Whitman, and he wrote an impassioned essay celebrating the poet as the embodiment of moral individualism, one who went beyond the dichotomies of good and evil to the sheer vitality of the human spirit.

Martí's great intuition was that the irreversible changes of his time were not always positive. From his deeply moral perspective, to which he steadfastly adhered, the final decades of the nineteenth century were a time of physical and spiritual decay. Martí remained a singular voice in appreciating the disastrous consequences of the second industrial revolution, especially for Latin America. Nothing worried this Cuban poet more than the negative effects of this new colonization—not by military occupation, but by foreign investment.

"Nuestra América" [Our America], published in 1891, is indispensable

266 · Anthology of Spanish American Thought and Culture

for understanding Latin American thought. No other text describes with such clarity the contemporary adversities facing the region. Nothing before had ever named the dangers so precisely or articulated so positively the directions to genuine freedom. In magnificent prose and with extraordinary courage, Martí defies the dominant trends of his time, challenging deeply rooted prejudices and common-sense "truths" about public education, politics, and society. At the risk of being thought irrational or delirious, Martí confronts several key issues: the servile imitation of foreign models; the palpable treason of those allied with the new colonizers, like the United States; the manipulative use of race; the contemptuous disregard for the customs and values of individual nations; the careless dismissal of history and its implications.

No one had yet expressed with such brevity and simplicity this basic truth: "There can be no racial animosity, because there are no races." Martí was not, of course, denying ethnological and anthropological realities, but he was rejecting the concept of race to justify discrimination against Indians and blacks, a tactic that unfortunately continues into the present. Before Martí, no one had directly accused government officials in Latin America of disregarding the social composition of their own people: governing as if there were no Indians in Mexico or in Peru or Bolivia, or as if no blacks lived in Cuba and Colombia and the Dominican Republic. Even worse, as Martí explains, governments deliberately exploit those peoples—Indians and blacks—for the benefit of those who would then go abroad to Europe or the United States and deny their own origins: "[t]hose carpenter's sons, that are ashamed that their fathers are carpenters!. . . . [T]hese deserters who take up arms in the armies of a North America that drowns its Indians in blood."

But even beyond the sheer power of Martí's prose and his incisive critique, what stands out in this essay is the uniqueness of his solution: not weapons but ideas will bring change to "Our America." Martí understood that the necessary changes were spiritual, not solely material. He appreciated that adopting different behaviors or forms was unimportant compared to transformations in substance, in essence, in values. He saw that the enemy cannot be defeated by using its own aggressive, violent methods. Instead, true victory would be achieved by demonstrating an independent spirit and an authentic identity, by adopting governments that emerge from within the country and its people: "The spirit of the government must be that of the country. Its structure must conform to rules appropriate to the country." As Martí emphasizes, such structures must be inclusive—of

Indians, blacks, mestizos, creoles, peasants, workers, artisans—and not just "learned and artificial men." The true evil, the real blindness in Latin American history, he claims, has been the rejection of our own nature: by this ignominy, "the tyrants of America have climbed to power." It is remarkable that so few have seen this surprisingly obvious formula for success: "In a new nation a governor means a creator." To be a creator is simply to govern a nation as it is, faithful to its lived realities.

Martí's eloquent expression of the need to create an America that is truly "ours" follows in a remarkable tradition of thought beginning with BOLÍVAR and SIMÓN RODRÍGUEZ. It was, however, a perspective directly opposed to the era's dominant ideology, particularly in Argentina. Inherited from those who defeated Juan Manuel de Rosas, that opposite view was articulated by Juan Bautista Alberdi, who proclaimed that "to govern is to populate"—meaning, with Europeans, purposefully exterminating Indians and blacks.

All the power of hope in Martí fell useless before the realities of the late nineteenth century. With few exceptions, instead of disappearing, the traitors and cynical leaders who denied their roots and promoted foreign models only increased in the region, as the capitalist system, strengthened by innovations in manufacturing, power-generation, and armaments, gained momentum. This second phase of global occupation and colonization quickly engulfed Latin America by the end of the nineteenth century. In spite of Martí's warnings, and with few exceptions, such as Mexico's Revolution in 1910, the region entered a somber period of dependence.

Few essays in Latin American history have maintained their relevance as richly as "Nuestra América." A perfect balance between an imaginative style and forward-looking ideas, its language does not age; moreover, its message remains, if unhappily germane, reassuringly rejuvenating.

Martí himself continued to write and lecture and raise money for the Cuban cause until 1895, when he helped to organize an expedition to the island in support of the revolution. He was killed by Spanish troops in the Battle of Dos Rios on May 19 of that year.

This essay is from a collection that applies its title to the whole, *Our America: Writings on Latin America and the Struggle for Cuban Independence*, edited with an introduction and notes by Philip S. Foner; translated by Elinor Randall with additional translations by Juan de Onís and Roslyn Hel Foner (New York, London: Monthly Review Press, 1977), 85–88. Reproduced by permission of Monthly Review Press via Copyright Clearance Center.

From **Nuestra América (1891) [Our America]**

We can no longer be a people of leaves living in the air, our foliage heavy with blooms and crackling or humming at the whim of the sun's caress, or buffeted and tossed by the storms. The trees must form ranks to keep the giant with seven-league boots from passing! It is the time of mobilization, of marching together, and we must go forward in close order, like silver in the veins of the Andes.

Only those born prematurely are lacking in courage. Those without faith in their country are seven-month weaklings. Because they have no courage, they deny it to others. Their puny arms—arms with bracelets and hands with painted nails, arms of Paris or Madrid—can hardly reach the bottom limb, and they claim the tall tree to be unclimbable. The ships should be loaded with those harmful insects that gnaw at the bone of the country that nourishes them. If they are Parisians or from Madrid, let them go to the Prado under lamplight, or to Tortoni's for a sherbet. Those carpenters' sons who are ashamed that their fathers are carpenters! Those born in America who are ashamed of the mother who reared them, because she wears an Indian apron, and who disown their sick mother, the scoundrels, abandoning her on her sickbed! Then who is a real man? He who stays with his mother and nurses her in her illness, or he who puts her to work out of sight, and lives at her expense on decadent lands, sporting fancy neckties, cursing the womb that carried him, displaying the sign of the traitor on the back of his paper frockcoat? These sons of Our America, which will be saved by its Indians and is growing better; these deserters who take up arms in the armies of a North America that drowns its Indians in blood and is growing worse! These delicate creatures who are men but are unwilling to do men's work! The Washington who made this land for them, did he not go to live with the English at a time when he saw them fighting against his own country? These "iconoclasts" of honor who drag that honor over foreign soil, like their counterparts in the French Revolution with their dancing, their affectations, their drawling speech!

For in what lands can men take more pride than in our long-suffering American republics, raised up from among the silent Indian masses by the bleeding arms of a hundred apostles, to the sounds of battle between the book and the processional candle? Never in history have such advanced and united nations been forged in so short a time from such disorganized elements.

The presumptuous man feels that the earth was made to serve as his pedestal because he happens to have a facile pen or colorful speech, and he accuses his native land of being worthless and beyond redemption because its virgin jungles fail to provide him with a constant means of traveling over the world, driving Persian ponies and lavishing champagne like a tycoon. The incapacity does not lie with the emerging country in quest of suitable forms and a utilitarian greatness; it lies rather with those who attempt to rule nations of a unique and violent character by means of laws inherited from four centuries of freedom in the United States and nineteen centuries of monarchy in France. A decree by Hamilton[4] does not halt the charge of the plainsman's horse. A phrase by Sieyès[5] does nothing to quicken the stagnant blood of the Indian race. To govern well, one must see things as they are. And the able governor in America is not the one who knows how to govern the Germans or the French; he must know the elements that compose his own country, and how to bring them together, using methods and institutions originating within the country, to reach that desirable state where each man can attain self-realization and all may enjoy the abundance that Nature has bestowed on everyone in the nation to enrich with their toil and defend with their lives. The government must originate in the country. The spirit of the government must be that of the country. Good government is nothing more than the balance of the country's natural elements.

That is why the imported book has been conquered in America by the natural man. Natural men have conquered learned and artificial men. The native halfbreed has conquered the exotic Creole. The struggle is not between civilization and barbarity, but between false erudition and Nature. The natural man is good, and he respects and rewards superior intelligence as long as his humility is not turned against him, or he is not offended by being disregarded—a thing the natural man never forgives, prepared as he is to forcibly regain the respect of whoever has wounded his pride or threatened his interests. It is by conforming with these disdained native elements that the tyrants of America have climbed to power, and have fallen as soon as they betrayed them. Republics have paid with oppression for their inability to recognize the true elements of their countries, to derive from them the right kind of government, and to govern accordingly. In a new nation a governor means a creator.

In nations composed of both cultured and uncultured elements, the uncultured will govern because it is their habit to attack and resolve doubts with their fists in cases where the cultured have failed in the art of governing. The

---

4   Alexander Hamilton (1757?-1804), Secretary of the Treasury (1789–1795) in George Washington's cabinet, with whom Francisco de Miranda had several contacts and relations.

5   Emmanuel Joseph Sieyès (1748–1836), a French clergyman prominent in the French Revolution, who helped draft the Declaration of the Rights of Man (August 26, 1789) and whose views on government influenced Bolívar.

uncultured masses are lazy and timid in the realm of intelligence, and they want to be governed well. But if the government hurts them, they shake it off and govern themselves. How can the universities produce governors if not a single university in America teaches the rudiments of the art of government, the analysis of elements peculiar to the peoples of America? The young go out into the world wearing Yankee or French spectacles, hoping to govern a people they don't know. In the political race entrance should be denied to those who are ignorant of the rudiments of politics. The prize in literary contests should not go for the best ode, but for the best study of the political factors of one's country. Newspapers, universities, and schools should encourage the study of the country's pertinent components. To know them is sufficient, without mincing words; for whoever brushes aside even a part of the truth, whether through intention or oversight, is doomed to fall. The truth he lacks thrives on negligence, and brings down whatever is built without it. It is easier to resolve our problem knowing its components than to resolve them without knowing them. Along comes the natural man, strong and indignant, and he topples all the justice accumulated from books because he has not been governed in accordance with the obvious needs of the country. Knowing is what counts. To know one's country and govern it with that knowledge is the only way to free it from tyranny. The European university must bow to the American university. The history of America, from the Incas to the present, must be taught in clear detail and to the letter, even if the archons of Greece are overlooked. Our Greece must take priority over the Greece, which is not ours. We need it more. Nationalist statesmen must replace foreign statesmen. Let the world be grafted onto our republics, but the trunk must be our own. And let the vanquished pedant hold his tongue, for there are no lands in which a man may take greater pride than in our long-suffering American republics.

Rubén Darío (1867–1916)

In 1898, Spain lost the final remnants of its formerly vast colonial empire in Asia and America. The defeat of Spain in the so-called Spanish American War left Cuba, Puerto Rico, Guam, and the Philippines under the control of the United States. For Spanish Americans, the outcome was problematic, at best, since Cubans and Puerto Ricans had fought for decades to achieve independence from Spain and now found themselves simply transferred to a new empire. While Spain's defeat resulted in a general malaise throughout most Hispanic countries, that depression also sparked a movement for social renewal in the Spanish peninsula itself spearheaded by "The Generation of 98."

One of the texts associated with this reformist spirit had been written in Chile a decade earlier by a young Nicaraguan, Rubén Darío. *Azul* (1888), along with Darío's collections from the next decade, *Prosas profanas y otros poemas* [Secular Hymns and Other Poems] and *Los raros* [The Eccentrics], both published in 1896, was rapidly becoming a classic by defining a new way of thinking and a fresh sensibility in Latin America: *modernismo*. Not to be confused with the Modernism of England and North America, which dominated the arts between the World Wars, Latin American *modernismo* was an aestheticist, "art for art's sake" movement that began in the 1880s and was followed by the Spanish American avant-garde shortly before 1920. By contrast, European Modernism (in the United States and much of Western Europe) was associated with the French avant-garde, including surrealism, from the early decades of the twentieth century. Certainly, in its most basic meaning, modernity—being up-to-date and in sync with other western nations—had never been much evident in the Hispanic world. Ironically, however, modernity came first to the ex-colonies before the Spanish metropolis, whose decadence was by this point reaching its nadir.

Félix Rubén García Sarmiento was born in Metapa, Nicaragua, and after his parents' separation, was raised by his mother's aunt and uncle, though he used the surname first adopted by his paternal great-grandfather. He showed an early talent for poetry and published several verses in newspapers when he was still a child. With some official encouragement and after fruitful encounters with other poets, especially with Francisco Gavidia (1863–1955) in El Salvador, Darío moved to Chile in 1886, where he began producing his characteristically *modernista* poems.

Although he became part of a continental movement, Darío's work represented the moment at which *modernismo* reached its most self-conscious expression. Working as a journalist and writing prolifically, Darío became increasingly well known, especially after the publication in 1896 of *Prosas profanas y otros poemas* and *Los raros*. Traveling throughout Central and South America, serving as Colombian consul in Buenos Aires and as Nicaraguan ambassador in Madrid, being honored for his writing and then falling ill in New York, Darío finally returned to his native Nicaragua in 1915 and died the following year.

His literary achievement reflects one of the most original voices in the entire Hispanic tradition. Not since Calderón de la Barca's death in Spain (1681) or SOR JUANA INÉS DE LA CRUZ in Mexico (1695), did language and poetic form in Spanish achieve such brilliance. Among his contemporaries, Darío's artistry is matched only by the Spanish poet Gustavo Adolfo Bécquer (1836–1870) and JOSE MARTÍ, both of whom were important influences. Darío's poetry profoundly couples aesthetic insight with his own experience, even as he draws on—indeed, revels in—the complex traditions of Spanish, European, and American literature. Echoing Spanish classics like Cervantes, Góngora, and Quevedo as well as French poets like Victor Hugo and Verlaine, and North American writers like Walt Whitman, Darío transmutes disparate styles, attitudes, and forms into a completely original voice. For Darío, such appropriations were natural, an accurate image of the diversity, disparity, and contrariety that were proper to his own historical moment—that is, to *modernismo* itself.

One of the basic elements of *modernismo* was the recognition that Spanish American identity was a historical phenomenon. To identify Indians, for example, as barbaric or as cannibals was not to describe their "natural" or inherent characteristics but only to rehearse terms imposed by the dominant nations. Among the most useful justifications for conquest was the specific accusation of cannibalism. Darío exploits this negative association to reconfigure the relationship of conqueror and conquered in one of his most influential essays, "El triunfo de Calibán" [The Triumph of Caliban]. Darío draws the name Caliban from Shakespeare's final play, *The Tempest* (1611), evoking a character who represents barbarity—his name an anagram of cannibal—the direct opposite of Ariel, a figure of spirituality and civility. Darío follows a rich tradition of reinterpreting these complex figures, but he also creates a deeply original version by inverting their values, making Caliban an image of the barbarism of the United States, which was emerging as the bitter culmination of Western civilization. That decisive inversion opened the way for Uruguayan writer José Enrique Rodó (1871–1917) later to identify Latin Americans with Ariel in his eponymous book published in 1900.

"The Triumph of Calibán" (1898) exemplifies the complex attitude that most Latin Americans had toward the United States since the beginning of the nineteenth century: admiration and rejection, attraction and fear. Some Latin American countries had copied the U.S. Constitution and often yearned to imitate its progressive values. But Latin Americans also saw the greed informing U.S. expansionism and recognized the inconsistency of proclaiming liberty while profiting from slavery. The profound racism of American society and its internal contradictions were only too apparent, elaborated in numerous articles, books, travel diaries, and other texts throughout the period. Darío himself both admired and repudiated the United States, particularly after its intervention in separating Panama from Colombia in 1903, a blatant attempt to control the construction of the Panama Canal. Darío's response to this intervention was a poetic version of "Triumph of Caliban." Addressed "To Roosevelt," then U.S. president, the final line of the poem epitomizes the sentiments of this great Nicaraguan poet:

Y, pues contáis con todo, falta una cosa: Dios.
[You have everything on your side, only one thing is missing: God]

Translated by Isabel Bastos and Marvin Liberman with revisions by Carlos Jáuregui, the text and most notes (as indicated) are from Carlos Jáuregui's "Calibán: icono del 98. A propósito de un artículo de Rubén Darío" y "El triunfo de Calibán." Published in Balance de un siglo (1898–1998), a special number of Revista Iberoamericana 184–85 (1998): 441 –55 (coordinated by Aníbal González).

The Triumph of Caliban (1898)

No, I can't, I don't want to side with these buffaloes with silver teeth. They're my enemies, they're the ones who despise Latin blood, they're the Barbarians. Thus, anyone with a noble heart shivers, and every honorable man who keeps in his blood any vestige of the she-wolf's milk protests.

I've seen those Yankees, in their overwhelming cities of iron and stone; and the hours that I've lived among them I've spent in maddening anguish. It seemed to me that I was weighted down by a mountain; I felt that I was gasping for air in a country of Cyclops, eaters of raw meat, in a country of brutish blacksmiths, occupants of Mammoth houses. Red-faced, fat, vulgar, they walk their streets like animals, pushing and brushing against each other, chasing the dollar. The ideals of those Calibans[6] are reduced to the stock market and the factory. They eat, eat, and calculate, they drink whiskey and make millions. They sing Home, Sweet Home! but their home is a checking account, a banjo, a Negro man, and a pipe. Utter enemies of idealism, they are perpetual magnifying mirrors in their apoplectic quest for their progress; their eminent Emerson is like the moon to Carlyle's sun; their Whitman, with his rough-hewn verses, is a democratic prophet, à la Uncle Sam; and their Poe, their great Poe,—a poor swan drunk from sorrow and alcohol—was the martyr of his own dream in a

---

6   In Shakespeare's final play, The Tempest (1611), Caliban was a brutish creature who tried to seduce Miranda, the innocent daughter of the shipwrecked Prospero, who was aided by Ariel, a beneficial spirit. The play's island setting is generally associated with Bermuda and the Americas.

country where he will never be understood. As for Lanier, the single drop of Latin blood that shines in his name rescues him from being a poet solely for Protestant ministers and for buccaneers and cowboys.

"We have"—they say—"all the greatest things in the entire world!" Indeed, there we are in the country of Brobdingnag: [7] they have Niagara Falls, the Brooklyn Bridge, the Statue of Liberty, twenty-story cuboid buildings, dynamite and cannons, [Cornelius] Vanderbilt, [Jay] Gould,[8] and their newspapers and cronies. They look down at us, as if we were inferior to them, and belittle anyone who doesn't gulp down beef steaks and doesn't say *all right*, for those enormous *enfants sauvages*, Paris is simply their *grand guignol*.[9] There they go to party and leave their checks—because even their enjoyment is rude, and their women, although beautiful, are made of malleable rubber.

They coddle the British—*but English, you know?*—as a *parvenu* adulates a gentleman of noble lineage.

They have temples for all kinds of gods and don't believe in any; apart from [Thomas] Edison, their greatest men are called [Charles] Lynch, [James] Monroe, and that [Ulysses] Grant, whose character you could find in [Victor] Hugo's series of poems, *The Terrible Year*.[10] Huge red simians, they imitate and counterfeit everything in art and science. Not even the winds of centuries will be able to polish up this enormous Beast.

No, no I can't side with them; I can't support Caliban's triumph.

That is why, my soul was filled with joy the other night, when three men, representative of our race attended a dignified and cordial gathering to protest the Yankee's aggression toward the noble and now-tormented Spain.

---

7 Country of giants in *Gulliver's Travels* (1726) by Jonathan Swift. Groussac makes the same comparison: "We are like Gulliver in the kingdom of Brobdingnag" (*Del Plata al Niágara* 337). [Note by Carlos Jáuregui.]

8 Jay Gould (1836–1892), a railroad magnate and speculator who provoked "Black Friday" (September 24, 1869) by maneuvering gold prices, was harshly characterized by José Martí as "a great monopolist. . . . on the back of workers" and "a harsh and disdainful millionaire" (*Obras Completas* X, 84–86; 423). [Note by Carlos Jáuregui.]

9 *Guignol* is the name of a French marionette created in Lyon at the end of the seventeenth century; by Darío's time, *guignol* was the name of cabarets where decadent shows were presented, the sense here. By 1897, it designated horror theatre that used special effects or tricks. It seems hardly probable, but not impossible, that Darío would be cognizant of this theatre's success. [Note by Carlos Jáuregui.]

10 *L'année terrible* (1872). In "To Roosevelt" (1905), Darío repeats this idea: "Hugo already told Grant: The stars are yours." Hugo had attacked Grant in many articles. [Note by Carlos Jáuregui.]

One of these men was Roque Sáenz Peña,[11] the Argentine whose voice in the Pan-American Congress opposed Monroe's loudmouthed slang with his grand continental vision, and showed the redskin[12] in his own house that in our republics there are vigilant guards against the trickery of the barbarian's rapacious mouth.

On that Spanish night, Sáenz Peña spoke movingly, and one could not help but recall his [diplomatic] triumphs in Washington. With similarly refined eloquence, he surely had surprised the swindler Blaine[13] and all his cronies, the tycoons of cotton, bacon and railroads!

In this speech at La Victoria Theater,[14] the statesman and gracious gentleman rose up again. He repeated what he has always asserted, namely, his ideas about the danger of that boa constrictor, jaws still open after swallowing up Texas; about the greed of the Anglo-Saxon, about the infamous appetite of the Yankee, about the political disgrace of the government of the North; and the usefulness, the necessity for the Spanish American nations to be ready for and to expect an attack by the boa constrictor.

Apart from Sáenz Peña only one other soul has been as far farsighted about this issue, as perceptive and persistent: I am referring—oh, curious irony of our times!—to the insight of the father of free Cuba, José Martí. Martí never ceased to preach to the nations of his own blood that they had to be wary of those predatory men, and to see in all that talk about "alliances" and Pan-Americanism nothing but the bait and trickery of the merchants of Yankee-land. What would the illustrious Cuban say today, seeing how, under the pretense of assisting the magnificent Pearl of the Caribbean [Cuba], the [North American] monster swallows it up, oyster and all?

---

11 Roque Sáenz Peña (1851–1914) was a prominent Argentine politician, lawyer, congressman, secretary of state, senator, founder of a newspaper, and an extraordinary public speaker. He opposed Blaine during the Conferencia Internacional Americana (1889–1890), speaking against the Monroe Doctrine and its slogan, "America for Americans," and opposing it with the formula: "America for humanity." He became president of Argentina in 1910, including among his achievements the Suffrage Law, extending the vote to many thousands of disenfranchised citizens and breaking the political monopoly of the aristocracy. [Eds. and Carlos Jáuregui.]

12 Darío uses here the ethnic term *redskin* [piel roja] as an epithet for what he sees as the "savage" and brutish United States.

13 James G. Blaine (1830–1893) was in the railroad business and a Republican candidate in the presidential elections of 1884. He became the spokeman for U.S. interests in Latin America as well as the leader in political and economic U.S. intervention in the area under the geopolitics of *Pan-Americanism*. [Note by Carlos Jauregui.]

14 On May 2, 1898, Groussac, Tarnassi, and Sáenz Peña gave speeches here presenting their views on the Spanish-American War, an event sponsored by the Club español of Buenos Aires. [Note by Carlos Jáuregui.]

In the speech mentioned I reported that the statesman walked arm-in-arm with the gracious gentleman. Sáenz Peña's life attests precisely to these virtues. As such, he was bound to speak out in defense of the noblest of nations, already in the hands of these modern *yangüenses*.[15] He spoke in defense of the unarmed gentleman who accepts a duel with the dynamiting and mechanical Goliath.

On behalf of France, spoke Paul Groussac.[16] What a comforting spectacle, to see this eminent and reclusive man come out of his grotto of books, from the studious isolation in which he lives, also to protest the injustice and material triumph of brute force. The maestro is not an orator, but his lecture moved and excited everyone, especially the intellectuals in the audience. His speech, literary refined as with everything he writes, was art transformed into a vigorous defense of the noble cause of justice. And one would hear people say: "What? Is this the [same irascible] man who devours people alive? Is this the [literary] butcher? Is this the constable of cruelty?"

Those who have read his latest work[17]—intense, metallic, solid—in which he judges the Yankee, his strange culture, his civilization, his instincts, his propensities, and threats he poses [for us]—probably wouldn't be surprised at hearing him speak as he did after the band played *La Marseillaise*. Yes, France had to be at Spain's side. The vibrant Gallic lark could not but curse the axe that strikes at one of the most distinguished branches of the Latin tree. And after Groussac shouted with emotion—"Long live Spain with honor!"—there has never sprung from Spanish breasts a more fitting and united response than this: "Long live France!"

For Italy, Mr. Tarnassi.[18] In enthusiastic, fervent, Italian, Manzoni-like[19] music,

---

15 *Yangüenses* derives from Yanguas, a community in northwest Spain. In Cervantes's *Don Quixote*, the Yangüenses are a group of rude merchants who beat Rocinante. In defense of his horse, Don Quixote attacks the Yangüenses, a deed that results in the Knight's and Sancho's defeat. [Note by Carlos Jáuregui.]

16 Paul Groussac (1848–1929) was born in Toulouse, France, but immigrated to Argentina at eighteen. A respected historian and critic, he became director of Argentina's National Library and was much admired by his successors, Alfonso Reyes and Jorge Luis Borges. Darío makes him—somewhat hyperbolically—a representative of France.

17 *Del Plata al Niágara* (1897). [Note by Carlos Jáuregui.]

18 Giuseppe Tarnassi was born in Rome in 1861, where he studied law. Around 1884, he joined his uncle Antonio Tarnassi, who was dean of the Buenos Aires "foro." Giuseppe Tarnassi achieved acclaim as a scholar, translator, and professor of Italian and Latin literature at the University of Buenos Aires.

19 Alessandro Manzoni (1785–1873) was a writer whose musical prose was regarded as the ideal of Italian literature. Darío shifts Manzoni's "musicality" to praise the language of an orator, exemplifying the best of nineteenth-century Italian letters. Manzoni's major work was *I promessi sposi* (1827) [The Betrothed].

he spoke for the blood of Latium; old Mother Rome spoke through him: his decasyllables rang out fiercely like a warrior's clarion. And the large audience felt itself shaking before such a blazing *squillo di tromba* [trumpet blast].

And so, everyone of us who heard these three men, representatives of three great nations of the Latin race, all thought and felt how appropriate was that cathartic release, how necessary that stand; and we saw the palpable urgency of working and fighting so that the Latin Union does not continue to be [illusory] Fata Morgana[20] of the kingdom of Utopia, because, when confronted with hostile foreign policies and interests, our people sense the powerful call of our common blood and spirit. Don't you see how the English rejoice at the North American triumph, putting away old rancor and the memory of past disputes in the safe of the Bank of England? Don't you see how the democratic and plebeian Yankees, shout their three "hurrahs!" and sing *God Save the Queen*, when a ship passes nearby, flying the British flag? And together they think: "The day will come when the United States and England will be the owners of the world."

Our race should also unite, just as the soul and heart are one amidst tribulations; we are the sentimental race, but we have also been masters of power. The sun has not abandoned us and rebirth remains natural to our historic stock.

From Mexico to Tierra del Fuego there lies an immense continent where our ancient seed germinates and prepares in its vital sap the future greatness of our race; from Europe, from the universe, blows a vast, cosmopolitan gust of wind, that will help us to invigorate our own forests. But [beware] that the North, is extending its railroad tentacle, its iron arms, its voracious mouths.

It won't now be against the buccaneer Walker[21] that those poor republics of Central America will have to struggle, but the Yankee canal diggers of Nicaragua; Mexico is carefully watching and still feeling the pain of mutilation; Colombia has its isthmus stuffed with American coal and iron; Venezuela remains enthralled by the Monroe Doctrine and mesmerized with what happened in the recent crisis with England, without realizing that despite their own Mon-

---

20 Fatamorgana: a mirage in the Strait of Messina, attributed to Morgana, King Arthur's sister. [Note by Carlos Jáuregui.]

21 William Walker (1824–1860) was a lawyer, journalist, and soldier of fortune who exploited the Spanish American civil wars for North American investors and politicians. In 1855, with other mercenaries, he joined one of the factions in the Nicaraguan civil war and, after a chaotic victory, proclaimed himself the country's president. Later defeated by a coalition of Central American forces, he was taken prisoner by the intervening U.S. army and repatriated to the United States. Recaptured in Nicaragua by the British Navy, he was turned over to the Honduran government, which executed him in Trujillo in 1860.

roe Doctrine, the Yankees allowed Queen Victoria's soldiers to occupy the Nicaraguan port of Corinto; in Peru there are demonstrations sympathetic to the U.S. victory; and Brazil—painful to say—has shown a rather visible interest in games of give-and-take with Uncle Sam.

When a dangerous future is pointed out by leading thinkers, and when the gluttony of the North is in plain sight, there's nothing left but to prepare a defense.

Sure there will be those who would say to me: "Don't you see they're the strongest? Don't you know the terrible law that says we must perish, that we must be swallowed up or crushed by the colossus? Don't you recognize their superiority?" Yes, how can I not see the mountain that is the Mammoth's back? But despite Darwin and Spencer, I'm not going to put my head on the stone so that the great Beast can crush my skull.

Behemoth[22] is gigantic; but I don't have to freely sacrifice myself under its paws, and if I get trapped, at least my tongue will complete its last curse, with my last breath of life. And I, who have always sided with a free Cuba—at least to be able to share with so many dreamers their dream, and to share with so many martyrs their heroism—at this moment, I'm a friend of Spain, seeing it attacked by a brutal enemy, waving violence, force and injustice like a flag.

"And you, have you not always attacked Spain?" Never. Spain is no fanatical priest, or crushing pedant, or wretched cleric, disdainful of an America that he doesn't know; the Spain that I defend is one of Graciousness, Ideals, Nobility; it is Cervantes, Quevedo, Góngora, Gracián, Velázquez; it is the Spain of el Cid, Loyola, Isabel; it is the Daughter of Rome, the Sister of France, the Mother of America.

Miranda will always prefer Ariel; Miranda is the grace of spirit; and all the mountains of stone, of iron, of gold and of beefsteaks, can never be enough for my Latin soul to prostitute itself to Caliban!

In Context | Monument to Cuauhtémoc, Mexico City

In Mexico, the term *Reforma* describes the political process that emerged after the civil wars in the first half of the nineteenth century. The French invasion of 1862, followed by the imposition of an empire, ended that earlier struggle; the victory of the liberals in 1867 marked the ultimate success of the *Reforma* and the restoration of the republic. One critical reform that resulted was the elimination of the jurisdictional authority of the Church

---

22 A giant animal described by Job (40:15–24). [Note by Carlos Jáuregui.]

Figure 6.2. Cuauhtémoc statue and monument. Paseo de la Reforma, Mexico City, Mexico. Photograph by Protoplasma Kid (2007). License CC BY-SA 4.0.

and the privatization of ecclesiastical property. The Mexican state assumed numerous functions that formerly had been the exclusive province of the Church: education, the recording of births and marriages, and the issuance of death certificates.

In this new era, successive governments began to express their political ideologies along the great diagonal avenue of the capital city, the Paseo de la Reforma. One of the first monuments, constructed in 1802 and located at the head of the Paseo for many decades, was the statue of Charles IV—popularly known as El Caballito—"the little horse." Next came an homage to Columbus and Spanish evangelization in 1877, and then ten years later, during the second presidential period of Porfirio Díaz, the monument to Cuauhtémoc.

An official monument to the Spanish conquerors stands prominently in many cities of Latin America, like the statue of Pizarro in the heart of Lima. No such monument to Hernán Cortés exists in Mexico. Since independence, Mexico has considered the conquest and colonization as "interruptions" in the nation's history, an attitude that has generated some curious contradictions. For example, even those who believe that independence represented a resumption of pre-Hispanic history never really meant to defend actual native peoples but only to reclaim the symbols of their indigenous cultures. One favorite among those symbols was Cuauhtémoc, the last Aztec emperor, defeated by Cortés and his indigenous allies—and by the smallpox epidemic that the conquerors transmitted.

During his second presidency, Porfirio Díaz wanted to reinforce the official ideology of México's indigenous tradition even as he was approving the legalization of the largest expropriation of Indian land since the first few decades of the conquest. Although an Indian himself, Díaz was echoing the stance of most Mexican creoles, including CARLOS DE SIGÜENZA Y GÓNGORA. Exalting the authenticity of indigenous symbols, the powerful continued their shameless exploitation of living Indians and the flagrant confiscation of their lands. This striking monument was inaugurated in 1887.

Franz Tamayo (1878–1956)

Franz Tamayo excelled in many fields: writer, poet, journalist, diplomat, and politician; he was also the founder and leader of Bolivia's Partido Radical [Radical Party] (1911). Born in La Paz to an Aymara mother and a creole father, Tamayo often felt the sting of prejudice as a result of his mixed-race heritage. He spent much of his childhood on his father's haciendas and with private tutors; he mastered the piano as well as several languages, including Latin, Greek, German, French, and English. He later studied in France and then met and married Blanca Bouyon in London. The couple returned to Bolivia but soon separated.

Well-regarded as an accomplished poet, Tamayo published several notable collections of poetry, including *Odas* (1898), *La Prometheida* (1917) [The Promethiad], and *Epigramas griegos* (1945) [Greek Epigrams]. His most enduring work, however, is his book of essays, *Creación de una pedagogía nacional* (1910) [The Creation of a National Pedagogy]. The collection was originally a series of fifty articles Tamayo composed during an intense debate with Felipe Segundo Guzmán, the minister of education under the

Liberal Party president, Ismael Montes (1904–1908). Tamayo articulates his strident opposition to the government's educational policies, which were being fashioned according to western models, and he was particularly opposed to the plan of sending a delegation to Belgium to study and import their pedagogical practices.

His belief that pedagogy had to be developed by and for the people it serves is only one aspect of Tamayo's vision. While capturing a certain political moment, the essays also reveal Tamayo's anticipation of several of the most forward-looking theoretical positions of the twentieth century. Tamayo comprehended that a society was not an unchanging, essentialist, metaphysical entity but a product of the physical environment, of history and geography. More important, race was to be seen as a cultural category, created through historical circumstances and shaped by human imagination. To implement a Bolivian educational system, one thus had to study the complex needs of the Bolivian child, not just import a foreign pedagogy. Tamayo understood that history is not a developmental process toward an ideal, especially an externally defined ideal. He firmly rejected contemporary historicism and the models that posited the superiority of Western cultures, thus compelling their imitation. Instead, Tamayo pointed out that some of these utopian social ideals, such as Herbert Spencer's stateless, autonomous society, had already been achieved by the Indian cultures of Bolivia. Tamayo insisted that these desirable conditions were not evolutionary goals, but historical realities, based in fundamental characteristics of the people themselves.

This inversion of Spencer's evolutionary process also provided the basis for a radical new theory of race. Rejecting biological determinism, Tamayo posited a notion of race as constructed by a specific history and geography. In Bolivia, the "racial" character of Indians—which defined the character of the nation as a whole—epitomized a strong work ethic and a deep sense of autonomy—exactly the qualities that Spencer and others understood to be the evolutionary goal of developing societies. According to Tamayo, Bolivians were already there.

By defining race in terms of production and labor, of course, Tamayo's thought was consistent with much contemporary social theory. In 1903, for example, the Argentinian Octavio Bunge opined in his *Nuestra América: Ensayo de psicología social* [Our America: An Essay in Social Psychology] that "progress and decadence can be explained after all in terms of the greater or lesser activity of a people. The only remedy for decadence in South America is to become European through work." But Tamayo recognized that production in Bolivia was already firmly grounded in Indian labor, a point that even became a governmental slogan after the Chaco War (1933–1936), fought with Paraguay over natural resources: "Ninety percent of our national energy resides in the Indian." By construing indigenous peoples as essential to national identity, Tamayo began the slow transformation of negative racialized views of the Indian, which became part of the nationalist discourse after the 1952 Bolivian Revolution. More typical of the era was the view of his rival, Alcides Arguedas, who in his 1910 essay characterized Bolivia as *Pueblo enfermo* [A Sick People].

Tamayo served his party in a number of positions and was even elected president of Bolivia in 1935, although a military coup prevented him from taking office. An eloquent orator, he later became a distinguished representative in the National Congress. His lasting legacy was, however, making the Indian central to national identity, a notion that eventually helped to trigger the Indianista movements at the end of the twentieth century. The selection here anticipates a version of today's demands for decolonizing Bolivian society. Rejecting foreign cultural forms and reexamining internal cultural traditions, Tamayo argues, is the only way that Bolivia—or any nation—can choose what is truly best for its people.

The selection is from chapter 3 of *Creación de una pedagogía nacional* (La Paz: El Diario, 1910), 15–17, translated by Isabel Bastos and Marvin Liberman.

From Creación de una pedagogía nacional (1910) [Creation of a National Pedagogy]

We have arrived at this conclusion: we need to separate, scientifically, all the racial elements constituting our essence as Bolivians, through a comprehensive critique, in order to extract from these, methods and comprehensive laws on which to base a national and scientific pedagogy.

So then: how many men in Bolivia would be sufficiently prepared to undertake and lead such a study and such an enterprise? Do we have psychologists and psychiatrists with enough experience for this? Is there one single anthropologist who would do enough research for such an undertaking? Do we have a complete set of statistics, any demography? None of these exist, nor can they exist yet, nor should we be embarrassed by this fact. We are an unwise nation; we have just recently begun to become self-conscious, and we are experiencing the same processes that other nations have experienced before us.

But if we do not have national experts and we urgently need them, one must look for them elsewhere.

The creation of a national pedagogy is impossible without the supervision of a European scientific expert; we cannot deceive ourselves about one thing: in Bolivia neither elementary nor higher education exists. Beyond the basics, which is all one really learns, anyone who knows more than that, has either acquired it on his own, or had a European education; but advanced learning is never the result of a Bolivian education.

An example? Ask around what any of our high school graduates knows about natural sciences, mathematics, living and dead languages . . . and those high school graduates have had on average ten years of education! One has to have seen our students in Europe, trying to enroll in universities, and to have seen them suffer a complete lack of preparation, forcing them to start all over and redo an incomplete or useless education.

We, then, must create a national pedagogy, in other words, a pedagogy of our own, custom-made to our strengths, compatible with our traditions: matching our natural tendencies and tastes and harmonizing with our physical and moral nature. We must not believe that any method is absolute. At Cambridge they work in one way, at the Politécnica [in Paris] in another; and, indeed, the entirely autonomous English student would find himself exhausted by French methods.

The idea would thus be not to send our pedagogues (which they are not) to Europe, but to bring experts here, capable of studying and investigating the foundations of Bolivian pedagogy, putting themselves in the service of our studies, supplying us with all the available scientific knowledge of Europe, which we ourselves lack and will continue to lack indefinitely.

This writer believes that the only way to accelerate our new countries' civilization is to place them in immediate contact with European thought and purposes. Two different examples can demonstrate what foreign influence means both in and outside Bolivia.

The small amount of large-scale commerce that exists in the country is in foreign hands; the few great mining concerns are owned or managed by foreigners; all railroad construction, present or planned, is in foreign hands; the few genuinely scientific books about Bolivia are written by foreigners. Consider where that leaves us as native-born Bolivians! Knowing these facts, what can we expect to accomplish without foreign assistance, especially when dealing with this extremely serious and important issue, public education and the creation of a national pedagogy!

Another example: What would the marvelous Argentine Republic be without its foreigners? What existed before—actually much like Bolivia—was both similar and often worse; this situation remains true in the parts of Argentina where foreigners haven't yet arrived, and those Argentines are just like we are right now.

Unquestionably, bringing experts here is not going to be easy. One has to choose the right individuals and one has to pay them; but the need remains undeniably real. Indeed, if the governments of Chile, Argentina and Brazil have achieved anything in this area, we all know who is responsible, and we all know that the public education system in those countries is under the control of foreign influences.

—July 6, 1910

Jorge Luis Borges (1899–1986)

Jorge Luis Borges is one of the best—and perhaps the best-known—prose writers of the Spanish language in the twentieth century. Many of his short stories and essays are brilliant for their imaginative intelligence and inventive style, as in this selection—one of Borges's most accomplished pieces.

Born in Buenos Aires, Borges was the son of cultured parents and grew up speaking both English and Spanish. For reasons of health, the family settled in Geneva in 1914 and then returned to Buenos Aires in 1921. Always encouraged by his father to write, Borges had encountered the avant-garde movement while traveling in Spain and soon became active among the innovative young Argentine writers of his time, publishing poetry and essays in various journals.

In Europe, the avant-garde movement was fundamentally international, seeking to transcend all borders. In 1908, for example, the Italian poet Filippo Marinetti published "The Futurist Manifesto" in a Parisian newspaper; a few years later the Roman-born French poet, Guillaume Apollinaire, coined the term "surrealism" to describe his antitraditional aesthetic and its rejection of conventional poetic forms; and during the First World War, the Dadaist movement took shape in Zurich, drawing artists from many countries, including the Romanian, Tristan Tzara. Identified as "Modernism," this European version of the avant-garde was distinct from the *modernismo* of Latin America, exemplified in the works of RUBÉN DARÍO and others who also adopted a cosmopolitan, internationalist stance. But in reacting against the *modernismo* of the 1890s, the young avant-garde writers of Latin

America also rejected its cosmopolitan stance, and in countries like Peru, Argentina, and Mexico, the avant-garde acquired a distinctly nationalist character.

In Argentina, the style was known as *criollista* and adopted the principles of Xul Solar, a visionary painter and writer, who sought a return to popular modes characteristic of the Rio de la Plata region. The journal founded to feature such work was called *Martín Fierro*, appropriately named after a poem by José Hernández (part I, published in 1872; part II, 1879), the paradigm of gaucho poetry. Ironically, the gaucho had emerged as a nationalist symbol at a moment when—in the 1920s—most Argentines were neither Spanish-speaking nor American-born. Seen as the model for an authentically "country" manner in its vocabulary and colloquial style, *Martín Fierro* was a prototype for the new *criollismo*.

Borges was among the many young writers who enthusiastically adopted *criollismo*, especially in his first published book of essays, *Inquisiciones* (1925) [*Inquisitions*]. The essays were a series of inquiries into various writers and thinkers, past and present, including the Baroque writer Francisco Quevedo, the poet Miguel Unamuno, Irish writers James Joyce and George Berkeley, as well as several of Borges's contemporaries. One of those was the young Argentine avant-garde writer, Norah Lange, whom Borges had courted in vain. Almost as soon as the collection appeared, however, Borges recognized that *criollismo* was an inadequate stylistic vehicle for his ideas and even downright distracting. He tried to stop the circulation of *Inquisitions*, buying up the 500 copies of the first limited edition and prohibiting its reprinting during his lifetime.

Despite its self-conscious style, *Inquisitions* contains most of the defining ideas of Borges's oeuvre. Demonstrating his remarkable ability to gather ideas from different philosophical traditions and reveal their coherence, Borges contends in several pieces that personal identity does not exist, that we are, instead, a collection of wills, desires, deeds, and random occurrences that we falsely identify as "a person." This negation of the personality was central to Borges's thought: for images, for stories, for characters—for himself. In his best-known texts (short stories, poems, and essays), the central figure is a "person" called "Borges." But "Borges," the person, is also the act of writing, of narrating. Borges is not only a body, a place, a moment in time, but also a language. "Borges" became, quite literally, the discoverer of a particular aspect of being in the world, a perspective so distinctive that it is known as "Borgesian." Borgesian elements include his understanding of how time defines life; his impartial recognition of our internal multiplicity;

his matter-of-fact inclusion of temporal and spatial totalities; his serene skepticism in defining an unknowable reality; and his unique perspectives on his beloved Buenos Aires.

Though Borges wrote many poems about Buenos Aires, the one included here articulates not only his affection for his native city, but also its role as both source and object of Borges's principal ideas and passions. Few among Borges's contemporaries united thinking and expression so seamlessly: his poems, like his prose, brilliantly match precise thought with well-crafted language and form. While Borges rarely addressed political and social themes directly, he was an insightful psychologist and an expert metaphysician. Similarly, while his canon includes no long fictions or poems, his short stories often have the perspicacity of a novel and even brief poems can convey epic depth and scope.

Of course, Buenos Aires offers an extraordinary canvas for Borges's talents. Representative of the best and the worst in Latin America for most of the nineteenth century and for at least the first half of the twentieth, Buenos Aires sprang up from the emptiness of the pampa. As a social and aesthetic construction, the city manifested the creole dream of populating the American territory with European people. But the result also embodied the nightmare of those desires: a society without unity, an immense territory disproportionately dominated by its capital city. Such incongruities nonetheless had some surprising outcomes: Buenos Aires became a deeply cosmopolitan city, alive with neighborhoods that are at once Parisian and deeply *porteñas*—as the people of this major port are called; its cultural traditions are unsurpassed in the Americas, including a long and distinguished history of notable writers, musicians, and artists, and many vibrant popular institutions, like the tango, or creole theater, with its distinctive gaucho characters, and lively immigrant drama. Architecturally, the city boasts magnificent avenues that rival any in Europe and numerous fine buildings and public spaces. But Buenos Aires also resonates throughout Latin America as a storied city full of poignant and mysterious characters, exceptional singers, and loyal, passionate sons and daughters who die far away, still dreaming of their beloved city. As Borges writes in another of his poems, however, even those lost children are linked to this great metropolis not solely by love but by fear: "that might be why I love it so."

Borges's literary career developed steadily after the 1920s, as he perfected his craft, writing the innovative fiction he collected in *Ficciones* (1944) and *El Aleph* (1949), and becoming increasingly well known outside Argentina. Under surveillance during the Perón regime, he published another major volume of essays, *Otras inquisiciones* [Other Inquisitions] in 1952 and began teaching at the University of Buenos Aires. By the 1960s he was an international figure, lecturing abroad and having his work translated into scores of languages. Borges died in 1986 in Geneva, where he is fittingly buried in the Cemetery of Kings.

The poem is from Jorge Luis Borges, *In Praise of Darkness*, translated by Norman Thomas di Giovanni, a bilingual edition (New York: E. P. Dutton, 1974). "Buenos Aires, copyright © 1969, 1974 by Emece Editores, S.A., and Norman Thomas di Giovanni, from *In Praise of Darkness* by Jorge Luis Borges, translated by Norman Thomas di Giovanni. Used by permission of Dutton, an imprint of Penguin Publishing Group, a division of Penguin Random House LLC.

Buenos Aires

What is Buenos Aires to me?
It's the Plaza de Mayo, to which tired and happy men
    came home after having fought all over the conti-
    nent.
It's the growing maze of lights we glimpse from a return-
    ning plane, below us the flat roofs, the sidewalks,
    the innermost patios—these quiet things.
It's the wall of the Recoleta, against which one of my
    ancestors was executed.
It's that great tree at the head of Junín Street which,
    all unknowing, gives us coolness and shade.
It's a long street of low houses, lost and transfigured by
    the sunsets.
It's the South Docks, from which the *Saturno* and the
    Cosmos once sailed to Uruguay.
It's the sidewalk on Quintana Street where my father,
    who had been blind, cried when he saw the ancient
    stars again.
It's a numbered door behind which I lay rigid, in utter
    darkness, for ten days and ten nights—days and
    nights that in memory are a single moment.
It's the rider cast in heavy metal, throwing its rhythmic
    pattern of shadows from on high.

It's the same rider under the rain.

It's a certain corner on Peru Street, where Julio César
    Dabove told us that the worst sin a man can commit
    Is to father a son and sentence him to this unbear-
    able life.

It's Elvira de Alvear, writing a long novel in painstaking
    notebooks—at the beginning it was made of words and at
    the end of meaningless scrawls.

It's Norah's hand, drawing the face of a friend that is also the face of an
    angel.

It's a sword that once served in old wars and is now less a
    weapon than a memory.

It's a discolored political ribbon or faded daguerreotype
    —things that belong to time.

It's the day we left a woman and the day a woman left us.

It's that archway on Bolívar Street from which the National Library can be
    glimpsed.

It is that room in the Library where, around 1957, we
    discovered the tongue of the harsh Saxons—the
    tongue of courage and sadness.

It is the next room, in which Paul Groussac died.

It's the last mirror to have reflected my father's face.

It's the face of Christ I saw in the rubble, smashed to
    pieces by hammer blows, in one of the naves of La
    Piedad.

It's a tall house on the Southside, where my wife helps me
    translate Whitman (his great voice, I hope, echoes on
    this page).

It's Leopoldo Lugones by a train window, looking at the
    shapes that fly past and thinking he no longer has to
    put them into words, for this will be his last trip.

It is, in the uninhabited night, a corner of the Once where
    Macedonio Fernández, who is dead, keeps explaining to
    me that death is a fallacy.

I go no further—these things are too individual, too much
    what they are, also to be Buenos Aires.

Buenos Aires is the next street, the one I've never walked;
    it's the secret heart of its city blocks, its
    deepest patios; it's what house fronts are hiding;

it's my enemy, if I have one; it's the person who does
not like my poems (I too dislike them); it's that
shabby bookshop we may once have entered and
now have forgotten; it's a snatch of whistled *milonga*
that we cannot place and that moves us; it is all
that's been lost and all that's to come; it is what
lies beyond, what belongs to others, what is around
the corner—the neighborhood which is neither yours nor
mine, the things we do not understand yet love.

In Context | Avenida de Mayo, Buenos Aires

In the 1880s, after a near revolt by the *porteños*—as the citizens of Argentina's major port like being called—Buenos Aires was finally named the federal capital, and a new city, La Plata, was established as the provincial capital. Like many other economic and political centers of the era, Buenos Aires promptly began to construct numerous urban projects to symbolize its primacy. Argentina's great wealth during the 1870s and 1880s supported an unusually ambitious building spree. Even the great nationalist SARMIENTO complained that La Plata was becoming more modern than Buenos Aires, so that the older city really was living up to its nineteenth-century nickname as "the large hamlet."

Buenos Aires was, in fact, becoming a stunning capital. In the decade of the 1880s, construction of the magnificent Avenida de Mayo began,

Figure 6.3. Avenida de Mayo, Buenos Aires, c. 1910.

symbolically connecting the Plaza de Mayo, where the chief executive offices were housed—the elegant Casa Rosada or Pink House—with the Plaza of the Constitution, where the new national congressional building was to stand. The avenue was finally inaugurated in 1894, and a short time later work on the Congressional Palace began, to be completed in 1906.

The Avenida de Mayo is among the world's most beautiful. Lined with sophisticated buildings of harmony and proportion, the great tree-lined avenue testifies to the immense natural wealth yielded by the Argentine pampas as well as to the dedicated industry of its many immigrants, who flocked to the city to create its impressive cultural and material prosperity. This grand avenue appropriately denotes the status of Buenos Aires as one of the world's most powerful capitals since the 1880s.

In Context | Pancho Villa (1878–1923)

Pancho Villa was born and raised among the oppressed, during one of the most repressive and exploitative periods in Mexican history—the decades around the turn of the nineteenth century. For most of his early life, he was a fugitive from justice, a justice that primarily benefited the rich. That injustice was particularly blatant in the northern border state of Chihuahua, where mining and cattle farming were the leading sources of wealth. Villa raised cattle himself and profited from both the legal and illegal aspects of that trade.

By the end of the nineteenth century, in Chihuahua as in Argentina, the cattle business began to change. Historically, livestock roaming loose on the vast prairies could be herded and sold by anyone enterprising enough to do so. But then affluent cattlemen began fencing off their holdings and branding their herds. What had belonged to everyone was now the private property of an elite few, and selling free-roaming cattle became a crime. Supported by the central government, some individuals became powerful ranchers and politicians in Chihuahua. To resist their growing power (like the Argentine gauchos), a few defiant *bandidos* (bandits) or leaders began to appear in northern Mexico. Pancho Villa was one of those.

After 1910, as the Mexican Revolution spread north, Villa became part of its military forces. He knew Chihuahua "like the back of his hand," having traveled most of it on horseback, and his army, known as the Northern Division, consisted largely of hardy *vaqueros* or cowboys. Villa's greatest weapons were his mobility (thanks to his horses) and his men's knowledge of the terrain, often acquired as fugitives on the run. These advantages

Figure 6.4. General Francisco "Pancho" Villa on horseback, 1914. Bain News Service. Library of Congress.

more than compensated for Villa's ignorance about artillery and infantry tactics, and he was very successful for several years.

Short of military matériel and forced to fight outside his native territory, Villa was eventually defeated in 1915 by Alvaro Obregón, the leader of a rival faction, in a series of battles at Celaya. The decimation of his troops caused the collapse of the Northern Division and reduced his followers to barely two hundred. Even with so few followers, Villa continued to fight a guerrilla war, using his most effective weapons—his swift cavalry and his intimate knowledge of Chihuahua.

Ramón Puente (1879–1939)/Rafael F. Muñoz (1899–1972)

The reputation of Mexico's most famous revolutionary, Pancho Villa (1878–1923), has been shaped by several writers, none more significant than Ramón Puente. Like his fellow chronicler, Mariano Azuela, Puente was a medical doctor who joined Villa's forces to aid the wounded. However, he soon assumed the role of journalist, reporting the military and political victories of the Villistas and often serving as Villa's secretary. In 1919, Puente completed his purported autobiography: *La vida de Francisco Villa contada por él mismo* [Pancho Villa's Life as Told by Himself]. Using information from numerous interviews and conversations with Villa, Puente adopted a narrative voice that is not quite Villa's or his own, but one that nonetheless conveys a strong sense of verisimilitude. The book was published in 1919 in Los Angeles, California, by Octavio Paz, who had served in Emiliano Zapata's army—and was the father of the poet and essayist, his namesake OCTAVIO PAZ.

When Puente's autobiography appeared, Pancho Villa was leading his remaining guerilla troops against the government of Venustiano Carranza in northern Mexico. The next year Villa signed a truce with Adolfo de la Huerta, who had succeeded Carranza as interim president, and then retired to a ranch provided by the government. But in 1923, Villa was slain in a barrage of bullets while driving in nearby Parral, Chihuahua. Though the leader of the assassins claimed that Villa's murder was a personal vendetta, most believed that the assassination was ordered by president, Alvaro Obregón, or by Plutarco Elias Calles, Obregón's designated presidential successor.

Upon Villa's sensational death, a major newspaper in Mexico City asked the journalist Rafael F. Muñoz to prepare a low-cost pamphlet featuring Villa's biography for quick sale. Muñoz thought that the most efficient process would be simply to republish Puente's work and then continue the narration from 1919 to Villa's death. The printing press, however, neglected to put Puente's name on the cover, only appending it at the end of his portion of the text. Without Puente's name on the title page, Muñoz appeared to be the sole author. The pamphlet was republished many times with several different titles, the final edition in 1955 reading only: "*Pancho Villa, rayo y azote* [Pancho Villa: Lightning and Whip] by Rafael F. Muñoz." Few readers have noticed or understood why, at the end of a chapter, the name "Ramón Puente" suddenly appears in small print while the text continues without explanation, suggesting a misprint or a typesetter's mistake.

For many years Puente's biography constituted the most authentic portrait of Villa, capturing his worldview as well as that of the Villista movement he had inspired. With the exception of other Villistas, most Mexicans had a distorted image of Villa, one created by his enemies and a hostile press. Villa was consistently portrayed as a bandit, a pillager, an impulsive assassin, a womanizer, and a rebel with no real political cause. It was many years before Villa was recognized as a true revolutionary, in stark contrast to Emiliano Zapata, who was assassinated in 1919 and whose reputation as a revered Indian leader from the south was almost immediate. Only four years after his death, even Zapata's enemies acknowledged that he was an authentic representative of the poor peasants and Indians.

Between 1919 and 1936, very few publications defended Villa: Puente's biography, Muñoz's novel, *Vámonos con Pancho Villa* (1931) [Let's Go with Pancho Villa], a few articles, and two books by Nellie Campobello—*Cartucho* (1931) and *Las manos de mamá* (1937) [My Mother's Hands]. Then, with the election of the reformist president Lázaro Cárdenas (1934–1940), a government-funded film based on Muñoz's novel was produced in 1936, attempting to reexamine Villa's image. That same year Silvestre Terrazas, a man who knew and understood Villa remarkably well, published *El verdadero Pancho Villa* [The True Pancho Villa], and the next year Puente himself wrote another intelligent book entitled *Pancho Villa en pie* [Pancho Villa, Standing]. In 1938, the first volume of Martín Luis Guzmán's five-volume biography appeared, *Memorias de Pancho Villa* [Memoirs of Pancho Villa]. In 1928, Guzmán had published his own memoir, *El águila y la serpiente* [The Eagle and the Serpent], painting a more ambiguous image of his former commander. After 1936, then, Villa's image had been fully recuperated, though it took another sixty years before a scholarly biography appeared. Using archival material, contemporary accounts and extensive research, *The Life and Times of Pancho Villa* (1998) by Friedrich Katz finally took the study of Villa's life to another level of scholarship.

In this excerpt from Puente, Villa emerges as a true revolutionary, identified with the needs of the people. This was the strength of the Villista movement: a deep regard for the demands for social justice, irrespective of political ideology. Villa was not a politician, nor was he an ideologue. He fought to change the living conditions of his *hermanitos de raza*, a brotherhood not strictly of race but of the most abject oppression. Villa's identification with these others went far beyond humanity, expressing a communion with Nature itself. No one, not even Zapata, expressed such sentiments during the Mexican Revolution: only Pancho Villa.

Ramón Puente was also the author of a chronicle, *Pascual Orozco y la revuelta de Chihuahua* (1912), a novel, *Juan Rivera* (1936), and a number of historical essays, including an intriguing piece on the Mexican president Plutarco Elias Calles (1924–1928). The present text is translated by Sarah Taylor Cook from *Pancho Villa, rayo y azote* (Mexico City: Populibros "La Prensa," 1955), 96–99.

From **Pancho Villa, rayo y azote (1919; 1923) [Pancho Villa, Lightning and Whip**

And Still He Refuses Defeat

In broad brush-strokes, here is the story of my defeat. And although I can never really give up, I know perfectly well that many of those who were my friends will repudiate me and will regret ever having followed my orders because of my past—a past that they were well aware of and that I never concealed. But I also know that there are those who see in me a man that could never change his convictions as others change their shirts or as some politicians change parties.

I will forever be an enemy to Carranza. He can claim to be a radical revolutionary for a few more years. And before the workers and the people, he can continue to accuse my party of being backward and reactionary. But his extremism and his tolerance for a lack of zeal, demonstrated by his weakness when it comes to punishing the greed of his bosses, who only wanted to win to get rich, making the people starve like never before—this behavior will merely discredit the Revolution and endanger his own ideals.

Carranza will continue to damage me; he won't skimp on using his influence or his money to slander me in the papers. It's easy enough to buy a pen that will insult. And there is plenty to say to discredit me, since I've not been a saint. But I was one of the first to embrace this struggle, even as a simple soldier, and because I have been driven by my conscience, I don't think my actions seem shameful to anyone who understands them. I have fought and—unless a bullet hits home and traitorously slashes the thread of my life—I will continue to fight, so that in Mexico there is justice and education for my blood brothers. Justice, as I understand it, means that the land is not in the hands of a few owners, or that these landlords can make big deals that take advantage of Mexicans, without paying them fairly or giving them the treatment they deserve. And education, the way I see it, means not only that schools teach students how to read and colleges create lots of professionals. All too often our Indians, once they graduate, forget the poor, and so we also need schools of agriculture, where they teach our young people how to cultivate the earth properly, so that they do not remain stuck in the old ways as so many still are. It's a shame to see everywhere these "pigeons," farmhands in their white britches, opening furrows with a thousand-year-old plow, at the slow pace of an ox. We also need workshops to train workers so that labor is dignified in every trade and our industries are improved. Take care of our people and create what they need: this is what we must do. But this will only be accomplished with hard and honest effort by our presidents. And so far, their interest has only been to seek the luxury of palaces as if they were kings. They and their court live in comfort and feasting. They take pride in their beautiful buildings but they do not care at all about the bread or shelter or the clothes of the poor.

We need leaders that aspire to power not imagining themselves to be a Porfirio Díaz or a Carranza—these so-called essential men. In fact, wretched is the nation that believes only one man can save it, and cursed is the man who thinks he alone can save his country.

Sentimental Villa

I mourn this struggle; and all of the blood it has cost Mexico gives me pain. But my hopes are for a future when those rich, idle compatriots who have learned how to work in foreign countries, who have seen other ways of doing things and educated their children in other schools, when they return to our homeland. When they bring something new to their brothers, bound by blood and race, sharing with them modern conveniences: because only the stoniest hearts would not be softened by these misfortunes.

My hopes lie in a time when our hatreds cease, since, as in all conflicts between brothers, such hatred is particularly bitter and can only be lessened by great suffering.

Certainly, Carranza has the advantage over me. More astute for having been a good rancher and wiser because he is older, he reduces me to the nothingness from which I came; but he forgets that in this very long race his horse might tire before mine does, because I am not spoiled by comforts, and sacrifice has never been a big deal to me.

I have witnessed up close the birth of an army, with leaders who became corrupted largely by the love of money. In those first days of the revolution, money was easy to find and everyone was keen to spend it. But I still have the energy to create another army, even in the midst of this adversity, and I know that the soldier that hardens himself in such necessity will be the son of better times for Mexico. I am confident that these men are out there, because among the simple folk that follow me are the grandest souls that our land produces. While Carranza perverts his own destiny, which will dissolve like a sugar cube in water, I, being patient, will—as the poor say—fulfill my fate, facing difficulties with resolve.

His Cause: That of the Poor

I am not unaware that one of the worst hidden dangers for me is the tongue of my enemies, slashing me to the bone every day, pretending to believe that I am a heartless man. But my cause is that of the poor, and that of the multitude in every place, among people of all nations, among men of courage everywhere. This cause has its adherents, and it will find those who will defend it until the final victory. I am convinced that any scandal created by lies will be in vain, because while the truth may sometimes be hidden, it neither flinches nor dies. Even if I am entangled as I climb this thorny hill, someone else will reach the summit and make many things clear.

Pedro Henríquez Ureña (1884–1946)

Pedro Henríquez Ureña was born in Santo Domingo in the Dominican Republic, to well-educated and talented parents, who schooled him at home until he was eleven. In some sense, Henríquez Ureña never left that rich intellectual environment throughout his nomadic life, comprising travel and brief residencies all over the world. His experience was characterized by constant activity: teaching and lecturing at universities in the United States, in Spain, in Mexico, in Chile, and in his native country, where he was named superintendent of education for Santo Domingo in 1932–1933. He lived and worked in Mexico from 1906 until 1913 and again in 1921, after spending several years in Washington, in New York, and at the University of Minnesota. In 1924 he moved to Argentina, where he remained, a dedicated teacher, with enthusiastic students forming literary circles around him such as *el cenáculo estudiantil*. Henríquez Ureña also edited one of the most prestigious collections in Latin America, *Las cien obras maestras* [One Hundred Masterworks]. He died in Buenos Aires in 1946 catching a train to his work at the Colegio Nacional de la Universidad de La Plata, an hour outside the capital.

Three volumes of Henríquez Ureña's complete works were published posthumously in 1976, but his writing reflects only a portion of his intellectual activity. He was a memorable teacher, giving numerous lectures and informal talks, staying up late with his students, teaching them (as one student recalled) how to live and think, listen to music, read the classics, learn about science, appreciate art, and, above all, work for justice. Widely respected as a literary historian and distinguished critic, Henríquez Ureña's real task was the integration of thought into an active and committed life. He revealed how literary criticism can become part of a creative historical process, shaping both individual lives and the larger social fabric. His own cosmopolitan lifestyle, living in many different cultures, doubtless contributed to his own rare, nonnationalistic view of literature.

La utopía de América [America, the Utopia] conveys just this sense of how different cultural expressions constitute an interpretive process that actually creates a future. What one critic has called Henriquez Ureña's "dialectical thought" is already evident in this early piece. Describing how Mexico creates its "own life," its "own distinct character and civilization," Henríquez Ureña proceeds to explain how the continent becomes a single entity: "the unity of its history and the unity of purpose in its political and intellectual life make America a single entity, a great fatherland, a conglomeration of peoples." As critic Gutiérrez Girardot observes, this dialectical thought is not based on speculation or abstract principles. Instead it derives from solid empirical knowledge, for example, delineating the role of popular culture and Indian traditions to reshape a common Spanish heritage into distinctive nations, peoples, and regions.

Another central idea in Henríquez Ureña's work is his conception of the role that literature and the arts play in creating the autochthonous elements of each culture. Henríquez Ureña recognizes the roots of authenticity in strong Indian traditions, but he also appreciates the unique character that everything Spanish assumes in the Americas. These notions form the backbone of a major collection of essays based on lectures delivered at Harvard between 1940 and 1941. Originally written in English, *Literary Currents in Hispanic America* (1945) was posthumously translated into Spanish in 1949. In these essays, Henríquez Ureña positions the works of artists, writers, and poets within a network of social and historical periods, which are then reconfigured by the artist's specific role in those environments. With the precision of a witness simply recording events, Henríquez Ureña allows the underlying theory of his critical assessments to remain almost undetected—a quality that is perhaps his greatest asset as a writer, critic, and teacher.

The selection is from *La utopía de América*, compiled by Angel Rama and Rafael Gutiérrez Girardot (Caracas, Venezuela: Ediciones Ayacucho, 1978), 3–6. Translated by Charles Becker.

From La utopía de América (1925) America, the Utopia

I have not come to speak to you on behalf of the University of Mexico, not only because it has not authorized me to represent it in public events, but rather because I would not dare hold it responsible for the ideas that I will expound. And yet, I must begin by speaking at length of Mexico, because that country, which I know as well as my own Santo Domingo, will provide me with an exemplary case for my thesis. Mexico is now in one of the active moments of its national life, a moment of crisis and of creation. It is carrying out a critique of its past life; it is investigating what currents from its formidable tradition tow it toward apparently insurmountable shoals and what forces will be able to drive it to a safe port. Mexico is creating a new life for itself, asserting its own character, declaring itself ripe for founding a new type of civilization.

You will note that I do not speak of Mexico as a young country, as it is customary to speak of our America, but rather as a country of a formidable tradition. This is because underneath the Spanish organization, the indigenous heritage, albeit impoverished, persevered. Mexico is the only country in the New World where there is a long, enduring, uninterrupted tradition, in all things, in every sort of activity: in the mining industry as well as in textiles, in the cultivation of astronomy as well as classical letters, in painting and in music. Any of you who has visited one of the exhibits of popular art that are beginning to become a salutary custom for Mexico, could testify as to what variety of traditions were represented there; for example, in ceramics: Puebla's, where the Talavera pottery takes on a New World character; Teotihuacán's, where primitive figures are drawn in white on black; Guanajuato's, with an interplay of red and green over a yellow background, as in the landscape of this region; Aguascalientes', with vegetable ornamentation in white or black over dark red; Oaxaca's, where the blue butterfly and the yellow flower rise as if amidst splotches of cacao, over white soil; Jalisco's, where the tropical forest places its entire richness of lines and assertive color over the fertile native mud. And those among you who may have visited the ancient cities of Mexico—Puebla, Querétaro, Oaxaca, Morelia, Mérida, León—could say how they appear to be sisters, not daughters, of their Spanish namesakes; because, other than the extremely archaic cities, such as Ávila and Toledo, the Spanish cities do not have a medieval appearance, but rather reflect the sixteenth to the eighteenth centuries, precisely when the old Mexican cities were built. The capital, in the end, the triple Mexico—Aztec, colonial, post-independence—is the symbol of the ongoing struggle and occasional equilibrium between ancient traditions and new impulses, conflict and harmony that give character to one hundred years of Mexican life.

And so it is that, in spite of how great the tendency to de-civilize it, in spite of the frightful commotions that have shaken it and stirred it to its very foundations, in extended periods of its history, Mexico has possessed in its past and in its present the wherewithal to create, or perhaps more accurately, to continue and to broaden a life and a culture that are uniquely its own.

This enterprise of civilization is thus not absurd, as it may appear in the eyes of those whose only knowledge of Mexico is through the biased slander of cinema and wire services; this is not whimsical, this is not a simple desire to celebrate what is autochthonous, as the skeptics would hold. No. In Mexico, what is autochthonous is a reality; and what is autochthonous is not only the indigenous race, with its formidable dominion over all the activities in the country, the race of Morelos and of Juárez, of Altamirano and of Ignacio Ramírez: that is autochthonous, but so too is the special character that everything Spanish takes on in Mexico, since the beginning of the colonial era, whether it is Baroque architecture in the hands of the artists of Taxco or Tepozotlán or the theatrical comedy of Lope and Tirso in the hands of Don Juan Ruiz de Alarcón.[23]

With such foundations, Mexico knows what instruments must be employed for the task that it has taken on; and these instruments are culture and nationalism. But culture and nationalism are not, thankfully, understood in the manner of the nineteenth century. The idea is not of the dominant culture in the era of capital disguised as liberalism, a culture of exclusivist dilettantes, a walled-in garden where artificial flowers are raised, an ivory tower where dead sciences are kept, as if in a museum. The idea is of social culture, offered to and given to all, and built on the basis of work: learning is not simply learning of knowledge, but learning how to do and to make. There should be no high culture, because it would be false and ephemeral if it did not recognize popular culture. Nor is the idea of nationalism one of political nationalism, whose sole moral justification remains the need to defend the genuine character of each people against the threat of being reduced to a uniformity under types that under a delusion of the moment would appear to be superior; the idea is of another type, a spiritual nationalism born of the qualities of each people when translated into art and thought, which was humorously referred to, in the International Congress of Students, held in Mexico, as a nationalism of native ceramic cups and poems.

The nationalist ideal in Mexico now invades every field of endeavor. I shall cite the clearest example: Drawing is now being taught in a purely Mexican fashion. Instead of using the mechanical copying of trivial models, painter and

---

23 Juan Ruiz de Alarcón (1580–1639), a native of Taxco, is considered one of Mexico's best playwrights, especially for *La verdad sospechosa* [The Suspicious Truth].

researcher, Adolfo Best[24] ("penetrating and subtle as a sword") has created and widely shared his most original system, which consists of providing the child, when he or she begins to draw, with only the seven linear elements of indigenous Mexican popular arts (the straight line, the broken line, the circle, the semi-circle, the wave-like figure, the S, and the spiral) and telling him or her to use them in the Mexican fashion; that is, according to the rules also derived from the arts of Mexico: Thus, not to cross two lines, unless the thing represented inevitably requires them to cross.

But in speaking of México as a country of autochthonous culture, I do not mean to isolate it within America: I believe to a greater or lesser extent, all of our America shares similar natures, although it might not achieve the richness of the Mexican traditions everywhere. Four centuries of Hispanic life have given our America distinguishing features.

The unity of its history and the unity of purpose in its political and intellectual life make America a single entity, a great fatherland, a conglomeration of peoples destined to come together closer and closer every day. Were we to maintain that infantile audacity with which our forbearers would call any city of the Americas, "Athens," I would not hesitate to compare us with the politically disjointed but spiritually unified cities and peoples of classical Greece and of Renaissance Italy. But I would dare to compare us with them so we might learn from their example that disunity is disaster.

Our America must affirm its faith in its destiny, in the future of civilization. I do not, of course, base my assertion on the present or future development of our material wealth, not even on those implacable arguments for industrialization known as Buenos Aires, Montevideo, Santiago, Valparaíso, and Rosario.

No. These populaces demonstrate that when forced to compete in contemporary activity, our peoples know, just as well as in the United States, how to create within a few days formidable beehives, new types of cities, radically different from the European variety, and even how to accomplish, as in Río de Janeiro, feats never before imagined by North American cities. Nor do I base my point, to avoid opening myself up to the puerile censures of pessimists, on the work, as of yet scant, that represents our spiritual contribution to the world cultural heritage, regardless of how high the values in Mexican colonial

---

24 A prominent painter, Adolfo Best Maugard was born in Mexico City in 1881 and died in Greece in 1964. In his promotion of artistic nationalism, Best Maugard proposed that Mexican modern art adopt the basic linear elements of pre-Hispanic painting, sculpture, and architecture. He defined seven such elements to create a method of drawing. In 1923, he published an influential textbook for public schools, *Manuales y tratados: Método de dibujo: Tradición, resurgimiento y evolución del arte mexicano* [Manual of Drawing: Tradition, Renaissance and Evolution of Mexican Art].

architecture, and in contemporary poetry throughout our America, and in our marvelous popular arts.

I base my argument on the fact that in each one of our crises of civilization it is the spirit that has saved us, struggling against apparently more powerful elements; the spirit alone, and not military force or economic power. In one of his moments of deepest disappointment, Bolívar said, that were it possible for people to return to the void, the communities of Latin America would do so. The fear was not unfounded. Researchers of history tell us today that Central Africa, not so long ago, went from the organized social life of a creative civilization to the dissolution by which we know it today in which it has been easy prey for the greed of outsiders: the bridge was warfare without end. And Sarmiento's *Facundo* is the description of the acute instant in our struggle between the light and chaos, between civilization and barbarism. For a long time, barbarism had the sword on its side; but it was conquered by spirit, as if by a miracle. Thus, those magisterial men, such as Sarmiento, Alberdi, Bello, and Hostos,[25] are sometimes the true creators or saviors of our peoples, sometimes more so than the liberators of our independence. Forced to create their own work tools, in places where economic activity was sometimes reduced to the bare minimum within the patriarchal economy, men such as these are the true representatives of our spirit. It is our habit to demand, even of amateur writers, a magisterial aptitude: because he had it, José Enrique Rodó[26] is emblematic. And this is how we explain why today's youth, demanding like all youth, is embittered against those men of intelligence with little taste for meddling in the issues that interest today's youth, who in turn seek the guidance of their teachers for the solution to their problems.

If spirit in our America has triumphed over interior barbarism, there is no room to fear that it will surrender to barbarism from the outside. We are not dazzled by others' power: power is always ephemeral. Let us broaden the spiritual ground: let us provide the alphabet to all men; to each of them let us give

---

25 Eugenio María de Hostos y Bonilla (1839–1903) was a Puerto Rican lawyer who lectured throughout Latin America on the abolition of slavery. He helped women gain admittance to professional schools in Chile, and sought to reform the educational systems both there and in the Dominican Republic. Among his numerous books and essays was *La peregrinación de Bayoán* [The Pilgrimage of Bayoán], a seminal work promoting Cuban independence.

26 José Enrique Rodó (1871–1917) was a Uruguayan writer best known for his long essay, *Ariel* (1900), a classic of Latin American literature. Taking the form of a farewell address, the essay features a professor urging his students to uphold artistic and humanistic values over contemporary mechanization, technology, and the lure of material goods. In *Ariel*, Rodó makes the famous distinction between Latin America standing for art and the United States as subservient to economic and technological values.

the best instruments with which to work for the sake of all; let us redouble our efforts to achieve social justice and true freedom; therefore, let us go forward to our utopia.

José Carlos Mariátegui (1894–1930)

The agrarian community is one of the most enduring institutions of indigenous culture in Spanish America. Two basic factors support the cohesiveness of these communities: a complex network of family relationships and communal ownership of land. The Spanish crown tolerated indigenous communities, since they posed few obstacles to the *encomenderos* or landowners who tried for three centuries to appropriate Indian land and dissolve their societies in order to secure their valuable semislave labor. The *Leyes de Indias* [Laws of the Indies], the body of Spanish regulations imposed as early as 1512, actually prohibited Indians from legal enslavement as well as from the Inquisition. Unfortunately, independence in Spanish America coincided with an economic liberalism that emphasized private property as a basic principle. Blind adherence to this doctrine led several new governments to declare many indigenous communities illegal, and some even proposed their dissolution—to the obvious detriment of the indigenous people themselves.

Ruthless repartitioning of their lands deprived Indians of their communal power and left them with small plots that could barely support their families. Land was cheapened in the process, an outcome that only encouraged the voracity of landowners. In spite of such severe pressures, many Indian communities did survive—in Mesoamerica, especially in Mexico and Guatemala, and in the Andes, in Ecuador, Peru, and Bolivia. In the regions under Incan influence, the *ayllu* was an economic and social system that became key to the radical thought of José Carlos Mariátegui.

Mariátegui was born in Moquegua, a small city in southern Peru. When he was barely ten, a severe accident and a long convalescence left him with a limp and a physical fragility that affected him the rest of his life. Recurring infections led to the amputation of his left leg in 1924 and then the other leg a year before he died. But neither the loss of his legs nor the persistent infections that caused his premature death in 1930 ever deterred Mariátegui. Unable to continue in school, Mariátegui began working for a printing press. While still an adolescent, he began his career as a journalist, poet, and playwright, also becoming involved in Lima's political, intellectual and artistic circles. His enduring friendship with another Peruvian intellectual, Abraham Valdelomar, introduced Mariátegui to the European avant-garde, though politics and journalism remained his primary focus.

After Augusto Bernandino Leguía became president for the second time through a coup d'état in 1919, Mariátegui left Peru for Europe. It remains unclear whether his exile was voluntary, but after traveling in France and Germany, Mariátegui settled in Italy—partly because of his delicate health. His years there were decisive: he met and married Ana Chiappe, with whom he had four children, and he also encountered the ideas that were to become fundamental to his own intellectual development. Though Mariátegui had already declared himself a socialist in Peru, in Italy he was able to further his reading and acquaint himself with European political movements. Italian Marxism was then under the influence of a brilliantly heterodox thinker, Georges Sorel (1847–1922), who was already famous for three basic ideas: the power of violence for revolutionary change, the impact of social myths, and the superiority of unions over political parties as a vehicle for change. While Mariátegui discarded violence, he made the latter notions central to his thought.

Sorel understood social myths as events or concepts that produced "the determination to act." The French Revolution was such a myth, motivating any number of social and political movements of the nineteenth century. Sorel's confidence in the power of labor unions, however, placed him at odds with contemporary socialist and communist movements that insisted that leadership of the workers must come from the party, not from workers' unions. While Mariátegui eventually recognized the importance of the Peruvian workers' movement, he focused on applying Sorel's notion of social myth to indigenous communities. In his best-known work, *Siete ensayos de interpretación de la realidad peruana* (1928) [Seven Interpretative Essays on Peruvian Reality], Mariátegui points out that Peru's historical evolution was anomalous, lacking the transition from the feudal to the bourgeois stage. The feudal period had been prolonged because the colonial *latifundios* [large estates] had increased throughout the nineteenth century, perpetuating a system of feudal relationships and ownership. Mariátegui argued that the bourgeoisie had failed its historic role by co-opting the benefits of a feudal system to exploit Indian labor and expropriate communal lands.

Mariátegui concluded that an orthodox socialist revolution was not possible in Peru because there was neither a bourgeoisie nor a working-class consciousness. But there was a powerful social myth, one maintained by the Indians though not by the creoles, or the landowners, or the bourgeoisie, or even the workers. Communal landownership had consistently motivated the Indians to action, defending their lands and even recovering what had been lost in the conquest. This was Mariátegui's most powerful idea, and he used it to examine all political phenomena in Peru. With it, he confronted the politics of the dictator Agusto Bernardino Leguía y Salcedo whose second regime lasted eleven years, the so-called *oncenio* (the eleventh) from 1919 to 1930, and who proclaimed himself protector of the Indians even as their lands were being seized.

From the moment Mariátegui returned to Peru in 1923, he never stopped promoting his ideas, despite personal illness and government persecution. In 1926, he created *Amauta*, one of the most important journals in twentieth-century Latin America, disseminating Marxist ideas, clarifying the significance of the Mexican Revolution and the avant-garde. The same year that he published his *Seven Essays*, he also founded the Peruvian Socialist Party (Partido Socialista del Perú)—not to be confused with its successor, the Peruvian Communist Party (Partido Comunista Peruano).

The distinction between socialist and communist was ideologically and politically crucial in this era. Despite pressure from Moscow's Komintern, already under the control of Stalin following Lenin's death in 1924 and Trotsky's exile, Mariátegui stubbornly refused to change the name of his party to Communist. Mariátegui simply would not recognize the Komintern as the party's sole governing authority, a point he elaborated at a Montevideo conference organized by Moscow in 1929. Mariátegui had not forgotten Sorel's lesson about the primacy of workers' unions over political parties in representing workers' interests. That same year, he founded the Confederación General de Trabajadores del Perú (CGTP) (General Confederation of Workers of Peru), today the nation's largest labor union.

Despite his individual resistance to the Komintern, Mariátegui recognized the growing tendency to give in to Moscow and probably realized that he would lose that battle in the Socialist Peruvian Party. He began making plans to emigrate to Buenos Aires. But a recurrence of the infections that had plagued him all his life overtook him; Mariátegui died on April 16, 1930. Barely a month later, on May 20, Eudocio Ravines changed the party's name to Partido Comunista Peruano (the Peruvian Communist Party). Only three months later, a military rebellion broke out, which ultimately led to the resignation of President Leguía.

In spite of all the cultural and political changes that have occurred in the decades after his death, Mariátegui continues to be one of the most original thinkers in Latin America. A sharp political and social analyst, he was also a visionary cultural critic. His incisive essays and ground-break-ing magazine stimulated the avant-garde movement all over the Americas, promoting the literary merits of César Vallejo, Alberto Hidalgo, MARTÍN ADÁN and many other creative writers. Even today, his understanding of community as the basic "myth" of Indian culture remains not only valid, but operative in many activist organizations.

The text is from *José Carlos Mariátegui: An Anthology*, edited and trans-lated by Harry E. Vanden and Marc Becker (New York: Monthly Review Press, 2011), 145–50. Copyright © 2011 by Harry E. Vanden and Marc Becker. All rights reserved. Reprinted by permission of Harry E. Vanden and Marc Becker.

From El problema del indio (1928) [On the Indigenous Problem]

The population of the Inca empire, according to conservative estimates, was at least ten million.[27] Some people place it at twelve or even fifteen million. The conquest was, more than anything, a terrible carnage. The Spanish con-querors, with their small numbers, could not impose their domination, but only managed to terrorize the Indigenous population. The invaders' guns and horses, which were regarded as supernatural beings, created a superstitious impression. The political and economic organization of the colony, which came after the conquest, continued the extermination of the Indigenous race. The viceroyalty established a system of brutal exploitation. Spanish greed for precious metals led to an economic activity directed towards mines that, under the Incas, had been worked on very small scale because the Indians, who were largely an agricultural people, did not use iron and only used gold and silver as ornaments. In order to work the mines and *obrajes* (sweatshops) where weaving was done, the Spanish established a system of forced labor that decimated the population. This was not only a state of servitude, as might have been the case had the Spanish limited the exploitation to the use of land and retained the agricultural character of the country, but was in large part a state of slavery. Humanitarian and civilizing voices called for the King of Spain to defend the Indians. More than anyone, Father BARTOLOMÉ DE LAS

---

27 José Carlos Mariátegui wrote this essay at the request of the Tass News Agency in New York, and it was translated and published as "The New Peru" in *The Nation* 128 (January 16, 1929). It was reprinted in *Labor* (Year 1, No.1, 1928) with the title "On the Indian Problem: Brief Historical Review." An editorial note from Mariátegui preceded it indicating that these notes "in a sense complement a chapter on 'The Problem of the Indian' in *Seven Interpretive Essays on Peruvian Reality*." For this reason, the editors of *Obras Completas* added it to this essay beginning with the third edition, April 1952. [Trans. note to this edition.]

CASAS stood out in their defense. The Laws of the Indies were inspired by the purpose of protecting the Indians. It recognized their traditional organization into communities. But in reality the Indians continued to be at the mercy of a ruthless feudalism that destroyed the Inca economy and society without replacing it with something that could increase production. The tendency of the Spanish to settle on the coast drove away so many aboriginals from the region that it resulted in a lack of workers. The viceroyalty wanted to solve this problem through the importation of African slaves. These people were appropriate to the climate and challenges of the hot valleys and plains of the coast and, in contrast, inappropriate for work in the mines in the cold sierra highlands. The African slave reinforced the Spanish domination that in spite of the Indigenous depopulation was still outnumbered by the Indians who, though subjugated, remained a hostile enemy. Blacks were devoted to domestic service and other jobs. Whites easily mixed with blacks, producing a mixture of a type characteristic of the coastal population that has greater adherence to the Spanish and resists indigenous influences.

The independence revolution was not, as is known, an Indigenous movement. It was a movement of and for the benefit of *creoles* and even Spanish living in the colonies. But it took advantage of the support of Indigenous masses. Furthermore, as illustrated by the Pumacahua,[28] some Indians played an important role in its development. The liberal program of the revolution logically included the redemption of the Indian as an automatic consequence of the implementation of its egalitarian principles. And so, among the first acts of the republic, were several laws and decrees in favor of the Indians. They ordered the distribution of land, the abolition of forced labor, and so on. But the revolution in Peru did not bring in a new ruling class, and all of these provisions remained on paper without a government capacity to carry them out. The colony's landholding aristocracy, the owner of power, retained their feudal rights over the land and, therefore, over the Indians. All provisions apparently designed to protect them have not been able to do anything against feudalism even today.

The viceroyalty seems less to blame than the republic. The full responsibility for the misery and depression of the Indians originally belongs to the viceroyalty. But in those inquisitorial days, a great Christian voice, that of Fray [Friar] Bartolomé de Las Casas, vigorously defended the Indians against the

---

28 Mateo Pumacahua (1740–1815) was a cacique, or chief, of a region in Cuzco. In 1781, he sided with the Spanish against the rebellion of Tupac Amaru. In 1811, he opposed the forces for independence in Bolivia, but later, in 1814, he demanded that the colonial authorities implement the Cadiz Constitution and rebelled when they refused. He was defeated and executed in 1815.

brutal methods of the colonizers. There has never been as stubborn and effective an advocate of the aboriginal race during the republic.

While the viceroyalty was a medieval and foreign regime, the republic is formally a Peruvian and liberal regime. The republic, therefore, had a duty the viceroyalty did not have. The republic has the responsibility to raise the status of the Indian. And contrary to this duty, the republic has impoverished the Indians. It has compounded their depression and exasperated their misery. The republic has meant for the Indians the ascent of a new ruling class that has systematically taken their lands. In a race based on customs and an agricultural soul, as with the Indigenous race, this dispossession has constituted a cause for their material and moral dissolution. Land has always been the joy of the Indians. Indians are wed to the land. They feel that "life comes from the earth" and returns to the earth. For this reason, Indians can be indifferent to everything except the possession of the land, which by their hands and through their encouragement is religiously fruitful. *Creole* feudalism has behaved, in this respect, worse than Spanish feudalism. Overall, the Spanish *encomendero* often had some of the noble habits of feudal lords. The creole *encomendero* has all the defects of a commoner and none of the virtues of a gentleman. The servitude of the Indian, in short, has not decreased under the republic. All uprisings, all of the Indian unrest, have been drowned in blood. Indian demands have always been met with a military response. The silence of the puna[29] afterward guards the tragic secret of these responses. In the end, the republic restored, under the title of the road labor draft, the system of mitas.

In addition, the republic is also responsible for the lethargic and weak energies of the race. The cause of the redemption of the Indians became under the republic a demagogic speculation of some strongmen. *Creole* parties have signed up for their program. And thus the Indians lost their will to fight for their demands.

In the highlands, the region mostly inhabited by Indians, the most barbaric and omnipotent feudalism remains largely unchanged. The domination of the earth in the hands of the gamonales,[30] the fate of the Indigenous race, falls to an extreme level of depression and ignorance. In addition to farming, which is carried out on a very primitive level, the Peruvian highlands also have another economic activity: mining, almost entirely in the hands of two large U.S. companies. Wages are regulated in the mines, but the pay is negligible, there

---

29 Cold, desolate highland region. [Trans. note.]

30 *Gamonales* were administrators or bosses of large haciendas whose owners lived mostly in the capital cities, such as Lima, Quito, and La Paz.

is almost no defense for the lives of the workers, and labor laws governing accidents are ignored. The system of *enganche* (forced recruitment), which through false promises enslaves workers, puts the Indians at the mercy of these capitalist companies. The misery of agrarian feudalism is so great that Indians prefer the lot offered by the mines.

The spread of socialist ideas in Peru has resulted in a strong movement reflecting Indigenous demands. The new Peruvian generation knows that Peru's progress will be fictitious, or at least will not be Peruvian, if it does not benefit the Peruvian masses, four-fifths of whom are Indigenous and peasant. This same trend is evident in art and in national literature in which there is a growing appreciation of Indigenous forms and affairs, which before had been depreciated by the dominance of a Spanish colonial spirit and mentality. *Indigenista* literature seems to fulfill the same role of Mujik literature in pre-revolutionary Russia. Indians themselves are beginning to show signs of a new consciousness. Relationships between various Indigenous settlements which before were out of contact because of great distances grow day by day. The regular meeting of Indigenous congresses that are sponsored by the government initiated these linkages, but as the nature of their demands became revolutionary they were denatured as advanced elements were excluded and the representation was made apocryphal. *Indigenista* currents press for official action. For the first time the government has been forced to accept and proclaim *indigenista* views, and has decreed some measures that do not touch *gamonal* interests and are ineffective because of this. For the first time the Indigenous problem, which disappears in the face of ruling-class rhetoric, is posed in its social and economic terms and is identified more than anything as a land problem. Every day more evidence underscores the conviction that this problem cannot find its solution in a humanitarian formula. It cannot be the result of a philanthropic movement. The patronage of Indigenous chieftains and phony lawyers is a mockery. Leagues of the type of the former Pro-Indigenous Association provide a voice clamoring in the wilderness. The Pro-Indigenous Association did not arrive in time to become a movement. Their action was gradually reduced to the generous, selfless, noble, personal actions of Pedro S. Zulen and Dora Mayer. As an experiment, the Pro-Indigenous Association served to contrast, to measure, the moral callousness of a generation and an era.[31]

---

31 The Asociación Pro-Indígena (Pro-Indigenous Association) was a moderate Peruvian association dedicated to advancing Indigenous rights. It operated in the first part of the twentieth century. [Trans. note.]

The solution to the problem of the Indian must be a social solution. It must be worked out by the Indians themselves. This concept leads to seeing the meeting of Indigenous congresses as a historical fact. The Indigenous congresses, misled in recent years by bureaucratic tendencies, have not yet formed a program, but their first meetings indicated a route for Indians in different regions. The Indians lack a national organization. Their protests have always been regional. This has contributed in large part to their defeat. Four million people, conscious of their numbers, do not despair of their future. These same four million people, though they are nothing more than an inorganic mass, a dispersed crowd, are unable to decide their historical course.

In Context | *The Exploitation of Mexico by Spanish Conquistadors* (1929–1945) by Diego Rivera (1886–1957)

Diego Rivera's murals, together with those of José Clemente Orozco, David Alfaro Siqueiros, and others, constitute the most striking artistic product of the Mexican Revolution. Prior to 1922, no single artistic form seemed capable of capturing the powerful impact of the social movement that had stunned the country and caused the death of nearly one million people.

Figure 6.5. Diego Rivera (1886–1957), *The Exploitation of Mexico by Spanish Conquistadors*. Palacio Nacional, Mexico City, Mexico. Photograph by Jennifer Saracino. Banco de México Diego Rivera & Frida Kahlo Museums Trust, Mexico, D.F. / Artists Rights Society (ARS), New York.

Among the literary works that sought to reflect this moment was Mariano Azuela's *Los de abajo* [The Underdogs]. But this 1915 novel doesn't celebrate the revolution so much as it denigrates some of its participants, offering a bestialized view of popular insurgents and a skeptical judgment of their leaders. Five years later, in a second edition, Azuela altered some passages and characters trying to attenuate his disillusioned and violent vision, but his changes did little to reveal the motives of the rebellion or elucidate the profound social conflicts that had fueled revolution. It was not until 1931 that these objectives were fulfilled in the works of Nellie Campobello in *Cartucho* and of Rafael F. Muñoz in *Vámonos con Pancho Villa* [Let's Go with Pancho Villa].

Meanwhile, the mural as a form was undergoing a dazzling renewal, both in artistic techniques and in its capacity to make art relatable with the people. The earliest murals in this era were created in Mexico City in the early 1920s by Gerardo Murillo (Dr. Atl) in the historic church of San Pedro and San Pablo, and were soon followed by the artwork decorating the galleries of the National High School (formerly the Jesuit School of St. Ildefonso), largely painted by José Clemente Orozco.

In 1922, Diego Rivera began a mammoth project to retell Mexican history: an ambition reflected both in the sheer size of his murals and the diversity of his artistic ideas and themes. Rivera's great project took shape on the walls of the Department of Public Education, in the Agricultural School of Chapingo, and at the Palacio Nacional. The mural reproduced here, from the Palacio Nacional, demonstrates the effects of the conquest, utilizing a narrative technique that combines the methods of medieval European painters, portraying biblical episodes and the lives of the saints, with those of indigenous artists, like those at Bonampak, an ancient Mayan city like Palenque, that flourished in the Yucatán during the Classic period (500 to 800 BCE). CORTÉS is the central figure, but in contrast to most representations of the conquistador, he appears here as monstrous, a hunchbacked weakling with a deathly pallor.

While these public murals are extremely expressive, one paradoxical aspect of the muralist movement is that the era's most intense images do not appear in works of Dr. Atl or Orozco or Rivera. Instead, perhaps the most powerfully authentic impressions of the muralist heyday emerge on the private canvasses of Frida Kahlo, Rivera's model and inspiration, as well as his primary supporter and, of course, his wife.

7

New Civil Wars and Dictatorships,
1930–1980

No single description of Latin America from the 1930s through the 1980s can adequately comprehend its complexity. After a hundred years of independence (a mere thirty for Cuba), the historical development of each country, with distinctive social, economic, and political components, had irrevocably differentiated each of them from the others. In some cases, nations had not changed significantly since independence—or since colonial rule, for that matter. Certainly, the condition of Indians was not much altered in many places, as in JOSÉ CARLOS MARIÁTEGUI's Peru, or in Bolivia and Guatemala. Few major economic shifts had occurred since the previous century, with some nations still dependent on the exploitation of a single raw material, like Bolivian tin, needed by Europeans and increasingly by the United States. While some countries were starting to diversify production, there was also an effort to reach the stage of "import substitution": closing markets to imports that could be locally produced, despite the fact that those products were often manufactured by foreign companies, which then took their profits abroad.

Latin America was also deeply affected by the international economic crash of 1929, and it was beginning to react to the intense political currents sweeping Europe and the United States. The sudden loss of markets and increasing economic inequality led some countries—at very different times—to adopt populist measures, occasionally tainted with fascism, but quite specific to each nation. In Mexico, for example, Lázaro Cárdenas responded to the demands of the Revolution with a vigorous program of land redistribution and by nationalizing the oil industry. At the same time, Cárdenas imposed strict controls on political activity by creating national labor unions, which ultimately were more oppressive than liberating for their members. Finally, Cárdenas strengthened his own political party, founded in 1929 by Plutarco Elías Calles, to become the *sui generis* instrument of a new power caste designed to hold the reins of government permanently. Significantly, the party changed its name from the Partido Nacional Revolucionario (PNR) (National Revolutionary Party) to the Partido de la Revolución Mexicana (Mexican Revolution Party); a bare eight years later, another president changed the name again to the Partido Revolucionario Institucional (Institutional Revolutionary Party), the PRI of today, which controlled Mexico until 2000, and, after a brief hiatus, regained the presidency in 2012.

Many of Cárdenas's measures were later implemented in Argentina by Juan Domingo Perón, with suitable modifications. But while there were some parallels between these regimes, the differences were significant. Cárdenas was president between 1934 and 1940, while Perón took office for the first time in 1946. And while both were military men, their earlier careers were quite dissimilar and the symbolic roles they played in their respective countries could hardly have been more disparate.

Cárdenas, for example, renewed the myth of the peace-loving *caudillo*, a benefactor of the peasantry; indeed, after his death, many still referred to him as "Tata Lázaro" (Daddy Lázaro). Years later, Cárdenas's son Cuauhtémoc attempted to harness his father's reputation in his unsuccessful presidential campaign in 1988—though a suspicious computer system "failure" probably deprived him of victory. Cárdenas's legacy was decidedly mixed: on the one hand, he established the conditions for a corrupt and corrupting union system; on the other, he secured the resource that would become the nation's most important source of revenue, the oil industry.

Perón, though democratically elected, governed even more forcefully, closing universities and newspapers, and was often accused of dictatorial tactics, despite his efforts to improve the conditions of workers and the poor. For many, Perón was a contemporary manifestation of the fundamental Argentine duality once described by DOMINGO FAUSTINO SARMIENTO in *Facundo* (1845) as "Civilization and Barbarism." For Sarmiento, barbarism had the specific face of the dictator Juan Manuel Rosas but such barbaric practices, as ESTEBAN ECHEVERRÍA suggested, also defined a place—the abattoir or "slaughterhouse." These nineteenth-century assessments of Argentine culture are echoed in a 1947 short story "La fiesta del monstruo" [The Monster's Feast]. Written by Jorge Luis Borges and Adolfo Bioy Casares under the pen name Bustos Domeq, the story retells the events of October 17, 1945. On that day, a massive assembly gathered in the Plaza de Mayo to demand Perón's reinstatement as vice president, effectively marking the onset of his power. Pointedly alluding to ECHEVERRÍA's famous short story, "El matadero" [The Slaughterhouse], "La fiesta del monstruo" renders Perón and his followers as emblems of a resurrected Rosas and his barbarians.

After Obregón's assassination in 1928, consecutive or nonconsecutive reelection was banned in Mexico, so Cárdenas was unable to run for a second term as president in 1940, but his nationalization of oil had already changed the course of Mexican history. Though Perón was elected for two terms, in 1946 and 1952, his second term was cut short by a coup d'état in 1955. Eighteen years later, in 1973, Perón was elected again, only to die a few months later in July 1974. Juan Perón and his charismatic wife Evita—who died in 1952 at the height of her popularity—were without a doubt the most influential figures in Argentine history in the second half of the twentieth century, while Peronism itself continues to be the country's most decisive political force.

Mexico and Argentina were, of course, not alone in producing formidable politicians who shaped their country's evolution. In Ecuador, the powerful orator José María Velasco Ibarra occupied the political landscape from 1934, when he was first elected president, until 1972. But while Velasco Ibarra was elected five times, he completed only one full term, 1952 to 1956, having been deposed every other time. Similarly, Augusto César Sandino left a deep and lasting imprint on his native Nicaragua. Between 1927 and 1933, Sandino was an ardent opponent of the U.S. occupation, which had begun in 1926. When North American troops finally departed, Sandino was assassinated by the leader of the Nicaraguan National Guard, Anastasio Somoza, who two years later established a dictatorial regime that lasted over fifty years. However, Sandino himself became the inspiration for the guerrilla movement that finally brought down the Somoza family dictatorship in 1979.

Sandino's crusade and his Sandinista successors highlight one of the most decisive factors in twentieth-century Spanish America, U.S. interventionism. Such interference assumed a number of forms. Often the intervention was complicit with particular social or governing sectors of a country. Sometimes the United States utilized the covert actions of transnational North American businesses, such as ITT (International Telephone and Telegraph) in Chile in 1973 or the United Fruit Company, which served that function on several occasions and in several countries. Another tactic was the application of diplomatic and economic pressure through organizations like the Alliance for Progress or the Organization of American States. Spying agencies, like the CIA, often took action outright, precipitating, for example, a coup d'état against Guatemalan president Jacobo Árbenz in 1954. And finally, of course, there was direct intervention by the U.S. military, invading and occupying nations south of its borders.

Twentieth-century invasions by the United States began in 1898 with the so-called Spanish American War, resulting in the occupation of Cuba and of Puerto Rico, which is still a U.S. colony. Interference in Latin American affairs continued with several intrusions into Mexico: the seizure of Veracruz in 1914 and General Pershing's massive invasion of the northern border in 1916. In the following decade, the United States also began occupations of Haiti, the Dominican Republic, and Nicaragua. All of these interventions had a twofold result: the establishment of long-lasting dictatorships and the emergence of costly and prolonged armed rebellions.

The twentieth century thus begins and ends in Spanish America with liberation and revolutionary movements—directly coinciding with anticolonial wars throughout the world—but one rebellion in the region remains exceptional. The Cuban Revolution began in 1953 with a failed attempt by Fidel Castro to seize Moncada Barracks, controlled by the Cuban president and dictator Fulgencio Batista. After a historic trial, Castro and many of his fellow fighters were sent to jail. More than a year later, they were granted amnesty by Batista and were released. Fidel and several comrades went to Mexico, where they organized a guerrilla group that included CHE GUEVARA. Having landed in Cuba late in 1956, the insurgents eventually took power on January 1, 1959. The success of the rebellion both inspired and directly supported other uprisings throughout Latin America, from Nicaragua, El Salvador, and Guatemala to Venezuela, Peru, and Bolivia. Beyond the specific outcomes of these insurgencies, the Cuban Revolution became during the 1960s and 1970s an unprecedented social and cultural force. The revolution renewed the sense of Latin American solidarity, of a common identity with a shared troubled history. Especially at first, the revolution seemed to realize the declaration of JOSÉ MARTÍ in "Our America": If Latin American countries do not follow their own traditions and the will of their peoples, true liberation will be impossible.

Under these circumstances, it is not surprising that thinkers throughout the region began to explore the significance of "a national identity." In many cases, countries were responding to a particular defining moment. In Mexico, it was the Mexican Revolution; in Cuba, it was political instability and dependence on the United States; in Argentina, it was the restoration of the oligarchy following a coup d'état against a reformist president, Hipólito Irigoyen (1930). Several writers here—EZEQUIEL MARTÍNEZ ESTRADA, FERNANDO ORTIZ and OCTAVIO PAZ—address these issues of national identity. Others, like PEDRO HENRÍQUEZ UREÑA, MARTÍN ADÁN and JOSÉ LEZAMA LIMA, concern themselves with broader questions about Latin America as a whole. And finally, a few works examine national identity more obliquely, as in RODOLFO WALSH's superb short story, "That Woman," in which the enigmas of Argentine history and its inescapable mythologies are scrutinized in an allegorical search for the body of a woman who can only be Evita Perón.

All of these texts share two further elements. First, the search for origins is abandoned in favor of understanding the consequences of history. Profoundly historicist, these essays evaluate and contextualize their subjects in a self-aware, historicized moment of configuration. And second, they all exemplify some of the best contemporary prose written in Spanish.

Ezequiel Martínez Estrada (1895–1964)

Ezequiel Martínez Estrada was born on September 14, 1895, in San José de la Esquina in the province of Santa Fe, Argentina. His parents divorced when he was twelve, and he moved to Buenos Aires to live with one of his aunts. Though he briefly attended the Colegio Avellaneda, financial constraints forced him by 1914 to take a position as a postal employee, a job he held until his retirement in 1946.

Working full time and largely self-taught, Martínez Estrada launched his literary career by publishing poems in literary journals. In 1921, he married Italian-born artist Agustina Morriconi, who provided both inspiration and encouragement. In 1924, he began teaching literature at the Colegio Nacional de la Plata. He published six volumes of poetry between 1918 and 1929; he later wrote drama, short stories, and literary history. But even in this early period, he was writing essays that were sharply critical of Argentine society. His most famous book, *Radiografía de la Pampa* [X-Ray of the Pampa], was published in 1933. A social psychoanalysis of Argentina, *X-Ray of the Pampa* was the first text of its kind in Latin America; it received the National Prize for Literature in 1937.

As many critics have suggested, *X-Ray of the Pampa* remains relevant because it captures how the spirit of specific historical moments shaped people's mentality, urban architecture, and social and political events in Argentina. In writing about the gauchos, for example, Martínez Estrada connects their solitude on the pampas, their self-sufficiency, the physicality of their labor—dealing with cattle and meat and manure—with the rugged mentality of the Federalists. Thus Martínez Estrada provides a social and psychological explanation for the politics of a Juan Manuel de Rosas and for the construction of the Argentine state. In the present selection, Martínez Estrada suggests that Buenos Aires is, like the pampas, constructed in layers. Like "the sand and the loess that covers the plain," the desires of the newcomers from the countryside successively impose their individual wills on the shapes of the city, rather than conforming to any existing or uniform social aesthetic.

After the publication of *X-Ray of the Pampa*, Martínez Estrada became increasingly dedicated to the essay, though he never really stopped composing verse. One of his most impressive analyses of Argentine culture and literature is *Muerte y transfiguración de Martín Fierro*, 1947 [The Death and Transfiguration of Martin Fierro]. This two-part essay examines the epic poem by José Hernández, whose central character is the gaucho Martín Fierro. Martínez Estrada creates a dialogue with the protagonists, who are rebelling against Hernandez's authorial control. This remarkable piece cleverly subverts traditional literary analysis even as it transforms the meaning of one of Argentina's most canonical texts.

Always harshly critical of Perón, especially in his book, *¿Qué es esto?* [What is this?], Martínez Estrada found himself during the Perón regime bedridden with a debilitating skin disease that lasted five years (1951–1955). In 1959, shortly after his recovery, feeling discouraged by his evident failure to affect Argentine society, Martínez Estrada departed for Mexico in what became a self-imposed exile. In 1960, he moved to Cuba, where he was warmly welcomed. Encouraged about the usefulness of his writing, Martínez Estrada became chair of the Center for Latin American Studies of the Casa de las Américas Publishing House; he also began a definitive biography of Cuba's great poet and revolutionary, JOSÉ MARTÍ. His completed manuscript of 1,000 pages established Martí as one of Latin America's premier writers. By 1962, after the Cuban missile crisis and facing the deterioration of his health, Martínez Estrada returned to Argentina. He died at his home in Bahía Blanca in 1964.

The selection is from *X-Ray of the Pampa* by Ezequiel Martínez Estrada, translated by Alain Swietlicki (Austin: University of Texas Press, 1971), 235–41. Copyright ©1971. Courtesy of the University of Texas Press and Fundación Ezequiel Martínez Estrada.

From X-Ray of the Pampa (1933)

Face and Cosmetics

Buenos Aires can appear as a beautiful city in the eyes of an observer who contemplates it as a huge mass quickly erected in the solitude. There is nothing like it in the Southern Hemisphere. It offers a certain attraction for the outsider if he has not imagined the city to be possible; the interest quickly evaporates after the initial impression. For the native born, or for the one who inhabits it from childhood or judges it within a known context, the city is of no interest by itself or as a world wonder. Buenos Aires is a city without secrets, without viscera or glands, without deep convolutions or caries. Everything is in the open; once the city is known on the outside, it ceases to interest. It lacks a yesterday and does not possess a true shape; when it stops growing and developing, it might have an entirely different configuration. Today it possesses the beauty of youthful bodies; the limbs have acquired their definitive size but have not as yet defined their function or achieved the robustness of maturity. Its defects may well be blamed on factory blunders. But this undoubtedly grandiose city, is it related to the area in which it lies, to the nation to which it belongs, as Paris is related to the other French cities, and as Berlin, London, Amsterdam, and Moscow are related to theirs?

The city is beautiful because it sprouted while overcoming enormous difficulties pertaining to its outline, its area, its location, and its inhabitants. It is beautiful precisely because against all those difficulties it embodies a will more powerful than the will to build and to populate; it is a vigorous assertion in a landscape that conspires against all things exalted. Whatever its faults, it will remain famous as a monument to an aspiration. In the first place, it suffers from improvisation defects, and they are most difficult to detect by those people who are themselves improvised. We are disgusted and indignant whenever we witness a structure that will not be able to stand tomorrow, because we see it as an unnecessary squandering of power and someone's autonomous will, whereas cooperation would have produced a more desirable result. The marvelous aspiration is full of crevices. Next to finished pieces there are others barely sketched; within the finished pieces there are others that are provisional or unfinished and other incomplete parts impossible to finish. This defect is particularly true of those sections which are well hidden, such as the back part of Congress, the interior of the Tribunals, or the drainage of the main Post Office. These hidden sections are the digital impressions, the factory's

318 · Anthology of Spanish American Thought and Culture

stamp of incapacity, and the differentiation between a project in which the entire city has collaborated and one that has been erected treacherously. Buenos Aires is ugly if one views it as a city and not as an effort. It has been conceived with beauty; the attempts at beautification, wastefully and very expensively done, produce ugliness and are the ostentation of the provincial parvenu. Beauty cannot be arbitrarily placed in various artificial locations of the city, such as corners, monuments, and promenades; poverty also can be beautiful in a city where even ruin speaks of life and of forms of existence and not of the hastened pace. Along one block, the different buildings speak assorted languages of time, of economic eras, and of styles, allowing us to see, as does the earth, in its strata, the various cataclysms suffered. Unfortunately, that diversity perpetuates the precarious, the fortuitous, and what is already past, and not what is everlasting and protected from catastrophes under the assurance of an already successfully tested formula.

Next to the one-floor houses are the two-floor houses; between them are the empty lands and the *skyscrapers* of twenty and thirty stories that rise with the predominant ambition, like a personal triumph that annuls the effort of others and proves the omnipotence of the empty plot adjoining the skyscraper. A skyscraper located in a block of low-lying buildings, next to pasture lands, indicates the same—but just the reverse—as a cave-in: the fracture of a piece of ground on which everything is settled, on which is built a city that does not oscillate or change. The empty plot is correlated with three million square kilometers, and the skyscraper relates to adventure and to the dream spoken aloud. The smaller houses are the older ones; the new ones have been erected when the economic out-look of Buenos Aires has improved—although not the architectural outlook. The earlier city was made up of one-floor dwellings; over these constructions is rising a multistory city. The buildings that are above average height are like the old one-floor dwellings that looked down on the ground, the oldest flooring of Buenos Aires. Today's one-floor houses are yesterday's empty plots of land. At the beginning, construction was sporadic and was erected directly on the soil; today, the first floor is used as the ground, and thus the one-floor houses are the idle lands in comparison to the higher houses. Buenos Aires has the structure of the pampa: layers form on top of layers, resembling the sand and the loess that cover the plains. This process has not been even and homogeneous, but fractured and selective. The diversity of styles and elevations indicates the difference in methods employed in the conquest of fortune and demonstrates the malleability of the medium to the impetuous attack of events or to unforeseen disasters. Although at some time houses may become stabilized at a certain height as they are in the old

European cities where the ordinances, the economic capacity, the architecture, and the mayors' talents are well-balanced, there will be a lack of harmony in the growth, in the styles, and in the ages that will be immediately perceived. The materials age quickly, the styles are outmoded, and the sojourner outlasts the buildings and watches them crumble and be demolished. Each building is a cement shape that pays for itself and triumphs in an easy victory. The styles are as independent as the buildings; they are quickly out of tune with the general taste or with the passing whim, which inflates certain values in the market of triumph and of defeat. The buildings age in their ornaments, in their adornments, and in their cornices before their masonry becomes old. The houses of Buenos Aires, although relatively new, have a withered face; they are experiments, provisional houses to occupy the land and to increase its value. They will not remain long; they are merely part of a passing Buenos Aires. Neither the wealth of the proprietors, nor the faith in the future, nor the architect's love for construction has conspired to make these houses last indefinitely. A city like Florence, where mansions built five hundred years ago still stand, is an honest city; but the portable fair of the gypsies is the swindle and the flight. Although Paris and Berlin may perish as soon as New York—the architect's taste, the administrative regulations, the constructor's city built to last thirty years—they have the stamp of eternity. The experience, the orientation of activities that enriched the owner, the glance of the passer-by, and the care of the artisan give a look of eternity, of stability, and of symmetry to each house in relation to the city, to each building in relation to the whole, and to each family in relation to its home. In that which wishes to endure there is the gaiety of life; in that which must perish there is the sadness of the fleeting moment. "Only gaiety desires eternity."

The man who conquered the plain, who made money on the plain, who bent the plain's defense with his tactics and methods, and who came to the city brought with him a rural breath that may be observed not only in the general flatness of construction but also in the manner in which, suddenly, that flatness is shattered in hand-to-hand combat and the jewel of economic victory is shown off. As far as Torcuato de Alvear, the northern part of the city was not an aristocratic zone; the opulent physiognomy arose from the success of export business, and the age of a whole neighborhood coincided with the age—why not with the forms?—of that prosperity, that eagerness to trade wools for architecture. The southern part of Buenos Aires is at present, as it was before the economic outbreak of 1880, more authentically Buenos Aires, as Argentina was more authentic in 1860 than in 1932. Whether in the northern or in the southern part of the city, the one-floor house will yield to the two-floor house; irremittably it will become the foundation. The city grows over the palaces and the miserable huts.

Urban Image of Rawhide Wealth

Among compact constructions, amid the massiveness of buildings struggling for every centimeter of light and air, suddenly, the magnate opens a tennis court to show off his millions—like a yawn. As if he were tying a horse to the palisade, he introduces a fragment of the pampa into the city, and in a piece of forest he affirms the nostalgia and the resentment of the pampa. To open his park, he has probably demolished some houses that, in a painful twenty-year encroachment, have barely cleared one-fourth of a hectare. The passer-by scorns a vanity that overdoes itself when aiming to arouse envy; the city is wild in its empty lands and ill-bred in its palatial parks. The countryside's influence on the city is evident in the egotistical conduct and in the whimsical manner of edification. To build a house to one's taste implies the rupturing of social unity and coincides with the desire to impose one's personality on the world. It is the affirmation not only of the ego and the fickleness of exhibited wealth but also of an unpolished rebellion. The proprietor has no intention of submitting to the architectural canons; his personality lacks style because he imagines that respect for esthetic values is equivalent to individual submis-sion. For this reason, the ordinances have taken into account the fancy of the lord of the pampa, and they adjust to his uncivil judgment. The proprietor is always able to find an architect who shares his opinion and who knows how to reflect the owner's personality in the façade so that people will not be able to say that the house does not resemble him, like some child of suspected origin. Those owners conceive of the dwelling as a salting place or as a silo; their idea of beauty is like that of a rubric they can barely sketch. It would be useless to try to make them understand that the acquisition of a good style is in good measure related to the style of others.

Each house in the city represents the magisterial and architectural shape of a fortune; in turn, each fortune stands for a way of life. That is why we have such a diversity of styles, of elevations, and of colors, which causes each build-ing to appear isolated, in the heterogeneity of the whole, as an unsociable personality with a temperamental idiosyncrasy. Nowhere in their façades, floors, or overhead views do the houses breathe the collective spirit of the city; they loathe to integrate into a similar group or to form one of the same age, and so they agglutinate into a chaos of unconnected fragments in which we can easily perceive the economic differences from decade to decade.

The people who own the houses differ in their long-pursued goals; contrasting systems of life, of morality, and of comprehension of reality have delivered into their hands the wealth with which to erect their dwellings—which will condense their biographies. Each house is more similar to a unique dream than to the city. Vestiges of individual struggles endure in the physiognomy of frontispieces. Each house takes advantage of another not only by sharing a common wall but also by infringing, as much as possible, on the neighbor's air and light. Whoever obtained more suffocates whomever procured less; a ten-story building proclaims to all winds the barely muttered ideal of the two-story house. The eagerness to possess real estate tramples respect for the laws of style and of edification that make a great city the collective home of millions of people. The ostentation of power reaches its apex in construction, and, since the housing industry provides—together with the food and clothing industries—the safest investment, the ten stories assert the ability to edify. The building represents a capital invested to the utmost; the mortgage usually starts from the sixth floor upward. The last four floors correspond to the disproportionate ambition and to the confidence in a successful outcome for that type of business.

The effort of the poor man who writes, paints, or plays music is not enough to absolve the city from the judgment, so richly deserved, that renders it barbarous; the city has grown at a time of maximum wealth but has paid no heed to aesthetics. Fifty thousand structures that proclaim fifty thousand surly wills fashion a formless city, a mosaic of souls who operate against the harmony of the whole: a cosmopolitan and polyglot city. A room in a house changes into the prison cell of a captive spirit whose most anxious desire is emancipation. The totality of souls constitutes more than an architectural people or a necropolis; it is a multitude compounded of brick, iron, and wood, without unity or spirit. The city is invaded by the pampa on all sides; the ranches and fields are sold or leased and transformed into buildings. At the end of the street we once again meet the horizon. Except for the skyscraper, which scrambles over the aggregate like a ram over its flock, the only variety among low-level constructions is provided by the balustrades devised for the upper stories. The roofs are not at one level and the fronts are not of one style, nor has the material acquired the patina that results after prolonged exposure to bad weather. If the houses are designed to exceed one story, they almost always have a balcony as an entablature: the balcony of a nonexistent upper parlor, similar to the dirt square in front of humble dwellings, which is kept in reserve for better times. The owner's project went beyond his means, and that second-story fragment, that balcony to the sky, oppresses the house with its nonexistent weight. A whole family lives in expectation of the floor that is not yet there. The sky's temporary habitation rests on bare hands and shoulders; often, the house must be demolished before the upper story is completed. It is an imaginary floor, with the mystery of an attic seen in a postcard of a city that will never be visited. It is an aspiration, but it is also a hole through which disappear, in a vain attempt to fill it, many things essential to life. The floor has its own preexistence, like a child who begins to rule from the first months of its gestation: everything has to revolve around it, submit to it, and be at its service. To labor toward the dream means to suffer deprivation, ignorance, hostility, and many lost years that float by as mere phantoms of an ideal; each year is a small unpardonable fault, though solid as the bricks piled on the stumps of amputated walls to encase the sky with nonexistent walls. It sometimes occurs that the long-desired dream is achieved. It may have cost ten or twenty years of sacrifices, of slavery to ambition. The head of the family is happy: his house, instead of one story, has two.

Fernando Ortiz (1881–1969)

The son of a Cuban mother and a Spanish father, Fernando Ortiz was born in Havana, Cuba, though he spent most of his childhood on the island of Minorca, Spain, where he completed high school. He finished a degree in law in Madrid in 1901, but after a short visit to Cuba in 1902, he was appointed consul to Italy, a position that changed his career. There Ortiz met and befriended the social theorist Cesar Lombroso and became interested in criminology, contributing to Lombroso's journal, *Archivio di Antropologia Criminale* [Archives of Criminal Anthropology]. When Ortíz returned to Cuba in 1905, he began studying criminal psychology among blacks, which led to a life-long immersion in Afro-Cuban culture.

Ortiz taught constitutional law at the University of Havana and completed his second book on criminal ethnology in 1916, *Hampa afrocubana: Los negros esclavos* [Afro-Cuban Underworld: Black Slaves]. A productive scholar, Ortiz was also politically active throughout his life. He served in the House of Representatives between 1917 and 1927, where he supported legislative reforms to reduce crime and prison corruption and programs to resocialize ex-prisoners. In protest against the government of Gerardo Machado, Ortiz went into exile in the United States (1931–1933), returning to Cuba with a renewed commitment to the cultural life of Havana.

He founded several important journals, including *Ultra* (1936–1947), and organizations, like the Society of Afro-Cuban Studies (1937). In 1950, he published *La africanía de la música folklórica de Cuba* [The Africanness of Folkloric Music of Cuba], a standard source in the field of African-Cuban Studies, which Ortiz himself largely created.

But Fernando Ortiz's most important intellectual contribution remains his ground-breaking book *Contrapunteo cubano del tabaco y del azúcar* [Cuban Counterpoint: Tobacco and Sugar]. Originally published in 1940, with an English edition in 1947, *Cuban Counterpoint* consists of two parts. The first features an imaginative debate between tobacco and sugar—as if they were characters in a drama. In the second part, Ortiz introduces the term *transculturation* to describe how cultural exchange occurs when two cultures meet or coexist to form a new society. Using the genealogy of two distinctly American products, tobacco and sugar, Ortiz illustrates the concept by showing what happens when these new commodities travel to other cultures and contexts, developing new social functions and significance. Tobacco, for example, which was originally an element of sacred rituals in Indian societies, becomes in Europe a symbol of wealth and social status. While tobacco thus loses its religious meanings, it retains the hedonistic associations that were also present for its early users. In making his case, Ortiz provides a thorough review of the literature, from the colonial to the republican period, offering textual descriptions, contemporary critiques, and extended accounts of the production, economic competition, and social uses of these essentially American products. *Cuban Counterpoint* is an impressive demonstration of the materiality of culture, from its physical impact on the body to the ways in which the production of these commodities determines social and labor structures, which, in turn, generate far-reaching economic conflict and competition.

The excerpt here is from the first part of the book, where the term that established Ortiz's fame never occurs. But transculturation is everywhere evident in this inventive counterpoint between these two products. Ortiz begins with the natural plants. Sugar cane is a sturdy stalk, requiring a machete for harvesting and machines for processing. Tobacco, on the other hand, is a delicate leaf that can only be harvested by hand. Sugar production is thus established as a trade, while tobacco production is an art. This dialectical relationship defines every level of production and the social status of its producers. Since sugar requires a division of labor among many, from grinding to filtering, its manufacture is a collective enterprise. More individualized, tobacco depends on the skill of a worker, who creates a distinctive reputation—like a brand—and confers on the cigar-maker the social standing of an artist. Impressively, Ortiz interprets cigar production—individuals laboring in a quiet workroom—as conducive to forming workers' associations, which are able to protect their own class interests. The general practice of reading aloud to cigar-makers in workrooms, for example, directly contributes to the social and political consciousness of tobacco workers. As JOSÉ MARTÍ had noted some decades earlier, the reading sessions were "an advance pulpit of liberty." And as Ortiz explains, this consciousness led many workers to support "José Martí's revolutionary efforts on behalf of Cuban independence."

One dimension of Fernando Ortiz's accomplishment is that he recognized two of Cuba's (indeed America's) most typical products making material culture a source of consciousness and national identity during the years of the Great Depression. In presenting these physical commodities as a counterpoint to colonization as well as to abstract symbolic identity, Ortiz enters contemporary discussions of postcolonialism and postmodernism, a half-century before their time.

The selection is from *Cuban Counterpoint: Tobacco and Sugar*, by Fernando Ortiz, translated by Harriet de Onís, with an introduction by Bronislaw Malinowski (New York: Alfred A. Knopf, 1947), 39–42. Translation copyright © 1947, renewed 1974 by Penguin Random House LLC. Used by permission of Alfred A. Knopf, an imprint of Knopf Doubleday Publishing Group, a division of Penguin Random House LLC. All rights reserved.

From **Cuban Counterpoint (1940)**

There is no type of trading that affords such a margin for subtle fraud as that in tobacco. For this reason the good repute of a dealer, based on past dealings, is almost a *sine qua non* for staying in business and doing well at it. Uprightness and reliability are the accepted thing in the tobacco business, not out of virtue or principle, but because experience has proved, even to those least burdened with scruples, that honesty is the best policy. In the same way the development of trade and credit since the sixteenth century has made it necessary to glorify as a cardinal virtue the honoring of agreements and the prompt payment of loans and interest when due. This was the underlying motive of Puritan morality as typified in the Protestant middle class, and the same thing may be said to have taken place in the agricultural aspect of the tobacco industry. José Aixalá, in his interesting *Recuerdos Tabacaleros del*

Tiempo Viejo (Horizontes, Havana, August 1936), has left us this typical picture of the old Vueltabajo [tobacco region in the province of Pinar del Río, Cuba]: "I still remember seeing negroes meet the train running from Villanueva to Batabanó on Thursday, with wheelbarrows loaded with sacks of gold doubloons, which were unloaded at Punta de Cartas, Bailén, and Cortés, and then carried on muleback through the tobacco country, leaving at each vega [field where tobacco was cultivated] payment for its crop."

But when tobacco begins to circulate commercially on a large scale, it becomes frankly knavish and seizes upon every opportunity to get the highest returns on the lowest investment. As soon as tobacco hits the European market, it loses its virtue. Especially is this true of Havana tobacco, whether in cigars or as cut tobacco, which, because of its exquisite quality, its reputation, and the high price it brings on the foreign market, has always been the victim of every manner of adulteration. The sugar industry, on the other hand, is laced with fraud at every step, from the scales on which the cane is first weighed to the shrinkage in weight and polarization that the buyer falsely claims from the warehouse at the port of embarkation, and to the refiner who bleaches and markets the final product abroad.

The sugar trade always involved contracts, promissory notes, foreign drafts, and complicated litigation in the Cuban courts. Dealings in tobacco have always followed the system of "cash on the barrel head," the money passing directly from buyer to seller, and of credits extended by a simple country storekeeper. A deal in sugar had to be written out on paper; with tobacco a man's word was enough. Nevertheless, sugar boasts of its orderly methods, and accuses tobacco of carelessness. But it has already been observed that the one is a conservative and the other a liberal, and each has its own prejudices, likes, and dislikes.

One might say that working with sugar was a trade, and with tobacco an art. In the first, machines and brute strength are the essential skills; in the latter, it is always a matter of the individual skill of the workman. From the utilitarian point of view, tobacco is all leaves, cane all stalk. And this fundamental difference between a pliable leaf and a tough stalk gives rise to the greatest divergences between the two industries, with striking social and economic repercussions. In the harvesting of tobacco all that is needed is a little knife to cut the stem of the leaf; even without a knife, with the hands alone, it can gently be pulled from the plant. For the harvesting of cane a long, sharp machete is required, which hacks down the stalk, trims off the leaves, and cuts it into lengths.

All the operations in the preparation of tobacco are carried out without machinery, using only the complex apparatus of the human body, which is the tobacco central.[1] In leaves cut by hand and one by one, the vega yields its harvest to the grower, and from his hands the leaf passes into other hands, and from hand to hand it reaches the warehouse and the factory, where still other hands work it up into cigars or cigarettes that will be consumed in another hand, that of the smoker. Everything having to do with tobacco is hand work—its cultivation, harvesting, manufacture, sale, even its consumption.

In the tobacco industry delicate hands are required, of woman or man, to manipulate the leaves and cut them with a slender-bladed knife. In the sugar industry human hands alone cannot crush the tough, woody canes, which must be ground and shredded in mills before they yield the treasure of their juice. For tobacco, deft and gentle hands; for sugar, powerful and complicated machinery.

In reality, the enjoyment of tobacco, like that of sugar, does not come until after a series of complicated operations beginning with the harvesting of the plants and ending in the consumer's mouth. Like sugar, tobacco has to go through a series of physical and biochemical phases, such as cutting, sweating, drying, curing, pressing, and combustion; like sugar it, too, needs the heat of fire to yield its substance, and it gives off a refuse of waste and ash which are its bagasse and settlings. But the operations involving sugar consist of machete strokes, shredding, crushing, boiling, dizzy rotation, and continual filtration and separation, while those having to do with tobacco are all delicate and caressing touches, "as though each plant were a delicate lady," to use José Martí's phrase.

This explains why the tobacco worker is better-mannered and more intelligent. And why he is generally a more individualized and prepossessing person; this holds true of the grower as of the selector, and of the man who works and shapes the tobacco. In the tobacco business each individual has a reputation of his own, like a brand, and a standing that has a price value. Just as there are planters and selectors famous for their special ability, so there are workers who are gifted in the manufacture of certain types of cigars and receive higher salaries for their work. It is said that part of their skill depends on the length of their fingers and their sense of touch; it is generally believed that the colored tobacco worker of Cuba excels those of other countries. Possibly

---

1   The *central* is a group of adjacent workshops where sugar is processed. Ortiz describes a similar "central" for tobacco, though tobacco production requires no machinery, only human hands. For Ortiz, the human body is the "central" for tobacco, and he later details this basic opposition between the mechanized production of sugar and the manual processing of tobacco.

this is a racial distinction of a somatic character; but whether it is an inherited trait or merely individual, the result of habit and training, lacks scientific proof. A French journalist wrote that Havana cigars owed their excellence to the fact that they were rolled by beautiful mulattoes on their bare thighs. This smacks of lewdness, and probably has its origin in the custom of old tobacco-growers who rolled their *monteras*, flattening out the leaves with their hands across their right leg, as is still done in certain selection operations.

The great secret lies in the individual ability of the worker. A man who was once a tobacco worker and is now a professor has said of the members of his erstwhile profession: "This work demands not only apprenticeship and practice but aptitude and a natural gift. Whoever lacks this and taste will never be anything more than a maker of plug tobacco. The good cigar-maker is an artist. The variety in the form, size, and workmanship creates different classes of cigar-makers, from those known as master cigar-makers to those who make *brevas* or *londres*.[2] The lowest level is represented by the *bonchero*[3] who works with a mold" (G. M. Jorge: *El Tabaquero Cubano*.) If there had been cigar-makers in the middle ages, they would have formed a guild and a secret society like the Masons, by reason of the diabolical fame of the leaves they worked with and the strict system of apprenticeship and rank. The master cigar worker had to serve an apprenticeship of three or four years; even today he represents only two per cent of his profession. The good cigar worker is a "master." At every step tobacco is the work of a tobacco worker, while sugar is the product of a whole mill.

For this reason, also, the division of labor in a sugar factory is different from that in a tobacco workshop. In the sugar central many workmen are needed to carry on the different industrial operations necessary from the time the cane is put on the conveyor belt to the grinder until the sugar comes out of the centrifugals into the sacks in which it is packed. In the making of sugar certain workmen tend to the fires, others to the grinding, others to the syrup, others to the chemical clarification, others to the filtering, others to the evaporating, and so on, through the successive steps involved in the sugar cycle. Each workman attends to one single job. No workman of the mill can by himself make sugar out of the cane; but each cigar worker can make a cigar out of a leaf of tobacco unassisted. The same tobacco worker can take charge of making each cigar from beginning to end, from cutting with his own knife the leaf

---

2 *Breva* or *londres* are types of cigars; the former is made with dark seasoned tobacco and the latter is a straight cigar about 4¾ in. long.

3 The person who shapes the bunches (bunching). The bunch is the semi-finished product, usually consisting of three to five filler tobacco leaves and the binder, which is rolled around them.

for the filler to twisting the wrapper to its final turn. And any smoker can do it, too, as the tobacco planter does with the leaf of his own harvest for his own smoking. He can cut the leaf, dry it, shred it, stuff it into a pipe or roll it in a cigarette paper, and light it and smoke it, as he pleases. At the mill many work together in joint and successive operations, which in their totality produce sugar in great quantities. In the tobacco industry many workers are occupied in individual but identical tasks, all of which when added together produce many cigars. The manufacture of sugar is a collective job; that of tobacco is by individual efforts.

The consumption of tobacco is likewise individual, and this is borne in mind during its processing; but this is not the case with sugar. One cigar or one cigarette for each smoke. No smoker smokes two cigarettes at the same time. Even when made up in big factories, tobacco is put out for the exclusive use of each smoker; in the singular, by portion and form, thinking of the potential consumer. Not so sugar, which is packed and consumed in bulk. And even though now certain refined sugar is made up in cubes, equivalent to the lumps into which the old sugarloaves used to be broken, these are not individual portions, but rather small doses of granulated sugar, like spoonfuls without a spoon, of which the consumer uses one or several, without selection, according to his needs.

Sugar comes into the world without a last name, like a slave. It may take on that of its owner, of the plantation or mill, but in its economic life it never departs from its typical equalitarian lack of caste. Nor does it have a first name, either in the field, where it is merely cane, or in the grinding mill, where it is just juice, or in the evaporating-pan, where it is only syrup. And when in the dizzying whirl of the turbines it begins to be sugar and receives this name, that is as far as it goes. It is like calling it woman, but just woman, without family name, baptismal name, name of hate or of love. Sugar dies as it is born and lives, anonymously; as though it were ashamed of having no name, thrown into a liquid or a dough where it melts and disappears as if predestined to suicide in the waters of a lake or in the maelstrom of society.

From birth tobacco was, and was called, tobacco. This was the name the Spaniards gave it, using the Indian word; so it is called in the world today, and so it will be known always. It is tobacco in the plant, in the leaf, while it is being manufactured, and when it is going up in smoke and ashes. Moreover, tobacco always had a family name, that of its place of origin, which is the vega; that of its epoch, which is the harvest; that of its school, which is the selection; that of its gang, which is the tercio; that of its regiment, which is the factory;

that of its distinguished service, which is its commercial label. And it has its citizenship, which, if it is Cuban, it proudly proclaims.

Martín Adán (1908–1985)

Martín Adán is the pseudonym of Rafael de la Fuente Benavides, a native of Lima, and one of Peruvian letters' most original writers. Although Rafael de la Fuente never explained his odd nom de plume, JOSÉ CARLOS MARIÁTEGUI recalled that the poet chose "Martín" from the name that organ grinders gave their monkeys who collected tips from passersby, while "Adán" alluded to the creation of the first man. Thus "Martín Adán" is an incongruous reference to both evolution and religion. Even if Mariátegui's account is not precisely true, it does accurately describe the contradictions of Rafael de la Fuente's personality. Devoutly Catholic, he espoused liberal, even antireligious beliefs. A private, even reclusive, individual who struggled with alcoholism all his life, he consistently tried, in his life and in his work, to unite ideological extremes and historical opposites. Identified by his pseudonym in some of his earliest publications, pieces that appeared in Mariátegui's pioneering journal, *Amauta*, "Martín Adán" became the first expression of the poet's fundamentally Baroque view of the world.

Though Adán is best known for his superb, complex poetry, he also wrote extraordinary prose. Before he was even twenty years old, he had written a novel that has become a Latin American classic: *La casa de cartón* (1928) [The Cardboard House]. Ten years later, determined to obtain his doctorate, Adán wrote the first version of *De lo barroco en el Perú* [On the Baroque in Peru] under his real name. For a decade, Adán continued to edit and revise his dissertation, publishing several chapters in journals in Lima. Finally, in 1968, he published a definitive version of this extraordinary work. Adán's goal was to discover a national identity—a task resembling that of a number of writers of the 1950s, including Samuel Ramos and OCTAVIO PAZ in Mexico; Scalabrini Ortiz and MARTÍNEZ ESTRADA in Argentina; and FERNANDO ORTIZ and LEZAMA LIMA in Cuba.

Adán's title asserts the author's clear, if apparently paradoxical, purpose. Identifying the writer RICARDO PALMA or, for that matter, the Peruvian Romantics, as Baroque was a radical assertion. In fact, Adán was simply articulating what many critics believed but had not dared to express: that the Baroque has defined Spanish American perspective and expression since the conquest. As Martín Adán insists, the Baroque is essentially more of a worldview than a style: a perspective on the sensible shape of the world and not simply the external reflection of some interior content. Indeed, Adán's essay highlights the Peruvian tendency to attend to exteriors, to the ceremonial and the ritual, at the expense of firm ideological positions, of political or social convictions that might contradict those surfaces. Adán also differentiates the literary legacy of Góngora from the Baroque as a distinctive Hispanic attitude. Indeed, as Adán observes, the Góngora of Spanish America was already a mixture or *mestizaje:* combining Arab influences (the "arabesque") with Gothic and Renaissance elements—a phenomenon earlier noted by JUAN ESPINOSA MEDRANO.

For Adán, the Baroque as worldview is both a mode of capturing reality and a manner of approaching it. Deeply skeptical of transcendental entities and embracing a hedonistic sensuality, the Baroque defines an attitude that endured long after colonization but that also encompassed an essentially Romantic point of view: the awareness of the singularity of being Spanish American. Within these defining contexts then, Hispanic and Indian cultures confront each other to produce a unique *mestizaje.* That resulting tension is also what LEZAMA LIMA addresses in *La expresión americana* [The American Expression].

One particularly interesting contribution that Adán makes to the definition of the Baroque spirit is its identification with the Jesuits. Throughout their tenure in Spanish America, the Society of Jesus kept the Baroque style and sensibility quite robust—as the works of JUAN ESPINOSA MEDRANO ("El Lunarejo"), HERNANDO DOMÍNGUEZ CAMARGO, FRANCISCO JAVIER CLAVIJERO, and FRANCISCO JAVIER ALEGRE and others demonstrate. In the selection here, Adán notes the irony that, though the Jesuits were not part of the wars of independence, they played a decisive role in shaping the spirit that motivated the colonies to break away from Spain.

Moreover, as Adán explains, the expulsion of the Jesuits in 1767 interrupted Andean—indeed, Spanish American—history. That disruption caused Romanticism to fail in the republics, despite the presence of several critical conditions for its success: an "uncontrollable" nature; a republican tradition following a monarchy; a problematized notion of freedom (though one that never really generated a "new consciousness"); and the appalling poverty of the population. All the elements for the development of Romanticism were there—except for the "human subject capable of carrying it out." There was in the new republics no sense of the individual, of a self capable of translating these conditions at once into consciousness and into discourse.

Martín Adán's terminology can be disconcerting, in part because he refers to the Baroque and the classical as if they occurred simultaneously, even as if they were identical. For Adán, the Baroque, the classical, and the Romantic are not simply literary styles, but forms of being, methods of assessing discourse and reality. Thus a Baroque sensibility can be expressed in a classical style, or a classical perspective articulated in a Baroque manner, or, as was frequently the case, Romantic views can find their expression in fundamentally Baroque modes.

On the Baroque in Peru contains an enormous wealth of ideas, interpretations, and speculations, along with uncommon and daring statements expressed in—of course—a Baroque style. Though the impact of Martín Adán's critical work has largely been confined to Peru, his thought deserves to be recognized as one of Latin America's most original contributions to understanding the region's artistic and cultural heritage. He died in Lima in 1985.

The selection is translated by Isabel Bastos and Marvin Liberman from *De lo barroco en el Perú* (Lima: Universidad Nacional Mayor de San Marcos, 1968), 375, 381, 383. Reproduced by permission of the Sociedad de Beneficencia de Lima Metropolitana.

From De lo barroco en el Perú (1968) [On the Baroque in Peru]

Romanticism could have no better place to fully develop if it had, in fact, encountered a Hispanic America that was a single peaceful and sophisticated nation. Indomitable natures, consummate despotism, an imperial tradition, the presence of poverty everywhere, all were ideal to produce Romantic outcomes. Nonetheless there lacked a competent human subject. The canonical norms and Aristotelian doctrine remained the trophies of colonial culture, and the reading of the Encyclopédie, with its enormous collection of raw material, simply ended up confusing [the] mechanical and literal mind of the cultivated son of the colonial world. In the course of the republic, we will realize that liberty does not become a new awareness of life, but is instead only a version of a new concept; that around it, things continue to be ordered by an old-fashioned human gullibility, that the question is dealt with in polite academia and that it is suppressed violence or the resistance of the oppressed that must bring order to the opposing strata and to *mestizajes* [mixed-race peoples], while the colonial bourgeoisie, presumably a model for discernment and a source of power, decays away, exhausted and wounded by its own convulsive symptoms.

Because I care, what I am trying to do is to establish and celebrate national continuity, in its superior expressive forms, attributed to a dominant social class, originating in the colonial period and struggling to become cultivated and to protect itself in the shadow of the Republic. It has been said, unreasonably, but not without reason, that the colonial period left hardly any structure and that the colonial spirit is nothing but an embrace of those structures when they are tangible: obsessive sensuality, barren selfishness. I believe—passionately—that the essential colonial order, Catholic and hierarchical, even with its material flaws and its enduring complications, has always functioned according to everlasting ideals; that it made possible our present; that it still nourishes us in our surest goals. If it is true that colonial literature was barren aesthetically, it is also true that, in a critical way, it collaborated decisively in creating and maintaining larger categories and essential forms; and that its poverty derives from that of the historical model—disfigured, odd and unavoidable. Even so, it is obvious that in republican literature the critical innovations were not modified forms, but the revelation of new purposes. The classicism of our most important writers of the last century is based their social status and political opinions, and it only brings them to an inner self and empty gestures of a supposedly romantic pursuit of liberal doctrines and an expressive life. This false and imitative Romanticism prolonged Góngora's style making its difficulties only more subtle, abstract and just bad.

Doubtless the best American literature, the most realistic and truthful, is one that reorganizes, that establishes, that moves away from truisms and returns to expressive style, in short, a classic. A good *writer in a classic sense* is the one who best handles the most recent techniques, the one who knows how to distinguish between topics and expression, who captures the best from what is immediate and then brings it back in an indelible, intelligible way, like Espinosa Medrano.[4] Although today we believe that we really do understand *El Lunarejo*—[Espinosa Medrano], someone might argue that the book is disorganized, and someone else will argue against that perception, and that defense would be legitimate and supported by time. In *La apología de don Luis de Góngora*, the *indiano* was indeed employing an organizing hermeneutics, an acknowledgement of the imperial origins of our Góngora style, a compromise with the sacred art through scholasticism, a confirmation of the excellence of the summarized statement and the nobility of Polyphemus's anguish. *El*

---

4   JUAN DE ESPINOSA MEDRANO is considered the major proponent of Gongorismo in America and the first literary critic in Spanish America. See chapter 3 of this anthology.

Lunarejo guesses that the truth is, naturally, convention; that sincerity is, in essence, form; that Góngora's gongoresqueness includes the Arab spirit, which provoked a gothic expansion of the immortal blood of the mestizo Spanish Goth; that it removes the sour taste for all things Italian; that it lends humanity to academic Platonism, genuine life and death, spirit and flesh, disillusion and destiny. Spain, diverse and unique, African and Romantic, brutal and ascetic, Catholic and Jewish, covetous and generous, Roman, almost Carthaginian, enters in Góngora's poetry with the most delicate respect for the Renaissance, the flower of the Gothic [. . .]

[W]ith the fall of the Society of Jesus in the Indies, mainly in the Andes, the last possibility disappeared for maintaining an understanding of the world in the Colonial period and thus for establishing the American Baroque, for an all-embracing reconciliation, for an authentic Catholicism, for a productive idealism, all of which were indispensable for the Cesarean birth [of the republics]. The politics of Ignatius of Loyola, which were suitable for world government, were predestined and had enormous capacity to unify the form and the patience of America. So in the struggle for freedom, the Society was still present and active, with the Jesuits in exile, taking their belated revenge: the social body and the universal ideas did not help the liberators, instead, what helped them was their absent enemy, the shadow of Loyola—the sensualist, the mason, the romantic. Unfortunately, the noblest, most profound and firmest unifying force of the Indies, let us say the only one, is not present at the birth of the republics.

José Lezama Lima (1910–1976)

In 1927, the third centennial of the death of Luis de Góngora was celebrated throughout the Hispanic literary world. After two centuries of being deemed "in bad taste" or even "monstrous," Góngora's work was being reappraised by a new generation, sparking lively interest in the author and in the Baroque itself. Writers throughout Spain and Latin America began to realize their debt to this poet from Córdoba, Spain, and the artistic vitality of the style he espoused. More critically, they recognized ways to harness its aesthetic power in comprehending the modern world.

The revival of the Baroque in the twentieth century marked a renewed appreciation for its congruence with the Hispanic spirit. A neo-Góngoran style emerged in Hispanic poetry, producing notable poems like "Muerte sin fin" [Death without End] by the Mexican José Gorostiza, "El rayo que no cesa" [The Lightning That Never Ceases] by the Spaniard Miguel Hernández, and *El diván del Tamarit* [The Divan at Tamarit] by his countryman Federico García Lorca. Among the most accomplished of these writers was the Cuban José Lezama Lima, whose poetry spanned four decades, from *La muerte de Narciso* (1937) [Narciso's Death] through the posthumous *Fragmentos a su imán* (1978) [Magnetized Fragments].

Born in Havana, the son of an army colonel, Lezama Lima left his island home only once or twice, on a short excursion to Jamaica and perhaps a visit to Mexico. He studied law at the University of Havana, but his true vocation was literature. A voracious and eclectic reader, noted for his erudition, Lezama Lima became an active cultural advocate, founding several short-lived literary reviews in the 1930s and then the influential arts journal *Orígenes* (1944–1956), which published writers from around the world. Following the poetic and editorial credo of the Spanish poet Juan Ramón Jiménez, whom he greatly admired, Lezama Lima believed that the arts, and especially poetry, offered access to a superior level of consciousness. Lezama Lima also wrote two novels, *Paradiso* (1966), which won immediate international recognition, and its unfinished sequel, *Oppiano Licario* (1979). Lezama Lima's poetic skills transferred to his prose, producing a subtle and evocative Spanish.

While Lezama Lima's poetry and fiction provide outstanding examples of the practice of twentieth-century Baroque, his collection of essays *La expresión americana* (1957) [American Expression] superbly lays out the sources of that resurgent style—both its historical presence in Latin America and its profound resonance with the region's culture. As Lezama Lima takes pains to explain in this selection, the Baroque was not a decadent Spanish style—as was often asserted in the eighteenth and nineteenth centuries. Traditionally associated with the Counter-Reformation, the Baroque was a rebellious, vital, and flamboyant style; and while, in Spain, it was associated with an opposition to the austere aesthetics of Protestantism, in Spanish America, it emerged as a vehicle of resistance to the conquest. As Lezama Lima suggests, the Baroque was the style of "counter-Conquest," a mode adopted by the Indians, the mestizos, and the creoles as a challenge to Spanish dominance as these emerging cultures developed their own unique cultural forms, modes of thought, and points of view. The tension and rupture implicit in the Baroque is thus perfectly adapted to these historical contexts, creating new wholes, ultimately reuniting what it tears apart and melting down what it fragments.

In addition to his reflections on the Baroque as a style, Lezama Lima attempts to explain how the Latin American spirit is defined by these reconsiderations of the past. By exploring the past, Lezama Lima discerns new paths for the future, or what he calls "futurity," a process of looking back to see ahead that models the Spanish American mission of identity in the twentieth century: recapturing the past to define the frontiers of the future.

Like his contemporaries, OCTAVIO PAZ and Julio Cortázar, Lezama Lima also helped bring Latin American writing and thought onto an international stage. For many years, he worked with Cuba's National Cultural Council, though the publication of *Paradiso*, with its daringly homoerotic scenes, earned the disfavor of the Castro regime and harassment by government censors. Already too famous to repress, Lezama Lima remained in Havana until his death, Cuba's most highly regarded writer, continuing to sponsor and protect other young talented writers.

The selection is translated by Isabel Bastos and Marvin Liberman, from the essay "La curiosidad barroca" in *La expresión americana y otros ensayos* (Montevideo: Arca Editorial, 1969), 30–35. Reproduced by permission of Agencia Literaria Latinoamericana.

From La curiosidad barroca (1957) [The Baroque Curiosity]

Our evaluation of the American Baroque will highlight three points: first, a fundamental tension shapes the Baroque; second, there is within the Baroque a plutonic force,[5] an original fire breaking up and reunifying fragments; third, rather than being a degenerative style, it is prolific and productive, serving in Spain and in Spanish America—perhaps uniquely—as an enrichment of language; indeed, the Baroque furnishes our homes, offers us modes of life and curiosity, reveals a mysticism that unfolds new methods of prayer, provides ways of savoring and handling delicacies, which exhale a complete, refined and mysterious life-force—theocratic and self-conscious—of ever-changing forms and deeply rooted essences.

Adapting Weisbach's[6] phrase to the case of Hispanic America, we can say that for us the Baroque was an art of the counter-conquest. It represents a triumph of the city, inhabited by a satisfied American living out a normal

---

5   Plutonism, or vulcanism, is a geological theory proposing that continual volcanic activity forms the earth's layers.
6   Werner Weisbach (1873–1953), a Swiss professor of art history, contributed to an early twentieth-century re-evaluation of the Baroque style. He was one of the first to write an analysis of Italian Mannerism.

course of life and death. It is a monk, pursuing the bounteous subtleties of theology; an Indian, poor or rich; a master of sumptuous Latin; a captain of rhythmic idleness; a farmer with repeated complaints, an aimless solitude in the heart; all of these begin to weave a web, wandering through the poor quarters like friendly shadows, a prototype, a distinctively American figure, like a plumb line in his seriousness and fate. The first American that begins to dominate these riches is our Lord Baroque; with the lovingly worn spine of his Dutch copy of Ronsard, with his thick volume of the Mantuan Swan [Virgil], his surreptitious and risqué poems by Góngora or Polo de Medina,[7] like a Gongorist sonnet cast in silver or a Quevedian sonnet with its ribcage prison. Before resting from this idleness, a cup of fine chocolate, a gift for the sternly paternal bishopric, is consumed with Cartesian caution, just to prevent gout, that purple peril. And now sitting in the concave armchair of the *oidor*,[8] he [the Lord Baroque] observes an apparition of the *sans culottes* in slow, gray waves, true and eternal.

That American Lord Baroque, our first authentic settler on his estate, with his sinecure or inherited house, this poverty that amplifies the pleasures of the intelligence appears just when the commotion of the conquest and the colonizer's parceling of the landscape all receded. He is the man who goes to the lookout, who slowly dusts the sand from the all-consuming mirror, and who lingers beside the moonlit waterfall constructed in the dream of his own making. Language, when savored, braids and proliferates itself; relishing one's life fills the mind and rouses fervor. Enjoying and savoring were the first acts of this American lord: like a carefully studded artifact, if a single stud is removed, it shrieks and goes out of tune. His life becomes transformed into a giant, subtle ear, in the corner of a very spacious room, disentangling intricate confusions and unfolding simple solutions; this room, a *galpón*, which, as the Inca Garcilaso reports, is a word from the Windward Islands. "The Inca kings had such big rooms," says the same Garcilaso, "that they were used as plazas in which to have their festivities when it was raining." That lord demands only one space: his great living room, where there is singing, with all the chandeliers multiplying their ignis fatuus in the mirrors, and out of which death emerges with her cowbells, her procession of oxen, and her blankets absorbing the mournful dampness of the Venetian mirrors.

---

7   Salvador Jacinto Polo de Medina (1603–1676), Spanish poet and one of the best followers of Góngora, thus considered one of the greatest inventors of the Spanish Baroque.

8   Spanish for "judge," but literally a "hearer."

If we contemplate one of the church interiors of Juli and the façades of the Puno Cathedral in Peru,[9] they reveal a certain tension. Amongst the luxuriant arcs of the trefoils, of emblems reminiscent of the distant Inca, of braided rosettes, of niches like seaside grottos, we soon perceive that the effort to arrive at some unified form is disrupted by a tension, an impulse, perhaps not the verticality of the Gothic, but a thrust toward some symbolic purpose. In the Basilica of the Rosary in Puebla,[10] where this Lord Baroque can feel quite comfortable, the whole interior, the walls and the columns, are a relentless surging of ornamentation without pause or any spatial parenthesis. There, too, we perceive this tension, as if amidst that abundant Nature, as if amidst the absorption of a forest by the unfriendly stone, amidst that Nature that seems at once to rebel and to recuperate, the Lord Baroque wanted to create a measure of order but one embracing everybody and everything, an impossible feat where all the vanquished could maintain the requirements of their pride and their profligacy.

In addition to that inherent tension there is a plutonism that burns the fragments and compels them, transformed, towards their destined end. In those remarkable works by the [Quechua] Indian [José] Kondori, from whose creative fires, contemporary architects—in their arrogant banality—could learn a great deal, one observes the introduction of an audacious wonder: the *Indiátide*. On the façade of San Lorenzo of Potosí,[11] among the emergent angels, from the dangling leaves of granite, from the keystones, navigating like galleys through the carved stone, there appears, sumptuous, hieratic, an Inca princess, full of native power and royal disdain. In a closed theological world, with so much of its divine fury still deriving from the medieval, that figure, that fearless stone, obliged to become symbolic, has caused all of these elements to blaze forth so that the Indian princess can walk forth amidst an entourage of praise and reverence.

That Baroque of ours, that we locate from the end of the seventeenth century through the eighteenth, behaves as a steadfast friend of the Enlightenment; on occasion, relying on Cartesian scientific ideas, the Baroque even anticipates the Enlightenment. The five hundred controversial volumes that Sor Juana kept in her cell, increased to four thousand by the excessive admiration of Father [Diego] Calleja [her first biographer]; many "precious and exquisite mathematical and musical instruments"; her skillful handling of the fifth part

---

9   The Jesuit Church of Santa Cruz of Jerusalem in the town of Juli and the Basilica of St. Carlos Borromeo in Puno.

10   Lezama is misremembering the Chapel of the Rosary in Puebla, which is not, in fact, a basilica.

11   The façade is attributed to Kondori.

of the *Discourse on Method* in her *First Dream*; her knowledge of the *Ars Magna* [The Great Art] of Kircherio (1671),[12] that returns to the old [medieval] compendia of the learning of an epoch; all of that takes her Baroque toward a thirst for universal, scientific knowledge, which brings her closer to the Enlightenment. Likewise, in the friend of the Hieronymite nun, Don Carlos Sigüenza y Góngora, the language and the hunger for physics and astronomy sparkled like Juno's tail. Sigüenza y Góngora—an extraordinarily sympathetic figure, of unrelenting curiosity and profligate by nature, a womanizing priest—unites the most sophisticated, flamboyant style with the most careful scientific approach. With their surprising titles, his *Philosophical Manifesto against the Comets* and his *Libra Astronómica* do not disappoint in their innovative poetic language coupled with the thirst for understanding physics and the laws of nature, going well beyond nature, to the point of being tempted to its domination, as for Doctor Faust himself.

Those "marvels of the new world" first seen by the conqueror reappear in this amazing "cabinet of physics" owned by these Baroque lords of the Enlightenment. When Gracián[13] remembers the Salastano Palace, he recalls Brazil's crystalized delicacies, as he says, mixing the charms of Seneca's essences with a floury crust, realistic, bursting with immediacy. Not only in its proximity to the Enlightenment has our Baroque defined itself so effectively, but also in the paradise constructed by the Jesuits in Paraguay, which tried to be a *falansterio*.[14] With these missions, our Baroque was returned to an innocence, which placed it at a pure new beginning. And though in the Enlightenment, a Voltaire, a Diderot, seemed to ridicule that work by the Society of Jesus, in the Jesuit spirit can be seen their mockery of both: the Jesuit Fathers Sejee and Poré,[15] both mocked Voltaire in their mastery of the humanities, as well as Diderot in his Encyclopédie. But before examining the new paradise, let us talk about the subtlety of the stories that heralded and revealed it.

In their Hispanic echoes of Gongorism, we realize that neither Bernardo Soto de Rojas,[16] with his unhurried pleasure and his prolonged voluptuousness, manages to capture the crackling, the metallic fire of Don Luis [de Góngora], forcing Góngora to walk through numerous doors and fruit-bearing

---

12 Athanasius Kircher (1602–1680), a German Jesuit scholar.
13 Baltasar Gracián y Morales (1601–1658) was a Spanish Jesuit writer of the Baroque.
14 The phalanstery was a utopian community, a concept of communal living.
15 Gabriel François Le Jay and Charles Porée were French Jesuits of the eighteenth century.
16 Pedro Soto de Rojas (1584–1658) was a poet who imitated Góngora's style. His friend and another poetic follower of Góngora was Francisco de Trillo y Figueroa (1618–1680), who wrote the prologue to one of Soto de Rojas's books. Polo de Medina (1603–1676) was another Baroque poet influenced by Góngora.

gates and dissipating [Soto de Rojas's] intentions; nor does [Francisco de] Trillo y Figueroa capture the dilettante sonnet, the magic is not ripe; while Polo de Medina, lingering for a short time in the myrtle of Murcia, surrenders to the somber apologues of Quevedo. It is in America where Góngora's project regarding life and poetry—of crackling forms, of a plutonist content that attacks all forms as up against the executioner's wall—reappears in the Colombian Don Hernando Domínguez Camargo. The same frenzy, the same wild thrust, the same disdain for what commoners consider bad taste. "What is intoxicating in bad taste," Baudelaire tells us, "is the aristocratic pleasure of being unpleasant." [. . .]

More than voluptuousness, more than a delight in Cordovan charms and in the crystallized fruits of Granada, in Hernández Camargo, Gongorism assumes a very American manifestation, appearing as a craving for frenzied innovation, for defiant rebellion, for wild pride. All of this leads him to devilish excesses, in order to achieve, like an authentic Gongorist, an excess even more excessive than that of Don Luis [de Góngora], intending to destroy the very element that he employs in trying to domesticate a verbal style that is already in itself fertile and bold.

Octavio Paz (1914–1998)

Octavio Paz is Mexico's iconic poet and intellectual of the twentieth century, a towering figure in all Hispanic literature. Though he hoped to be remembered as a poet, he himself predicted that only a few of his poems would survive, hopefully including his masterful *Piedra de sol* [Sun Stone] (1957). Instead, Paz wrote essays, which are indeed among the finest written in Spanish, especially *El laberinto de la soledad* (1950) [The Labyrinth of Solitude], which, after 1970, included a postscript, "Postdata," also known as "Return to the Labyrinth of Solitude."

Paz was a native of Mexico City. He developed his passion for literature in the extensive library of his paternal grandfather, a respected political journalist. Octavio Paz's father was a lawyer and a supporter of Emiliano Zapata during the Mexican Revolution (1910–1917). Paz published his first volume of poems, *Luna Silvestre*, in 1933; and a visit to the United States in 1943 deepened the influence of Anglo-American Modernism on his poetry. Two years later, he joined the Mexican diplomatic corps, serving in several positions, notably in France and as ambassador to India in 1962. Paz was an influential cultural critic, and he founded and edited a number of important literary journals, including *Taller* (1938) [Workshop] and *Vuelta*

(1976) [Return]. After leaving the diplomatic service in 1968, he went first to Paris and later to Mexico City, where he became the central figure in many cultural and even political activities. He lectured all over the world, including at Harvard University, while continuing to publish poetry and essays. He won the Nobel Prize for Literature in 1990 and died in 1998 in Mexico City.

Paz began writing his critical commentary on Mexican identity, *The Labyrinth of Solitude*, in postwar France. There was already a solid current of thought on the topic, notably Samuel Ramos's *El perfil del hombre y la cultura en México* (1934) [A Profile of Man and Culture in Mexico]. A contemporary group, known as Hiperión, was also producing a number of works on Mexican identity, including *Los grandes momentos del indigenismo en México* (1950) [Great Moments of the Indigenous Movement in México] by Luis Villoro; *Análisis del ser del mexicano* (1952) [An Analysis of Mexican Being] by Emilio Uranga; and the posthumously published *La fenomenología del relajo*[17] (1966) [The Phenomenology of Relaxation] by Jorge Portilla. What distinguishes Paz's text is his admirably holistic vision of Mexican identity, fusing the grand sweep of the historical—from preconquest to the 1910 revolution—with luminous transhistorical characteristics.

The Labyrinth of Solitude is divided into four parts. The first section is a reflection on "Pachucos"—youthful Mexican immigrants to the United States who sought to assert their native identity even as they integrated themselves into a different society. Building on Ramos's insight that Mexicans experienced a persistent psychological sense of inferiority, Paz suggests that one source of that inferiority complex was the historic encounter between Mexican Catholicism and U.S. Protestantism. Defined by very unequal economic and political power, these two Christian traditions offered quite distinctive perspectives on life and death, as well as on the relationship between the individual and the community.

The second section covers a number of characteristics, in an effort to isolate the most essential Mexican social attitudes. One of these is the mask; intrinsic to many Indian ceremonies, the mask also provides a means of concealment, a way to disguise identity and emotion. Paz also singles out

---

17 *La fenomenología del relajo* [The Phenomenology of the Relajo] by Jorge Portilla gathers essays published between 1948 and 1962, reprinted posthumously in 1966. *Relajo* has no English equivalent, but in Mexico the term describes a moment of shared enthusiasm that shifts between disorder and amusement. *Echar relajo* means to have fun, but the pleasure could turn chaotic, disorderly, excessive, or even violent. Portilla sees the Mexican *relajo* as a form of nihilism, that is, as a lack of values, a denial of values or a rejection of any meaning in social conduct.

the "historic trauma" of the sexual encounter between conquistadors and Indian women—a harrowing occurrence that many historians and anthropologists have labeled massive rape. La Malinche represents this ambivalent memory: an Indian woman, who by force or necessity, collaborated with the conquistadors, becoming CORTÉS's sexual partner and the mother of at least one of his sons. This uneasy relationship gave La Malinche mythic status as the mother of the first mestizo, a quality that became essential to the Mexican character. But symbolically the actions of La Malinche reflect a more negative dimension, Mexican submission to foreigners. As the original *chingada*—raped woman—La Malinche inspired some of Paz's most beautiful prose, seamlessly combining elements of history, psychology, and poetry.

The third section of *Labyrinth* surveys Mexican history from the conquest to the 1940s. Paz interprets this past as positivist stages in the growth of an individual. But instead of applying the usual positivist phases (theological, philosophical, and positivist)—as GABINO BARREDA might have done—Paz adopts the midcentury ideologies of Freudian psychology, phenomenology, and Hegelianism to describe the search for a national identity. Paz viewed the revolution as the culmination of that quest, when Mexicans entered modernity to become finally "self-conscious," or "contemporary of all men." Concluding this section at the end of World War II, Paz construed many global trends quite accurately, and his analysis, even seventy years after the war's end, has not lost its initial brilliance.

The final section turns from an examination of Mexican identity to a surrealist reflection on eroticism, a notion that also became central to his best poem: *Piedra de sol*.

Paz's concept of Mexican identity remains deeply contradictory, in part because he himself could never abandon his position as a Mexican Creole, proudly untainted by Indian blood. His Eurocentric perspective on Indian culture borders on racism, particularly in *Postdata*. Paz roots his explanation of the violence in Mexico, for example, in Aztec human sacrifice, and in general finds nothing original or creative about Indian culture or art. His continuing ambivalence about Indians is only underlined by his evident respect for Emiliano Zapata as marking a return to genuine community.

The first excerpt here is taken from the second part of *The Labyrinth of Solitude*. Paz brilliantly interprets death in Mexican life and culture, though he bases his comments on a misreading of a popular phrase from the Mexican Revolution: "If they're going to kill me tomorrow, let them kill me right away." This expression reflects the sentiment of prisoners facing execution, but it refers, not—as Paz suggests—to their indifference to life, but rather to a desire to choose the moment of their deaths themselves, rather than allow the executioner such control. Paz could never fully appreciate the vital passions that had precipitated the revolution, and instead faulted that pivotal moment as lacking a "clear ideology"—as if any social movement required well-defined principles to become transformative.

The second excerpt, from the "post-scriptum," recounts Paz's reaction to the notorious massacre of Tlatelolco on October 2, 1968, when the Mexican army disrupted a student-led protest shortly before the Olympics, killing hundreds of citizens. Paz connects these events with the ancient pyramid of Tlatelolco, situated near the Plaza de las Tres Culturas where the protests occurred. By associating the massacre with the sacrificial rituals once performed on that site, Paz rejects both the violence of the government (which led him to resign from the diplomatic service) and that barbaric Indian past, represented by the goddess COATLICUE. For Paz, that famous sculpture is not even art, but only an expression of the bloody spirit of Aztec religion.

The first excerpt from *The Labyrinth of Solitude* by Octavio Paz, and the second and third, from *Postada* (in English, The Other Mexico), are compiled in *The Labyrinth of Solitude and Other Writings* by Octavio Paz, translated by Lysander Kemp, Yara Milos, and Rachel Phillips Belash (New York: Grove Press, 1985), 57–59, 298–300, 306–8. Copyright © 1961 by Grove Press Inc. Used by permission of Grove/Atlantic, Inc. Any third-party use of this material, outside of this publication, is prohibited.

From El laberinto de la soledad (1950) [The Labyrinth of Solitude]

Death also lacks meaning to the modern Mexican. It is no longer a transition, an access to another life more alive than our own. But although we do not view death as a transcendence, we have not eliminated it from our daily lives. The word death is not pronounced in New York, in Paris, in London, because it burns the lips. The Mexican, in contrast, is familiar with death, jokes about it, caresses it, sleeps with it, celebrates it; it is one of his favorite toys and his most steadfast love. True, there is perhaps as much fear in his attitude as in that of others, but at least death is not hidden away: he looks at it face to face, with impatience, disdain, or irony. "If they are going to kill me tomorrow, let them kill me right away."[18]

---

18 From the popular folk song La Valentina. [Trans. note] *Si me han de matar mañana, que me maten de una vez.* [Eds.]

The Mexican's indifference toward death is fostered by his indifference toward life. He views not only death but also life as nontranscendent. Our songs, proverbs, fiestas and popular beliefs show very clearly that the reason death cannot frighten us is that "life has cured us of fear." It is natural, even desirable, to die, and the sooner the better. We kill because life—our own or another's—is of no value. Life and death are inseparable, and when the former lacks meaning, the latter becomes equally meaningless. Mexican death is the mirror of Mexican life. And the Mexican shuts himself away and ignores both of them.

Our contempt for death is not at odds with the cult we have made of it. Death is present in our fiestas, our games, our loves and our thoughts. To die and to kill are ideas that rarely leave us. We are seduced by death. The fascination it exerts over us is the result, perhaps, of our hermit-like solitude and of the fury with which we break out of it. The pressure of our vitality, which can only express itself in forms that betray it, explains the deadly nature, aggressive or suicidal, of our explosions. When we explode we touch against the highest point of that tension, we graze the very zenith of life. And there, at the height of our frenzy, suddenly we feel dizzy: it is then that death attracts us.

Another factor is that death revenges us against life, strips it of all its vanities and pretensions and converts it into what it really is: a few neat bones and a dreadful grimace. In a closed world where everything is death, only death has value. But our affirmation is negative. Sugar-candy skulls, and tissue-paper skulls and skeletons strung with fireworks . . . our popular images always poke fun at life, affirming the nothingness and insignificance of human existence. We decorate our houses with death's heads. We eat bread in the shape of bones on the Day of the Dead, we love the songs and stories in which death laughs and cracks jokes, but all this boastful familiarity does not rid us of the question we all ask: What is death? We have not thought up a new answer. And each time we ask, we shrug our shoulders: Why should I care about death if I have never cared about life?

From Postada (1970) [The Other Mexico]

Critique of the Pyramid

The fact that the whole country was given the name of the city of its oppressors is one of the keys to the history of Mexico, her unwritten, unspoken history. The fascination that the Aztecs have exerted has been such that even their conquerors, the Spaniards, did not escape from it: when Cortés decided that the capital of the new kingdom would be built on the ruins of México-Tenochtitlán, he became the heir and successor of the Aztecs. Although the Conquest destroyed the indigenous world and built another and different one on its remains, there is an invisible thread of continuity between the ancient society and the new Spanish order: the thread of domination. That thread has not been broken: the Spanish viceroys and the Mexican presidents are the successors of the Aztec rulers.

If there has been a secret political continuity since the fourteenth century, is it any wonder that the unconscious basis of that continuity is the religious-political archetype of the ancient Mexicans: the pyramid, the implacable hierarchies, and, over all, the hierarch and the platform of sacrifices? When I speak of the unconscious basis of our idea of history and politics, I am thinking, not of those who govern, but of the governed. It is apparent that the Spanish viceroys were unaware of the mythology of the Mexicans, but their subjects were not, whether Indians, mestizos, or Creoles: all of them, naturally and spontaneously, saw the Spanish state as the continuation of Aztec power. This identification was not explicit and never assumed a rational form: it was something that was in the nature of things. Besides, the continuity between the Spanish viceroy and the Aztec lord, between the Christian capital and the ancient idolatrous city, was only one aspect of the idea that colonial society had of the pre-Columbian past. That continuity could also be seen in the realm of religion. The appearance of the Virgin of Guadalupe on the ruins of a shrine sacred to the goddess Tonantzin is the central example, but not the only one, of this relationship between the two worlds, the indigenous and the colonial. In The Divine Narcissus, an auto sacramental[19] by Sor Juana Inés de la Cruz, the ancient pre-Columbian religion, despite its bloody rites, is shown as a prefiguration of the arrival of Christianity in México. The Spaniards' historical model was imperial Rome: México-Tenochtitlán and, later, México City were simply reduced versions of the Roman archetype. Christian Rome prolonged, while rectifying, pagan Rome; in the same way, the new México City prolonged, rectified, and in the end affirmed the Aztec metropolis. Independence did not alter this conception radically: it was decided that the Spanish colonial period had been an interruption in Mexico's history and that, by freeing it from foreign domination, the country had re-established its liberties and resumed its traditions. From this point of view, independence was a kind of restoration.

---

19 The auto sacramental were allegorical dramas where a secular or pagan story represented religious ideas or states. A common practice was to Christianize classical mythological figures to represent Christian themes. They were performed mainly during Corpus Christi, a feast that reveres the presence of the body of Christ in the Eucharist (that is, in the sacrament of communion). The celebration of Corpus Christi does not have a fixed date.

This historical-juridical fiction consecrated the legitimacy of Aztec domination: México-Tenochtitlán was and is the origin and source of power. After independence the process of sentimental identification with the pre-Hispanic world became so important that following the Revolution it became one of the most notable characteristics of modern México. What has not been said is that the vast majority of Mexicans has made the Aztec point of view its own and has thus, without knowing it, strengthened the myth that is embodied in the pyramid and the sacrifice stone.

*   *   *

Our art critics wax ecstatic about the statue of Coatlicue, an enormous block of petrified theology. Have they ever *looked* at it? Pedantry and heroism, sexual puritanism and ferocity, calculation and delirium: a people made up of warriors and priests, astrologers and immolators. And of poets, too: that world of brilliant colors and somber passions was crisscrossed with lightning flashes of poetry. And in all the manifestations of that extraordinary and horrifying nation, from the astronomical myths to the poets' metaphors, from the daily rites to the priests' mediations, there is always the smell of blood, the obsessive reek of it. The Aztec year, like those wheels-of-torture circles that appear in the novels of Sade, was a circle of eighteen blood-soaked months, eighteen ceremonies, eighteen ways of dying: by arrows, by drowning, by beheading, by flaying . . . Dance and penitence.

What religious and social aberration caused a city as beautiful as México-Tenochtitlán—water, stone, and sky—to be the scene of a hallucinatory and funereal ballet? And what obfuscation of the spirit is responsible for that fact that no one among us—I am speaking, not of our outdated nationalists, but of our philosophers, historians, artists, poets—wishes to see and to admit that the Aztec world was one of history's aberrations? The case of the Aztecs is unique because their cruelty was the result of a system impeccably and implacably coherent, an irrefutable syllogism-dagger. That violence can be explained as a result of sexual puritanism, repression of the senses, and the crushing weight of religion; but what stuns and paralyzes the mind is the use of realistic means in the service of a metaphysic both rigorously rational and delirious, the insensate offering up of lives to a petrified concept. It was not the homicidal rage of Genghis Khan and Tamerlane nor the White Huns' intoxicated delight in killing and burning. Instead, the Mexicans are reminiscent of the Assyrians, and not only because of the splendor of their capital and the grandiose and liturgical nature of their slaughters: the Assyrians, too, were inheritors of a high culture and were equally partial to the truncated pyramid (the ziggurat). But the Assyrians were not theologues. In fact, the real rivals of the Aztecs are not to be found in the East at all but rather in the West, for only among ourselves has the alliance between politics and metaphysics been so intimate, so exacerbated, and so deadly: the inquisitions, the religious wars, and, above all, the totalitarian societies of the twentieth century. I do not presume, of course, to judge the Aztec world, and still less to condemn it. México-Tenochtitlán has disappeared, and what concerns me, as I gaze upon its fallen body, is not the problem of historical interpretation but the fact that we cannot contemplate the cadaver face to face: its phantasm inhabits us. For this reason I believe that a critique of México and its history—a critique resembling the therapeutics of the psychoanalysts—should begin by examining what the Aztec worldview meant and still means. The image of México as a pyramid is one viewpoint among many others equally possible: the viewpoint of what is on the platform at its top. It is the viewpoint of the ancient gods and of those who served them, the Aztec lords and priests. It is also that of their heirs and successors: the viceroys, the generals, the presidents. And, furthermore, it is the viewpoint of the vast majority, of the victims crushed by the pyramid or sacrificed on its platform-sanctuary. The critique of México begins with the critique of the pyramid.

In Context | Plaza de Tlatelolco, Mexico City

On October 2, 1968, shortly before the opening of the first Olympic Games ever to be held in Latin America, a peaceful demonstration against the policies of the Mexican government was being conducted in this square by students and community members. The army decided to break up the protest, firing on the crowds and blocking exits. According to eye-witnesses, between two hundred and four hundred people were killed in the chaos, and many more injured, although the government later claimed that deaths numbered only slightly more than thirty.

In the sixteenth century, the early Spaniards had built a church and a convent here on top of the ruins of an Aztec pyramid. In 1964, the Mexican government constructed a massive housing project for people of scarce resources. Thus the official name of the square, the Plaza of the Three Cultures: pre-Hispanic, colonial, and modern (fig. 7.1, 347).

This spot was also the inspiration for OCTAVIO PAZ's notion of a "substrate"—a subterranean indigenous presence in Mexican history. Just as the ruins of the pyramid—a place where human sacrifices likely occurred—lie beneath the square, PAZ saw in the Tlatelolco massacre a sym-

Figure 7.1. Plaza de Tlatelolco, Mexico City, Mexico. Photograph by Jennifer Saracino. By permission of the Instituto Nacional de Antropología e Historia.

bolic event, one congruent, according to him, with the history of Mexico, as if the modern massacre had been a reenactment of pre-Hispanic ritual deaths.

Ernesto "Che" Guevara (1928–1967)

"Che" Guevara is perhaps the most iconic Latin American figure of the twentieth century. Born to middle-class parents of Irish and Basque descent in Rosario, Argentina, Ernesto Guevara was the eldest of five children. His famous nickname, adopted later in life, is a common Argentine term for "buddy" or "friend." By the time of his execution at the hands of the Bolivian army in La Higuera, Che Guevara had played an unusual variety of historic roles in his short 39 years, including acting as a key figure in the Cold War between the United States and the Soviet Union.

An avid reader and enthusiastic athlete, Guevara studied medicine in Buenos Aires. In 1951, when he was twenty-three years old and about to graduate from medical school, he decided to take a trip with his friend Alberto Granado to see South America. They began the journey on a motorcycle, but when it stopped working, they resorted to various other types of transportation, taking them across the Andes from Argentina to Chile and along the Pacific coast. In Peru, the friends separated, and Che continued

Figure 7.2. Ernesto "Che" Guevara (1928–1967). Courtesy of the Cuban Heritage Collection, University of Miami Libraries, Coral Gables, Florida.

his travels alone. Relying on Guevara's travel notes as well as on Alberto Granado's recollections, the first portion of that famous trip became the subject of the film directed by Walter Salles, *The Motorcycle Diaries* (2004).

The two men's encounters with the harsh working conditions at the vast Anaconda copper mines and the dire poverty everywhere along the journey were transformative. These experiences, coupled with Guevara's understanding of Argentina's social and political conditions, sharpened his civic consciousness and determined his lifelong commitment to the oppressed and the poor. He completed his medical degree in 1953 and set out again, arriving in Guatemala at a moment that proved crucial both for him and for the country. President Jacobo Árbenz had begun implementing major land reforms in a pioneering effort to relieve the miserable conditions of the Guatemalan peasants, who were—not surprisingly—Indians. In 1954, Guevara witnessed the overthrow of Árbenz by members of the army, trained, organized, and funded by the CIA. Identified as part of the resistance, Guevara fled to Mexico, where another decisive experience occurred: his meeting with two young Cuban revolutionaries, first Raul and then Fidel Castro. The events in Guatemala clarified for Guevara the pernicious influence of the United States in Latin America, while the encounter with the Castro brothers provided an immediate channel for his outrage at these injustices.

Fidel Castro was by 1955 already an accomplished militant. As a law student in Havana, he had been involved in organizations dedicated to the removal of dictatorships throughout the Caribbean, including Rafael Trujillo in the Dominican Republic and General Fulgencio Batista in Cuba. On July 26, 1953, with a small group of comrades, Castro attacked the Moncada army barracks. The effort failed miserably and the few survivors, including the Castro brothers, were incarcerated. Six months later, trying to win popular support for the coming elections, Batista granted the rebels amnesty. Castro and some of his closest followers sought refuge in Mexico to continue the struggle. It was at that point that he met the remarkable Argentinian, Che Guevara.

Married to fellow activist Hilda Gadea and working as a doctor in Mexico City, Guevara began training with the Cuban revolutionaries as they prepared to invade the island and start a guerrilla war, which Castro believed was the only way to defeat Batista. In a flimsy boat, the guerrilla expedition of eighty-two men reached the Cuban swamps in early December 1956. Only a small number survived the army's assault, but the remnant escaped to the mountains and gradually regrouped. After two years of fighting, on January 1, 1959, the rebels triumphed, with Che Guevara leading the troops into Havana.

In the next few years, Che Guevara became one of the pillars of the revolution, serving as chief of appeals of the revolutionary tribunals that tried and often executed war criminals; as the supervisor of aggressive agrarian reform; as minister of industry; as a fervent supporter of literacy; as the director of education for the Cuban army; as finance minister and president of the National Bank (where he contemptuously authorized bills signed only "Che"); and as the preeminent spokesperson of the Cuban revolution throughout the world, including at the United Nations.

By 1965, having publicly criticized the U.S.S.R., Cuba's primary economic supporter, Che Guevara concluded that his mission in the Cuban revolution had ended, and he retreated from public life. Though few knew his whereabouts, he had in fact gone to the Congo to continue the struggle against dictatorships and injustice. But he soon became disillusioned with the lack of national resolve and the absence of Marxist guerrilla organizations. By this time, Guevara was also being actively pursued by CIA-backed troops as well as by mercenaries from South Africa, still the site of apartheid. Che Guevara disappeared again, though by 1966 it was known that he was fighting somewhere in Latin America. Guevara was actually in Bolivia, trying to organize a guerrilla resistance. But his efforts against the Bolivian government's offensive, supported by the CIA, fell short, in part because the Bolivian Communist Party failed to support him. By then, Che Guevara was reviled both by the United States for his outspoken criticism of capitalism as well as by the U.S.S.R., which believed that he had "abandoned Marxism."

Soon after Che first disappeared at the end of 1965, he composed a long letter, answering a question posed by the editor of Uruguay's *Marcha*, one of the most important magazines in Latin America at that time. Though Che said nothing new in this letter, he did reiterate two decisive points in his thinking: that both the creation of a "new man" and the formation of a new state could only occur through pedagogical institutions.

The new man—defined as honest, joined in solidarity with other human beings, hard working, and free—shares many characteristics with Rousseau's ideal. Rousseau also believed that the natural "man" would be recovered through new forms of education. These themes were likewise pillars in the thought of SIMÓN RODRÍGUEZ, FRANCISCO BILBAO, JOSÉ MARTÍ, and JOSÉ CARLOS MARIÁTEGUI.

Among these great figures of Latin American thought, Che most resembles JOSÉ MARTÍ, who shared his inexhaustible enthusiasm in fighting for justice, equality, and freedom. Like Martí, Che Guevara seemed called to martyrdom, or more aptly, had a clear appreciation of his need to be an example. Very few figures in the history of Spanish America have awakened popular fervor like Martí or Che Guevara. Other political figures, like Juan Domingo Perón or his wife Evita, generated reverent public enthusiasm, but both had political power. Neither Martí nor Che Guevara ever had any real personal or lasting authority. More important, both men are distinguished by never separating the emergence of a new humanity from a rigorous morality. No one else has spoken so eloquently and passionately about developing the values that would allow each man and each woman to reach their full potential. From the onset of modernity, beginning with the French Revolution, the true revolutionary dream has been not just to change society but to change human beings. Such a goal may be utopian or an unreachable dream, but it remains the enduring aspiration of true revolutionaries for the last several centuries: to retrieve an authentic human nature, to reclaim the goodness, the generosity, the ethics, the solidarity of humanity. Che Guevara did everything he could to realize that dream of human possibility. And while he failed in that aim, he did provide a memorable example of commitment. His life, and his death, will continue to serve as a beacon for all those who seek to make life better for all human beings.

The text is from *Che Guevara Speaks: Selected Speeches and Writings*, edited by George Lavan (New York: Grove Press, 1968), 132–35.

From Notes on Man and Socialism in Cuba (1965)

Guevara wrote "Notes for the Study of Man and Socialism in Cuba" in the form of a letter to Carlos Quijano, editor of *Marcha*, an independent radical weekly published in Montevideo, Uruguay. It bore the dateline "Havana, 1965." In addition to appearing in *Marcha*, it was printed by *Verde Olivo*, the magazine of the Cuban armed forces.

*   *   *

Socialism is young and has made errors. Many times revolutionaries lack the knowledge and intellectual courage needed to meet the task of developing the new man with methods different from the conventional ones—and the conventional methods suffer from the influences of the society which created them.

(Again we raise the theme of the relationship between form and content.)

Disorientation is widespread, and the problems of material construction preoccupy us. There are no artists of great authority who at the same time have great revolutionary authority. The men of the party must take this task to hand and seek attainment of the main goal, the education of the people.

But then they sought simplification. They sought an art that would be understood by everyone—the kind of "art" *functionaries* understand. True artistic values were disregarded, and the problem of general culture was reduced to taking some things from the socialist present and some from the dead past (since dead, not dangerous). Thus Socialist Realism arose upon the foundations of the art of the last century.

But the realistic art of the nineteenth century is also a class art, more purely capitalist perhaps than this decadent art of the twentieth century which reveals the anguish of alienated man. In the field of culture capitalism has given all that it had to give, and nothing of it remains but the offensive stench of a decaying corpse, today's decadence in art.

Why then should we try to find the only valid prescription for art in the frozen forms of Socialist Realism? We cannot counterpose the concept of Socialist Realism to that of freedom because the latter does not yet exist and will not exist until the complete development of the new society. Let us not attempt, from the pontifical throne of realism-at-any-cost, to condemn all the art forms which have evolved since the first half of the nineteenth century for we would then fall into the Proudhonian mistake of returning to the past, of putting a straitjacket on the artistic expression of the man who is being born and is in the process of making himself.

What is needed is the development of an ideological-cultural mechanism which permits both free inquiry and the uprooting of the weeds which multiply so easily in the fertile soil of state subsidies.

In our country we don't find the error of mechanical realism, but rather its opposite, and that is so because the need for the creation of a new man has not been understood, a new man who would represent neither the ideas of the nineteenth century nor those of our own decadent and morbid century.

What we must create is the man of the twenty-first century, although this is still a subjective and not a realized aspiration. It is precisely this man of the next century who is one of the fundamental objectives of our work; and to the extent that we achieve concrete successes on a theoretical plane—or, vice versa, to the extent we draw theoretical conclusions of a broad character on the basis of our concrete research—we shall have made an important contribution to Marxism-Leninism, to the cause of humanity.

Reaction against the man of the nineteenth century has brought us a relapse into the decadence of the twentieth century; it is not a fatal error, but we must overcome it lest we open a breach for revisionism.

The great multitudes continue to develop; the new ideas continue to attain their proper force within society; the material possibilities for the full development of all members of society make the task much more fruitful. The present is a time for struggle: the future is ours.

To sum up, the fault of our artists and intellectuals lies in their original sin: They are not truly revolutionary. We can try to graft the elm tree so that it will bear pears, but at the same time we must plant pear trees. New generations will come who will be free of the original sin. The probabilities that great artists will appear will be greater to the degree that the field of culture and the possibilities for expression are broadened.

Our task is to prevent the present generation, torn asunder by its conflicts, from becoming perverted and from perverting new generations. We must not bring into being either docile servants of official thought, or scholarship students who live at the expense of the state—practicing "freedom." Already there are revolutionaries coming who will sing the song of the new man in the true voice of the people. This is a process which takes time.

In our society the youth and the party play an important role.

The former is especially important because it is the malleable clay from which the new man can be shaped without any of the old faults. The youth is treated in accordance with our aspirations. Its education steadily grows more full, and we are not forgetting about its integration into the labor force from the beginning. Our scholarship students do physical work during their vacations or along with their studying. Work is a reward in some cases, a means of education in others, but it is never a punishment. A new generation is being born.

The party is a vanguard organization. The best workers are proposed by their fellow workers for admission into it. It is a minority, but it has great authority because of the quality of its cadres. Our aspiration is that the party will become a mass party, but only when the masses have reached the level of the vanguard, that is, when they are educated for communism.

Our work constantly aims at this education. The party is the living example; its cadres should be teachers of hard work and sacrifice. They should lead the masses by their deeds to the completion of the revolutionary task which involves years of hard struggle against the difficulties of construction, class enemies, the sicknesses of the past, imperialism . . .

Rodolfo Walsh (1927–1977)

The Argentine writer, journalist, and political activist Rodolfo Walsh—born in Choeke-Choel in the Province of Río Negro—always lived on the edge. When his parents, both of Irish descent, fell on hard times, he was sent to Buenos Aires, where Walsh attended a Catholic boarding school run by Irish priests for three years. He later re-created that oppressive environment— with refreshing humor—in the short stories of *Los oficios terrestres* (1965) [Earthly Skills]. After a series of jobs in publishing, including proofreading, Walsh found his vocation as a journalist. He worked for several magazines in Buenos Aires and later in Cuba for the press agency, Prensa Latina. But his real work was investigative reporting, deployed as a weapon in the fight against political oppression—a path that would ultimately lead to his assassination in 1977.

Walsh excelled at investigative journalism. His *Operación masacre* (1957)

Figure 7.3. Eva Perón
(1919–1952). Archivo
General de la Nación
(Argentina).

[Operation Massacre] is the first example of a nonfiction novel, preceding by nine years Truman Capote's famous *In Cold Blood* (1966). *Operation Massacre* examines the clandestine executions of workers in trash dumps near the José León Suarez neighborhood of northern Buenos Aires in 1956. The victims were suspected of being involved in a failed coup against the de facto government of Pedro Eugenio Aramburu (1955–1958) that overthrew Juan Perón in 1955. The characters of the story are the murder victims, one of whom actually survived and told his story to Walsh. In an interview, Walsh later explained that he wrote *Operación masacre* "so that it would act," that is, so that his words would incriminate the guilty. Walsh was quite conscious of the power that this genre possessed, particularly in its ability to denounce political crimes. He published several other pieces, including *¿Quién mató a Rosendo?* (1969) [Who Killed Rosendo?] and *El caso Satanovsky* (1973) [The Satanovsky Case].

Rodolfo Walsh's fiction and his life as a fighter against oppression, especially of the working class, run along close parallel lines. Walsh's fiction consistently reflects the realities of his life—its political contexts, the abuses of power, the world of criminals—presented from an experiential point of view, either as a political observer or an investigative journalist. The short story "Esa mujer" (1965) [That Woman] is a compelling example of these parallels. The story consists of a dialogue between a reporter and a drunken colonel involved in the disappearance of a woman's corpse. "Esa mujer" can be read solely as macabre fiction, or as informed by an actual occurrence in 1955, when the embalmed body of Eva Perón was stolen by military officers in the coup that forced Juan Domingo Perón into exile. Walsh brilliantly links fiction and historical events so that they merge for the reader. The text stands alone as fiction, since it makes no reference to Evita; but for knowledgeable readers, the story is deepened by its historical contexts. Walsh differentiates himself from Borges by not challenging the categories of fiction and nonfiction *within* the story, but rather by juxtaposing these categories as a coincident in the text. Such juxtapositions are also anticipated in Walsh's early detective stories, where various versions of reality are proposed until one emerges as acceptable. In *Variaciones en rojo* (1953) [Variations in Red], for example, the murder scenes are interpreted and reinterpreted by inspector Jiménez and his friend, Daniel Hernández, until one version (typically Hernández's) solves the mystery.

Especially in the 1970s (a decade of military dictatorships), writers in Latin America were rarely able to negotiate the dual roles of writer and political activist. Walsh is unusual in having been able to integrate these functions; for him, good writing *is* political activism. As Walsh says, his writings "act." The truth of that statement was demonstrated in the final years of his life. Though both of Walsh's daughters became actively involved in political resistance, in 1976, his elder daughter, María Victoria, died in a gun battle with military forces, a result of her involvement in protests over the ongoing disappearance of Argentine citizens. Though heartbroken, Walsh himself never stopped his own activism—his writing. On March 24, 1977, the day before his own murder—in broad daylight on the streets of Buenos Aires—Walsh had just mailed his last newsletter, "Carta abierta de un escritor a la Junta Militar" [Open Letter from a Writer to the Military Junta], articulating the vulnerability of dictatorships to a powerful pen. The next day, he was murdered. His body has never been recovered. Like all those whose unjust deaths he fought so hard to prevent and expose, Rodolfo

Walsh himself remains among the disappeared, *los desaparecidos*, those whose lives were taken by the military dictatorship. But his words continue to act for justice. "Esa Mujer" [That Woman] by Rodolfo Walsh, translated by Cindy Schuster, originally appeared in *Prose Tangos*, a special issue of the online journal *Words without Borders*, February 2004. Translation of "Esa Mujer," from the collection *Los oficios terrestres* (Editorial Jorge Álvarez, 1967; Ediciones de la Flor, 1986). Translation © 2006 by Cindy Schuster. By permission of *Words without Borders* (www.wordswithoutborders.org). All rights reserved."

That Woman (1965)

The Colonel compliments me on my punctuality:

"You're a punctual man, like the Germans," he says.

"Or the English."

The Colonel has a German surname.

He is a corpulent, graying man, with a broad, tanned face.

"I've read your work," he advances. "I congratulate you."

As he serves two generous shots of whisky, he informs me, casually, that he worked in intelligence for twenty years, that he studied humanities, that he takes an interest in art. He doesn't dwell on anything, he simply establishes the terrain on which we can operate, a vague zone of common ground.

From the picture window of his tenth-floor apartment you can see the twilit city, the pallid lights of the river. From here it is easy, if only for a moment, to love Buenos Aires. But it is not any conceivable form of love that has brought us together.

The Colonel is looking for some names, some papers I might have.

I am looking for a dead woman, a point on the map. It's not an investigation yet, it's barely even a fantasy: the kind of twisted fantasy certain people would suspect me of concocting.

The day will come (I think in moments of anger) when I will go in search of her. She means nothing to me, but even so I will pursue the mystery of her death, track down the distant graveyard where her remains lie slowly rotting. If I find her, fresh swells of rage, fear, and thwarted love will surge up; powerful, vengeful waves, and for a moment I will no longer feel alone, I will no longer feel like a wretched, bitter, forgotten shadow.

The Colonel knows where she is.

He moves easily around the ornately furnished flat, adorned with ivories and bronzes, delicate Meissen china and Cantonese porcelain. He smiled before the forged Jongkind,[20] the dubious Figari.[21] I imagine the look on his face if I were to tell him who fabricates the Jongkinds, but I compliment his whisky instead.

He drinks vigorously, robustly, enthusiastically, happily, haughtily, contemptuously. His expression alters from one moment to the next, as he slowly turns the glass in his beefy hands.

"Those papers," he says.

I look at him.

"*That woman,* Colonel."

He smiles.

"Everything is interconnected," he says philosophically.

A shard is missing from the base of a Viennese porcelain pot. The crystal lamp is cracked. The Colonel, bleary-eyed and smiling, talks about the bomb.

"They planted it on the landing in front of my apartment. They think it's my fault. If that scum only knew what I've done for them."

"Was there much damage?" I ask. I couldn't care less.

"Quite a bit. My daughter. I'm sending her to a psychiatrist. She's twelve years old," he says.

The Colonel drinks, with anger, sadness, apprehension, remorse.

His wife comes in, with two small cups of coffee.

"You tell him, dear."

She leaves without answering; a tall, proud, woman, with a neurotic rictus. Her scorn lingers in the air like a little cloud.

"It took quite a toll on her, poor thing," explains the Colonel. "But that's of no concern to you."

"Of course it is! . . . I heard that Captain N and Major X also had trouble after that business."

The Colonel laughs.

"People get carried away," he says. "That's how rumors get started. But they never really come up with anything new. They only repeat."

He lights a Marlboro, and leaves the pack on the table within my reach.

"Tell me a joke," he says.

I think. I draw a blank.

---

20 Johan Barthold Jongkind (1819–1891) was a Dutch landscape painter, who mainly lived in France where he was highly esteemed by the artistic community. He is regarded as the forerunner of Impressionism.

21 Pedro Figari (1861–1938) was a Uruguayan painter, lawyer, journalist, educator and author of many books. Many of his paintings depict Afro-Uruguayans and their dances, rituals, and celebrations, re-creating images from memories of his youth.

"Tell me a joke about politics, any one you want, and I'll prove to you they were telling the same joke twenty, fifty, a hundred years ago. After the defeat of Sedan, or about Hindenburg, Dollfuss, or Badoglio."[22]

"What's your point?"

"King Tut's tomb," says the Colonel. "Lord Carnarvon.[23] It's shit."

The Colonel wipes off his perspiration with his fat, hairy hand.

"But Major X had an accident, he killed his wife."

"So what?" he says, clinking the ice in his glass.

"He shot her in the middle of the night."

"He thought it was a burglar," the Colonel smiles. "These things happen."

"But Captain N . . ."

"He had a car accident. It could happen to anyone, especially him—he can't even see the side of a barn when he's tanked."

"What about you, Colonel?"

"My situation is different," he says. "They're out to get me."

He stands up, walks around the table.

"They think it's my fault. That trash has no idea what I've done for them. But someday the story will be written, it will go down in history. Maybe you'll be the one to write it."

"I'd like to."

"And I'll come out clean, I'm going to look good. I don't care what the trash thinks of me, but I want to look good in the history books, understand?"

"With any luck, I may have something to do with that, Colonel."

"They'd been hanging around. One night, one of them got up the nerve. He left the bomb on the landing and ran away."

He reaches into a glass cabinet, takes out a polychrome porcelain statuette, a shepherdess carrying a basket of flowers.

"Look."

The little shepherdess is missing an arm.

---

22 Two battles occurred in Sedan, France, one in 1870 and another in 1940; both were won by Germany. The first, in 1870, marked the end of Napoleon III's Empire. The characters that the Colonel mentions in this story (Engelbert Dollfuss, Paul von Hindenburg, and Pietro Badoglio) are historical figures that share the element of defeat. Perhaps this explains the Colonel's statement: "I'll prove to you they were telling the same joke twenty, fifty, a hundred years ago." Badoglio and Hindenburg were leading generals defeated in World War I: the former in Italy and the latter in Germany. As the second president of Germany, Hindenburg appointed Adolf Hitler as chancellor of Germany, thus handing over power to the Nazis. After the war, Badoglio served as chief of staff for many years during Mussolini's regime. Engelbert Dollfuss was an Austrian chancellor in the early 1930s who was killed by a Nazi group in 1934.

23 Lord Carnarvon was an English aristocrat who sponsored the excavations that led to the discovery of Egyptian King Tutankhamun's tomb.

"Derby,"[24] he says. "Two hundred years old."

The shepherdess is swallowed up in his suddenly tender fingers. The Colonel clenches his jaw into a grimace on his pained, nocturnal face.

"Why do they think it's your fault?"

"Because I moved her from where she was, that's true, and I took her to where she is now, that's also true. But they don't know what was in the works, the trash doesn't know anything, and they don't know that it was me who stopped it."

The Colonel drinks: passionately, proudly, fiercely, eloquently, methodically.

"Because I've studied history. I can see things in historical perspective. I've read Hegel."

"What did they want to do?"

"Dump her in the river, throw her out of a plane, burn her up and toss her remains down the toilet, dissolve her in acid. How much shit one has to listen to! This country is covered in shit, nobody knows where so much shit comes from but we're all up to our necks in it."

"Yes we are, Colonel, all of us. Because when you come right down to it you and I agree, don't we? It's time to destroy everything. Tear it all down."

"And piss on it."

"But with no regrets, Colonel. Blithely brandishing the bomb and the cattle prod. Cheers!" I say, raising my glass.

He doesn't answer. We're sitting by the big window. The lights of the port glow: mercury-vapor blue. From time to time you can hear the honking of automobiles, trailing off into the distance like voices in a dream. The Colonel's face is little more than a blurry gray face over a blurry white shirt.

"*That woman,*" I hear him murmur. "She was naked in the coffin and she looked like a virgin. Her skin had turned transparent. You could see the metastases of the cancer, like those little pictures you draw on a fogged-up window."

The Colonel drinks. He's tough.

"Naked," he says. "There were four or five of us and we didn't want to look at each other. That ship captain was there, and the Spaniard who embalmed her, and I don't remember who else. And when we took her out of the coffin"—the Colonel wipes his brow—"when we took her out, that filthy Spaniard . . ."

It gets dark by degrees, like in the theater. The Colonel's face is almost invisible. Only the whiskey glows in his glass, like the embers of a fire. Muffled noises reach us through the open door of the apartment. The elevator has closed on the ground floor, and opened nearer to us. The enormous building

---

24 Derby is a kind of porcelain produced in Derby, England, after 1750.

whispers, breathes, gurgles with the noise of its pipes, incinerators, kitchens, children, televisions, maids. And then the Colonel is on his feet, clutching a semiautomatic that he seems to have pulled out of nowhere, and he tiptoes toward the landing, turns on the light abruptly, looks at the austere, geometric, ironic emptiness of the landing, the elevator, the stairway, where there is absolutely no one at all, and comes back slowly, dragging the gun.

"I thought I heard something. That scum won't catch me off guard, like the last time."

He sits down, closer to the window this time. The gun has disappeared and the Colonel continues his digression about that great scene in his life.

" . . . that filthy Spaniard, he threw himself on top of her. He was in love with her corpse, he touched her, he groped her nipples. I punched him so hard, see that?" the Colonel looks at his knuckles, "that I knocked him into the wall. Everything's rotten, shot to hell, nobody even respects death anymore. Do you mind the dark?"

"No."

"Good. I can see the street from here. And I can think. I think all the time. It's easier to think in the dark."

He pours himself another whiskey.

"But that woman was naked," he says, arguing against an invisible foe. "I had to cover her pubis, I wrapped her in a shroud and a Franciscan belt."

He laughs gruffly.

"I had to pay for the shroud out of my own pocket. Fourteen hundred pesos. That proves it to you, doesn't it? That proves it."

He repeats, "That proves it," several times, like a windup toy, without saying what it is that it's supposed to prove.

"I needed help to move her to another coffin. There were some workers around, and I called them over. Imagine their reaction. For them she was a goddess, who knows what kind of nonsense they put in the heads of those poor people."

"Those poor people?"

"Yes, those poor people." The Colonel struggles against a slippery internal rage. "I'm Argentinean too, after all."

"So am I, Colonel, so am I. We're all Argentineans."

"All right," he says.

"Did they see her like that?"

"Yes, I already told you, that woman was naked. A goddess, naked, dead. Laid out for all the world to see. With all her, all her . . ."

The Colonel's voice is lost in a surrealist perspective, those few words receding further and further into the vanishing point, his voice falling in perfect proportion to whatever. I pour myself another whiskey too.

"For me it's no big deal," says the Colonel. "I'm used to seeing naked women. I've seen many in my life. Dead men too. A lot in Poland, in '39. I was a military attaché, you know."

I want to know. I try to calculate the sum of naked women and dead men, but it just doesn't add up, it doesn't add up, it doesn't add up . . . With a single jolt of my muscles I sober up, like a dog shaking off water.

"I'd seen it all before. But they . . ."

"Were they shocked?"

"One of them fainted. I slapped him awake. I said to him: 'Faggot, is this how you act when you have to bury your queen? Remember Saint Peter, who abandoned Christ in his agony.' Later he thanked me."

I look out at the street. The sign says *Coca*, silver on red. The sign says *Cola*, silver on red. The gigantic pupil expands, one red circle after another red, concentric circle, invading the night, the city, the world. *Drink.*

"Drink," says the Colonel.

I drink.

"Are you listening?"

"I'm listening."

"We cut off her finger."

"Was that necessary?"

The Colonel is silver now. He looks at the tip of his index finger, marks it with his thumbnail and holds it up.

"Just this little bit. To identify her."

"Didn't you know who she was?"

He laughs. His hand turns red. *Drink.*

"Yes, we knew. Things have to be legal. It was a historic act, understand?"

"I understand."

"The fingerprint doesn't take if the finger is dead. It must be hydrated. We stuck it back on her later."

"And?"

"It was her all right. That woman was her."

"Was it hard to tell?"

"No, no, you don't get it. She was exactly the same. It seemed like she was going to speak, that she was going to . . . The finger was so that everything would be legal. Professor R. was in charge of everything, he even took X-rays."

"Professor R.?"

"Yes. It couldn't be done by just anyone. It had to be somebody with scientific and moral authority."

Somewhere in the house a bell rings, distant, cut off. I don't see the Colonel's wife come in, but suddenly she's there, her bitter, unyielding voice:

"Should I turn on the light?"

"No."

"Telephone."

"Tell them I'm not here."

She disappears.

"They're trying to break my balls," explains the Colonel. "They call me at all hours of the night. At three in the morning, at five."

"They just want to fuck with you," I say cheerfully.

"I changed my phone number three times. But they always find out."

"What do they say?"

"That my daughter should get polio. That they're going to cut off my balls. Shit."

I hear the ice in the glass, like a distant cowbell.

"I gave them a speech, I stirred them up. I respect your ideas, I told them. That woman did a lot for you. I'm going to give her a Christian burial. But you have to help me."

The Colonel is standing and he drinks with courage, with exasperation, with great and lofty ideas that crash over him like great and lofty waves against a rocky outcrop, leaving him untouched and dry, silhouetted and black, red and silver.

"We took her out of there in a truck. I kept her on Viamonte St., and then on May 25th St., always taking care of her, protecting her, hiding her. They wanted to take her away from me, do something with her. I covered her with a sheet of canvas, she was in my office, on top of a closet, up high. When they asked me what it was, I would tell them it was the radio transmitter from Cordoba, The Voice of Liberty."

I don't know where the Colonel is anymore. The silver reflection searches for him, the red pupil. Maybe he's gone out. Maybe he's walking around the furniture. The building has a vague smell of soup in the kitchen, cologne in the bathroom, diapers in the crib, medicine, cigarettes, life, death.

"Rain," says his strange voice.

I look at the sky: Sirius the dog, Orion the hunter.

"It rains every other day," says the Colonel. "Every other day in a garden where everything is rotting, the roses, the pine tree, the Franciscan belt."

Where, I think, where.

"She's standing on her feet!" shouts the Colonel. "I buried her standing, like Facundo, because she had balls!"

Then I see him, at the other end of the table. And for a moment, when he's bathed in the iridescent glare, I think that he's crying, that thick tears roll down his face.

"Don't pay any attention to me," he says, and sits down. "I'm drunk."

And it rains for a long time in his memory.

I stand up, I touch him on the shoulder.

"Huh?" he says. "Huh?" he says.

And he looks at me with suspicion, like a drunk who wakes up on a train he doesn't remember boarding.

"Was she taken out of the country?"

"Yes."

"Did *you* take her out?"

"Yes."

"How many people know?"

"Two."

"Does the Old Man know?"

He laughs.

"He thinks he knows."

"Where?"

He doesn't answer.

"This must be written about, it has to be published."

"Yes. Someday."

He seems tired, distant.

"Now!" I've lost my patience. "Aren't you concerned about history? I'll write the story, and you'll look good, Colonel, you'll look good once and for all!"

He keeps his mouth shut, his teeth clenched.

"When the time comes . . . you'll be the first . . ."

"No, now is the time. Think about it. *Paris Match. Life.* Five thousand dollars. Ten thousand. As much as you want."

He laughs.

"Where, Colonel, where is she?"

He gets up slowly, he doesn't know who I am. Maybe he's going to ask me my name, what I'm doing there.

And as I walk out defeated, thinking that I will have to come back, or that I will never come back. Even as my index finger has already begun to trace that laborious trail across maps, compiling rainfall indices, probabilities, intrigues.

Even as I know that it no longer interests me, and that I'll never lift a finger, not even on a map, the Colonel's voice strikes me like a revelation:

"She's mine," he says simply. "That woman belongs to me."

In Context | *The Two Fridas* of Frida Kahlo

Frida Kahlo was born in Coyoacán, Mexico, July 6, 1907, to a Hungarian-Jewish father and a Mexican mother of Spanish-Indian descent. When she was eighteen, she was injured in a serious bus accident and took a year to recuperate—from fractures of her spine and collar bone, a shattered pelvis,

Figure 7.4. Frida Kahlo (1907–1954), *The Two Fridas*, 1939. Oil on canvas, 173.5 × 173 cm. Museum of Modern Art, Mexico City, Mexico. Banco de México Diego Rivera & Frida Kahlo Museums Trust, Mexico, D.F. / Artists Rights Society (ARS), New York.

and shoulder and foot injuries. During her convalescence, she began to paint.

At twenty-two, she married the well-known muralist DIEGO RIVERA, who became central to her art and to the world of pain and love reflected in this painting. According to Kahlo's diary, the other Frida was an imaginary friend of childhood, but this portrait, completed after her divorce from DIEGO RIVERA in 1939, shows her turmoil after their separation. One Frida is dressed in European clothes, while the one Diego liked wears a Tehuana costume. The painting depicts the split self, created by love, or the two Fridas, in pain. Such pain is a common element of Kahlo's work, represented here as physical, in the bleeding, cut-open heart of the European Frida. But the amulet bearing Diego's portrait as a child passes through a vein between the Fridas, suggesting that the pain is also related to a self that is being denied. The connection between the two Fridas is vital and cannot be undone.

In this painting, physical and emotional states are *one*. Emotional pain is not simply being represented by physical pain; Kahlo instead shows how love *is* pain, defining one aspect of a person, one Frida—and how her love cannot be separated from her suffering. The shocking wounds, the blood on the dress, the realistic organs in much of her painting—these elements give a new dimension to the body, as a spiritual materiality, sharply reminiscent of colonial Indian images of Christ or even the pre-Hispanic images of sacrifices.

8

The Contemporary Period:
Speaking from the Margins

Contemporary Latin America has reacted forcefully to many powerful twentieth-century trends, among them the desire to create homogenous modern nations, to establish free market economies, to standardize education, and to resemble more closely its powerful neighbor to the north. These are not, however, sudden responses to contemporary politics and events, but a continuation of attitudes that were already manifest in the nineteenth century. Fighters for independence like JOSÉ MARTÍ and intellectuals like SIMÓN RODRÍGUEZ and FRANCISCO BILBAO believed that it was possible to create a new and culturally authentic society in Spanish America. That desire for authenticity has resurfaced with a vengeance during the last three decades of the twentieth century and continues into the twenty-first.

This final section introduces some of the innovative social and cultural forces that sprang up to oppose the long years of dictatorship and neoliberal policies in countries like Argentina, Chile, Bolivia, Mexico, Guatemala, and Cuba. Many selections represent these new forces in inventive forms of writing and representation, some of which are unclassifiable in traditional genres. While familiar categories, like testimony, have been applied to some indigenous texts, such categorizations are not really consistent with traditional Western notions. That so many of these texts so often defy classification underlines the intent of the title: "Speaking from the Margins." Each text generates its own unique category, speaking for itself and claiming its unique space as a voice of the voiceless—indigenous peoples, women, homosexuals, and members of the Latin American New Left who joined indigenous movements, like the ZAPATISTAS and like ÁLVARO GARCÍA LINERA, the vice president of Bolivia.

Two indigenous voices that emerged toward the end of the twentieth century were those of RIGOBERTA MENCHÚ and LUCIANO TAPIA. When it was published in 1984, *I, Rigoberta Menchú: An Indian Woman in*

Guatemala garnered international attention and was quickly translated into several languages. Menchú's testimony reflected an urgent situation, the killing of her people during the long civil war in Guatemala. Tapia's *Ukhamawa Jakawisaxa (Así es nuestra vida) Autobiografía de un aymara* (1995) [(That Is How Our Life Is) An Aymara Autobiography] is a very different text, still not well known, and in its scope, it covers seventy-five years of Bolivian history from the perspective of an Aymara Indian and the Aymara people, who have been condemned to poverty and harsh labor. Both texts provide new insights into the survival of indigenous cultural practices—often in unfamiliar urban contexts—insights that challenge Eurocentric views about race, history, writing, social structures, and beliefs. The printed version of these texts often combines taped transcriptions and written accounts, and, more important, they differ substantially from conventional genres, not just in their forms, but in their objectives and purposes.

One significant difference is that these indigenous texts are not viewed by their authors as representations of experience; rather, the text and the experience are one and the same. These texts do not seek to capture experiences that are in any way distinct from their authors: the text *is* their experience as a cultural and communal other, grounded in a specific ethnicity. The "I" here is not the familiar first person singular, but rather the collective "we" of a culture, defying the Western understanding of testimony as the report of an individual account. "My" personal experience barely counts, since the possessive cannot exist without the others of one's culture. Writing itself, for these indigenous authors, is a function of otherness, a simultaneous act of affirming a culture and assuring its physical survival, since survival is only possible as an ethnic group, an outcome that remains in doubt as long as Hispanic culture is regarded as superior and destined to absorb their identities and culture into its own.

Neither Menchú nor Tapia can be separated from their appeals for cultural recognition, a recognition that was essential to any effective defiance of unjust treatment, persecution, and racism. But this insistence on the integrity of cultural identity brings us full circle to pre-Hispanic civilizations. These readings mark not only the impressive survival of pre-Columbian civilizations, but their pivotal role in combating notions of national, linguistic, and educational homogeneity that dominated the first half of the twentieth century. Integral to larger indigenous social movements in Latin America, these texts challenge the nation-state as a homogenous entity. That challenge is reflected in the renaming of plurinational countries like Bolivia and Ecuador to indicate the inclusion of distinctive indigenous nations. There has also been a continental movement to recognize Indian territories as extending beyond the borders of nation-states, to claim the territories of indigenous peoples before they were divided by colonization and independence. But these large-scale efforts have their roots in local struggles. In Mexico, the ZAPATISTAS (1994) were the first to establish international links and reinvigorate an identification with worldwide struggles against oppression, meanwhile insisting on remaining an essentially local force with no ambition to take over the seat of government.

Nonetheless, the connection between indigenous and leftist groups that first appeared in Guatemala at the end of the last century have emerged in the early decades of this century as crucial to effective social and political change, particularly on a national scale. That critical link was missing for earlier revolutionaries, like CHE GUEVARA, who died in Bolivia in 1967, lacking sufficient indigenous support. But in 2005, Bolivia became the first nation in South America to elect an Indian president. And Bolivian vice president ÁLVARO GARCÍA LINERA emphasizes in his interview the magnitude of this historic juncture between Indianism and Marxism. García Linera came to power only after members of the left joined with Indian movements, like the Movimiento al Socialismo (MAS)[Movement to Socialism], to elect an Aymara president, Evo Morales.

While leftist movements seem moribund in the West, García Linera is enacting many of its radical ideas. The new Bolivian nation challenges the state as a monolithic institution, proposing a model that incorporates indigenous perspectives and questions Eurocentrism. Declaring itself plurinational (like Ecuador), Bolivia seeks to include into its new constitution indigenous groups with their unique systems of governance and distinctive notions of democracy, elections, and communal rights.

Another revolutionary effort is that of the Zapatistas. Using the Internet to broadcast their rebellion on January 1, 1994, the Zapatistas claimed immediate international attention. Though composed by one of the movement's leaders, the text included here does not reflect a personalized or individualized voice; instead, it is a voice speaking out of the struggles, oppression, and poverty of the indigenous peoples in Chiapas. While the Zapatistas have steadfastly retained their regional focus, García Linera, for one, would criticize that stance on principle. For the Bolivian, revolutionary change cannot remain local if it is to be effective in fighting the advances of capitalism and its myriad forms of exploitation.

Of course, oppression and exploitation are not restricted to the indigenous poor. Women are also among the subjugated voices emerging from the chronicles, autobiographies, and fiction of Latin America, many of them victims of military regimes in Argentina, Uruguay, and Chile. Many of these writers have achieved international recognition, including Luisa Valenzuela, Christina Peri Rossi, Isabel Allende, and ELENA PONIATOWSKA. While they all challenge patriarchal dominance, they differ in their approaches: Christina Peri Rossi, for example, calls into question heterosexuality as normative while Luisa Valenzuela portrays the victims of patriarchy, particularly under brutal dictatorships.

The political oppression of homosexuals has generated another silenced voice. Perhaps the most radical and best-known of these writers is Manuel Puig, whose masterful novel, *El beso de la mujer araña* (1976) [Kiss of the Spider Woman], manipulates the role of fiction itself in maintaining gender categories—a perspective often overlooked by the political left. Puig's novel exposes the false dichotomy that designates politics as real and the imagination as fictive, revealing that this dichotomy is just another ideology that the revolutionaries must topple. At the same time, the creations of the imagination become a means of liberation for both imprisoned men, the homosexual Molina as well as the leftist Valentín. But Puig's most radical achievement is his depiction of the homosexual body as defying definition, a body that subverts other bodies, including the heterosexual Valentín, who eventually has a sexual relationship with his cellmate.

Literature has always offered writers a space to pose provocative ideas, a function that is often feared by the repressive governments who recognize that power. Such was the case of the Cuban writer REINALDO ARENAS, whose representations of homosexuality attracted the enmity of the Castro regime, which imprisoned Arenas because his work was regarded as subversive. Like RODOLFO WALSH, however, Arenas understood the potency of writing and of all art, and his works are in themselves a gesture of freedom from social, familial, and sexual oppression.

These voices from the margins reveal the revolutionary energies that exist at every level of society in today's Latin America. They are the voices that are bringing rapid and needed change to the twenty-first century, opening the way to new visions of Hispanic America, inventing novel ways to contest domination, and producing transformations as profound as any that these remarkable peoples and diverse cultures have ever known.

Rigoberta Menchú Tum (1959–)

Rigoberta Menchú Tum is best known as the Maya-Quiché woman from Guatemala who, in 1992, won the Nobel Peace Prize, bringing international

Figure 8.1. Rigoberta Menchú Tum (1959–). Photograph by David Fernandez (2013).

attention to the atrocities committed against her people by the Guatemalan armed forces during the long civil war (1960–1996) waged against leftist rebels. The military's scorched-earth tactics, designed to eliminate all support for the guerrillas, brought tremendous violence to Mayan communities in the highlands. One result was an increase in Mayan resistance, as the people fought for their survival, joining the rebels to defend their families and land. As many as 200,000—mostly Mayan—civilians were killed or disappeared, 626 Mayan villages were razed to the ground, and over a million people were displaced during this protracted war.

Rigoberta Menchú fought with the Ejército Guerrillero de los Pobres (EGP) [Guerrilla Army of the Poor] after joining the Committee of the Peasant Union (CUC) in 1979. Targeted by the Guatemalan army, she was forced to flee to Mexico in 1982. Once abroad, Menchú found a new way to continue the struggle, speaking out about her plight and that of her people. In 1983, she was interviewed by the anthropologist Elisabeth Burgos-Debray, who recorded and edited her testimony, which became *I, Rigoberta Menchú: An Indian Woman from Guatemala*.

In her new environment, Menchú accomplished two things: providing a moving first-hand account of the disappearances and murders of her people, including many of her own family members; and harnessing the media as a weapon in the fight. Critics have complained that Menchú was being used by guerrilla leaders, like Arturo Taracena, a member of the EGP, who was a silent editor of Menchú's testimonial—along with Burgos-Debray. But as the scholar Emilio del Valle-Escalante has confirmed, by the time Menchú was interviewed, she had already begun to speak out, trying to raise international public awareness about the suffering of her community. Moreover, the recordings made by Burgos-Debray in Paris in 1982 took place in the very midst of the civil war, at a point when speaking out seemed particularly urgent. Far from being exploited by those around her, it was Menchú who used every means available to bring attention to this cruel war.

Most Westerners expect firsthand witness accounts to reflect some kind of "objective truth." But this expectation does not hold across every culture. Menchú's account is indeed first hand, but it is in a communitarian rather than in an individual sense. Her account isn't confessional, since she deliberately withholds secrets about her culture that are not meant to be disclosed to outsiders. Her testimony thus challenges many notions of what this form implies: that nothing should be withheld, that the individual is herself a unified being who stands apart from her society and can speak about it rather than only with and through it.

Menchú's testimony reveals a different conception of the individual. From the very first paragraph, Menchú signals that distinctiveness, insisting that she is speaking not for herself but for her entire community. She points out that, even from childhood, actions are nonindividualized. As early as three, a child begins to "work" and plays a critical social role within the family, with every activity shaped by specific cultural traditions. The self of Menchu's testimony cannot be separated from her community because the self is essentially a communal entity. However, the title of Menchú's work—both in Spanish (*Me llamo Rigoberta Menchú y así me nació la conciencia*) and in English (*I, Rigoberta Menchú. An Indian Woman in Guatemala*)—belies this communal self, reflecting an outsider's assessment of her testimony. Menchu's text accordingly occupies a space between two cultures, that of the editors who created the titles and that of the author: the Mayan culture to which Menchú belongs and the culture of her exile, which enables her to speak out about and for her people.

This doubled aspect of Menchú's text, which opens it to interpretations that depend on the reader's cultural perspective, generated controversy when it was published, particularly because of how the text frames and recounts actual occurrences. Several scholars challenged its veracity—and Menchú's integrity—because not all events were corroborated by eye-witnesses and some events seemed patently untrue. These assessments were thoroughly examined in 2001 by Arturo Arias in *The Rigoberta Menchú Controversy*, and Menchú's book emerged intact. This remains a singular text, one that questions the boundaries of truth and fiction, the role and notion of testimony, and the concept of selfhood—all from the perspective of a culture whose integrity has been steadily undermined by the hierarchies of Western epistemology. But Menchú's work also has immense historical value in demonstrating the early connections between indigenous groups and leftist movements. Initiated in the guerrilla wars as a pragmatic response to the common repression suffered by both groups at the hands of the military, the subsequent collaborations between these movements have proved vital to their mutual success—both for survival and for the creation of a more just society.

Rigoberta Menchú was awarded the Nobel Peace Prize in 1992. With the endowment from this prestigious award, she created the Rigoberta Menchú Tum Foundation to promote the cause of indigenous peoples around the world. Menchú also became more politically involved and ran as a candidate for the presidency of Guatemala in 2007 and again in 2011. Her second book, *Rigoberta: La Nieta de los Mayas* (1998) [Crossing Borders] continues the account of her life after the Nobel Prize. The award permanently changed Menchú's life, and she recounts her efforts to manage her role as an international figure while remaining in touch with the Mayan communities of her home.

The selection here demonstrates the centrality of community life in Mayan culture, as well as the function of religion in building that community. Menchú's role as a catechist further suggests how Catholicism has been appropriated by her culture to express its own beliefs.

The selection is from *I, Rigoberta Menchú: An Indian Woman in Guatemala*, edited by Elisabeth Burgos-Debray, translated by Ann Wright (London, New York: Verso, 1984), 79–81. Reproduced by permission of Verso Books.

From I, Rigoberta Menchú: An Indian Woman in Guatemala (1984)

XII: LIFE IN THE COMMUNITY

Don't you understand that the game is a sign of freedom, of death, and of fate, which governs the sentences of the judges. The only ones daring enough to play are dead.
—Popol Vuh
I am a catechist who walks upon this earth, not one who thinks only of the kingdom of God.
—Rigoberta Menchú

I remember things very, very well from the time I was twelve. It's then that I thought like a responsible woman. When we do collective work, to have something extra in case someone in the community dies, or is ill, only the adults work. Of course, we have this relationship with our community from the very beginning but, even so, it becomes much stronger when we start having a real obligation to the community. Each member of the family always has a duty to perform. Like visiting neighbours, for instance, spending time talking to them in any free moments. Not quarrelling with neighbours since that sometimes causes bad feeling. And children don't have petty rows like grown ups. They start fighting with other children, with their neighbours.

Well, at twelve, I joined in the communal work; things like harvesting the maize. I worked together with others. It was also then that I began making friends, closer friends, in the community. I began taking over my mother's role too. My mother was the woman who coordinated certain things in the community. For instance; 'What shall we sow prior to the maize?' 'Should we only sow beans?' 'How shall we do it?' Most of this is our work—sowing beans, sowing potatoes, or any kind of vegetables which can be grown on the same land as the maize. Putting in little sticks for the beans so they don't harm the maize, or tying up the tendrils of the *chilacayotes*[1] or whatever vegetables we've sown in with the maize. We define a task; what we have to do step by step. Every *compañero*, every neighbour, has his little bit to tend, to harvest, to pick the crop. He tends it from the first day it is sown, looking after the plant right through until it bears fruit and he picks the fruit. We all make a promise to do this. It's a collective obligation, naturally.

It was during that time that I began to take on responsibility. The Catholic

---

1   *Chilacayote*, sometimes called the Asian pumpkin or fig-leaf gourd, is an edible American squash.

religion had already come to our region. The Catholic religion chooses, or at least the priests choose, people to become catechists. I was a catechist from the age of twelve. The priest used to come to our area every three months. He'd bring texts for us to teach the doctrine to our community. We did it on our own initiative as well, because my father was a dedicated Christian. By accepting the Catholic religion, we didn't accept a condition, or abandon our culture. It was more like another way of expressing ourselves. If everyone believes in this medium, it's just another medium of expression. It's like expressing ourselves through a tree, for example; we believe that a tree is a being, a part of nature, and that a tree has its image, its representation, its *nahual*,[2] to channel our feelings to the one God. That is the way we Indians conceive it. Catholic Action[3] is like another element which can merge with the elements which already exist within Indian culture. And it confirms our belief that, yes, there is a God, and yes, there is a father for all of us. And yet it is something we think of as being only for what happens up there. As far as the earth is concerned, we must go on worshipping through our own intermediaries, just as we always have done, through all the elements found in nature. And this helped us a lot in becoming catechists and taking on the responsibility of teaching others; in the way we teach in our community, by being an example to others who are growing up. Many of the images of Catholic Action are similar to ours, although ours are not written down. A lot of it is familiar. For example, we believe we have ancestors, and that these ancestors are important because they're good people who obeyed the laws of our people. The Bible talks about forefathers too. So it is not something unfamiliar to us. We accept these Biblical forefathers as if they were our own ancestors, while still keeping within our own culture and our own customs. At the same time, it often refers to leaders, to kings. For instance the Bible tells us that there were kings who beat Christ. We drew a parallel with our king, Tecún Umán, who was defeated and persecuted by the Spaniards, and we take that as our own reality. In this way we adjusted to the Catholic religion and our duties as Christians, and made it part of our culture. As I said, it's just another way of expressing ourselves. It's not the only, immutable way of keeping our ancestors' interme-

---

2   *Nahual*, among the most fundamental in pre-Hispanic Mesoamerican religions, is the belief that every human being has a "double" in the animal kingdom. Miguel Angel Asturias's novel, *Hombres de maíz* (1949) [Men of Maize] deals in large part with the consequences of the death of a deer that was a *nahual* or double of one of the characters.

3   Catholic Action refers to groups of laity engaged in various forms of social and religious activism. In Central America, such groups were helping to Christianize Indian populations and helping them to escape persecution by military regimes. Rigoberta Menchú became a member of such a group.

diaries alive. It's twice the work for us, because we have to learn the doctrine, and we have to learn to pray. We pray in our ceremonies in our own culture, so that's not so different. We just have to memorize the prayers they tell us to use and add them to our own. Everything has to be in our language. Well, sometimes it's something we do, not because we understand it, but because that's the way it has to be. Because I remember that at first the prayers weren't even in Spanish but in Latin or something like that. So although it's something we say and express with all our faith, we don't always understand what it means. Since the priests don't know our language and they say the prayers in Spanish, our job is to memorize the prayers, and the chants. But we didn't understand exactly what it meant, it was just a channel for our self-expression. It's very important to us, but we don't understand it.

Elena Poniatowska (1932–)

Elena Poniatowska was born in Paris in 1932; her father was French and Polish, and her mother was Mexican. Poniatowska and her mother fled Europe for Mexico during the Second World War, when she was ten. After a stay in the United States she settled in Mexico permanently in 1953. Fluent in three languages, she began working as a journalist in Mexico City when she was eighteen and acquired an early reputation for her astonishing talent at interviewing. Elena Poniatowska virtually transformed this standard journalistic genre. Her reporting uniquely combines chronicle, personal testimonies (both of the interviewed and the interviewer) and the literary imagination. No other Mexican journalist—and very few in all of Latin America—has been able to explore the personal dimensions of experience in interviews like Elena Poniatowska. Her questions are never formulaic in seeking information, nor do they intrude on the interviewee as unjustified curiosity. Instead, Poniatowska's inquiries appear to open doors for the interviewees to enter a welcoming, confidential space, where they can reveal truths that might otherwise remain hidden. Poniatowska's unrivaled talent for communicating even seems to extend to the dead, who have been among her most successful subjects.

Though many of Poniatowska's books of interviews are classics of Mexican letters, they remain very difficult to classify. Is *Hasta no verte Jesús mío* (1969) [Here's to You Jesusa!]—based on the life of a spirited working-class Mexican woman—a novel or a chronicle? *La noche de Tlatelolco* (1971) [Massacre in Mexico] is manifestly history, recounting the killing of the protesters in 1968, but is it a collage of voices, or is it a testimony? *Nada, nadie* (1985) [Nothing, Nobody], which gathers the words of the victims of an earthquake in Mexico City in September 1985, similarly confounds genres. How can one begin to classify the 1991 book, *Tinísima*? A nonfiction novel about the activist photographer, Tina Modotti, the book is based on solid research and thoroughly documented, but many segments are plainly products of the writer's imagination.

Many Latin American novels in the last two decades, the period of postmodernism, have used history as the foundation for otherwise purely imaginary narratives. Based on the conviction that history as event and as text cannot guarantee a single indisputable truth, these novels question both what has occurred and the texts that document them. Many postmodern works offer fictional solutions to what has become the elusiveness of truth: if we cannot determine the truth of the past, then we can use the imagination to construct our own versions of history.

While many of Elena Poniatowska's texts predate postmodernism, they offer prototypes of the form. Many writers have, in fact, adopted her narrative techniques, especially in combining oral and written components. Even so, Poniatowska's historical novels—like *Tinísima*—take a view of history that is decidedly not postmodern. For her, the imagination does not substitute for an absence of certainty but derives its legitimacy from the coherence established among the discrete events being researched. For Poniatowska, reality must always be rescued from obsolescence as well as from silence. She has often explained that the purpose of her writings is to give voice to the voiceless, but also to value the silence of the oppressed—a point underlined by the title of one of her finest collections of chronicles, *Fuerte es el silencio* (1980) [Strong Is Silence]. Like her contemporary Carlos Monsiváis (1938–2010), Elena Poniatowska is part of a generation of Mexican writers who have used the chronicle to expose hidden facts and repressed events—though Poniatowska remains unique in her discursive virtuosity, inviting the voice of the imagination to be history's essential companion in finding a glimpse of the truth.

Part of what sets Monsiváis and Poniatowska apart from others is the diversity of their topics—social conflicts, literary figures, politicians, film, theater, painting, daily events, historical sites, memorable dates. Their work explores the variety of Mexican life without insisting on a definitive image of the nation. Both of them are, of course, quite aware of the standard set by OCTAVIO PAZ in his commanding essay on Mexican identity, *El labe-rinto de la soledad* [The Labyrinth of Solitude]. But while they do not challenge

Paz's achievement, neither do they necessarily agree with his analysis. Both credit Paz for his insights, but they also suggest their ambivalence toward his notions of Mexico as based on ahistorical elements like masks or the preoccupation with death, or his understanding of Mexican history as a progression from "unconscious" to "conscious" to "self-conscious." For these two writers, the defining events and qualities of the nation must be more firmly rooted in the specific moment of their occurrence.

The protagonist of *Tinísima*, Tina Modotti, was herself a remarkable historical figure. Born in Italy in 1896, she died in Mexico in 1942. As an adolescent, she immigrated to the United States to be with her father in San Francisco. She began a career as an actress, but then in the 1920s moved to Mexico with the American photographer Edward Weston. Under his influence, Modotti took up photography as a form of art rather than as a visual recording. Though the two were lovers, they had very opposite views of photography, and while her early works bear Weston's unmistakable stamp, Tina Modotti's vision soon changed drastically, deeply affected by her allegiance to the Mexican Communist Party and the communist cause.

After Weston returned to the United States, he and Modotti maintained their relationship through letters, which reveal her increasing involvement in political activities that were often indistinguishable from her artistic aims. In that linking, she joined many artists of this era, who recognized an intense connection between their communist political views and their art, notably Xavier Guerrero and Diego Rivera, both of whom had artistic and intimate relationships with Modotti.

Modotti was exiled from Mexico in 1930, after the government fabricated charges that she was a militant foreign communist. After her expulsion, Modotti first lived in the USSR and Germany, and then in Spain during its civil war. Using a pseudonym, she finally returned to Mexico when republican sympathizers who had lost the war to Francisco Franco were welcomed into the country. Three years later, Tina Modotti died of a heart attack.

While there are many books about Modotti, none are like Elena Poniatowska's. Any objective or neutral narration of events is overtaken by the flow of the imagination, offering a deeply truthful chronicle that never neglects or overlooks the rich diversity of life.

The selection is from *Tinísima*, translated by Katherine Silver (New York: Farrar, Straus, Giroux, 1996), 111–19. Reproduced by permission of Elena Poniatowska.

From **Tinísima** (1991)

When Tina received the new batch of Edward's photographs, her first impulse was to go out and buy a pepper, examine its curves and slopes, for never before had she imagined that one could be so suggestive. Weston always searched for the unexpected, and now he had found it. What did it matter how many hours he had worked if this was the result?

Edward's photographs shook the foundations of her renunciation and temporarily released her from the colorless world in which she had immersed herself. As she wrote of her feelings, her reactions to his photos, she knew that she was speaking out of the past as the woman of the world she once was and who now existed only in these brief flashes. He had, after all, taught her to discover beauty.

Edward—nothing before in art has affected me like these photographs. I just cannot look at them a long while without feeling exceedingly perturbed—they disturb me not only mentally but physically. There is something so pure and at the same time so perverse about them. They contain both the innocence of natural things and the morbidity of a sophisticated distorted mind. They make me think of lilies and of embryos at the same time. They are mystical and erotic.

The seashells, the peppers, Weston's images were still capable of overcoming misery and inoculating her momentarily against anxiety. But could she really choose to shoot roses, lilies, and crystal glasses when Gómez Lorenzo was urging her to photograph the peasants reading *El Machete*.[4] "Tina, we live on a continent of starvation, as horrible as India's." Could she really waste film on the stairway of Tepotzotlán while the streets were exploding with human misery?

"A photograph," Gómez Lorenzo continued, "is an irrefutable document. The pictures you take are a slap in the face of the bourgeois conscience."

"A photograph is also a form . . ."

Misery, on the other hand, had no form, or had all of them. And since that misery did not allow her to breathe, she wanted to transcend it, go beyond it, turn it into art.

Tina took Edward's photos to Diego; he looked at them for a long time. "Has Weston been ill lately?"

Then he added: "Perhaps I am the one who is ill."

She continued to send packages of her own new work to her master and

---

4   *El Machete* was initially founded in 1923 by an artists' union but later became the official newspaper of the Mexican Communist Party.

waited for glory or ruin, praise or condemnation by return mail. Maybe he would appreciate the form of the bandolier, guitar, and ear of corn, her synthesis of the Mexican Revolution, even though he would reject it as a symbol.

When she was asked if she wanted to travel to Texcoco to take pictures of a peasant rally, she felt as if she had been offered the keys to life. She would wear her overalls and go wherever she wanted, take pictures from different angles, approach the people, for this was also what *El Machete* wanted her to do: show that a sea of straw hats answered the Party's call. Yes, this was her profession. She spent days on the photo of the bum who hid his despairing face as he sat under the advertisement for a fashionable clothing store: *"We have everything a gentleman needs to dress elegantly from head to toe. Estrada Hermanos, Segunda de Brasil 15, Primera de Tacuba 15."* Of course that one was a montage, and Weston would criticize it. The Mexico that moved her most—Mexico humble, beaten, profound—that Mexico should be left in peace and not tampered with.

Despite it all, she still spent time on the kind of photograph that was more likely to earn Weston's praise and Xavier's scorn. Two calla lilies—elegant purity of form—had caught her eye, the eye of the artist, not the militant. Developing the negative, she had felt as if she were giving birth. She broke into a cold sweat as she imagined herself with Weston again at her side. "The negatives are going to slip out of my hands; how much time do I leave them in?" Her arms felt stiff. "I must get hold of myself. If it weren't for this excellent equipment you left me . . ." "It's got nothing to do with the equipment: you're a fine photographer." She had to turn the negative every thirty seconds so the liquid would cover it uniformly; Weston himself had prepared the developing fluid, and she repeated the formula like a spell against failure: sodium hyposulfite, two grams; hydroquinone, ninety grams; boric acid crystals, thirty grams. "It's a bit dark," she blamed herself as she held out the finished negative. "You spoiled it," Edward growled. How much longer? My God, what an anguished process! "You don't know how to determine the difference between technique and magic." The shapes outlined in the emulsion seemed the result of a magic spell cast in the darkness; two, three minutes, an eternity. The calla lily was pure and sensual. "Will it retain both its limpid and its carnal quality?" Diego Rivera could retouch his paintings, change colors as he searched for a particular effect, but this wasn't possible in photography. Art was created or lost in the blink of an eye.

Now with the negative in the enlarger, she whispered, "Eduardito, help me." She was going to use the most expensive, fine-grained paper.

Then they appeared, her two dear callas, exactly as she had wanted them in front of the dirt-mottled wall, the shadow on the long spadix culminating in the glaring whiteness of the cups, the sap on the fiber of the petals terminating in that thin black line, a prelude to death. Cruelty is implicit in the beautiful; there is a flaw in nature; death takes the opposite direction from life. The emulsion has repeated its miracle. She hung up a copy to dry, like a small sheet of her imagination.

She wondered why she had been thinking so much about Edward if their last few months together had been so hostile. Hadn't she followed Xavier's lead, forgotten about aesthetics, and turned into a witness, photographing people on the streets, whoever happened by? It wasn't easy for her to forget her formal considerations, think only about portraying the life of the poor, forget what she had been taught by Weston, that photography was also an art form, yes, Xavier, just like painting. And in addition, of course, there was her equipment, her heavy Graflex that made it almost impossible to catch those fleeting moments, the flukes, the urgency. The picture of the flag-bearer on the bridge had been planned in advance. She still wanted her photographs to captivate the viewer's attention by the story they told, by their own value, and for this, she needed to think each one through before she snapped the shutter.

In her ever more encompassing role as a Communist militant, Tina was no longer that creature of endlessly renewed sensuality, but rather a cautious copy of herself. Even so, she couldn't prevent people from looking at her; every one of her movements exuded sexual energy, especially when she walked. Still, she made an effort to be more like Consuelo Uranga, Gachita Amador, María Luisa López.[5] She spoke almost in a whisper: "Excuse me," "Good morning," "I'll be back in a moment." She almost wished Diego had not known her from "before." Her comrades would have judged any of her former activities as extravagant; Weston in drag: a faggot, decadent; Tina, dressed as a man, walking down the street on his arm: degenerate; Brett, wearing her brassiere stuffed with oranges: a pervert; Weston dancing with excited, tremulous Elena the maid: a deviation, a lack of respect for the poor, a nameless malignity; and Weston's attempts at sexual apocalypse that would lead to the intensification of pleasure: an activity for maniacs. What was morality? Was

---

5   Consuelo Uranga, Graciela (i.e., Gachita) Amador, and María Luisa López were Mexican feminists in the decades of the '20s, '30s, and '40s. Consuelo Uranga fought militantly for women's suffrage. She was married to the secretary general of the Mexican Communist Party, Valentín Campa. Graciela Amador was also a militant communist who befriended many leftist writers, including Pablo Neruda. She was married to the muralist painter, David Alfaro Siqueiros until 1929 when he asked for a divorce to live with the Uruguayan poet, Blanca Luz Brum.

X normal? How did the comrades channel their sexuality? How did Hernán Laborde make love? And Frijolillo? What was the reality of their desires? How did peasants make love with their callused feet covered with mud, their legs and arms scarred by their daily labor, their chests panting like the earth, the flames of their breath? How about the women, wrapped in their shawls, their eyes like timid pools, their hands always hidden? The poor beat each other. The wives, the children, the dogs, the burros, the mules, all received their fair share of beatings. To beat was to educate. "Don't hit me, don't hit me, papa," Tina would hear. "Why shouldn't I hit you if it's for your own good?" According to the code of ethics of the Communist Party, the comrades got up every morning to struggle, not to be creative. They would construct a new society, a Mexico for all the disinherited, and above all, a Mexico for the people, the peasants, the true Mexicans.

When they brought in Comrade Raúl Álvarez—his nails bloodied, his face smashed, his swollen flesh beginning to rot—Tina realized that the Communists were putting their lives on the line.

She had been drawn to Raúl the first time she met him. Regardless of directives from Moscow, he had gone out to the impoverished settlements to be with the squatters and find out what they really needed.

"Specifically, they need toilets, sinks, drinking water, garbage cans."

"Why are they coming to the city?"

"Because they are dying of hunger in the countryside."

The children's cries were sharp and piercing, but the Party had to turn everything into committees, then divide these into subcommittees, and meetings could last for whole days while typhoid infested the settlements. They hadn't finished discussing possible strategies and they were already buying coffins.

Raúl Álvarez told the squatters to arm themselves with stones and sticks, whatever they could find, anything rather than give themselves over to the authorities. They should resist, demand what was rightfully theirs. "What is ours? We don't own anything." They didn't feel they had the right to life, much less to a piece of earth. The poor readily adjusted to their predictably bad luck. "Don't give up. React." He advised them, "Don't urinate or defecate near where you are sleeping; we're going to get shovels and picks to dig holes. In the meantime, here is some cardboard to make yourselves a shelter." They listened to Álvarez distrustfully, as if they were unaware of the degree of their misery.

The comrades disapproved of his activities. "You're wearing yourself out for nothing, and one of these days you're going to pay for it. You must make the government accountable, assign responsibility where it belongs. Write an article for *El Machete* denouncing the situation. They say that the President has our newspaper on his desk. What do you gain by going over there every day?"

Tina shared Raúl's concerns. How could the comrades abandon those poor people to the elements and the authorities?

Again she was reminded that the Party was not a charity organization, that the Party's work was political.

"But I'm willing to do it myself," Tina said, asserting herself. "I have friends, I can get blankets, cots, whatever is needed."

"Tina, our job is to denounce the problem, not solve it. We simply don't have the means. Next, you and Raúl are going to ask us to build a hospital."

"And why not?" she asked angrily.

"That is not the role of the Party. We must force the government to do it. You want us to turn into a branch of the Red Cross?"

On her own, Tina decided to approach some of her wealthy friends from the past and ask them to support her new cause.

Tita and Tomás Braniff welcomed Tina effusively into their opulent home in Puente de Alvarado, which she remembered from her days with Weston.

She came directly to the point. "I've come to ask for your help."

"By all means. What do you need? I'm sorry you had to wait, but Tomás has taken a great interest in aeronautics. We've just arrived from a test flight in Balbuena."

"We at the Party are committed to helping some families who are about to be evicted."

"Tina, we're leaving for Europe in a few days. Maybe we can help you when we get back. In the meantime, here is one hundred pesos, just to see you through."

"It's not for me," Tina said proudly. "I'm here on behalf of thousands of Mexicans."

On the table, in a silver bowl for visiting cards that stood between the candlesticks, Tina left the one-hundred-peso note. On her way to their house, she had felt the same joy and anticipation she used to feel when she went there with Weston. Now, the Braniffs' response only helped to define even more clearly the distance between Weston's Tina and Guerrero's Tina.

Next, she made her way to the corner of Juárez Avenue and San Juan de Letrán, to the building where Monna, widow of Rafael Sala and now wife to Felipe Teixidor, had her apartment. Here she would not feel the aversion she had felt at the Braniffs'. The Teixidors' rooms were filled with books; they were intellectuals. How silly she had been to go to the Braniffs'. She hugged Monna, who immediately asked about Edward and offered Tina tea. "How well you look, beautiful as always!" They sat on a plush green velvet sofa and Tina told her about the squatters' needs and her commitment to help them. Monna listened with a generous expression in her intelligent eyes, an expression that did not change as she replied.

"We've known each other, Tina, for a long time, so I'm sure you are aware of our way of thinking—Rafael's, may he rest in peace, Felipe's, and mine. You must remember that we have always remained marginal to ideologies. To help you, Tina, would be to betray myself, because I don't share your current beliefs. I don't believe in the dictatorship of the proletariat. This is my response to the militant. Nevertheless, I am willing, and I am sure Felipe would be too, to help you as our friend."

"Your friend is not asking for anything. Your friend doesn't need anything."

Tina hid her disappointment from Xavier. He would have blamed her. "Why did you go? You asked for it. That's the way they are. You should have known." Their rejections confirmed for her that something had been reborn within her that had brought her back to a distant time, to that child on Giuseppe's shoulders at the rallies, the goddaughter of Demetrio Canal, her fist raised in the air. Those arduous days at the offices of *El Machete* on Mesones Street had prepared her for this reencounter with herself. She felt no resentment toward her rich friends from before. She simply knew she would never see them again; the path she was following was different, and she believed it to be sacred. That night she gave herself fully to Xavier, merging with him through all his fibers and his consciousness. The next day, she gratefully became a card-carrying member of the Communist Party.

During the ceremony, Xavier's pride in his comrade was so great that even his stone features betrayed emotion.

Tina was also deeply moved. She received her membership as if she had been knighted, and Xavier Guerrero, a member of the Central Committee and her lover, had armed her. She owed this to him, her commitment unto death. Enea Sormenti told her about cards that had been perforated by bullets and religiously put on display in glass cases by the Russian Communist Party, about the Reds who had gloriously fallen in the struggle, like young girls who died of love. Yes, Tina, like those who die of love.

"I felt very honored," said Enea Sormenti, "when I received my card as a member of the Mexican Communist Party."

"Oh, but you are international."

"You can also be one day, Tina."

"From now on," El Canario joked, "no relaxation, no love affairs, not even a glass of red wine; goodbye to good times, wasted time, to even one single day without serving the cause."

"Here's to one hell of a life you will lead," toasted Ratón Velasco.

Those were the jokes they told the new members, those who joined the various cells named after Karl Marx, Engels, Zapata, as if each one were a saint of the Church. Soon there would be a Klara Zetkin cell, once she was canonized. Tina felt that in the coming years life would live her, her time would not be her own. Would there be one day a Tina Modotti cell?

When Raúl Álvarez finally obtained authorization to take a brigade to the Bondojo settlement, Tina asked to be included. Raúl refused. Squatting was for the young, the unattached, not for Tina. "I don't want anything to happen to you. Don't take it personally, Tina. In the struggle, obedience is the most important thing. There is no room for pity. The comrades are also poor. They barely make ends meet."

"But I prefer to work in the field, look for a pot, a blanket, anything rather than listen to their interminable speech-making."

"Such individualism! You can't use the Party to resolve your personal conflicts. Don't worry. As soon as this is over, we'll talk again."

And now there he was, lying on the desk, the soles of his shoes torn off, his skin transparent, emptied of blood, his hands clenching his genitals in an impotent gesture toward the blows. Dead. Gómez Lorenzo put his arm

Figure 8.2. Tina Modotti (1896–1942), *Mexican Sombrero with Hammer and Sickle* (1927).

around her. Tina instinctively moved away. "You see, you see what happens. We warned Raúl again and again. If you had been in that brigade, the same thing would have happened to you."

In Context | Tina Modotti: Photography as Art and Ideology

Italian-born Tina Modotti (1896–1942) spent much of her adult life in Mexico. Her photograph of a Mexican hat with a hammer and sickle reflects her belief that ideology and art are deeply connected. Having herself been a teenage worker in an Italian silk factory, helping to support her family, Modotti establishes her solidarity with all workers. The objects here reflect communism as both an ideological vision and intrinsic to the life of the Mexican people. The materiality of ideology is also revealed, since the hammer and sickle are simultaneously international symbols and functional tools of ordinary Mexican people.

Reinaldo Arenas (1943–1990)

The writing of Reinaldo Arenas represents an invaluable testimony about political, social, familial, and sexual oppression. His texts create a vivid image of an individual harassed by his family and then by the state bureaucracy. Like few other Latin American writers of the twentieth century, Arenas reveals in exact and dramatic language just how the desire for power determines everyone's behavior—whether friends or lovers, parents or neighbors, strangers, bureaucrats, or politicians. Even the title of Arenas's 1969 novel about the Mexican priest SERVANDO TERESA DE MIER, *El mundo alucinante* (1969), translated in 1971 as *Hallucinations: Being an Account of the Life and Adventures of Fray Servando Teresa de Mier*, reveals a world of delusions of power.

Three specific sources of these delusions emerge in Arenas's novels, poetry, and plays: the family, society, and the state. The collusion and omnipresence of these institutions allow only one means of escape, and those who do not pursue it risk annihilation. That escape is through small fissures in the suffocating web of social life—in intimate and personal relationships with other individuals, in friendships, in love, in fortuitous encounters with strangers. But even these precious openings are contaminated by those three repressive agents of illusion. There can be no secure relationship: parents can denounce their children; children can betray their parents; everyone can be an informer; anyone can belong to the state police.

Society itself deteriorates through this steady accumulation of betrayals, denunciations, and aggression.

Given these assumptions about society, Arenas's work nonetheless offers an obstinate practice of what he calls beauty: loving relationships, literature, art, and the physical world. In the most memorable pages of his posthumously published autobiography, *Antes que anochezca* (1992), published in 1993 as *Before Night Falls*, Arenas condemns repression precisely because it is a persecution of beauty and an imposition of ugliness. For Arenas, this condemnation is not aesthetic but a defense of freedom, love, expressiveness, and life at all levels.

Born in Oriente Province, Cuba, Arenas came to Havana in 1963 to study philosophy and literature. He began working at the National Library and won several prizes for his fiction and poetry. But as a dissident writer—as well as an openly gay man, proud of his homosexuality—Arenas soon ran awry of Cuba's antigay policies. The Cuban State was obsessed with maintaining "normality" among its citizens, and individuals like Arenas were viewed as subversive simply by the deviance of their attitudes. In 1974, Arenas was arrested and later confined in the infamous El Morro castle. Forced to renounce his writing in order to be released, he left Cuba in 1980 as part of the Mariel boatlift. He lived in New York City until, suffering from AIDS, he committed suicide, exhorting his Cuban countrymen to continue the fight for freedom. "Cuba will be free," he wrote, "I already am."

From Arenas's first novel to his final autobiography, sexuality and poetry remain in close proximity. Few authors in Spanish have achieved his mastery of erotic poetry—even in his prose. His novels rely on narrative as much as on poetic technique, and he legitimizes his experience through the concreteness of his testimony and the intimacy of its details. The pleasures of the body, the beauty of metaphor and physical reality, momentarily allow one to forget the power of repression, but Arenas's narrative itself never loses its sense of moral responsibility.

Early on, Arenas understood how his literary project would define life in Cuba—from before the revolution and through the violent, paranoid decade of the 1970s—as a series of death-throes. Begun in 1967 as *Celestino antes del alba* (later retitled *Cantando en el pozo*) [Singing from the Well], Arenas eventually included five novels in his *Pentagonía*: "five agonies," or "dyings." Three are masterpieces of twentieth-century Latin American literature: *Cantando*, *El palacio de las blanquísimas mofetas* (1980), translated in 1982 as *Palace of the White Skunks*, and *Otra vez el mar* (1982), translated in 1986 as *Farewell to the Sea: A Novel of Cuba*. Throughout these occasionally joyful narratives, Arenas never abandons the sense of pain, of effort, of suffering. An individual can briefly escape the totalitarianism of family, society, or the state, but struggle will always be required if one is to continue living.

As an autobiography, *Before Night Falls* is an exceptional testimony to the human desire for freedom. Described by the *New York Times* as one of 1993's ten best books, *Before Night Falls* represents its author's unrelenting search for release from the narrow constraints of a blind and ruthless culture. Arenas found that release in literature—and nowhere more poignantly and exuberantly than in the literature that he himself wrote.

The selection is from *Before Night Falls: A Memoir* by Reinaldo Arenas, translated by Dolores M. Koch (New York: Viking, 1993), 172–77, 294–96. Copyright © 1992 by the Estate of Reinaldo Arenas; translation copyright © 1993 by the Estate of Reinaldo Arenas and Dolores M. Koch. Used by permission of Viking Books, an imprint of Penguin Publishing Group, a division of Penguin Random House LLC.

From **Before Night Falls (1992)**

Several of my friends who were now informers (Hiram Prado was one) had called on Nicolás Abreu where he worked as a movie projectionist to inquire about me. The police not only were watching José; they threatened to put him in jail if he did not disclose my whereabouts. The person directing the group in charge of capturing me was a lieutenant by the name of Víctor.

Once an undercover cop sat next to José Abreu on the bus. The cop started to praise the United States and then added that Reinaldo Arenas was his favorite author. José just changed seats, without saying a word. When the surveillance intensified, Juan would go to the place where we had agreed to meet and instead of waiting for me, he would just leave me something to eat.

I started writing my memoirs in the notebooks that Juan had brought me. Under the title "Before Night Falls" I would write all day until dark, waiting for the other darkness that would come when the police eventually found me. I had to hurry to get my writing done before my world finally darkened, before I was thrown into jail. That manuscript, of course, was lost, as was almost everything I had written in Cuba that I had not been able to smuggle out, but at the time, writing it all down was a consolation; it was a way of being with my friends when I was no longer among them.

I knew what a prison was like. René Ariza had gone insane in one; Nelson Rodríguez had to confess everything he was ordered to and then he was executed; Jesús Castro was held in a sinister cell in La Cabaña; I knew that once there, I could write no more. I still had the compass Lagarde had given me and didn't want to part with it, although I realized the danger it posed; to me it was a kind of magic charm. The compass, always pointing north, was like a symbol: it was in that direction that I had to go, north; no matter how far away it might take me from the Island, I would always be fleeing to the north.

I also had some hallucinogenic drugs that Olga had sent me. They were wonderful; however depressed I was, if I took one of them, I would feel an intense urge to dance and sing. Sometimes at night, under the influence of those pills, I would run around among the trees, dance, sing, and climb the trees.

One night, as a result of the euphoria that those pills gave me, I dared to go as far as the park amphitheater, where none other than Alicia Alonso was dancing. I tied several branches to my body and saw Alonso dance the famous second act of *Giselle*. Afterward, as I reached the road, a car stopped all of a sudden in front of me and I realized that I had been discovered. I crossed near the improvised stage platform, which was on the water, dove in and came out on the other side of the park. A man with a gun was following me. I ran and climbed a tree, where I stayed for several days not daring to come down.

I remember that while all the cops and their dogs were searching for me in vain, one mutt stood under my tree, looking at me happily without barking, as if it did not want to let them know where I was. Three days later I came down from the tree. I was ravenously hungry; but it would have been difficult to contact Juan. Strangely enough, on the very tree in which I had been hiding there was a poster with my name, information about me, my picture, and in large letters the heading: WANTED. From the information supplied by the police, I learned that I had a birthmark under my left ear.

After those three days of hiding, I saw Juan walking among the trees. He had dared to come to the park. He told me my situation was desperate, that in order to mislead the police he had spent the day switching buses to get to the park, and that there appeared to be no way out. Moreover, he had not heard from anyone in France, and the international scandal caused by my escape was amazing; State Security had sounded the alarm. Fidel Castro had given the order to find me immediately; in a country with such a perfect surveillance system, it was inconceivable that I had escaped from the police two months before and was still on the loose, writing documents and sending them abroad.

In water up to my shoulders, I would fish with a hook and line that Juan had brought me. I would make a little fire to cook the fish near the dam, and try to stay in the water as much as possible. It was much harder to find me that way. And even in that situation of imminent danger I had my erotic adventures with young fishermen, those always ready to have a good time with anybody who cast a promising glance at their fly. One of them insisted on taking me home—he lived nearby—so that I could meet his parents. I first thought it was because of the wristwatch I had, another present from Lagarde, but I was wrong; he simply wanted to introduce me to his family. We had dinner, had a good time, and later returned to the park.

The hardest part was the nights. It was a cold December, and I had to sleep out in the open; occasionally I would wake up soaking wet. I never slept twice in the same place. I hid in ditches full of crickets, cockroaches, and mice. Juan and I had several meeting places because a single spot would have been too dangerous. Sometimes at night I would continue reading the *Iliad* with the help of my lighter.

In December the water behind the dam dried up completely and I sought protection against its great walls. I kept a sort of mobile library there; Juan had brought me a few more books: *From the Orinoco to the Amazon River*, *The Magic Mountain*, and *The Castle*. I dug a hole at the end of the dam and buried them there; I took care of those books as if they were a great treasure. I buried them in polyethylene bags, which could be found all over the country; I think they were the only item the system produced in abundance.

While hiding in the park I got together now and then with the young fisherman I had met there; he was alarmed by the excessive surveillance of the place. He told me that, according to the police, a search was in progress for a CIA agent hiding there. He also told me that other fishermen and State Security were spreading various stories to alarm the people of the area so they would inform State Security if they saw any suspicious-looking character. They were saying that the person they were looking for had murdered an old lady, raped a little girl; in short, he was supposed to have committed such heinous crimes that anyone would inform on him. It was unbelievable that he had not been captured yet.

The Capture

Since I scarcely had eaten in the last ten days, I ventured down a path leading to a little store in the town of Calabazar with the *Iliad* under my arm. I think at that moment I felt suicidal. That, in any case, is what a friend whom I had met in the park had already told me. His name was Justo Luis, and he was a painter.

He lived nearby and was aware of everything that was happening to me; the night I saw him he brought me something to eat, cigarettes, and some money, and said: "Here you are giving yourself away; you have to go somewhere else."

In Calabazar I bought ice cream and quickly returned to the park. I was finishing the *Iliad*. I was at the point when Achilles, deeply moved, finally delivers Hector's body to Priam, a unique moment in literature. I was so swept away by my reading that I did not notice that a man had approached me and was now holding a gun to my head: "What is your name?" he asked. I replied that my name was Adrián Faustino Sotolongo, and gave him my ID. "Don't try to fool me, you are Reinaldo Arenas, and we have been looking for you in this park for some time. Don't move, or I'll put a bullet in your head," he exclaimed, and started to jump for joy. "I'm going to be promoted, I'm going to be promoted, I've captured you," he was saying, and I almost wanted to share in the joy of that poor soldier. He immediately signaled other soldiers nearby and they surrounded me, grabbed me by the arms, and thus, running and jumping through the underbrush, I was led to the Calabazar police station.

The soldier who had captured me was so grateful that he selected a comfortable cell for me. Although my mind told me I was a prisoner, my body refused to believe it and wanted to continue to run and jump across the countryside.

There I was in a cell, the compass still in my pocket. The police had taken the *Iliad* and my autobiography.[6] Within a few hours the whole town was gathered in front of the police station. The word had spread that the CIA agent, the rapist, the murderer of the old lady, had been captured by the Revolutionary police. The people were demanding that I be taken to the execution wall, as they had so loudly shouted for so many others at the beginning of the Revolution.

Those people actually wanted to storm the police station, and some of them climbed on the roof. The women were especially incensed, perhaps because of the rumored rape of the old lady; they threw rocks at me, and anything else they could find. The cop who arrested me yelled that Revolutionary justice would take care of me and succeeded in calming them down a little, although they still remained outside in the street. At that point it was dangerous to take me out of there, but the police finally managed to do so with a heavy escort of high-ranking officers. I then met Víctor, who had been interrogating all of my friends.

Víctor had received orders from the high command to transfer me immedi-

---

6   It seems that R.A. was able to recover the *Iliad* later on. [Trans. note]

ately to the prison at Morro Castle. As we drove through the streets of Havana, I saw people walking normally, free to have an ice cream or go to the movies to watch a Russian film, and I felt deeply envious of them. I was the fugitive now captive, the prisoner on his way to serve his time.

Witches

Witches have played an important part in my life. First there are those I could consider peaceful and spiritual, those who reign in the world of fantasy. This kind of sorceress, which came to me through my grandmother's imagination, filled the nights of my childhood with mystery and terror, and summoned me later to write my first novel, *Singing from the Well*. But there is another kind of sorceress, of flesh and blood, who has also played an important part in my life. Maruja Iglesias, for example, whom everybody called "the Library Witch": she was the influence that made possible my job transfer to the National Library, there to meet another sorceress, even wiser and more enchanting, María Teresa Freyre de Andrade, who gave me protection and also imparted her extensive, ancient wisdom. María Teresa had the habit of blinking, just like the great witch in one of Shakespeare's plays. Then I met Elia del Calvo, so perfect a witch that she surrounded herself entirely with cats. Her character and personality were very important to me at one point in my life. A sorceress like her indirectly made it possible for me later to leave the country like a nonperson, like an unknown. In Miami I also met several witches dedicated to the traffic of words. Witch-like, they dressed in long black robes, and were thin, with prominent jaws; some of them wrote poems and, like Elia del Calvo, forced me to read them. The world is really full of witches, some more benign, some more implacable, but the kingdom of fantasy, as well as patent reality, belongs to witches.

When I arrived in New York I met the perfect witch. This lady dyed her hair violet, wanted her old husband to die quickly, and flirted with everyone who would come close to her. It was a platonic flirtation, no doubt she was only trying to fill the immense loneliness of her life, on the West Side of Manhattan, where she tried to communicate in an English impossible to decipher. This witch, a perfect "fag hag," collected homosexuals and welcomed me as soon as I arrived. Though her son was homosexual as well, she, being a witch, had forced him to have a girlfriend and later to marry and even to have several children. This witch, whose name was Alma Ribera, told me I had to stay in New York. Thus she helped me fulfill my destiny, my always terrible destiny. She managed to find me an empty apartment in the center of Manhattan. "Rent it at once," she said. And suddenly I, who had come to New York for only three days, now had a small apartment on Forty-third Street between Eighth and Ninth Avenues, three blocks from Times Square, the most crowded place in the world. I did rent the apartment at once and I entrusted myself, as always, to the mysterious, evil, and sublime power of witches.

A real witch was my aunt Agata, matchless in her wickedness; for more than fifteen years I had to live with her in terror and under the constant threat of being denounced to the police. But I cannot deny that I felt a strange attraction for her; perhaps the attraction of evil, of danger.

Another unforgettable witch in my life was Blanca Romero, who transformed Old Havana into a clog factory, and who gave up prostitution when her tits collapsed, and became an extraordinary painter while, at the same time, denouncing her admirers to State Security.

Witches have dominated my life: witches who never gave up their brooms, not so they would be able to fly but because all their longings and frustrations, all their desires were exorcised through their sweeping: sweeping the rooms, the passageway, the yards at home, as if in this way they could sweep away their own lives.

The image of one major witch stands out above all the others; that of the noble witch, the suffering witch, the witch full of longing and sadness, the most beloved witch in the world: my mother. Also with her broom, always sweeping as if nothing mattered but the symbolic meaning of the act.

Sometimes witches would assume a half-masculine form, which could make them even more sinister. Among the witches that were for so long part of my life, how could I forget Cortés, a fearsome witch with a perfectly witch-like shape, thanks to whom I had to rewrite my novel *Farewell to the Sea* so many times, and who branded my life with terror during the seventies. How could I forget Pepe Malas, another perfect witch, who seemed to be in a constant state of levitation, twisted and insidious in character, misshapen of body (and thanks to whom I landed in jail, in one of the most Dantesque circles of hell). And how could I forget the classic witch all in black, black gloves and black cape, with bulging eyes and wispy hair, the Witch with the huge jaws and sinister smile: Samuel Toca, the frightening witch from whom I learned the real meaning of betrayal and who, witchlike, would materialize wherever I happened to be, even riding in the same car with me through the streets of New York.

Witches, my companions since childhood, will escort me to the very gates of hell.

Subcomandante Marcos (1957–)

One of the most dazzling figures of twentieth-century Mexico is Subcomandante Marcos. With little exaggeration, it can be said that Marcos completes a circle begun in 1910 with the Revolution's legendary leaders, Emiliano Zapata and Pancho Villa. It is hardly coincidental that Marcos adopted from Zapata the name for his movement, Ejército Zapatista de Liberación Nacional (EZLN) (the Zapatista Army of National Liberation), nor is it surprising that many Zapatistas still invoke the legacy of Pancho Villa. Indeed the late twentieth-century vindication of these once-disparaged men confirms the persistence of indigenous and peasant struggles in Mexico, where both rural and urban poverty has increased and where citizens continue to be deprived of their civil rights by political and military repression that has not always been subtle.

The insurrection that was announced to the world on January 1, 1994, had a number of sources. When the Zapatistas took control of many local towns, notably San Cristobal de las Casas, several social and historical movements converged: the Indian struggle against exploitation, discrimination, and the plunder of their lands; mounting resistance to large-scale agrarian production; and the revival of democratic movements sparked by the student uprisings of 1968.

While Subcomandante Marcos's words were at first interpreted as calling for a Zapatista coup, any remnant of that military and political goal was soon abandoned. That fact sharply differentiates the EZLN from any other Mexican military rebellion in the twentieth century and particularly from the guerrilla wars of the 1970s. After nearly two decades as a political force, the EZLN has had an enormous influence on many other organizations and has served as an international model for revolutionary change. The EZLN has conducted international conferences for democratic movements; it has published manifestos that reflect a language and perspective on Mexican reality unprecedented for political parties; and, above all, it has modeled an unwavering focus on the demands of indigenous peoples throughout the Americas. Many of its former allies have been critical of this particularization by the EZLN and also of its distancing itself from national struggles that concern all exploited and dispossessed Mexicans. In fact, the EZLN has simply remained faithful to its roots. According to its own chronology, the group originated in 1974 at an Indian conference in Chiapas commemorating 500 years since the birth of BARTOLOMÉ DE LAS CASAS. One of the principal organizers was Samuel Ruiz, the bishop of Chiapas, who never resorted to armed struggle but also never flagged in his support of Indian demands for justice.

In his timeline, Subcomandante Marcos cites the student protests that began in Mexico in 1968. The national student strike between June and October 1968 had soon escalated into a political movement with larger demands: freeing political prisoners, abolishing anticonstitutional articles that curtailed freedom of expression, and punishing high-ranking officials for using excessive force. These issues went to the heart of the Mexican political system, controlled by an oligarchy for decades through the PRI (Institutionalized Revolutionary Party). The student movement was violently repressed by the army on October 2 in the massacre of Tlatelolco, a working-class neighborhood in Mexico City. Though the government claimed only 30 casualties, other witnesses alleged that there were between 200 and 400 deaths, with many people killed inside the apartment buildings surrounding the square in which the meeting was taking place. Many people believed that those corpses were secretly cremated by the army.

The violent suppression of the strike frustrated the hopes of many who thought that slow democratic change was possible in Mexico. A number of urban and rural guerrilla groups rose up in the 1970s; others, already disillusioned by the outcomes of other guerrilla movements, like that of Cuba's Fidel Castro, sought to fight repression by organizing its most immediate victims—the workers and peasants. The man who later became Subcomandante Marcos contacted the precarious indigenous organizations in Chiapas with the specific goal of starting with a base and avoiding any acceleration in the process of consciousness-raising or in the structure of the resistance.

The first cell of clandestine opposition emerged in the Lacandonian jungles in 1983 and, little by little, gradually formed the EZLN. The situation in Chiapas was particularly delicate. Since the early 1980s, thousands of Guatemalan Indians had been crossing into Mexico to escape the massacres of the Guatemalan army. Moreover, the drug cartels had chosen Chiapas as a principal passageway for their illegal merchandise en route to the United States. The EZLN had to toe a very thin line to avoid being associated with either the Guatemalan guerrillas or the drug traffickers—a task the EZLN managed admirably, distancing itself very effectively from activities that might taint its image. Subcomandante Marcos has proved to be a decisive presence in the movement's independence. Though he has repeatedly affirmed that he is only the spokesperson for the Indian leadership of the

EZLN, he has also helped to guide the organization through many political decisions with great wisdom and skill.

Clarity has seldom been a major feature of Mexican style in political speeches or written discourse. The declarations from the Lacandonian forest are unique precisely because of the fluidity with which they link the political and the moral, the moral and the racial, racial issues with social concerns, social problems with economic ones. The result is a complex and multidimensional image of Mexican reality. Soon after the declarations appeared, this connectedness was applied to other genres, using the same fresh and incisive language. Marcos even invented the character "Durito" [Little Tough Guy], drawing on both Indian oral traditions and the Spanish classics to create contemporary parables, using humor and wit to make points about relevant issues. Further evidence of Marcos's considerable literary talent was his coauthorship of the novel *Muertos incómodos* (2004) [The Uncomfortable Dead] with noted historian and novelist Paco Ignacio Taibo II. Marcos has, in fact, become an indispensable witness in the contemporary world, producing acute assessments of issues ranging from international politics to the intricate repercussions of social behaviors.

Though the early Zapatistas tried to protect their identities with masks and pseudonyms, the Mexican government was eventually able to reveal that Subcomandante Marcos was actually Rafael Sebastián Guillén, born in 1957 in the state of Tamaulipas in northeastern Mexico. The son of middle-class parents who were both teachers, Guillén attended a Jesuit school as a youth, where he probably first encountered Liberation Theology, a Catholic political movement asserting that the teachings of Jesus Christ insist on social and economic justice. Marcos's Jesuit education also suggests the origins of the shrewd political judgment that he has repeatedly demonstrated. Abandoning work on a doctorate in Mexico City, Marcos participated in several leftist organizations before immersing himself in the work of assisting the Indians of Chiapas.

One of the early supporters of the Zapatistas was the Bishop of Chiapas, Samuel Ruiz, who became a critical mediator in talks between the EZLN and the Mexican government. Like Marcos, Ruiz was deeply influenced by Liberation Theology, which, along with the Cuban Revolution, became one of the most potent forces in undermining exploitative regimes all over Latin America. While not all high-ranking members of the Catholic Church endorsed or collaborated in armed resistance, the explicit connections with Liberation Theology underline the critical, if ambivalent, role of the Church in these contemporary struggles. Some segments of the Church often suppressed or ignored the social and political demands of their constituencies, while other sectors made conscious efforts to satisfy those economic and social needs whenever it could.

As an able politician and as a compelling social symbol, Subcomandante Marcos has become an indispensable figure in Latin American culture, producing thoughtful commentary on social issues as well as making exceptional contributions to the Mexican literary tradition. The selection is from "EZLN Communiques." the *Struggle Site: Archive*, n.d. (http://struggle.ws/mexico/ezln/jung4.html).

From The Fourth Declaration of the Lacandon Jungle (January 1, 1996)

I

TO THE PEOPLE OF MEXICO: TO THE PEOPLES AND GOVERNMENTS OF THE WORLD: BROTHERS AND SISTERS:

The flower[7] of the word will not die. The masked face which, today has a name, may die, but the word which came from the depth of history and the earth can no longer be cut by the arrogance of the powerful. We were born of the night. We live in the night. We will die in her. But the light will be tomorrow for others, for all those who today weep during the night, for those who have been denied the day, for those for whom death is a gift, for those who are denied life. The light will be for all of them. For everyone everything. For us pain and anguish, for us the joy of rebellion, for us a future denied, for us the dignity of insurrection. For us nothing.

Our fight has been to make ourselves heard, and the bad government screams arrogance and closes its ears with its cannons.

Our fight is caused by hunger, and the gifts of the bad government are lead[8] and paper for the stomachs of our children.

Our fight is for a roof over our heads, which has dignity, and the bad government destroys our homes and our history.

Our fight is for knowledge, and the bad government distributes ignorance and disdain.

Our fight is for the land, and the bad government gives us cemeteries.

---

7 The flower (la flor de) is idiomatic for "beauty."

8 Lead (plomo) is a metaphor for "bullets."

Our fight is for a job, which is just and dignified, and the bad government buys and sells our bodies and our shames.[9] Our fight is for life, and the bad government offers death as our future.

Our fight is for respect for our right to sovereignty and self-government, and the bad government imposes laws of the few on the many.

Our fight is for liberty of thought and walk (movement) and the bad government builds jails and graves.

Our fight is for justice, and the bad government consists of criminals and assassins.

Our fight is for history and the bad government proposes to erase history.

Our fight is for the homeland, and the bad government dreams with the flag and the language of foreigners.

Our fight is for peace, and the bad government announces war and destruction.

Housing, land, employment, food, education, independence, democracy, liberty, justice and peace. These were our banners during the dawn of 1994. These were our demands during that long night of 500 years. These are, today, our necessities.

Our blood and our word have lit a small fire in the mountain and we walk a path against the house of money and the powerful. Brothers and sisters of other races and languages, of other colors, but with the same heart now protect our light and in it they drink of the same fire.

The powerful came to extinguish us with its violent wind, but our light grew in other lights. The rich dream still about extinguishing the first light. It is useless, there are now too many lights and they have all become the first.

The arrogant wish to extinguish a rebellion which they mistakenly believe began in the dawn of 1994. But the rebellion which now has a dark face and an indigenous language was not born today. It spoke before with other languages and in other lands. This rebellion against injustice spoke in many mountains and many histories. It has already spoken in nahuatl, paipai, kiliwa, cucapa, cochimi, kumiai, yuma, seri, chontal, chinanteco, pame, chichimeca, otomi, mazahua, matlatzinca, ocuilteco, zapoteco, solteco, chatino, papabuco, mixteco, cucateco, triqui, amuzzgo, mazateco, chocho, ixcaateco, huave, tlapaneco, totonaca, tepehua, populuca, mixe, zoque, huasteco, lacandon, mayo, chol, tzeltal, tzotzil, tojolabal, mame, teco, ixil, aguacateco, motocintleco, chicomucelteco.

---

9   Shames (vergüenza) also means "dignity."

They want to take the land so that our feet have nothing to stand on. They want to take our history so that our word will be forgotten and die. They do not want Indians. They want us dead.

The powerful want our silence. When we were silent, we died, without the Word we did not exist. We fight against this loss of memory, against death and for life. We fight the fear of a death because we have ceased to exist in memory.

When the homeland speaks its Indian heart, it will have dignity and memory.

In Context | The Zapatistas

The Zapatista National Liberation Army (abbreviated by its Spanish acronym as EZLN and named for the revolutionary leader Emiliano Zapata) was created when the Indians of the Lacandón region in the Mexican state of Chiapas started an armed rebellion in 1994. Like most guerrilla movements at the end of the twentieth century, they initially sought to take power from the central national government. However, they soon relinquished this aspiration, led toward more localized transformation by their chief spokesperson, SUBCOMANDANTE MARCOS.

Figure 8.3. The Zapatistas, Subcomandante Marcos, Chiapas, 1994. Photograph courtesy of Antonio Turok.

The EZLN is an army, but it also reflects the will of a people, an organization designed as a defensive tool. In addition, the EZLN and the people it represents have assumed another powerful instrument of defense: their identification with their natural environment. Nature is not, for them, merely a source of raw material, a depot of usable products. Their religion insists that nature is a living being, an intrinsic part of their lives, encompassing all aspects of their existence.

The ski masks worn by the Zapatistas are both a form of defense and symbolic. As anonymous Indians, they have been exploited; they also defend themselves anonymously.

Luciano Tapia (1923–2010)

Born in the copper mining town of Coro Coro (Corocoro) in the Department of La Paz, Luciano Tapia—whose Aymara name is Lusiku Qhispi Mamani—has always lived between two worlds. As a small child, he was part of the *ayllu* of Q'allirpa, where his father was born, and the mining town where his parents worked. A few years later, when the family moved to the capital, Tapia encountered a totally different culture and learned a new language, Spanish; he also experienced the social and psychological consequences of racism and the different poverty of the city.

Tapia eventually emerged as the first Indian leader to give political shape to critical ideas then circulating in Bolivia. He was, in some sense, the creator of Indianismo, a movement for the vindication of Indians articulated most effectively by Fausto Reinaga (1906–1994), an indigenous Bolivian activist and writer who sharply criticized Western influences on native society. In his many books and essays, including the influential *La revolución india* (1970) [The Indian Revolution], Fausto Reinaga advocated making culture central to politics. He sought, for example, to reclaim the name "Indian" from its pejorative uses and transform it into a positive affirmation of a proud way of life. Luciano Tapia expanded upon Reinaga's ideas; he used his experience as a union leader, party organizer, and representative in parliament to make Reinaga's intellectual framework a political reality.

Luciano Tapia's politics were honed in the mining industry, where he served as a union leader until the closures of the mines in 1985, followed by massive layoffs. Tapia then immigrated to the lowlands of the Alto Beni region and became a peasant leader during the presidency of Victor Paz Estenssoro. After Hugo Banzer was elected to office in 1971, Tapia was persecuted and arrested. As he became acquainted with other political prisoners,

Tapia began to understand the scope of Bolivia's political persecutions and the need for a different kind of political organization. In 1982, Tapia became one of the founders of MITKA (Movimiento Indio Tupak Katari) [Tupak Katari Indian Movement]. The new party grew in influence and national scope, allowing Tapia to be elected as its representative in Parliament from 1982 to 1985. Tapia was also the party's nominee for president in 1978, 1979, and 1982.

In 1995, Tapia recorded the major events of his life and those of the Aymara people from the highlands of Bolivia in his autobiography, *Ukhamawa Jakawisaxa (Así es nuestra vida) Autobiografía de un aymara*—in English: (That Is How Our Life Is) An Aymara Autobiography. The title itself is deliberately in Aymara and the Spanish serves *only* as a translation to underline how critical culture and language are in defining one's life. Throughout the book, Tapia relates the profound changes that have been occurring in Aymara culture, many of them imposed by a presumed inferiority to the dominant Hispanic values. Tapia insists that any successful Indian movement must first reaffirm the importance of its culture and heritage; that act will then allow the community to restructure its political forms in more appropriate—and effective—ways.

What is most original in Tapia's thought is his insistence on the wholeness of culture in redefining politics: cultural awareness is not just the adoption of superficial folklore and indigenous symbolism, but the incorporation of an authentic and complex understanding of the world. For Luciano Tapia, affirming Indian culture includes acknowledging communal property of the land (the *ayllus*) and recognizing the original Indian territories as a separate nation formed by the broader conglomeration of *ayllus* and *markas*[10] called Q'ullasuyu, the name it possessed in the pre-Colombian period. In its most basic terms, Tapia's position does not even acknowledge the Bolivian State as representing Indian groups like the MITKA. As the party's leader, Tapia unwaveringly maintained this approach when other indigenous groups, like the Tupak Katari Revolutionary Movement (MRTK), formed alliances with the left. Tapia considered any affiliation with leftist parties, such as the Revolutionary Leftist Party (PRI), a form of yielding to colonial hegemony.

Tapia's autobiography documents a broad scope of human experience: life in the mines and in the *ayllus*; the struggles of the unions in the highlands and the peasants' problems in the lowlands; the political persecution

---

10 *Marka* is a large area consisting of many *ayllus*.

of union leaders and the role of Indian leaders in Parliament; the dominance of the established parties over the poorly funded new Indian parties; political corruption and social subservience; the psychological and social effects of racism at every level. The enormity of Tapia's undertaking makes the book difficult to assign to a single category or genre. Narrating so many lives and recording so much change and migration in the lives of Tapia's people, *Ukhamawa Jakawisaxa* is not an autobiography per se. At the same time, it articulates—from a distinctly Indian perspective—a thoughtful critique of contemporary Bolivian society over a period of seventy-five years. One might simply call *Ukhamawa Jakawisaxa* a microhistory of a nation.

In the selection here, Tapia recalls his realization of how death in the mines is simply part of a broader system of labor exploitation. That realization later impels him to assume a role as union leader. Tapia's radical politics are thus formed in response to a concrete event, rather than by any indoctrination from the left. That connection resonates throughout Tapia's career in his repeated demonstrations of his commitment to making his words consistent with his deeds and to being grounded by the authenticity of his culture and beliefs. The failure of other politicians to connect their lives with their public agendas was often the target of Tapia's criticism. This selection also offers a glimpse into the hard life of miners and the utter disregard for their safety by the mining companies. A terrible accident, resulting in several deaths, generates a moment of deep sorrow among the workers and acts as a force to unite in a communal affirmation of life. Tapia later shows how that moment triggers his long life as union activist and leader, fighting for his people and trying to survive subsequent persecutions from dictatorships.

The selection is from Luciano Tapia, *Ukhamawa Jakawisaxa (Así es nuestra vida) Autobiografía de un aymara* (La Paz: Hisbol, 1995), 225–30. Translated by Isabel Bastos and Marvin Liberman. Reproduced by permission of the Estate of Don Luciano Tapia.

From Ukhamawa Jakawisaxa (That Is How Our Life Is) An Aymara Autobiography (1995)

Bitterness and Union Awakening

One morning, when we'd just started working, we got a general alarm for help because an entire crew had been caught in the *aysa* of the *tuxus* (a cave-in of the pit). That accident seemed particularly bad because it involved a significant number of dead and wounded. I arrived at the site along with other miners who'd also come to help with the rescue. From the narrow mine shaft I could only hear a disturbing silence. In spite of the presence of some twenty miners, all we could see was a gigantic mineral block covering the floor of the pit, nearly *llusk'a* to *llusk'a* [end to end], about 15 meters long and about 1.20 meters wide. That one huge slab covered the entire work crew so that, with the exception of two men whom we could see jammed between the rock wall and the giant block, there wasn't a single trace of the others nor could we even hear any moans. Even the two trapped miners, maybe owing to shock or because they had fainted, remained very quiet until someone was able to get them out. Then, between cries of pain, they related the details of the accident and pointed out precisely where their workmates could be found.

Because the mine floor was so uneven it was possible to find a gap where the light from the lanterns revealed the unmoving bodies of the dead; one miner was clearly dying, his feet moving from time to time in his death-throes. Another miner was scraping the dirt beneath him to get out on his own, and he miraculously made it, helped by the rescuers in the final part of his trench-digging. His feat was really astonishing, not just because of his courage, struggling to save his life, but just because he managed to survive the accident that had killed his workmates, when he too had been crushed just like them; it was an astonishing sight in the midst of that terrible scene.

Meanwhile, the thick iron pipes that we were using as levers were bending like molasses candy. We all felt powerless, and some of the men's faces were streaked with tears as they recognized the futility of all our efforts. Confusion began to spread; there wasn't a single engineer to direct the operation or a boss to keep order among the rescuers; nor did anyone have the composure or experience to initiate standard rescue procedures. Maybe because there were many miners, we only thought about applying brute force, without understanding that the enormous block was far beyond our strength, not only because of its tremendous weight but even more because its awkward position simply cancelled out our usefulness. However, if there'd only been any kind of direction or intelligent approach, it should have been possible to dig a trench in the floor, just like the one dug by our fellow worker who, by scraping at the dirt, managed to squeeze himself out from under the block; by digging a trench it would have been possible to get to those who were trapped. But in the confusion of the moment, there seemed to be no alternative except to smash up the block with chisels and sledgehammers, striking on it directly above the victims' bodies.

That decision finally made me nauseous enough to vomit; those agonizing death throes that were visible through the gap between the floor and the block made me sick, and I thought about how the area was becoming soaked with the blood of the dead. That thought, along with the nausea, finally forced me to draw away into an isolated corner so that I wouldn't see any more or join in on trying to shatter the block, which was in fact becoming a colossal headstone for those same workmates we were trying to save. It seemed sacrilegious, finishing off the work of death by crushing the rock over the men's bodies, finally even killing the poor worker whose last struggles had been visible under the stone block. I tried to stop this pointless effort. But in the general confusion the miners were like worker ants stirred up over their nest; the only thing anyone could think about was doing something to save the miners, even if their method was both misguided and cruel. I could not bear to watch that dreadful scene any longer; or maybe I just didn't have the courage to look directly into death's ugly face.

In all that noise of iron banging on rock and the miners' shouts, the rescue work continued until it was done. I just couldn't bear to witness that parade of dead men with broken bodies, their faces still marked by expressions of sudden panic, of pain and desperation. It was so emotionally overwhelming that I began to shake violently, with a bitterness reaching to the bottom of my heart. Without fully understanding my reactions, I soon realized that I was breathless and that my mouth was dry. The bitterness then gave way to an inner explosion of blind rage, bursting from my chest. I wanted to find out who was to blame here, who was hiding behind the fog of that cruel reality, even though I could see with my own eyes the heavy block of granite that had caused the disaster. In the violent emotional turmoil of that day, perhaps because it was the first time I'd had to witness such an immense calamity, that desire for some explanation became the search for a more fundamental truth: the source of that cruel reality in which we lived. Or maybe unconsciously I had already given myself an answer, one that explained my bitter explosion of rage.

After bodies of the dead miners had been retrieved, the site emptied out quickly; I walked away with the last of those who were leaving, still dazed and bewildered by what had occurred. I walked without intent, not knowing what to do; I knew I didn't want to go back to my own workplace, which, even though it was on another level, was just another pigeonhole of that same reality. But, what to do? Then I felt an involuntary shudder. I was afraid: the mine seemed to me now a dismal and horrific place, where I too could meet the same end as those poor miners who had died so wretchedly, doubtless leaving behind little children, now neglected and unable to understand the depths of misfortune that had befallen them. I also could have the same end. That thought made me break into a cold sweat; I understood that my fear wasn't so much for my own life, but for the fate of my little children should I die suddenly in the mine. At that point, my bitterness and rage turned into grief.

People in the village were by this time used to accidents; they were no longer even moved by these disasters, which had become instead objects of mere curiosity and occasions for Christian resignation. The death of a miner was, in some sense, normal, a common occurrence and just part of the realities of mining. However, this time the emotional upheaval was particularly intense, probably because of the sheer number of miners dead and injured— something that hadn't happened in a long time. Our labor union, which then was only in its early stages declared a state of mourning and a "work stoppage" for the day of the burial, although the company management, in order to make a point, changed the term from work stoppage to furlough or release time. In any case, on that occasion the company accepted the workers' request without further comment; the work attendance cards were signed even though the day shift had barely worked half a day and the night shift didn't even show up for work. Moreover, for the first time in memory, the miners held a wake for the corpses, raised up on biers, whose rental the company had paid for, further demonstrating their concern by providing coca, cigarettes and alcohol.

On the night of the wake, the new union hall, only recently opened, was completely full, with workers as well as neighbors and relatives of the victims. I was there, too. What most impressed me was the family members, their faces full of their intense grief, some crying out in loud laments, others weeping quietly with heartbreaking sobs. One woman epitomized the stark human grief of the mining disaster: surrounded by her three stunned children, she wept with such sorrow and distress that no one could fail to be touched by her suffering. That image of sadness and grief moved me so deeply that I wept openly, unable to hold back the trembling sobs that shook my shoulders.

As the *ponchecitos* [a warm alcoholic drink] that were being served began to take effect, several mestizo laborers, who were particularly gifted orators and poets, began the usual speeches, praising the dead workers' virtues in elaborate language that few of us Indian miners understood very well. In their competition for finding the best phrases, they declared the humble *ponchecito*, made with cinnamon and alcohol, "nectar," while the speaker himself was called a "lover of the arts" and all sorts of other complicated phrases whose meaning I didn't understand.

But as more and more of the attendees became willing to speak, the prayers began to be transformed into angry revolutionary speeches by people taking up the workers' struggle; their language was full of references to imperialism, to the tin barons, to the government, and, of course, to the company. For the first time, I was hearing incendiary speeches that demanded the recognition of our national interests and of the rights and dignity of the long-suffering miners, whose sacrifices were evident before us in the broken bodies of our former companions and in the desperation of their forsaken relatives and their innocent orphaned children, who would soon be mercilessly expelled from the camp. There were so many causes of our exploitation that the speeches seemed unable to end. Speaking roughly and without flourishes, these courageous individuals became the spontaneous voice of the mineworkers, hurling their anger directly against our oppressors. The core of rational argument was still embryonic, but that moment marked the beginning of a struggle that was not going to end that night.

For me that wake was the beginning of an education in union struggle. It's important to observe here that, at this early point in the movement, no politician ever spoke to us about the need for a socio-economic vindication. The strongmen who were candidates for office spoke about issues in the regional cantons, but they said nothing about the realities of the mines. Typically, they offered open-door canteens only to their supporters, and if they gave him a victory, they provided what the voters expected as a reward: a barbecue. Because of these practices, it's important to note that the leaders of the struggle of the miners of Corocoro were natives of Pacajes, well-known in the community, who, having worked in the larger mines of the tin barons, had returned home because of layoffs, persecutions and confinements, to which they were commonly subjected. Those plain, rank-and-file miners, through talk and speeches, were developing in us a revolutionary consciousness.

Despite the solidarity generated by that accident, leaving three wounded and four dead, there were, after all, two different worlds in the village. The difference was noticeable not only in cultural practices but also in racial and social prejudices. For example, despite the public homage rendered to the dead by all the workers, many relatives were irritated because we could not carry out our ancestral ceremonies. Indeed, with only one exception, all the victims were Indians, community members of the neighboring *ayllus*, whose relatives had come to reclaim the bodies and take them to their communities. A lot of persuasion had been necessary even to get their consent to have the wake at the union hall. Despite that early conflict, everyone agreed that the miners were being honored, even though the cultural roots of the victims were being ignored. All in all, the burial was a solemn event, with all the workers in attendance. For the first time, the union's banner was at the head of the funeral cortège, and several speakers representing different sections of the mine gave farewell speeches. It seemed natural that the union would represent the bereaved, and its prestige then grew among the workers, offering an example of their power in relation to the mine company.

Álvaro García Linera (1962–)

Born in Cochabamba, Bolivia, Álvaro García Linera is among Latin America's most significant leftist intellectuals. He has come full circle in his career: beginning as a radical revolutionary, he is at this writing vice president of Bolivia. Elected in 2005 with Evo Morales, who became Bolivia's first Indian president, García Linera has used his position to bring about major changes in Bolivia, relying on his sophisticated intellectual background to interpret social complexities and to resolve the conflicts of contemporary society.

García Linera began reading Marxist texts as an adolescent. In 1981, he moved to Mexico City to study at the Universidad Nacional Autónoma de México (UNAM) and earned undergraduate and graduate degrees in mathematics. In Mexico, he also became acquainted with the guerrilla movements of Guatemala, such as the EGP (Ejército Guerrillero de los Pobres) [Guerrilla Army of the Poor]. That experience, as he later recalled, allowed him to see more clearly the need to establish connections between Indian and leftist movements in his own country.

Shortly after his return to Bolivia in 1985, García Linera joined a clandestine political group that soon became involved with the mineworkers' union and the Katarista Indian movement. He met Felipe Quispe, an Indian leader who was in MITKA (Tupak Katari Indian Movement) at that time, and they later formed the EGTK (Ejército Guerrillero Tupak Katari) [Tupak Katari Guerrilla Army] to promote armed resistance. In April 1992, García Linera was arrested and charged with subversive activity and armed insurgency. Tortured by the secret police, he was confined in the maximum-security prison of Chonchocoro until 1997. During his imprisonment, he wrote one of his most important works: *Forma valor y forma comunidad* (1995) [Value Form and Community Form], collaborating with his companion, Raquel Gutiérrez Aguilar, a Mexican national and a member of the EGTK who had been arrested at the same time; they cowrote the introduction to the first edition of the book. In prison García Linera also

Figure 8.4. Álvaro García Linera, vice president of Bolivia (2005–). Photo by Matilde Mamani, from the Oficina de la Vicepresidencia of Bolivia. Taken on December 13, 2013, at the IV Conference of the European Leftist Party in Spain. Photo courtesy of the Office of the Vice Presidency.

undertook rigorous readings of Karl Marx's *Capital* and books on Andean culture, establishing the critical links between Marxism and Indianismo that form the basis of *Forma valor y forma comunidad* and his own political views.

The excerpt here is from a longer interview with García Linera in which he comments on *Forma valor y forma comunidad* and explains the principal dilemmas and challenges facing the new social movements in Bolivia. However, neither his book nor his comments can be understood without appreciating the culmination of García Linera's political trajectory with his election to the office of vice president in the administration of Evo Morales. The Morales government was the result of a period of intense social activism at all levels of Bolivian society. One such movement was that of the coca growers, who looked to Morales as their leader; other indigenous movements from the Altiplano and the Lowlands of Bolivia were also gathering strength.

Although *Forma valor y forma comunidad* is the text of a revolutionary and precedes García Linera's role as a government official, its relevance persists. As García Linera has commented, the book reflects his life: "things I have done in my life have a lot to do with the reading and the interpretation in this book, and what I am going to do in the future is also here." One of the tensions here is the relationship between local movements as a point of departure for social change and the need for a more general takeover of power as a way to produce a broader and deeper transformation of the social and state structures.

Having been a local revolutionary fighter, García Linera is concerned with the larger issues, such as the transformation of the state, and during his first term in office, with writing a new constitution, which (against strong opposition from traditional parties) included the participation of a large Indian constituency. Though the new constitution was approved by Congress in 2009, the document itself continues to be tested. One major challenge is to figure out how to contain within a general framework the constitutional provisions for representing and integrating different cultural notions of citizenship as well as various forms of political representation and juridical practices. In their multiplicity, these practices can seem to defy a general law of the state.

As vice president, García Linera is living the conflicts he explored in his book, including the tension between the state as a monopoly and the social movements that aim to destabilize that concentration of power to make their demands. As he explains, "There is no solution to this contradiction. You have to live that contradiction. . . . you have to be making decisions . . . you cannot enter into a three-year debate about whether a school should be built or not because the people will demand it . . . you have to be efficient and at the same time you have to consult the people, take into consideration the participation of the people."

As other intellectuals question the role of the Left in our changing societies, García Linera has been implementing leftist objectives and creating new spaces for the social forces that generated its convictions. The Office of the Vice President has actively launched major publications by international leftist intellectuals, including the Ecuadorian/Mexican writer, Bolivar Echeverría, and the Slovenian philosopher, Slavoj Žižek. García Linera has himself continued to publish, explaining Morales's government policies and responding to growing criticism from different political positions.

García Linera has put Bolivia on the map as a leader in implementing radical change. Many are watching the results closely, and some have begun to imitate the successes. García Linera himself remains only too aware that the labors necessary to create a more egalitarian society and a more communitarian distribution of wealth are not easily accomplished. As he himself states, full revolutionary change is yet to come, but the road to its realization depends not on overcoming its contradictions but rather on learning to ride with them.

The selection is from *Valor y comunidad: Reencuentro marxista y boliviano. Una conversacíon con Álvaro García Linera* [Value and Community: The Meeting of Marxism and Indianism. A Conversation with Álvaro García Linera." Interview conducted and edited by Josefa Salmón, November 18, 2011, and translated by Isabel Bastos and Marvin Liberman, transcribed by Vanessa Alfaro (La Paz: Plural Editores, 2016), 14–15, 19–23.

From Value and Community: The Meeting of Marxism and Indianism. A Conversation with Álvaro García Linera (2011)

And starting from that connection, of the indigenous and labor movements with the armed struggle, we started to form, among this small group of young people—all university students, who had not yet graduated—a political identity and an intellectual identity that we were going to consolidate, that we were going to prepare and were then going to project as a political structure. And that is how our military training began there [in Mexico], with our reading of indigenous history, our reading about the workers' movement, our reading of Marxism from its source—no longer following manuals but going straight to the classics in the strict and literal sense of the term—and the issue of armed struggle, the actual preparation for an armed struggle. And, so, it was essential to read the classics of armed struggle, from Sun Tzu, Clausewitz, Mao Ze Dong, Ho Chi Minh, right up to the Tupamaros[11] and the Latin American experience. In the end, these were the three sources for the construction of our thought in the '80s. And so, when we arrived here in Bolivia—we arrived in '84, '85—we built a very close, clandestine nucleus of young activists who quickly acted on two fronts, by connecting directly with the mineworkers' union movement and by trying to form an alliance with the Katarista Indian movement, which at that moment was losing its strength and becoming fragmented. What we wanted, then, was to train with them. This led us to meet with Felipe Quispe's group, which was coming from a divided MITKA [Tupak Katari Indian Movement], from a weakened MITKA and also with new segments of workers who could not identify with the ongoing [leftist] debate

---

11 Tupamaros was a guerrilla urban movement founded in Uruguay in the mid-1960s. The term derives from two leaders, both called Tupac Amaru, who resisted the Spanish. The first Tupac Amaru was the last Inca ruler, executed in 1572; the second led a major rebellion in 1780–1781 against colonial rule.

between the PC [Communist Party] and the POR [Revolutionary Workers' Party] within the workers' movement.

Regarding the question of [the proletariat] the mineworkers, we introduced the need for armed struggle, of resistance, the need to be armed faced with the imminent closure of this cycle of social democratization, and the need to connect with the indigenous/peasant movement on equal terms. Regarding our comrades from the MITKA movement, we saw the need to build a structure that would lead to a movement toward the emancipation of the indigenous nations through the use of armed struggle. It isn't very well known but, for example, in 1987, I don't know how but the COB [Bolivian Workers' Central Union] congress approved—when [Juan] Lechín[12] [Oquendo] was brought down—a declaration, at the last minute, when everyone was asleep, it must have been four in the morning, we were a small group, a delegation of five guys, made up of mining and community delegates, we got an historic resolution approved, the resolution for the self-determination of indigenous nations, in '87, of the Aymara/Quechua Nation. [. . .]

And around the years—'84, '85, '86—we were going to find the central axes. In the indigenous front, from what our fellow members told us, from our meeting with the Kataristas and the Indianistas[13] and from our reading of [Fausto] Reinaga, and our reading of Marx's *Grundrisse*, we would come to understand more [in depth] the idea of communitarianism. That is how we linked indigenous with communitarian movements, with the labor movement and the armed struggle. Those are the columns, the pillars for the interpretation of the world, of Bolivian history, and of the driving forces of the revolution; the emancipating horizon that then opened up would be articulated around these four axes.

*   *   *

The Marxists in Bolivia, all of them without exception, we thought—and I continue to believe—that they didn't understand the indigenous world; therefore, they had a mutilated view of Bolivian reality and of Bolivia's emancipatory

---

12 Juan Lechín Oquendo (1914–2001) was the head of the COB (Bolivian Workers Union) from 1952 to 1987. His long leadership allowed him to acquire significant political leverage for this important union.

13 The Indianistas of the MITKA (Tupak Katari Indian Movement) differentiated themselves from the Kataristas by claiming that they did not mix with leftist groups, in contrast to organizations like the Tupak Katari Revolutionary Movement (MRTK), which was led by its founder Jenaro Flores, who was also head of the Confederación Sindical Única de Trabajadores Campesinos de Bolivia (CSUTCB) [Unified Syndical Confederation of Rural Workers of Bolivia].

potential. All our activity from the '80s until today has been motivated by these ideas. The left never understood the indigenous issue. And I wagered—it was a question of faith, basically of faith—that Marxism would be able to explain the indigenous issue, the national issue, and to present a different reading of the peasant movement.

Then, if you notice, all my texts since '87 until '97 when I wrote this book *Forma valor y forma comunidad*, have to do with that: how to use the core tools of classical Marxism, of the founders, to reread peasant history, reread indigenous history in our country, to settle the issue with the left and to try to consolidate another point of view. My first text, in '87, *The Conditions of the Socialist Revolution in Bolivia*, fundamentally goes through Lenin and reports what he says about the peasant movement, about the communitarian movement. It's an examination of the complete works of Lenin.

Another thing that I would do before going to jail, between 1989 and 1990 or 1991 was to make another revision of my readings of Marx in Spanish up to *Grundrisse*, in order to find out what Marx says about the Nation, about the peasants and about the so-called diffuse identities.

*   *   *

So, my obsession was to find what he [Marx] said so that we could find powerful tools in Marxism with which to understand, to reinforce the (Aymara-Quechua) indigenous movement in order to understand national and class issues. How to assemble all this into one? The Indianist perception left aside the matter of classes and also lost sight of the organizational question. There was moral denunciation [on the part] of the indigenous movements but it was a moral criticism, not a political one, leaving aside the class issue, in other words [leaving] the contradictions and the struggles around interests which differentiate society and that are also a motor for change. So, I wanted to find that fusion, of Indianism and Marxism. And I was sure that it could be found through Marxism, that Marxism offered tools for that articulation, for that encounter of those two fundamental narratives of what we are as Bolivians. I worked up to that point [in my text]. This text was the product of what I read up to the *Grundrisse*. But I had to continue [reading], the hardest part: *Capital* and the ethnographic notebooks. Then I was arrested. And I might have remained there for decades; it was a good moment to continue the work that I began as a free man [. . .]

And I believed I had found this fusion between Indianism and Marxism as a productive force for indigenous emancipation in the country. Later the things that I've been doing in life have much to do with the reading, the interpreta-tion contained here [in my book], and what I did from this point forward is also contained here.

Now, what you were asking me is partly written in the introduction, though there are things that aren't there that I'm telling you right now. You asked me: how did I take on this debate between the particular and the general, which I picked up again in the last text of *Las tensiones creativas de la revolución*, 2011 [The Creative Tensions of the Revolution], where I analyzed, now as vice president, what was happening in the Bolivian process. That debate is there [in Value Form and Community Form]. I picked it up again twenty years after in other circumstances, there [in 1991] in prison and now governing, but it's the same debate. I'd sum it up like this: it's in the local sphere where it springs to the immediacy of life, in every day satisfactions and discontents, the accu-mulation of what one is, of how one uses what one has inherited to confront the adversities and the challenges of life, where one can visualize, experience the new social entities created by people or awakened by people through their experience, [all of this] different or potentially different from mainstream society and from the logics of domination.

How could the Water War[14] have occurred in 2000 given that the entire workers' movement, the large national structures, the large unions had been destroyed? Because what the decree 21060 [Víctor Paz Estenssoro's Supreme Decree of 1985 to impose neoliberal policies] had not destroyed were the lo-cal networks; where people rallied around the water issue, the land issue, the supply issue, around cultural revitalization, thus creating new types of associa-tive forces. And that was something neoliberalism couldn't destroy, couldn't devour, couldn't wipe out. And for this reason in a way that will surprise many, from morning to night, there emerges a network when previously there was nothing. Because before, the visible networks were the COB, the confedera-tions, the unions, but all that had been swept away by neoliberalism. And how is it that from one day to the next the structure that mobilizes all the people, the whole nation appears? Ah! It was [through] these invisible local networks of daily life. Therefore the local has a great deal of power, of strength. And in that sense those comrades and those texts are right when they say that from the local it's possible to construct processes of emancipation, of transforma-tion; from the small things of daily life.

---

14 The Water War was a social uprising during several months in 2000 in Cochabamba. Protesting the privatization of water in Bolivia, the effort resulted in the expulsion from Bolivia of the com-pany, Aguas del Tunari. This unprecedented movement drew people from all levels of society and provoked a wave of demonstrations, riots, and confrontations with the Bolivian Army.

*   *   *

Therefore, what we're saying here in this text—and it can be seen through all my reflections up until today, including now as Vice President, accompanying comrade President Evo—is that the local holds the strength, the energy, it is the key element. If in the local there is a new sociability there is a future; but if the local [change] remains local, refuses to spread, refuses to expand beyond itself, refuses to make itself present in the general totality [of society], it's all lost. This is what I call the will to power, well, in Nietzschean terms. And this is what differentiated the indigenous peasant movement from the workers' movement, when in '95 they said, Ah! We've taken the municipalities. Excellent. Are we happy with the municipalities? No. Let's go and take the power of the State, without giving up the municipality, without giving up the community, without giving up another form of communitarian economy. They didn't give up. Instead they said, just as we struggle here [at the local level]; let's struggle at the general level [of society] also. And this is what is happening. This is what Bolivia is living through today.

Suggested Further Reading

Chapter 1. The Pre-Hispanic Period

Broda, Johanna. "Geography, Climate and Observation of Nature in Prehispanic Meso-america." In *The Imagination of Matter: Religion and Ecology in Mesoamerican Traditions*, edited by David Carrasco. Oxford: BAR International series 515, 1989.

Carrasco, David. *City of Sacrifice: The Aztec Empire and the Role of Violence in Civilization.* Boston: Beacon, 1999.

Cereceda, Verónica, Johnny Dávalos, and Jaime Mejía. *A Difference and a Meaning: The Textile Designs of Tarabuco and Jalq'a.* Sucre, Bolivia: ASUR, 1993.

Duverger, Christian. *La flor letal: Economía del sacrificio azteca.* Translated by Juan José Utrilla. Mexico City: Fondo de Cultura Económica, 1983.

Gisbert, Teresa, Silvia Arze, Martha Cajías. *Arte textil y mundo andino.* La Paz: Plural Editores, [1988] 1992.

Gonçálvez Holguín, Diego. *Vocabulario de la lengua general de todo el Peru llamada lengua Qquichua o del Inca.* Lima: Universidad Nacional Mayor de San Marcos, Instituto de Historia, [1608] 1952.

The Huarochirí Manuscript: A Testament of Ancient and Colonial Andean Religion. Translated and edited by Frank Salomon and George L. Urioste. Austin: University of Texas Press, 1991.

Janusek, John Wayne. *Ancient Tiwanaku.* New York: Cambridge University Press, 2008.

Lafaye, Jacques. *Quetzalcóatl and Guadalupe: The Formation of Mexican National Consciousness, 1531–1813.* Chicago: University of Chicago Press, 1976.

Lambert, Peter, and Andrew Nickson, eds. *The Paraguayan Reader: History, Culture, Politics.* Durham, N.C.: Duke University Press, 2013.

Leon-Portilla, Miguel, ed. *The Broken Spears: The Aztec Account of the Conquest of Mexico.* Translated by Lysander Kemp, adapted from original codices painting by Alberto Beltran. Boston: Beacon Press, 1962.

Mendiburu, Manuel. *Apuntes históricos del Perú.* Lima: Imprenta del Estado, 1902.

Sá, Lúcia. *Rain Forest Literatures: Amazonian Texts and Latin American Culture.* Minneapolis: University of Minnesota Press, 2004.

Schele, Linda, and David Freidel. *Forest of Kings: The Untold Story of the Ancient Maya.* Color photographs by Justin Kerr. New York: Quill/W. Morrow, 1992.

Sullivan, William. *The Secret of the Incas: Myth, Astronomy, and the War against Time.* New York: River Press, 1996.

Tedlock, Dennis. *Popol Vuh: The Definitive Edition of 'The Mayan Book of The Dawn of Life' and 'The Glories of Gods and Kings'.* Translated by Dennis Tedlock. New York: Touchstone, 1996.

Tibón, Gutierre. *Historia del nombre y de la fundación de México.* Mexico City: Fondo de Cultura Económica, 1975.

Wilson, Jason. *The Andes: A Cultural History.* New York: Oxford University Press, 2009.

Young-Sánchez, Margaret, and Fronia W. Simpson, eds. *Andean Textile Traditions: Papers from the 2001 Mayer Center Symposium at the Denver Art Museum.* Denver, Colo.: Denver Art Museum, 2006.

Chapter 2. From the Conquest to the Consolidation of Colonial Society, 1530–1640

Adorno, Rolena. *Guáman Poma: Writing and Resistance in Colonial Peru.* Austin: Institute of Latin American Studies, University of Texas Press, 2000.

Barlow, Robert H. *The Extent of the Empire of the Culhua Mexica.* Berkeley: University of California Press, 1949.

Castro, Daniel. *Another Face of Empire: Bartolomé de Las Casas, Indigenous Rights, and Eccleciastical Imperialism.* Durham, N.C.: Duke University Press, 2007.

Edmonson, Munro S. *Sixteenth-Century Mexico: The Work of Sahagún.* Albuquerque: University of New Mexico Press, 1974.

Friede, Juan, and Benjamin Keen, eds. *Bartolomé de Las Casas in History: Toward an Understanding of the Man and His Work.* DeKalb: Northern Illinois University Press, 1971.

Gibson, Charles. *Spain in America.* New York: Harper Torchbooks, 1966.

Gutierrez, Gustavo. *Las Casas: In Search of the Poor of Jesus Christ.* Translated by Robert R. Barr. Maryknoll, N.Y.: Orbis Books, 1993.

Hanke, Lewis. *All Mankind Is One: A Study of the Disputation between Bartolomé de Las Casas and Juan Ginés de Sepúlveda in 1550 on the Intellectual and Religious Capacity of the American Indians.* De Kalb: Northern Illinois University Press, 1974.

Lafaye, Jacques. *Quetzalcóatl and Guadalupe: The Formation of Mexican National Consciousness, 1531–1813.* Chicago: University of Chicago Press, 1976.

Leonard, Irving A. *Books of the Brave: Being an Account of Books and Men in the Spanish Conquest and Settlement of the Sixteenth-Century New World.* New York: Gordian, 1964. First published in 1949.

López de Gómara, Francisco. *Cortés: The Life of the Conqueror by His Secretary.* Berkeley: University of California Press, 1964.

Pagden, Anthony. *European Encounters with the New World: From Renaissance to Romanticism.* New Haven, Conn.: Yale University Press, 1993.

———. *The Fall of Natural Man: The American Indian and the Origins of Comparative Ethnology.* London: Cambridge University Press, 1988. First published 1981.

Pease, Franklin. *Violence, Resistance, and Survival in the Americas: Native Americans and the Legacy of Conquest.* Edited by William B. Taylor and Franklin Pease. Washington, D.C.: Smithsonian Institution Press, 1994.

Sahagún, Bernardino de. *General History of the Things of New Spain: Florentine Codex.* Santa Fe, N.Mex.: School of American Research, 1950.

Stern, Steve J. *Peru's Indian Peoples and the Challenge of Spanish Conquest: Huamanga to 1640.* Madison: University of Wisconsin Press, 1993.

Wagner, Henry Raup, and Helen-Rand Parish. *The Life and Writings of Bartolomé de Las Casas*. Albuquerque: University of New Mexico Press, 1967.

Chapter 3. Colonization and the Expulsion of the Jesuits, 1640–1767

Arellano, Ignacio. "El zoológico de Domínguez Camargo en el poema heroico San Ignacio o el conceptismo como clave de lectura." *Hispanófila* 71.1 (2014): 29–43.

Arellano, Ignacio, and José Antonio Mazzotti, eds. *Edición e interpretación de textos andinos: Actas del congreso internacional*. [Pamplona, Spain]: Universidad de Navarra; Madrid: Iberoamericana; Frankfurt am Main: Vervuert, 2000.

Beverley, John. *Essays on the Literary Baroque in Spain and Spanish America*. Woodbridge, UK: Tamesis, 2008.

Carilla, Emilio. *Hernando Domínguez Camargo: Estudio y selección*. Buenos Aires: R. Medina, 1948.

Catalá, Rafael. *Para una lectura americana del barroco mexicano: Sor Juana Inés de la Cruz & Sigüenza y Góngora*. Minneapolis, Minn.: Prisma Institute, 1987.

de la Cruz, Sor Juana Inés. *Poems, A Bilingual Anthology*. Translated by Margaret Sayers Peden. Tempe, Ariz.: Bilingual Press, 1985.

Flynn, Gerald. *Sor Juana Inés de la Cruz*. Milwaukee, Wis.: Twayne, 1971.

Leonard, Irving Albert. *Don Carlos de Sigüenza y Góngora, a Mexican Savant of the Seventeenth Century*. Berkeley: University of California Press, 1929.

Mayers, Kathryn M. "American Artifice: Ideology and Ekphrasis in the *Poema heroico a San Ignacio de Loyola*." *Hispanófila* 155 (2009): 1–19.

Merrim, Stephanie, ed. *Feminist Perspectives on Sor Juana Inés de la Cruz*. Detroit: Wayne State University Press, 1999.

Paz, Octavio. *Sor Juana: Or, the Traps of Faith*. Translated by Margaret Sayers Peden. Cambridge, Mass.: Harvard University Press, 1988.

Rivers, Elias L. "Góngora y el Nuevo Mundo." *Hispania* 75.4 (October 1992): 856–61.

Ross, Kathleen. *The Baroque Narrative of Carlos de Sigüenza y Góngora: A New World Paradise*. New York: Cambridge University Press, 1993.

Vitulli, Juan M. *Instable Puente: La construcción del letrado criollo en la obra de Juan de Espinosa Medrano*. Chapel Hill: University of North Carolina Department of Romance Languages, 2013.

Chapter 4. The Wars of Independence, 1767–1824

Brading, D. A. *The First America: The Spanish Monarchy, Creole Patriots, and the Liberal State, 1492–1867*. Cambridge: Cambridge University Press, 1991.

Burrus, Ernest J. *Francisco Javier Alegre, Historian of the Jesuits in New Spain (1729–1788)*. Rome: Institutum Historicum S.J., [1953?].

Conway, Christopher B. *The Cult of Bolivar in Latin American Literature*. Gainesville: University Press of Florida, 2003.

Deck, Allan Figueroa. *Francisco Javier Alegre: A Study in Mexican Literary Criticism*. Tucson, Ariz.: Kino House, 1976.

De Nordenflycht, Adolfo. "Paratopia del exilio jesuita americano: Historia natural y narración literaria en Juan Ignacio Molina, Francisco Javier Clavijero, y Juan de Velasco." *Acta Literaria* 40 (2010): 91–109.

Gerbi, Antonello. *The Dispute of the New World: The History of a Polemic, 1750–1900.* Pittsburgh: University of Pittsburgh Press, 1973.

Junco de Meyer, Victoria. *Gamarra, o el eclecticismo en México.* Mexico City: Fondo de Cultura Económica, 1973.

Lynch, John. *Simon Bolivar: A Life.* New Haven, Conn.: Yale University Press, 2006.

Vargas De Luna, Javier. "Clavijero y la literalidad histórica del futuro." *Nóesis: Revista de Ciencias Sociales y Humanidades* 20.40 (2011): 126.

Velasco Gómez, Ambrosio, coordinador. *Significación política y cultural del humanismo iberoamericano en la época colonial.* Mexico: Universidad Nacional Autónoma de México; Plaza y Valdés, 2008.

Werner, Michael S. *Encyclopedia of Mexico: History, Society, and Culture.* Chicago: Fitzroy Dearborn, 1997.

Willingham, Eileen. "Imagining the Kingdom of Quito: Reading History and National Identity in Juan de Velasco's *Historia del Reino de Quito.*" In *Jesuit Accounts of the Colonial Americas: Intercultural Transfers, Intellectual Disputes, and Textualities,* edited by Marc André Bernier, Clorinda Donato, and Hans-Jürgen Lüsebrink, 81–106. Toronto: University of Toronto Press; UCLA Center for Seventeenth- and Eighteenth-Century Studies; William Andrews Clark Memorial Library, 2014.

Chapter 5. The Civil Wars, 1824–1870

Aguilar Mora, Jorge. *Una muerte sencilla, justa, eterna: Cultura y guerra durante la revolución mexicana.* Mexico City: Ediciones Era, 1990.

Cussen, Antonio. *Bello and Bolivar: Poetry and Politics in the Spanish American Revolution.* New York: Cambridge University Press, 1992.

Ewell, Judith, and William H. Beezley. *The Human Tradition in Latin America: The Nineteenth Century.* Wilmington, Del.: SR Books, 1989.

Frederick, Bonnie. *Wily Modesty: Argentine Women Writers, 1860–1910.* Tempe: Arizona State University Center for Latin American Studies Press, 1998.

Halperín Donghi, Tulio. *Sarmiento, Author of a Nation.* Berkeley: University of California Press, 1994.

Jaksic, Ivan. *Andres Bello: Scholarship and Nation-building in Nineteenth-century Latin America.* New York: Cambridge University Press, 2001.

Lipp, Solomon. *Three Chilean Thinkers.* Waterloo, Ont.: McGill University Press, 1975.

Mizraje, María Gabriela. *Argentinas de Rosas a Peron.* Buenos Aires: Editorial Biblos, 1999.

Ramos, Julio. *Divergent Modernities: Culture and Politics in Nineteenth-Century Latin America.* Durham, N.C.: Duke University Press, 2001.

Sorensen, Diana. *Facundo and the Construction of Argentine Culture.* Austin: University of Texas Press, 1996.

Chapter 6. Consolidation and Crisis of Liberalism, 1870–1930

Albarracín Millán, Juan. *El pensamiento filosófico de Tamayo y el irracionalismo alemán.* La Paz: Akapana, 1981.

Ameringer, Charles D. *The Socialist Impulse: Latin America in the Twentieth Century.* Gainesville: University Press of Florida, 2009.

Baines, John M. *Revolution in Peru: Mariategui and the Myth.* Tuscaloosa: Latin American Studies Program, University of Alabama Press, [1972].

Bell-Villada, Gene H. *Borges and his Fiction: A Guide to His Mind and Art*. Second Edition, revised and expanded. Austin: University of Texas Press, 1999.

Compton, Merlin D. *Ricardo Palma*. Boston: Twayne, 1982.

Mora, Gabriela. *El cuento modernista hispanoamericano: Manuel Gutiérrez Nájera, Ruben Darío, Leopoldo Lugones, Manuel Díaz Rodríguez y Clemente Palma*. Lima: Latinoamericana Editores, 1996.

Rama, Angel. *Rubén Darío y el modernismo*. Caracas: Alfadil Ediciones, 1985.

Sampson Vera Tudela, Elisa. *Ricardo Palma's Tradiciones: Illuminating Gender and Nation*. Lewisburg, Pa.: Bucknell University Press, 2012.

Tamayo, Franz. *Obra escogida*. Edited and prologue by Mariano Baptista Gumucio. Caracas: Biblioteca Ayacucho, 1979.

Valdez, Juan R. *Tracing Dominican Identity: The Writings of Pedro Herniquez Ureña*. New York: Palgrave Macmillan, 2011.

Vanden, Harry E. *National Marxism in Latin America: Jose Carlos Mariategui's Thought and Politics*. Boulder, Colo.: L. Rienner Publishers, 1986.

Chapter 7. New Civil Wars and Dictatorships, 1930–1980

Benitez Rojo, Antonio. *The Repeating Island: The Caribbean and the Postmodern Perspective*. Durham, N.C.: Duke University Press, 1992.

Bloom, Harold. *Octavio Paz*. Philadelphia, Pa.: Chelsea House, 2002.

Caistor, Nick. *Octavio Paz*. London: Reaktion Books, 2007.

Font, Mauricio A., and Alfonso W. Quiroz. *Cuban Counterpoints: The Legacy of Fernando Ortiz*. Lanham, Md.: Lexington Books, 2005.

Levinson, Brett. *Secondary Moderns: Mimesis, History, and Revolution in Lezama Lima's "American Expression."* Lewisburg, Pa.: Bucknell University Press, 1996.

Maharg, James. *A Call to Authenticity: The Essays of Ezequiel Martínez Estrada*. University, Miss.: Romance Monographs, 1977.

Palmié, Stephan. *The Cooking of History: How Not to Study Afro-Cuban Religion*. Chicago: University of Chicago Press, 2013.

Rosman, Silvia Nora. *Being in Common: Nation, Subject, and Community in Latin American Literature and Culture*. Lewisburg, Pa.: Bucknell University Press, 2003.

Salgado, César Augusto. *From Modernism to Neobaroque: Joyce and Lezama Lima*. Lewisburg, Pa.: Bucknell University Press, 2001.

Schaefer, Claudia. *Textured Lives: Women, Art, and Representation in Modern Mexico*. Tucson: University of Arizona Press, 1992.

Sebreli, Juan José. *Martínez Estrada: Una rebelión inútil*. Buenos Aires: Catálogos Editora, 1986.

Souza, Raymond D. *The Poetic Fiction of José Lezama Lima*. Columbia: University of Missouri Press, 1983.

Vargas Durand, Luis. *Martín Adán*. Lima: Editorial Brasa, 1995.

Chapter 8. The Contemporary Period: Speaking from the Margins

Arias, Arturo. *The Rigoberta Menchu Controversy*. Minneapolis: University of Minnesota Press, 2001.

Beverley, John. Testimonio: *On the Politics of Truth*. Minneapolis: University of Minnesota Press, 2004.

Bosteels, Bruno. *The Actuality of Communism*. London: Verso Books, 2011.

Cooper, Sara E., ed. *The Ties That Bind: Questioning Family Dynamics and Family Discourse in Hispanic Literature*. Lanham, Md.: University Press of America, 2004.

González, Eduardo. *Cuba and the Fall: Christian Text and Queer Narrative in the Fiction of José Lezama Lima and Reinaldo Arenas*. Charlottesville: University of Virginia Press, 2010.

Higgins, Nicholas P. *Understanding the Chiapas Rebellion: Modernist Visions and the Invisible Indian*. Austin: University of Texas Press, 2004.

Jorgensen, Beth Ellen. *The Writing of Elena Poniatowska: Engaging Dialogues*. Austin: University of Texas Press, 1994.

McMahon, Wendy-Jayne. *Dislocated Identities: Exile and the Self as (M)other in the Writing of Reinaldo Arenas*. New York: Peter Lang, 2012.

Olivares, Jorge. *Becoming Reinaldo Arenas: Family, Sexuality, and the Cuban Revolution*. Durham, N.C.: Duke University Press, 2013.

Poniatowska, Elena, and Beth Miller. "Interview with Elena Poniatowska." *Latin American Literary Review* 4.7 (1975): 73–78.

Schuessler, Michael Karl. *Elena Poniatowska: An Intimate Biography*. Tucson: University of Arizona Press, 2007.

Stern, Steve J. *Resistance, Rebellion, and Consciousness in the Andean Peasant World, 18th to 20th Centuries*. Madison: University of Wisconsin Press, 1987.

Van Cott, Donna Lee. "From Exclusion to Inclusion: Bolivia's 2002 Elections." *Journal of Latin American Studies* 35.4 (Nov. 2003): 751–75.

Author Index

Title Index

Jorge Aguilar Mora was born in Chihuahua, Mexico. Currently professor emeritus at the University of Maryland, College Park, he is the author of novels, several books of poetry and essays, and recipient of the 2015 Xavier Villaurrutia prize. His publications include *Una muerte sencilla justa y eterna: Cultura y guerra durante la revolución mexicana*, the novel *Los secretos de la aurora*, and most recently, *Sueños de la razón: 1799 y 1800 umbrales del siglo XIX*. He has also contributed to journals throughout the world. An international lecturer, he has taught at universities in Latin America, Europe, and the United States.

Josefa Salmón was born in Chulumani, Bolivia. She is professor emerita at Loyola University New Orleans where she taught for over three decades. She is the author of *El espejo indígena: El discurso indigenista en Bolivia 1900–1956* and *Decir nosotros: En la encrucijada del pensamiento indianista* and editor of several essay collections. She has contributed to international journals on Andean culture and film and was director of the *Bolivian Research Review/ Revista Boliviana de Investigación*, and she cofounded the Bolivian Studies Association *(www.bolivianstudies.org)*. Forthcoming publications include a series of monographs and DVDs, *Pensamiento boliviano*, which includes conversations with leading cultural and political figures in Bolivia.

Barbara C. Ewell, professor emerita, formerly Dorothy H. Brown Distinguished Professor of English, taught at Loyola University New Orleans for over three decades. She is author of *Kate Chopin* and coeditor of several essay collections, including *Louisiana Women Writers* (with Dorothy Brown), *Southern Local Color: Stories of Region, Race, and Gender* (with Pamela Menke), *"The Awakening" and Other Writings* (with Suzanne L. Disheroon, Pamela Menke, and Susie Scifres), and most recently (with Teresa Toulouse), *Sweet Spots: In-Between Spaces in New Orleans*. She has published numerous essays on a range of topics, from southern women writers and feminist pedagogy, to John Barth and the poetry of Michael Drayton.